Colin Wilson became famous as a young man in the 1950s with his remarkable book *The Outsider*. Since then he has written many books in such fields as literature, philosophy, psychology, mysticism, the occult and the paranormal. His interest in the often strange workings of the human mind has led him more than once to the subject of crime, and particularly of murder. His more recent works include *Access to Inner Worlds* (1983) and *A Criminal History of Mankind* (1984).

Robin Odell's first book, *Jack the Ripper in Fact and Fiction*, was published in 1965. His second, *Exhumation of a Murder*, the story of Major Armstrong, the only solicitor ever to be hanged in Britain, led to his successful partnership with crime historian Joe Gaute. Their *Murder* trilogy achieved considerable acclaim, the first title being awarded an 'Edgar' by the Mystery Writers of America. Robin Odell works in public relations, is married and lives in Oxfordshire.

J.H.H. Gaute has worked in publishing for sixty years, and has specialised in crime and criminals, on which he is a leading expert. He is the author of several books in collaboration with Robin Odell.

JACK THE RIPPER
Summing up and verdict

Colin Wilson & Robin Odell

Edited by J.H.H. Gaute

CORGI BOOKS

JACK THE RIPPER: SUMMING UP AND VERDICT
A CORGI BOOK 0 552 12858 9

Originally published in Great Britain by
Bantam Press

PRINTING HISTORY
Bantam Press edition published 1987
Corgi edition published 1988

Copyright © Colin Wilson and Robin Odell, 1987

This book is set in 10/11pt Baskerville

Corgi Books are published by Transworld Publishers Ltd.,
61–63 Uxbridge Road, Ealing, London W5 5SA, in Australia
by Transworld Publishers (Australia) Pty. Ltd., 15–23 Helles
Avenue, Moorebank, NSW 2170, and in New Zealand by
Transworld Publishers (N.Z.) Ltd., Cnr. Moselle and
Waipareira Avenues, Henderson, Auckland

**Printed and bound in Great Britain by
Cox & Wyman Ltd., Reading, Berks.**

Acknowledgements

The authors and editor wish to thank all those followers of Jack the Ripper who have contributed over the years to the fund of knowledge about the murders, which has led to the need for a summing up. We are especially grateful to Richard Whittington-Egan, the well-known commentator on criminal matters, for writing the Foreword, and to David Streatfield, in his guise as Alexander Kelly, for his invaluable guide to Ripperature. For their help and advice as the book progressed we should also like to thank John Kennedy Melling, Minna Fryman and Peter Brogan.

Contents

EDITOR'S PREFACE J.H.H. Gaute 9

FOREWORD Richard Whittington-Egan 11

AUTHORS' PREFACE Colin Wilson and Robin Odell 13

INTRODUCTION Psychological Portrait of Jack 15
the Ripper

CHAPTER ONE Ripper at Large 33

CHAPTER TWO Interlude 93

CHAPTER THREE Doctor Ripper 123

CHAPTER FOUR Jill the Ripper 179

CHAPTER FIVE Gentleman Jack 205

CHAPTER SIX Royal Jack 245

CHAPTER SEVEN Black Jack 263

CHAPTER EIGHT Jack of all Trades 283

CHAPTER NINE Summing-Up 307

APPENDIX ONE The Ripper's Disciples 323

APPENDIX TWO Sir Melville Macnaghten's 335
Notes

BIBLIOGRAPHY A Hundred Years of 340
Ripperature by Alexander Kelly
The Facts and the Theories 345
Fiction and Drama: A Selection 373
Films, Television and Radio 378

INDEX 379

Editor's Preface
by J.H.H. Gaute

It was more than fifteen years before I was born that Jack the Ripper had vanished for ever into the darkness, yet he somehow seems to have been hovering about me all my life.

When I joined the publishing house of Hutchinson towards the end of 1928, one of the first books to come on to my desk, and which incidentally, was to form the beginning of my crime library, was *The Mystery of Jack the Ripper* by Leonard Matters.

After the publication of Matters' book there was a long hiatus; the odd article on the Ripper appeared, but nothing else. Then, in 1935, I moved to Harraps where part of my work was looking after applications for permission to quote from our books. In 1964 a letter came into the firm from a Mr Robin Odell, of Southampton, saying he was writing a book on Jack the Ripper, and might he have permission to quote a paragraph from a work by A.T. Vassilyev entitled *The Ochrana*, which dealt with Russia and Rasputin. This I willingly granted, asking if his book had already been placed with a publisher, and saying that if not we would be very interested to consider it. Robin had not made any such arrangements, and so I invited him to come to my home in Surrey for lunch, and talk it over. I had brought with me a file on the case, on loan from Scotland Yard. It was a lovely summer afternoon and I don't believe in an after-life future, so when I opened the file and we were immediately attacked by a swarm of angry bees I didn't actually imagine that it was the ghosts of the Ripper or of his victims!

Robin's book, *Jack the Ripper in Fact and Fiction*, was published in 1965, and was immediately successful and, although there had been no other book on the subject for many years, Tom Cullen's *Autumn of Terror* appeared almost simultaneously. Since then quite a number of other

9

works have been published. We published the late Stephen Knight's *Jack the Ripper: The Final Solution* in 1976, and as time went on I realized that the centenary was coming up, and that a book was due reviewing the whole case together with the many theories that had been put forward. I talked it over with Colin Wilson, who has always found the affair fascinating, and with Robin Odell, who has been praised for his own contribution to the mystery. We agreed that it should be a complete summing-up.

The mystery of Jack the Ripper will never be solved. I am convinced that he was a nasty little man – like Christie and other sexual murderers – wearing an eighteen-eighties raincoat. As Don Rumbelow says in his excellent book, 'The answer must always be "perhaps". It can only remain conjecture. I have always had the feeling that on the Day of Judgment, when all things shall be known, when I and the other generations of "Ripperologists" ask for Jack the Ripper to step forward and call out his true name, then we shall turn and look with blank astonishment at one another when he announces his name and say, "Who?".'

Jack the Ripper escaped the prescribed and proper punishment for his crimes, a punishment so excellently described by A.E. Housman in his poem *Eight O'Clock* for one of his Shropshire lads:

> He stood and heard the steeple
> Sprinkle the quarters on the morning town.
> One, two three, four to market-place and people
> It tossed them down.
>
> Strapped, noosed, nighing his hour,
> He stood and counted them and cursed his luck;
> And then the clock collected in the tower
> Its strength and struck.

Foreword
by Richard Whittington-Egan

It is approaching fifty years now since I first began to look into the curious affair of the Jack the Ripper murders. While Colin Wilson was still in the kindergarten in Leicester, I, believed by my parents to be harmlessly busying myself in the innocent groves of the Natural History Museum, but having actually sneaked truant aboard the Metropolitan Railway line from South Kensington to Whitechapel, was padding around the East End – chiel with a penny notebook – meeting and cross-questioning the few of the last survivors who saw not Jack but his handiwork plain.

Nothing that I have learned or discovered in all the years since sounds any note of dissonance with the summing-up and verdict reached by Colin Wilson and Robin Odell. Accounts of the circumstances surrounding the Whitechapel murders are as tangled and jagged as the edges of a wound inflicted by Jack's lust-honed knife. The tidying up of the mutilations of Time requires careful surgery – which is precisely what we have in this painstaking volume. It comes as no surprise to me, as the authors, and the book's dedicatee, Joe Gaute, are familiar and respected figures in the ordinal of my criminological acquaintances.

Like them, I most vehemently eschew all suggestions of the famous-named Ripper. The miscreant was, I am perfectly convinced, a nominate nonentity. I cannot agree with Daniel Farson that Montague John Druitt is the most interesting and plausible suspect so far. The circumstance of his body having been found drifting in the vagrant-hospitable Thames some seven weeks after the despatchment of Mary Jane Kelly is no more than *post facto* police notional relevance. Neither, may I make it clear, do I, in my *Casebook on Jack the Ripper*, seriously propose the candidature of Roslyn D'Onston Stephenson, nor intend that my playful remark regarding the consequences to the homosexual prostitutes of the East End in the event of the blood guilt of Virginia Woolf's cousin should be taken for anything other than jocosity.

I consider Robin Odell's adumbration of some anonymous *shochet*, a Jewish slaughterman, possessed of the physical adeptness and psychological bizarrerie requisite to Ripper bill-fitting, as far more persuasive than the dredging-up–or out – of Druitt. Provided that one can countenance the shocking concept of a sadistic *shochet*, such an individual would seem to me to supply an entirely credible sitter for Colin Wilson's unfaultable psychological portrait of Jack the Ripper.

But it does not *have* to be a *shochet*. It *does*, however, have to be a likeness – whatever the sitter's trade, profession or avocation to Colin Wilson's artist's portrait of a young – or middle-aged – man.

A hundred years on, one is perhaps constrained to ask: Why all the fuss? Beside the serial murderer of today, Victorian Jack cuts a very modest figure. In a brilliantly conceived and coruscatingly argued introductory chapter, Colin Wilson explains all.

Happily, in subsequent chapters our authors do not explain–or, rather, explain away–all, do not mar their book by that sort of ill-founded special pleading, mandatory, it would seem, culprit-sacrifice, which has proved the ruination of so many another promising author, reckless in the Ripper minefield. Hunt-the-Ripper has indeed become for them a game, a kind of intellectual crossword puzzle, with the compiler providing clues to spell out the name which he has beforehand chosen for the ultimate acrostic. And, in this eternally repetitious pantomimic performance, they *will*, like the ugly sisters, make the foot fit the slipper instead of the slipper fit the foot. Those who seek equity should come with clean hands. Those who seek identity for the Ripper should come with clean feet!

I come, with pure heart, to recommend this as a most excellent and reliable account of all pertaining to Jack the Ripper, his murders and the circumstances surrounding and abutting upon their commission. So far as our present state of knowledge goes, this book could well have borne the title *Jack the Ripper: The Last Word* . . . and it would be a foolish – or exceptionally fortunate – investigator who could give it the lie.

12

Authors' Preface

The idea of this centenary study of Jack the Ripper originated with Joe Gaute, one of the leading experts on British crime. It was he who pointed out the enormous advances in 'Ripperology' (a word coined by Colin Wilson in 1972) in the past two or three decades. By the late 1920s – when Joe Gaute had just started his career in publishing – it was generally taken for granted that the mystery of the identity of Jack the Ripper would never be solved, and Leonard Matters' *Mystery of Jack the Ripper*, with its dubious tale of a deathbed confession, only seemed to confirm that view.

Thirty years later, Donald McCormick's *Identity of Jack the Ripper* proved at least one thing: that many clues had been overlooked. In the same year – 1959 – Daniel Farson discovered the identity of Sir Melville Macnaghten's leading suspect, Montague Druitt, and learned the possible existence of the pamphlet 'Jack the Ripper – I Knew Him' in Australia. Suddenly, the search was on again. And although this particular quest led nowhere, new suspects and new information began to appear almost year by year, resulting in the Clarence theory, Robin Odell's *shochet* suggestion, the J.K. Stephen story, the Gull theory and the Sickert angle. Donald Rumbelow's *The Complete Jack the Ripper* appeared in 1975, only to be rendered incomplete almost immediately by the appearance of Richard Whittington-Egan's *A Casebook on Jack the Ripper*, whose central section concerned newly discovered material by Aleister Crowley, and the emergence of a new suspect, Robert Donston Stephenson. And two years before beginning work on this present book, Colin Wilson received a letter from a Norwich accountant, Steward Hicks, telling him that he was convinced he had finally solved the puzzle of the identity of Jack the Ripper, and that his suspect was a completely new name. A preliminary scrutiny of Mr Hicks' material, whether he proves to have really produced the 'final solution' or not, certainly indicates that application and a flair for research can uncover completely new directions and information. A century after the murders, the message for 'Ripperologists' is that the solution may be just round the corner.

A word about the arrangement of the book. The introduction – 'Psychological Portrait of Jack the Ripper' – is by Colin Wilson. This is followed by an account of the murders in Chapter 1, 'Ripper at Large', and of the events surrounding them in Chapter 2, 'Interlude', both by Robin Odell. His account draws on material published by Harold Furniss in 1903 in the *Police Budget Edition of Famous Crimes*, illustrations from which are also included. The chapters dealing with the different theories are shared with the exception of 'Royal Jack' which is by Colin Wilson – and the book concludes with Colin Wilson's chapter giving a 'Summing-Up' and an appendix on 'The Ripper's Disciples'. Both authors think of the book as a tribute to the life and criminological researches of Joe Gaute.

Colin Wilson, Gorran Haven, Cornwall
Robin Odell, Sonning Common, Oxfordshire

July 1986

INTRODUCTION
Psychological Portrait of Jack the Ripper

On the afternoon of 8 September 1888 Mrs Mary Burridge, of 132 Blackfriars Road, south London, bought the Late Final edition of the London evening newspaper *The Star*, and when she read the headlines about the 'latest horrible murder in Whitechapel', collapsed and died 'of a fit'. The murder – the second in a fortnight – was that of a prostitute named Annie Chapman, who had been found disembowelled in a back yard that morning. The killer had not yet acquired the nickname that was to carry his notoriety all over the world: Jack the Ripper. But it is arguable that Mrs Burridge – described as 'a dealer in floor cloth' – deserves to be remembered as Jack the Ripper's third victim. For her death was curiously symbolic. The Whitechapel killer was a sadist who killed for pleasure, and out of a desire to cause shock and dismay. His crimes were *intended* to produce precisely the effect they produced on Mary Burridge; if he read about her death, he probably rubbed his hands with delight. At the end of Frank Wedekind's play *Lulu*, Jack the Ripper murders and disembowels the heroine, and as he slips quietly out of her room he murmurs with deep satisfaction, 'I was always a lucky fellow.' It was a brilliant psychological insight into the mind of what the Germans call a *lustmörd* – a 'joy murder'.

So before we begin this examination into the mystery of Jack the Ripper, let us see whether it is possible to understand the psychology of a man whose basic urges were so horribly different from those of the rest of us. For therein lies the key to the enigma.

First of all, we have to try to understand why the murders made such an impact on the minds of our great-grandparents of a century ago. The Victorians were brutally indifferent to many social issues – like child prostitution. But on closer examination, it proves to be a kind of insensitivity rather than callousness. When misery was actually brought to their attention, they were inclined to dissolve into floods of tears. Anyone who reads *The Pickwick Papers* for the first time will be struck by the little tales of sadness and misery that are scattered throughout the book – apparently as a kind of 'tragic relief' from the high-spirited comedy – tales of abandoned wives, wronged mothers, erring daughters, prodigal sons. But the Victorians could pass very easily from laughter to tears; their emotions were far less inhibited than ours, and a writer like Dickens took pleasure in his power to make them laugh or cry. The great bestseller of the 1870s was Mrs Henry Wood's *East Lynne*, the story of Lady Isobel Carlyle, who abandons her family to run away with a man of bad reputation, suffers horrible injuries in a railway accident after he has abandoned her, then goes back home to work as a governess to her own children, unrecognized by her family. The Victorians shed gallons of tears over the book – especially the scene where the mother has to watch beside the bedside of her dying child without betraying her identity. We are inclined to dismiss it as totally absurd – yet anyone who reads the book will have to admit that, absurd or not, it can still bring a lump to the throat of a modern reader. We are not really more sophisticated – or hard-hearted – than the Victorians; we have just had to learn to cope with a world that is unbelievably more complex. It was because the Victorians lived in a far less confusing world that their emotional reactions were far more open and spontaneous than our own.

Now it should be possible to see why the Jack the Ripper murders produced such a shock effect on the Victorians. They lived in a simple world of 'manly men and womanly women'. The kind of murders that fascinated them were murders committed by 'respectable people' – homicidal doctors, scheming solicitors, adulterous middle-class housewives, husbands who kept mistresses ... It gave them a pleasant *frisson* to think: that could easily happen in our street. Of course, there *were* a few homicidal maniacs who did gruesome things to women and children – like the Hampshire clerk Frederick Baker, who abducted eight-year-old Fanny Adams and hacked her to pieces, noting in his diary, 'Killed a young girl today – it was fine and hot', or Louis Menesclou, who hid his four-year-old victim under his mattress and slept on the body before he dismembered it. But such men were clearly insane: they belonged in 'bedlam'. In the world of normal, respectable people, murder was a sin committed only by those who had abandoned the moral teachings of the Church of England and allowed themselves to slide into disgusting self-indulgence. This is why the Victorians reacted with such indignation to the views of poets like Swinburne and Baudelaire, who implied that sin was wickedly alluring rather than nasty and ugly. These down-to-earth Englishmen felt that right was right and wrong was wrong, and that only a liar or a fool could take a different view. Even the Victorian poor shared the same moral viewpoint; they might pick pockets, but they would have been deeply shocked by Karl Marx's proposals for a classless society.

Then two women were found with their throats cut and their entrails torn out. It seemed almost a calculated insult, as if the murderer had shaken his fist at Victorian society, or spat in its face. He was like a man who shouts obscenities in church, or lowers his trousers in the midst of a royal garden party. Moreover, the victims were prostitutes – and this touched a deep spring of morbidity in the Victorian imagination. A woman who showed her ankle was regarded as 'fast'. Table legs were hidden by long tablecloths in case the very thought of 'legs' brought a blush to the cheeks of lady visitors. The word 'drawers' was coined for an undergarment that could be 'drawn' on, but this was soon abandoned because it evoked images of the same garment being drawn off. The very idea of a prostitute – a woman who sold her intimacy for money – caused morbid shudders in most Victorians. They were known as 'daughters of joy', apparently under the delusion that they chose their profession because they were nymphomaniacs. So the thought of such women being disembowelled by a sadistic madman aroused emotions that the Victorians found oddly disquieting.

As strange as it sounds, the Ripper murders were the first sex crimes in our modern sense of the word. In *The Newgate Calendar*, a compilation of crimes published in 1774, rape is very rare, and is usually committed in the course of an attempt at seduction – often of a servant girl by an upper-class 'rake'. The majority of the murders involve robbery. The work was reissued a century later, brought up to date by Camden Pelham, and this version is still notable for the absence of sex crimes. If Victorian criminologists gave any thought to the crimes of Frederick Baker or Louis Menesclou, they dismissed them with jargon like 'congenital psychopathic disposition' and 'inherited moral degeneracy'. (In fact, Menesclou *was* mentally subnormal, and there was insanity in Baker's family.)

And, indeed, rape was, in a sense, unnecessary in nineteenth-century England, as we can see from that incredible anonymous autobiography *My Secret Life*, which makes it clear that working-class women – and children – were readily available to anyone with a few shillings in his pocket. In the second volume, the writer describes how he was accosted by a middle-aged woman in Vauxhall Gardens, and invited to possess a ten-year-old girl. He des-

18

cribes spending the night with the two of them, and possessing the girl repeatedly. 'I longed to hurt her, to make her cry with the pain my tool caused her, to make her bleed if I could.' Yet he admits afterwards that the child cannot give the same pleasure as a grown woman. It is the *idea* of paedophilia that excites him, not the reality, which leaves him dissatisfied.

This offers us the vital clue to the rise of sex crime in the late nineteenth century. 'Walter' – the author of *My Secret Life* – finds sex exciting because he spends so much time *thinking* about it. By comparison, the seducers of the previous century – men like Casanova, Rousseau and James Boswell – took their sex for granted; it was a physical pleasure, like a good dinner, and they only thought about it when they were hungry. The late Victorians regarded sex as wicked and attractive because they had learned to use their imaginations. And this, in turn was the result of a habit that was scarcely a century old: the reading of novels. It is significant that the first novel – Samuel Richardson's *Pamela* (1740) – was about a wicked squire's attempt to seduce a virtuous servant girl. He leaps on her out of cupboards, flings her on beds, struggles to raise her dress above her waist, even tries to rape her with a procuress holding both her hands. His second novel, *Clarissa*, culminates in the rape of the heroine when she has been drugged. Rousseau's immensely popular *New Heloise* is about an aristocratic young girl who gives herself to her tutor. The literary sensation of the 1790s was *The Monk* by Matthew Gregory Lewis, which was about an abbot who learns that a young novice in the monastery is actually a girl who is in love with him. The temptation is finally too much for him. 'He sat upon her bed; his hand rested upon her bosom; her head reclined voluptuously on his breast. Who then can wonder if he yielded to the temptation? Drunk with desire, he pressed his lips to those that sought them; his kisses vied with Matilda's in warmth and passion; he clasped her rapturously in his arms; he forgot his vows, his sanctity, his fame; he remembered nothing but the pleasure and the opportunity.' And the abbot goes on to become a seducer, a rapist and a murderer. Lewis's *Monk* was the first in a long line of horror stories with strong undertones of sexual violence.

By the 1830s, there was a flourishing new industry: pornography. The first pornographic novel, John Cleland's *Fanny Hill*, had appeared in 1745, but found few imitators; the men of the eighteenth century were less interested in reading about sex than in doing it. Victorian prudery created a taste for the 'forbidden', and by 1853 it was necessary to pass an obscenity act to prevent pornography from flooding in from the Continent. The new pornography was no longer – like *Fanny Hill* – about straightforward couplings; little girls peeped through keyholes to watch their elder sisters losing their virginity, then gave themselves to the butler or the gardener's boy. Sex became associated with furtiveness. The number of rapes committed on children increased, although there was no corresponding increase in the rapes of adult women; they were still easily available – only children were 'forbidden'.

But towards the end of the century, even this was ceasing to be true. Victorian prosperity was creating a new type of working-class girl; she worked in shops and offices, and was sufficiently well paid to reject the advances of predatory males like 'Walter'. Middle-class girls went to night school and joined political movements like the socialists; they rode bicycles and wore 'rational dress' – a kind of divided skirt. Bernard Shaw's fellow socialist Hubert Bland took full advantage of this new class of young woman to make sexual conquests; so did H.G. Wells and Frank Harris, who detailed his seductions in *My Life and Loves*. Yet this partial breakdown of Victorian moral prohibitions only intensified the morbid preoccupation with the 'forbidden'. And it was at this point in history – just before the beginning of the 'naughty nineties' – that the Jack the Ripper murders seemed to crystallize that unwholesome Victorian obsession with wickedness and immorality.

It is interesting to note that one of the most popular of

the early theories about the Ripper was that he was a 'religious maniac' who was driven to murder by his hatred of prostitutes. In fact, nothing is less likely. It is practically impossible to imagine a clergyman – even one whose mind has been unbalanced by visions of hellfire – cutting the throats of his victims and then sexually mutilating them. But the Victorians were obsessed by their own morbid responses to sexual 'wickedness', and projected them on to the killer. And the first book about the crimes – *The Mystery of Jack the Ripper* by Leonard Matters – still displays this same tendency to think in terms of a moral avenger, even though it was published forty years later; according to Matters, 'Dr Stanley' was avenging the death of his son from venereal disease. Like the Ripper's contemporaries, Matters ignores the savagery of the multilations, which reveals a sick psychopath, and tries to create a picture of the killer as a heartbroken doctor whose motivations are relatively rational – to track down the woman who has caused his son's death.

The same objection applies to the theory presented in the second full-length book on the case, *Jack the Ripper, A New Theory* (1939) by 'William Stewart, artist'; this suggests that the killer was a sadistic midwife. Physically speaking, it might just be possible, if the midwife had powerful muscles; but again it overlooks the sexual mutilation of the women. The injuries reveal a man who hated women and who found them immensely attractive. No woman would have the motivation to cut open the victims and remove some of their organs.

This introduction is an attempt to construct a psychological profile of the Ripper, not to speculate about suspects – this will be done in later chapters. And the most significant clue so far is the comment in *My Secret Life*: 'I longed to hurt her, to make her cry with the pain my tool caused her, to make her bleed if I could.' Throughout the four thousand or so pages of the book, it becomes clear that 'Walter' is not at all sexually abnormal; his only peculiarity lies in the intensity of the obsession that leads him to devote his life to the pursuit of women. He is a coarse and unlikeable ruffian, but he is not a sadist or a masochist or a paedophile. Yet when he is in a state of sexual excitement, he wants to hurt the child and make her bleed. Walter is expressing the aggression that lies at the root of the male sex drive, the desire to feel himself 'the master'.

In the Victorian age, it was not fashionable to express the desire so crudely – hence the shock caused by the Ripper murders. But the twentieth century has seen an increasing number of crimes in which this element of male aggression is obvious. Until the 1960s, they were rare enough to be regarded as psychological oddities: Peter Kürten, Albert Fish, Earle Nelson, Neville Heath. But during the 1960s, this type of crime became increasingly commonplace – something that became clear to me (Colin Wilson) after I had compiled an *Encyclopedia of Murder* which appeared in 1960. Most of the crimes in the *Encyclopedia* were 'classic' murder cases – tales of greed, adultery, eternal triangles. During the 1960s, it became clear that there was a change in the pattern of murder. There was something oddly 'motiveless' about the Moors murder case in England and about the Charles Manson murders in America. It was as if the killers were committing murder to 'prove something' – the only parallel case in the *Encyclopedia* was that of Leopold and Loeb, the two rich Chicago students who decided to commit 'the perfect murder' to convince themselves that they were supermen. An increasing number of murderers seemed to want to demonstrate that they were 'above morality', that they lived according to their own laws. Both Charles Manson and Ian Brady made it clear that they felt they had turned their backs on normal society – that they regarded themselves as 'loners', outsiders.

Murder seemed to become far more casual. In August 1966, a young American named Charles Whitman went to the top of the tower on the campus of the University of Texas and began shooting with a rifle, killing nineteen people and wounding twenty-eight; he was finally shot by police. An autopsy revealed a brain tumour, and it was probably this, pressing on the amygdaloid nucleus – the brain's aggression centre – that led to the killings. But an increasing number of crimes of the past quarter of a century give the impression that something is stimulating the aggression centre and causing apparently motiveless violence. An eighteen-year-old student named Robert Smith walked into a beauty parlour in Arizona in November 1966, made five women and two children lie on the floor, and shot them all in the back of the head. Asked why he did it, he said, 'I wanted to become known, to get myself a name.' The motive sounds absurd. Yet it can be observed in more and more crimes of the late twentieth century.

But this change in the murder patterns – this increasing lack of inhibition – enables us to see more clearly the factors that lead to sex crime, particularly sadistic sex crime. The Ripper's contemporaries thought of him as a kind of ghoul, a madman with glowing eyes, like the *Punch* cartoon that appeared on the day before the 'double event' – the killing of Elizabeth Stride and Catherine Eddowes. But it is far more probable that he was a mild-looking little man whose family and friends had no idea that he had homicidal tendencies. That is one thing we have learned from modern cases in which mass murderers have been caught. It is hard to think of a single example of a killer who looked like one, or even who behaved like one. When Peter Kürten, the Düsseldorf sadist, was finally arrested in 1929, his neighbours were convinced the police had made a mistake. And when Donald Neilson, the 'Black Panther', and Peter Sutcliffe, the Yorkshire Ripper, were arrested, their neighbours appeared on the television news commenting that they found it impossible to believe that such pleasant, normal characters could turn out to be murder suspects.

The case of the Yorkshire Ripper throws an interesting light on the development of the sadistic impulse. The journalist Gordon Burn, who spent two years studying Sutcliffe's background, found no evidence of sadism or aggressive behaviour in his childhood; on the contrary, Sutcliffe was a

23

quiet, 'weedy' boy who on one occasion played truant from school for two weeks because he was afraid of bullies. As a teenager he was quiet, inarticulate, but obviously good-natured. His only peculiarity – one he shared with many of his friends – was a morbid fascination with prostitutes and red-light districts; a friend described how they used to sit in an old car, watching prostitutes 'for something to do'. But Sutcliffe never had the courage to approach one of them. At the age of twenty-one he began courting a sixteen-year-old Czech girl who was even more introverted and shy than he was. And it was during a quarrel with her that he picked up a prostitute 'to get his own back'. He proved impotent. The woman went off with a £10 note and failed to return with his £5 change. Some weeks later, he saw her in a pub and asked for the money; she jeered at him. 'Before I knew what was happening, most of the people were having a good laugh.' At last, the worm turned; he began attacking prostitutes. A few weeks later, eating fish and chips in a van with a friend, he thought he saw the woman who had cheated him. He followed her, and struck her on the back of the head with a brick in a sock. She noted the number of the van, and the next day he was arrested. But she decided not to press charges. A month later, he was again arrested lurking in the garden of a house, and was found to be in possession of a hammer; the police assumed he was contemplating burglary, and he was fined £25. Two years later, he again attacked a prostitute with a brick in a sock.

In 1972, Sutcliffe married the Czech girl, Sonia, but his sexual problems seem to have continued – one prostitute later reported that he told her he had been arguing with his wife about 'not being able to go with her'. In 1975, he followed a woman named Anna Rogulsky, and struck her on the head with a hammer, shattering her skull. As he was raising her blouse and was about to plunge a knife into her stomach, a man called out to ask what was happening, and he fled. His victim recovered after a twelve-hour operation to pick splinters of bone out of her brain. In the following month, he attacked a woman he assumed to be a prostitute,

24

and was beginning to slash her back with a hacksaw blade when he was disturbed by car headlights. This woman, too, recovered. Two months later, he picked up a prostitute named Wilma McCann; but again he proved to be impotent. When she told him to 'hurry up and get it over with', he hit her with a hammer, then mutilated her stomach with a knife. It was his first murder.

From now on, the stabbing ritual became an obsession; although Sutcliffe denied it, it seems certain that he achieved orgasm during these attacks. He had discovered a new sexual thrill; he was, in effect, committing rape with a knife. It made no difference that he was too nervous to achieve normal penetration. When, in January 1976, he picked up a part-time prostitute named Emily Jackson, he knocked her unconcious with a hammer, removed her bra and panties, and stabbed her a total of fifty-two times with a screwdriver; he also thrust a piece of wood into her vagina.

Sutcliffe was later to claim that he was driven by a hatred of prostitutes; in fact, several of his victims were innocent teenage girls, and he must have known it. Sutcliffe went on to kill eleven more women, and was sitting in his car with a black prostitute named Olive Reivers when a police patrol made a routine check, discovered that his car had false numberplates, and arrested him. By this time, the compulsion to kill and mutilate had become a fever; Sutcliffe said later that he felt he was driven by the Devil.

What seems clear is that Sutcliffe was not in the grip of a sadistic compulsion when he made his first attacks on prostitutes, but driven by rage and humiliation, a desire to get his own back. Ever since childhood, Sutcliffe had felt himself a victim; he was a quiet, inarticulate little man who never asserted himself; when upset or angry, he simply became silent. Yet he was convinced that his thoughts and feelings were of some value. A card displayed in his lorry was inscribed: 'In this truck is a man whose latent genius, if unleashed, would rock the nation, whose dynamic energy would overpower those around him. Better let him sleep?' Unleashing his violence against women became a form of self-expression, as if he had discovered a kind of perverted artistic talent.

It is important to recognize that almost any form of sexual self-expression can become a habit. In *Sex Perversions and Sex Crimes*, James Melvin Reinhardt cites a case of a man estranged from his wife who began an affair with a woman who 'gave him the greatest sexual satisfaction he had ever experienced', and whose eight-year-old daughter took part in their orgies. When this woman broke with him he returned to his family and seduced his own two youngest daughters. Before his affair he would probably have rejected the idea with horror; but it had become a habit. With Sutcliffe, the stabbing of women became a habit until the original hatred of prostitutes was forgotten; any woman would do.

What is so hard to understand is that the habit of sexual violence should become a repetitious compulsion, exactly like drug addiction. Burglars and pickpockets seem capable of taking a holiday from their profession, but the sex killer seems to experience an irresistible urge to go on until he is caught. The crimes often take place at shorter and shorter intervals, and become increasingly violent. In this respect, the Jack the Ripper case is typical. When he was interrupted during the murder of Elizabeth Stride, he hurried away and found another victim; he was not satisfied until he had left her with the typical mutilations. When he committed the last murder, in Miller's Court, he knew that he had been seen before he entered Mary Kelly's room; yet he spent several hours with the body, dissecting it until it looked like the remains of a butchered animal; the compulsion had become so overwhelming that it could only be satisfied by the virtual destruction of the victim.

This addictive aspect is again something the Victorians failed to understand; even forty years after the murders, Leonard Matters tried to explain it as 'Dr Stanley's' tireless search for the woman who had infected his son. A century later, with thousands of sex crimes to provide us with clues and parallels, we can recognize it as a typical aspect of the sex criminal's destructive urge. It seems capable of over-ruling all the laws of common sense. In one of the most curious cases of the 1980s, a successful Alaska businessman named Robert Hansen acted out his fantasies of sadistic violence with at least thirty prostitutes, killing twenty of them. Hansen's method was to pick up exotic dancers in the topless bars of Anchorage, Alaska, and ask them to engage in oral sex. One of the women became nervous and drew a knife; he took it away and stabbed her to death. 'When I thought about it, it was the sort of feeling I got when I bagged a trophy animal.' (Hansen was an expert big-game hunter.) Like Peter Sutcliffe, he was 'hooked'. Now he began fantasizing about hunting down naked girls in the forest; and since the topless bars were full of prostitutes, it was not long before he was turning the fantasies into reality. He would drive the girl out into the woods, have sex with her in the car, then order her out at gunpoint, and pursue her through the snow with a rifle. 'I'd let them think they'd got away, then flush them out and get them to run again.' Finally he would shoot them and bury the bodies. Even-tually, one of his victims succeeded in escaping, and ran – naked – into the arms of a policeman, a handcuff dangling from her wrist. She told how she had been picked up by an ugly, pock-marked little man who stuttered, and taken back to his home; then he had handcuffed her, and tortured her by biting her nipples and thrusting a hammer handle into her vagina. She had escaped when the man tried to take her to his private plane.

When Hansen – who was quickly arrested – confessed to the murders, he told the police about the problems of his childhood – how his stutter and the acne that covered his face with pimples made women regard him as a 'freak'. He came to hate women. In his twenties he moved to Anchor-age, set up a successful bakery business, and married. He also became a celebrated big-game hunter, winning many trophies. But his deepest desire was for oral sex. So he began picking up women in topless bars, and driving them out on to lonely roads in the woods. Those who left him

27

satisfied were allowed to go; the others were hunted like big game and finally despatched.

Through the Hansen case, we can begin to form a picture of the type of man who would have been capable of murdering five – possibly as many as seven – women in that summer and autumn of 1888: not a demented doctor or clergyman, not a moral reformer who was appalled by prostitution, but an introverted, unattractive little man whose lack of normal sexual outlet had embittered him until his desire could only be exorcized by stabbing and slashing. The murders were probably the culmination of months, perhaps years, of fantasizing about sex, with emphasis on the passivity and helplessness of the victim. James Melvin Reinhardt writes about a youth who had strangled and mutilated an eight-year-old boy: 'I gathered from conversations with him that his nature was such as to derive an overpowering satisfaction out of the contemplation of cruel acts upon another person. A combination of very bad training and a somewhat abnormal physical appearance had, in my opinion, helped to cut him off from normal social life and to shut him within himself.' This is the classic picture of a certain type of sex killer, and Reinhardt's next sentence is even more significant: 'His ego is the sort that demands cruelty, and he found a great deal of ego satisfaction in an abnormal sex act involving the infliction of cruelty on a relatively helpless creature.'

It is important to note that this type of sex killer – the ego distorted by frustration – is only one of two main classifications. The other is the outcome of an insatiable sexual urge, known as satyriasis, and which might be regarded as the sexual equivalent of the dipsomaniac's craving for alcohol. Such men are often physically attractive enough to have no difficulty finding willing partners; but they have no sooner satisfied the urge for conquest than it reappears. In his *Intimate Memoirs* the writer Georges Simenon estimates that he has slept with ten thousand women, eight thousand of them prostitutes, and admits that he no sooner finds himself in a strange city than he feels compelled to make for the brothel quarter. The Hungarian sex killer Bela Kiss was well known in the red-light district of Budapest, and was regarded as sexually insatiable. When he was reported killed in action in the First World War, police found in his house twenty-four petrol drums, each containing the body of a woman preserved in alcohol. Kiss had no problem persuading women to come to live with him in his farmhouse, but the intensity of his sexual urge meant that he experienced a continuous desire to replace them. Even so, the curious method of disposal suggests that he wanted to raise the lid periodically to gloat over his conquests.

In an American case of the 1980s, a millionaire businessman named Christopher Wilder suddenly went on a murder rampage across America, abducting attractive girls and taking them to motels, where they were raped, then tortured with an electric probe which sent shocks through their bodies and left burns on the breasts and genitals. Wilder committed suicide when about to be arrested. The curious feature of the case is that Wilder was an attractive man in his thirties, a racing driver who owned a luxury home, and who should have had no problem finding girls to share his bed. Yet the overpowering nature of his sexual drive meant that he could only be fully satisfied with rape and torture, usually followed by murder. Wilder is typical of the 'sadistic satyr'.

It is obvious that Jack the Ripper belonged to the other type of sex killer, the 'twisted ego', to which Sutcliffe and Hansen belong. This is made plain by his choice of victim: Kiss and Wilder chose attractive women; Jack the Ripper chose middle-aged drabs. It is even possible that, like Sutcliffe, he experienced a morbid fascination towards prostitutes. In the Ripper-type killer, the nature of the sexual impulse is determined by a feeling of inferiority.

One more parallel case will serve to underline this point. In Germany in the 1960s and 1970s, a sex killer made a habit of murdering girls – usually teenagers – then taking away parts of the body, usually slices from the thighs or

29

buttocks; he became known to the police as the 'Ruhr hunter'. On a hot day in 1976, a four-year-old girl, dressed only in knickers, was playing with friends when she was approached by a middle-aged man who persuaded her to go off with him. Police began a search of nearby apartment buildings, and discovered that a top-floor lavatory was blocked with a child's entrails. In an apartment belonging to a lavatory attendant, Joachim Kroll, they found parcels of the child's flesh and, on a stove, her hand boiling in a saucepan with carrots and potatoes. Kroll, who was mentally subnormal, admitted that he had been committing sex murders for twenty years – so many that he was unable to recall the precise number. He was too shy and nervous to attempt sex with a woman. In his flat, the police found a number of rubber female dolls, and Kroll admitted that he would strangle these with one hand as he masturbated with the other.

The murders were carefully planned. Periodically he would observe a young girl walking alone, perhaps on her way home from school, and would then watch her day after day to observe her routine. Finally, when the opportunity came, he would strangle her and commit rape. Then he would take a slice of her flesh, and take it home for dinner. Although Kroll insisted that this had no sexual motivation, it seems obvious that the cannibalism, like the rape, was a symbolic expression of conquest – of total power over the victim.

Jack the Ripper, we may recall, was believed to have sent part of a kidney to George Lusk, head of the Whitechapel Vigilance Committee, with a note claiming that he had fried and eaten the rest. 'It was very nise.' In the case of an earlier victim, Annie Chapman, he had taken away the uterus and upper part of the vagina. Yet in the last case, that of Mary Kelly, although the Ripper spent hours alone with the victim, no parts of the body were found to be missing. Why should that be so? The obvious explanation is that the work of dissection had left the killer completely satisfied; no further expression of 'power over the victim' was necessary.

It is true that all this brings us no closer to identifying Jack the Ripper. But at least it enables us to begin to see a dim outline of the kind of man who was capable of committing the crimes, and to begin to understand why they exercised such a horrible fascination for our Victorian great-grandparents. It is the necessary prelude to reading about the crimes themselves.

CHAPTER ONE
Ripper at Large

There was a prelude to London's 'Autumn of Terror' in 1888 when two women were murdered in separate incidents. These two killings were linked with the later Ripper murders and then discounted as true victims. Nevertheless they have featured in numerous of the theories which have sought to identify the elusive killer and it is important at least to put them in the correct chronological perspective.

On Easter Monday, 3 April, a common prostitute by the name of Emma Elizabeth Smith, a 45-year-old widow with two children and a reputation as a brawler, staggered into her lodgings at 18 George Street, Spitalfields, sometime during the afternoon. She told the lodging-house keeper that she had been attacked and robbed by four men in Osborn Street. She had cuts and bruises to her face and was persuaded, much against her wishes, to go to the London Hospital for treatment. The true nature of her injuries was discovered when she was examined by doctors. She was suffering from severe internal bleeding due to injuries to the vagina or, as a policeman's report of the day recorded with Freudian spelling, regina. It appeared that some object, not a knife, had been inserted into her body causing savage tearing of the tissues. The injured woman had placed her woollen shawl between her legs to soak up the blood while she made the painful journey first to her lodgings and then to hospital. Emma Smith died of peritonitis in the London Hospital on the day following the brutal attack.

Savage though this crime was, it was but one murder in many violent deaths which occurred in the East End. The immediate reaction was that Emma Smith had been a victim of one of the gangs which roamed the area and frequently terrorized the inhabitants. Old people were often assaulted in the streets and robbed in broad daylight.

The next Bank Holiday heralded another vicious murder, when, on 6 August, Martha Turner met her death at the hands of a killer using a knife. Turner, also known as Tabram, was a married woman who earned a living as a prostitute. Like most East Enders on that Bank Holiday, she had been out to enjoy herself which, in her case, meant a day spent mostly in the public houses.

She spent the evening drinking in the Angel and Crown near Whitechapel Church and talking to a soldier with whom she went off at closing time. This was the last time she was seen alive. At about 3.30 a.m., Albert Crow, a cab driver returning to his home at 35 George Yard Buildings, saw someone lying huddled up on the first-floor landing. He hurried past, no doubt keen to get to his bed and, in any case, thinking that the inert form was that of a drunk. At about 5 a.m., John Reeves, who was employed in one of the markets, left his room to walk to work. As he came down the stairs, he saw a woman lying on the landing in a pool of blood. He raised the alarm and the police quickly arrived at the scene as the new day dawned.

Dr Timothy Keleene examined the body and pronounced life extinct. It was only when he carried out the full post-mortem examination that the extent of the woman's injuries was realized. She had been stabbed in the chest thirty-nine times in what Dr Keleene thought was a twoweaponed attack. He believed that one was a long-bladed knife and the other, possibly a surgical instrument; he added, 'Whoever it was, he knew how and where to cut.'

It appeared that Martha Turner was something of an outcast, with few friends, and she was not known at George Yard Buildings where she met her death. The 35-year-old prostitute was known to the police on account of her regular soliciting in the docks and Tower Hamlets areas. Because she had last been seen in the company of a soldier, suspicion naturally fell on the garrison at the Tower of London. An identity parade was held and the man who had been in Turner's company came forward and was able to prove that he had rejoined his fellow servicemen at about 1.30 a.m. This was well before the woman was thought to have been killed and, in any case, she had been seen returning alone to the Angel and Crown at about 1.40 a.m.

Mr George Collier, the coroner at the inquest on Turner's death which opened on 10 August, returned a verdict of murder against a person or persons unknown. With no useful clues to pursue, once the dead woman's soldier companion had been cleared, the police had little option but to add the murder of Martha Turner to their list of unsolved crimes. The doctor's remark that two weapons had been used in the killing led to some discussion regarding the murderer's dexterity. Was he ambidextrous, or was the murder carried out by two individuals? While these questions were being discussed in a somewhat academic way, the events for which the deaths of Emma Smith and Martha Turner were merely a prelude began to erupt in Whitechapel.

About 3.45 a.m. on the morning of 31 August, Police Constable John Neil walked his beat through Bucks Row, Whitechapel. The thoroughfare, illuminated by a single gas lamp, had a warehouse on one side and a row of terraced houses on the other. In the gap between the houses and a board school was a gateway to some stables. The gates were closed, but lying next to them on the pavement was a dark form. Flashing the beam of his bull's-eye lamp into the gateway, PC Neil saw immediately that the amorphous bundle was the body of a woman. She lay on her back with one arm close to the stable gate and the other stretching across the pavement; her black straw bonnet lay close by. By the light from his lamp, PC Neil could see a frightful gash in the woman's throat from which blood had run in rivulets into the gutter.

What Neil did not know at that moment was that the body had already been discovered by a market porter on his way to work. George Cross had found the body in the semi-darkness while walking down Bucks Row at about 4 a.m. He thought at first that the dark shape was a tarpaulin which had fallen off a passing cart. On closer inspection, he realized the shape was that of a prostrate woman. Without the benefit of a light, he thought she was probably a drunk but when he saw her skirts had been pushed up to her waist he thought she was a rape victim.

Cross was still sizing up the situation when another early-morning worker, John Paul, came down the street. 'Come and look at this woman,' said Cross and, still thinking she was drunk, suggested that the two of them lift her up. Paul declined to assist in this course of action and instead bent down to feel the woman's face and hands; they were quite cold. He said he thought she was dead, and pulled her skirts down to preserve her decency. The two men decided to look for a policeman and went off in search of one quite unaware that the body they had found had been slashed across the throat from ear to ear and the abdomen ripped open.

PC Neil, whose flashing lamp had attracted another patrolling policeman, took in the horror of the cut throat and the open-eyed stare of the dead woman lying on the pavement. Dr Ralph Llewellyn who lived nearby was sent for and he confirmed what the bystanders already knew, which was that the woman was dead. The policemen directed the beams of their lamps on the body while the doctor examined its injuries. A livid incision about four inches long started an inch below the left side of the jaw and

36

below it was another larger, deeper incision which had cut the throat back to the vertebrae and finished about three inches below the right jaw. Two or three men, on their way home from work at the nearby slaughterhouse in Winthrop Street, stood uneasily in the knot of spectators.

Dr Llewellyn ordered the body to be removed to the Whitechapel mortuary which adjoined the workhouse. As the policemen lifted the corpse into the ambulance they realized that the woman's clothing was sodden with blood, the real cause of which they had yet to discover. The relatively small amount of blood left on the pavement was washed into the gutter by a resident throwing down a bucket of water. As daylight brightened the dark street, all that was left for sensation seekers to point out was rapidly drying blood in the cracks between the paving stones.

Two police inspectors from Bethnal Green followed the body to the mortuary where the progress of the crime investigation was halted while two workhouse inmates finished their breakfast. Fortified for their task, the two paupers began to strip the body of its clothing. Each garment was logged by one of the police officers. Immediately the petticoats were removed, exposing the naked body, the men were startled to see loops of bowel protruding from jagged cuts in the abdomen. Dr Llewellyn was hastily summoned and at once began a full post-mortem examination. Several jagged incisions had ripped the abdomen open down its full length and there were two stab wounds in the genitals. In addition to the cut throat, there were bruises on the right side of the jaw, possibly due to pressure exerted by gripping fingers. The doctor thought the mutilations might have been inflicted by a left-handed person using a long-bladed knife.

The body was that of a woman aged between forty and forty-five but her identity was not immediately apparent. Several women who thought they might be able to identify her visited the mortuary during the course of the day but, beyond satisfying their curiosity, none recognized the remains. One of the petticoats provided a clue in the form of the stamp of a workhouse in Lambeth. By this means, Inspector Helson was able to trace the dead woman. She was known to the residents of Thrawl Street, Spitalfields, as 'Polly' and was eventually named as Mary Ann Nichols, a 42-year-old prostitute.

She had not seen her husband, William Nichols, for three years and her five children lived either with relatives or in a home; her drunken habits were given as the reason for the break-up of the family. When last seen at 3.45 a.m. on the morning of her murder she was staggering down Whitechapel Road. About an hour and a quarter later she was found in Bucks Row and from the warmth still discernible in her legs Dr Llewellyn believed she had been dead no more than half an hour. William Nichols made a positive identification of his wife's body after the coroner's inquest opened.

Mary Nichols had been living for several weeks at 18 Thrawl Street where a bed cost fourpence a night. The coppers she earned by prostitution paid both for her drink and her doss. Early on the eve of her murder, dressed in a black straw bonnet and shabby clothes, she boasted to a friend that she had earned and spent her doss money three times that day and declared that she intended to earn some more. 'I'll soon get my doss money,' she laughed, adding, 'See what a jolly bonnet I've got now.'

The murder of Mary Ann Nichols was apparently motiveless. Those who gathered around the murder spot in Bucks Row and who lingered near the mortuary talked of a gang who ran a protection racket for prostitutes and beat them up if they failed to meet their payments. Reference was also made to earlier killings in the East End. There was a feeling of menace in the air and, for no good reason at all, people talked about the murder in whispers.

The inquest on Nichols opened on Saturday 1 September at the Working Lad's Institute, Whitechapel, under Mr Wynne E. Baxter. John Paul, one of the men who had stumbled across the body in the half-light, said: 'It was too dark to see blood. I thought she had been outraged and died

38

in the struggle.' Inspector Spratling of J Division related how he was called to the murder scene and accompanied the corpse to the mortuary. It was only then that the horrific mutilations were discovered. He said he had examined Bucks Row but found no suspicious blood stains apart from those washed away on the pavement. The surrounding area was searched but no further bloodstains were to be found nor any murder weapon.

The police questioned residents living close to the scene of the murder but no one heard any noise or scream amounting to an alarm. Walter King, who lived at Essex Wharf, opposite the entrance to the stables, said he was asleep in a room on the first floor and heard nothing. Harriet Lilley, whose house was two doors away from the scene of the murder, told the inquest that she heard whispering in the street at about 3.30 a.m. She thought she heard several gasps and moans and awakened her husband. They both strained their ears for any further sounds but the noise of a passing train denied them and they went back to sleep. Patrick Mulshaw, who was on duty as a nightwatchman at the warehouse situated some hundred yards from the murder spot, said he was standing in the street smoking for a while between 2.30 and 3.30 a.m. – he heard nothing and saw no one enter or leave Bucks Row. Thus were the murderer's phantom-like qualities nurtured.

Inspector Helson told the coroner, 'I first got news of the murder at 6.45 and went to the mortuary after eight.' He described the appearance of the body and there was considerable discussion of the stays worn by the dead woman. The relevance of the stays was that they had prevented any injuries being inflicted above the level of the diaphragm. It also appeared that the abdominal wounds had been caused while the body was still dressed – at least, none of the skirts or petticoats were torn.

Harold Furniss, a contemporary journalist, made a point of visiting Bucks Row in the early hours of the morning about a week after the murder. 'I was much struck with the decent and orderly character of the Row itself,' he wrote. 'It is fairly wide as compared with other thoroughfares round about, but it is dismally lighted.' Standing practically on the spot where the murder victim had lain, he considered the suggestion made during the inquest that Nichols had been murdered elsewhere and then dumped in Bucks Row. He concluded, 'I am of Inspector Helson's opinion, and believe the murder to have taken place in the mouth of the stable yard where the unhappy creature's remains were found.'

THE FRONT OF 29, HANBURY STREET.

THE REAR OF 29, HANBURY STREET.
(The + shows where the body was found.)

The inquest on Nichols was adjourned several times and the outcome was overtaken by events, for, on 8 September, another sensational murder occurred in the East End. The victim was found in the back yard of 29 Hanbury Street, no more than half a mile distant from Bucks Row. The three-storey house was one of a large number built to accommodate the workers of Spitalfields' once thriving loom-weaving industry. With the advent of steam-driven machinery the industry moved away and the character of the workers' houses changed. Many of them were turned into lodging houses so densely inhabited that each room would accommodate an entire family. Seventeen persons lived at 29 Hanbury Street at the time of the murder, a family of five occupying the attic. The house was entered by a front door which opened into a passageway leading either to the stairs or straight through to the yard at the rear of the house. In order to allow access to the rooms of the house at any time, it was the practice to leave both front and back doors of the passage unlocked.

Local prostitutes often used this arrangement to their advantage, taking customers out into the yard or even onto the first-floor landing. It was an arrangement which was to prove fateful for Annie Chapman when she was picked up and took her companion through the front door at 29 Hanbury Street and out into the yard beyond. Her body was found by John Davis, a carman, who lived on the third floor. He got up for work and went downstairs as the nearby church clock struck six o'clock. The door to the yard was closed. He pushed it open, set his foot on the top step, and froze; lying at the bottom of the steps close to the fence was a woman whose throat had been cut. Davis, horrified at what he had discovered, staggered back into the house and went out through the front door into the street. He crossed over to Barclays, a shop which made packing cases, and blurted out his story to two workmen. They took a look for themselves and then ran off to Commercial Street Police Station to fetch help.

Inspector Joseph Chandler, the senior duty officer, took a verbal report from the excited men and went immediately to Hanbury Street with several constables. A crowd had already begun to gather outside the house and the police had to force their way through The inspector cleared morbid curiosity seekers out of the yard and passageway and sent for the divisional police surgeon. Telegrams were despatched to a number of senior police officers including Detective Inspector Frederick Abberline at Scotland Yard. From the rear door of the house, the woman's body could be clearly seen lying on its back parallel to the fence, with the

41

head near the steps. Her hands and face were smeared with blood and her legs were drawn up with the knees turning outward and the feet flat on the ground. She was wearing a long black coat, the skirt of which, together with her other clothing, had been pushed up high over her legs.

Onlookers found the horror of the injuries difficult to take in. The throat had been cut right down to the backbone with savage force. It was rumoured that a handkerchief around the woman's neck had been tied there by the murderer to prevent the head rolling away from the corpse. This unlikely suggestion was later dispelled when it was proved that the neck scarf had been in place when the killer put the knife to his victim's throat. The woman had been disembowelled and part of the small intestine had been pulled over the left shoulder. Not surprisingly, the body was drenched in blood.

Inspector Chandler ordered the body to be covered with sacking while he made a search of the yard pending the arrival of the police surgeon. His every move was watched by local inhabitants who peered out from every conceivable vantage point. The inspector could find no evidence of any struggle having taken place in the yard. The fence was intact, though its wooden palings close to the dead woman's head had been splashed with blood, presumably from the cut throat. There were also a few blood spatters on the rear wall of the house, again close to the woman's head.

When Dr George Bagster Phillips arrived on the scene from his surgery at 2 Spital Square, a little more order was restored to the proceedings. He formally pronounced the woman dead, not that there was much doubt over her status but protocol required official certification. Dr Phillips, a man with twenty years' experience of police work, was destined for a modest place in history with his examination of the body in Hanbury Street and his involvement with her killer's other victims. He instructed that the body could be moved to the mortuary and it was borne away in the very same coffin shell that had been used a week previously to transport Mary Nichols from Bucks Row. With the body gone, the doctor made his own examination of the crime scene.

On the flattened earth of the unpaved yard he found several items of interest to the crime investigation. A piece of muslin, a comb and a paper case lay close to the body, having fallen from the woman's skirt pocket which had been torn open in the attack. Near the spot where the victim's head had lain was found part of an envelope bearing the seal of the Sussex Regiment on the reverse and, on the front, the letter 'M' and the post office franking mark, 'London, 28 Aug., 1888'. There was also a piece of paper enclosing two pills. Close to the position of the feet lay two rings, removed from the fingers of the victim, together with some pennies and two new farthings. The apparent ritualistic significance of these phenomena would be mulled over in great detail in the years to come. Perhaps of greater significance at the time was the discovery in the yard of a leather apron saturated with water and lying near an outside tap.

Just before 2 p.m. on that same day, Dr Phillips arrived at the mortuary to make a post-mortem examination of the body. He was surprised to see that the body had been stripped of its clothes save for the handkerchief which was still round the neck. The body had also been washed and consequently he was deprived of the opportunity to relate the flow of blood to the injuries. Not for the first time was Dr Phillips to have cause to complain about the conditions in which he was expected to carry out his work.

The doctor found that the woman's face and tongue were swollen and there were bruises on the face and chest; the ring finger was also abraded where the two brass rings had been wrenched off. The throat had been cut from the left side of the neck with two distinct parallel incisions about half an inch apart. The abdomen had been entirely laid open and a bundle of the intestines severed from their mesenteric attachments. These had been scooped out of the abdomen and placed on the left shoulder of the prostrate woman, while from the pelvic region of the body the uterus

43

with its ovaries, part of the vagina and a portion of the bladder had been cut out and entirely removed. Cause of death was ascertained as syncope or failure of the heart due to massive loss of blood from the cut throat. Dr Phillips' findings were judged to be so horrific that they were not generally made known but appeared later in an issue of *The Lancet*.

The murdered woman was soon identified as Annie Chapman, a 45-year-old prostitute living at 35 Dorset Street. She had been separated from her husband, a coachman at Windsor, for about four years. For a time she had lived with a man who made wire sieves, an association which earned her the nickname Siffey or Sievey. She fell on hard times when her husband died and she lost the meagre allowance he made her. Her two children were put into homes and she tried to earn money by selling flowers and crochet work. Eventually, she lapsed into drunkenness and prostitution and 'Dark Annie', as she was known to her friends, joined that hapless band of women in the East End who sold their favours at fourpence a time in order to earn the nightly price of a bed.

Some of her former neighbours were able to cash in on Annie's misfortune by charging sensation seekers a few pence each for a look into the yard where she was done to death. Excited crowds moved about the streets until night-fall and little groups of people stood in doorways discussing the day's horror and latest rumours. News of the discovery of a leather apron at the murder scene led to suspicion being directed at a local man who was a boot-finisher by trade. Known as 'Leather Apron' because he habitually wore the protective garment of his calling, this man's description was close to that of an individual said to have accosted a young woman in Flower and Dean Street on the eve of the murder.

A large body of detectives scoured the East End and several men were arrested and then released. Mobs gathered outside police stations in the area shouting 'Murderer' at a number of unlikely individuals arrested for a variety of trivial offences. On 10 September the police caught up with 'Leather Apron' who proved to be a man named John Pizer living with his stepmother and sister-in-law at 22 Mulberry Street, off Commercial Road. He was arrested by Detective Sergeant John Thicke and taken to Leman Street Police Station for questioning. A search of his house produced several sharp, long-bladed knives. Pizer declared his innocence of any involvement in murder and denied that he was known as 'Leather Apron'. His friends gave him a good character reference, describing him as harmless and inoffensive.

The air of excitement in Spitalfields and Whitechapel was kept alive by reports of further arrests and, following Pizer's detention, Inspector Abberline himself brought a man into Commercial Street Police Station. William Henry Piggott, who was said to resemble the descriptions of 'Leather Apron', had been drinking in the Pope's Head public house at Gravesend when a number of customers noticed that his clothes were bloodstained. The local police were sent for and a sergeant went to investigate. On questioning the man, who seemed dazed and whose hands bore the marks of recent injuries, the sergeant learned that he had been in Whitechapel on the previous Sunday. Piggott claimed to have been walking down Brick Lane at about 4 a.m. when he saw a woman stumble and fall. Thinking she was having a fit, he went to help her and was bitten in the hand for his trouble. He struck her angrily and ran off when he saw two policemen approaching. Understandably, the sergeant arrested Piggott and awaited instructions from higher authority.

Neither arrest helped the police find the real murderer; John Pizer was released from custody on 12 September and poor Piggott's rantings while he was in the cells caused him to be declared insane and he was sent to an asylum. The amount of blood on his clothes when he was arrested, which appeared unlikely to have resulted from a bite on the hand, was never satisfactorily explained. The 'Leather Apron' episode was, in any event, something of a red herring.

Ownership of the water-soaked apron found in the yard at 29 Hanbury Street was eventually traced to John Richardson, son of Emilia Richardson, a widow who rented the ground floor of the house. He wore the apron when he worked in the cellar and the article had recently been washed and left to dry in the yard where the police found it.

The Working Lad's Institute was again the venue for the coroner's inquest which opened on 10 September, with Mr Wynne E. Baxter presiding. There was a strong police presence and the public, not admitted to the proceedings, were kept away from the entrance of the building. After the jury had viewed the body and the clothing, the discoverer of the crime, John Davis, was called as the first witness. Elderly and rather feeble, he was plainly frightened by the formality of the inquest. When he said that his work had prevented him helping the police to locate the men working in Hanbury Street who had raised the alarm after he had found the body, the coroner was quite sharp with him. 'Your work is not of the slightest importance compared with this enquiry,' Davis was told. Mr Baxter was in no mood to trifle. When Mrs Emilia Richardson complained that she had lost a day's work by attending the inquest, he replied, 'I am afraid you will lose many days before this enquiry is over.'

Mrs Richardson confirmed that the door giving entry to the passageway to the yard at 29 Hanbury Street was usually left open for the convenience of the lodgers. She also said that women not resident in the house sometimes came there although she herself had not seen such persons, either on the night of the murder or at any other time. Nor did she hear any suspicious noises on the night in question. She was followed by her son John who reported that he had entered the house little more than an hour before the body was discovered. He thought the time was 4.40 to 4.45 a.m. and both front and rear doors were closed. As one of his boots was pinching, he opened the rear door and sat down on the top of the yard steps and trimmed off a piece of leather with a table knife which he had in his pocket. If the body had been in the yard at that time he could not have failed to see it.

By admitting that he had been at the scene with a knife only an hour or so before murder was committed, John Richardson was living dangerously. The coroner elicited the information that the knife was about five inches long and sent the witness home to fetch it. The article was retrieved and duly handed over to the police.

When Amelia Farmer gave evidence, the coroner gained a full appreciation of what life in the East End was like for those who had fallen on hard times. Farmer, who lived in the lodging house at 30 Dorset Street, had been on friendly terms with Annie Chapman for about five years and was able to provide details of her private life. She said that she had last seen Annie on Monday, 3 September in Dorset Street. She was without her bonnet or shawl and had evidently been in a scrap; she had bruises on her head and chest which she showed her friend. Her explanation was that she had become embroiled in an argument with a woman who sold butchers' meat hooks. In fact the real cause was a drunken fight with a fellow prostitute named Liza Cooper over a piece of soap. The altercation began in The Ringers public house and finished in a lodging house kitchen with Annie apparently coming off worst. She was in a poor state when Farmer saw her and commiserated with her over her condition. Annie said, 'It's no use my giving way. I must pull myself together and go out and get some money, or I shall have no lodgings.'

Amelia Farmer loyally defended her friend's character at the inquest, describing her as 'very civil and industrious when sober, but I have often seen her the worse for drink'. She added, 'Taking her altogether she was generally very respectable. I never heard her use bad language in my life, and I know no one who would injure her.' The picture was of a once respectable woman whom widowhood and the loss of a pension had cast down. She was distressed by not having her children about her and sought refuge in alcohol. As a contemporary report put it, she was 'done to death by a fiend while selling her body for the price of a bed in a common doss house'.

Timothy Donovan, the keeper at 35 Dorset Street, the lodging house which had been home to Annie Chapman, told the inquest that he had known her for about sixteen months. She had lived in his lodging house for the last four months although her appearances had been irregular during the last week of her life. She came in on Friday afternoon and asked to be allowed to go down to the kitchen. He gave her permission as he was sorry for her when he learned she had been hurt in a fight. She was still there at midday on Saturday when he asked her about her bed. 'I haven't sufficient money for my bed, Tim,' she said. 'Don't let it. I shan't be long before I'm in it.' When she left, she said again, 'Tim, I shall be back soon. Don't let it.'

When Donovan last saw her alive, she was making her way down Paternoster Row. He said, 'She was generally the worse for drink on Saturdays' and added that he had admonished her for finding 'money for beer when you can't find it for your bed'.

The watchman at 35 Dorset Street, John Evans, was one of the last persons, apart from the murderer, known to have seen 'Dark Annie' alive. That was about 1.45 a.m. on Saturday morning, a few hours before she met her death, when she left the lodging house, and Evans, standing in the doorway, watched her disappear on her regular track down Paternoster Row. He saw her turn into Brushfield Street and walk towards Spitalfields Church: 'I saw her no more. She was a little the worse for drink, but not badly so.'

Annie was possibly sighted several hours after this by Mrs Elizabeth Long in Hanbury Street. Mrs Long was walking down the street on her way to work at Spitalfields Market at about 5.30 a.m. on Saturday morning when she saw a man and a woman outside number 29. She was certain of the time as the brewers' clock had just struck the half hour. The couple were talking and she thought the woman was Annie Chapman. She did not recognize the man but thought he looked to be over forty and appeared to be a little taller than the woman. He was of shabby genteel appearance, wearing a dark coat and a deerstalker hat; she thought he was a foreigner. As she passed them, Mrs Long overheard him ask, 'Will you?' to which the woman replied, 'Yes.'

Dr Phillips in his evidence thought that the murdered woman had been dead for about two hours when he saw the body at 6.30 a.m. Being the experienced man he was, he was the first to admit that the heavy loss of blood and coldness of the early morning might have distorted his judgement. If the body had not been dead for so long it was possible that the bump against the fence separating the yards of 27 and 29 Hanbury Street heard by a neighbour was caused by Chapman collapsing under the killer's assault. Mr Cadosh was in the yard of number 27 between 5.20 and 5.30 a.m. when he heard a woman's voice utter the single word 'No', followed by the bump.

The doctor gave a summary of the injuries inflicted on the body, in which he stated, 'Obviously the work was that of an expert – or one, at least, who had such knowledge of anatomical or pathological examinations as to be enabled to secure the pelvic organs with one sweep of the knife.' He thought the murder weapon must have been a very sharp knife with a thin, narrow blade, at least six to eight inches long. He conjectured that a post-mortem knife might have been the murder weapon or a well ground down slaughterman's knife but he discounted a leather cutter's knife as being too short. The indications were that the murderer had some anatomical knowledge and Dr Phillips believed that even without a struggle he could not have committed all the injuries in under a quarter of an hour. Performed deliberately, in a professional way, he believed it would have taken him the best part of an hour.

It was left to the coroner in his summing-up on 26 September to introduce the final drama. He said:

The deceased entered the house in full possession of her faculties although with a very different object to

49

her companion's. From the evidence which the condition of the yard afforded and the medical examination disclosed, it appeared that after the two had passed through the passage and opened the swing door at the end, they descended the three steps into the yard. The wretch must have then seized the deceased, perhaps with Judas-like approaches. He seized her by the chin. He pressed her throat, and while thus preventing the slightest cry, he at the same time produced insensibility and suffocation. There was no evidence of any struggle. The clothes were not torn. Even in those preliminaries the wretch seems to have known how to carry out efficiently his nefarious work. The deceased was then lowered to the ground and laid on her back, and although in doing so she may have fallen slightly against the fence, the movement was probably effected with care. Her throat was then cut in two places with savage determination, and the injuries of the abdomen commenced . . . The body had not been dissected but the injuries had been made by someone who had considerable anatomical skill and knowledge. There were no meaningless cuts.

Mr Baxter went on to mention the uterus which had been removed from the body:

The organ had been taken by one who knew where to find it, what difficulties he would have to contend against, and how he should use his knife so as to abstract the organ without injury to it. No unskilled person could have known where to find it or have recognized it when it was found. For instance, no mere slaughterer of animals could have carried out these operations. It must have been someone accustomed to the post mortem room.

Winding up his speech for the bombshell he planned to drop, Mr Baxter continued:

The conclusion that the desire was to possess the missing abdominal organ seemed overwhelming . . . The amount missing would go into a breakfast cup, and had not the medical examination been of a thorough and searching character it might easily have been left unnoticed that there was any portion of the body which had been taken . . . The difficulty in believing that the purport of the murderer was the possession of the missing abdominal organ was natural.

The fact was, announced the coroner, that 'there was a market for the missing organ'. He explained that some months previously an American called on the sub-curator of a pathological museum and asked him to procure a number of uterus specimens. The man was willing to pay £20 each for specimens preserved in a flaccid condition in glycerine. 'Now was it not possible,' asked Mr Baxter, 'that the knowledge of this demand might have incited some abandoned wretch to possess himself of a specimen? If your views are like mine,' he told the jury, 'we are confronted by a murder of no ordinary character, committed, not from jealousy, revenge or robbery, but from motives less adequate than the many which still disgrace our civilization, mar our progress and blot the pages of our Christianity.' The coroner thanked the jury for their attention and assistance and the usual verdict of 'Wilful murder against some person or persons unknown' was announced.

One of the immediate results of the murders was a call to increase the strength of the police in the Whitechapel area which, it was reported, 'was infested by bands of thieves who almost hourly committed robberies in broad daylight with impunity, the courts and alleys in the locality giving ready means of escape'.

Sir Charles Warren, the Metropolitan Police Commissioner, was picked out as a target for public criticism at an early stage. He was never short of advice, most of it unasked for and irrelevant. Vigilance committees sprang up, some of them with responsible aims, but others with members whose motives had more to do with self-advertisement. One of the earliest of these committees was formed by a group of sixteen senior local tradesmen, with Mr J. Aarons as secretary. This committee offered a reward for information leading to the capture of the murderer and started to raise funds by public subscription. From these beginnings emerged the vigilance groups whose aim was to assist the police in their patrols.

There was a fund of good will available at this stage which the authorities could have used to good effect but the vigilance committees were generally treated in a high-handed manner. The Mile End Vigilance Committee wrote to the Home Office on the subject of rewards and received this reply:

I am directed by the Secretary of State to acknowledge receipt of your letter of 16th, with reference to the question of the offer of a reward for the discovery of the perpetrators of the recent murders in Whitechapel, and I am to inform you that had the Secretary of State considered the case a proper one for the offer of a reward, he would at once have offered one on behalf of the Government, but that the practice of offering rewards for the discovery of criminals was discontinued some years ago, because experience showed that such offers of reward tended to produce more harm than good. And the Secretary of State is satisfied that there is nothing in the circumstances of the present case to justify a departure from this rule.

I am, Sir,
Your obedient servant
G. Leigh Pemberton

This reply did little to reassure East Enders that the authorities had their best interests at heart. A large meeting of the Mile End Vigilance Committee was held at the

Crown Tavern to consider the best means of preventing further murders and of securing the capture of a perpetrator. A list of subscription pledges was announced and the attitude of the Home Office deplored.

Punch, in its issue of 14 September, drew attention to one of the facets of contemporary society which it thought relevant. Under the heading 'A Serious Question', the journal enquired, 'Is it not within the bounds of probability that to the highly-coloured pictorial advertisements to be seen on almost all the hoardings in London, vividly representing sensational scenes of murder, exhibited as "the great attractions" of certain dramas, the public may be to a certain extent indebted for the horrible crimes in Whitechapel? We say it most seriously; imagine the effect of these gigantic pictures of violence and assassination by knife and pistol on the morbid imagination of unbalanced minds. These hideous picture posters are a blot on our civilization and a disgrace to the drama.'

A mere four days passed after Mr Wynne Baxter made his revelation about the procurement of female organs before the murderer struck again. In the early hours of Sunday 30 September, two women were butchered within an hour of each other at locations no more than three-quarters of a mile apart. At 1 a.m., Louis Diemschutz, steward of the International Working Men's Educational Club in Berner Street, returned to the club with his pony and cart. Despite the late hour, the occupants of the club were still enjoying themselves singing and dancing, no doubt to the displeasure of the rest of the neighbourhood. The street lights were out and the high-walled narrow court which led to the club premises from the street was in complete darkness. As he turned into the court, Diemschutz's pony shied and refused to walk on. After a second refusal, Diemschutz got down and, sensing an obstruction in the darkness, poked about with his whip. Something lay on the cobblestones but he could not make out what it was until he lit a match. In the split second of light provided by the match before it was extinguished by the night breeze he saw a woman's body.

53

The steward's first thought was that she was a drunk. He went into the club to fetch a candle and, followed by several club members, returned to the entrance. They lifted the woman up and by the light of the candle saw the gash in her throat. Her clothes were wet, for it had been raining lightly, and her body was still warm. There was blood on the cobbles where her head had lain and the men noticed that tightly grasped in one of her hands was a bag of cachous. Several of the men ran off to fetch the police and in no time the court was seething with activity.

Dr Frederick Blackwell, a local physician, arrived at 1.15 a.m. and examined the woman whom he found to be dead from a deep cut in the throat. As far as he could ascertain at this stage there were no other injuries and the suggestion was quickly put about that the killer had been prevented from mutilating his victim by the arrival of Diemschutz. It was also suggested that the steward's pony may have shied less at the body lying on the ground than by sensing the presence of the killer in the pitch blackness. Dr Phillips, the police surgeon, was next on the scene. He conferred with Dr Blackwell and then examined the hands and clothing of the persons in the club while the police made a house-to-house search in the immediate vicinity. The dead woman's body was taken to the mortuary and, as the corpse was put into the ambulance, several people recognized the victim as Elizabeth Stride who was also known as 'Long Liz'. The doctors, their duty done, prepared to return home to their beds.

At what time the Berner Street investigators learned of events a few streets to the west in Aldgate is unknown. Doubtless, the sensational news travelled quickly that a second woman had been found murdered that night by a patrolling policeman in Mitre Square. The significance of the location for Dr Phillips was that it was in the City of London and therefore put the investigation in the hands of the City Police.

Mitre Square is situated in Aldgate and lies between Mitre Street and Duke's Place. It has three entrances or exits: via Mitre Street or by means of passages linking with Duke Street and St James's Place. Two sides of the square were lined with warehouses belonging to Kearley and Tonge, in one of which a nightwatchman was on duty. The other two sides contained houses, most of which in the autumn of 1888 were not occupied. The square was patrolled every fifteen minutes and on 30 September it was part of the beat walked by PC Watkins of the City force. He trudged through the square at 1.30 a.m., lighting his way with his bull's-eye lamp but nothing excited his suspicion. When he returned at about 1.45 a.m. he discovered the body of a murdered woman lying on the pavement in the south-west corner. He later described the victim as ripped up like a 'pig in the market' with the entrails 'flung in a heap about her neck'.

Watkins, a policeman of seventeen years' experience, had never before seen such a sight as lay in the beam of his lamp that night. He rushed across to Kearley and Tonge's warehouse to ask the nightwatchman for assistance. They blew several loud blasts on their whistles in traditional fashion and reinforcements quickly arrived. Dr George Sequiera, who lived locally, was sent for and Inspector Collard arrived with Dr F. Gordon Brown, the police surgeon. Major (later Lieutenant Colonel Sir) Henry Smith, Acting Commissioner of the City Police, was spending the night at Cloak Lane Police Station near Southwark Bridge. He was informed of the discovery at Aldgate and immediately dressed and rushed to the scene in a hansom with three detectives clinging to the outside of the vehicle.

He saw the murder victim lying on her back, the right leg bent and the other straight with her feet pointing towards the square. Her throat had been savagely cut and the clothing pushed up to her chest exposing the lower part of her body which had been hacked open. The woman's face bore a large gash across the nose and down one cheek; her black straw bonnet decorated with beads and velvet was still tied to her head. Her pockets contained a few commonplace items, probably all that she owned in the world.

The gruesome task of examining the body where it lay fell to Dr Gordon Brown, assisted by Dr Sequiera, a local physician. There was little they could do, other than note the gross injuries, until a full post-mortem was carried out. The two doctors stayed with the body until the ambulance came and they supervised the transportation of the remains to the mortuary.

The identification of the murder victim did little to help Major Smith's peace of mind when he learned that, using the name Kate Kelly, she had been in police custody earlier that evening for drunkenness. Catherine Eddowes, for that was her real name, had been found drunk and incapable in Aldgate at 8.30 p.m. and had been taken off to the cells at Bishopsgate Police Station to sober up. Shortly after midnight she asked to be set free and, as she could at least stand upright, she was allowed to go. She gave her name as Kate Kelly and her address as 6 Fashion Street, Spitalfields. Saying ' 'Night, old cock' to the desk officer she walked out into the night towards Houndsditch and Aldgate.

Somewhere along the way she encountered her murderer. In light of her grisly fate Major Smith was particularly incensed because he had given instructions that every man and woman seen together after midnight should be stopped for questioning.

The murder in Mitre Square, more than any of the other killings, provided the police with clues. Following the discovery of the body, the police searched the immediate area and then broadened out the pattern. At 2.55 a.m. PC Alfred Long found a piece of cloth lying in the passageway at 108–119 Wentworth Dwellings in Goulston Street. The material was bloodstained and it appeared as if it had been used to wipe a knife clean. Detectives dealing with the body at the Golden Lane mortuary had already noticed that the woman's apron had been cut. The missing piece, presumed to have been discarded by the fleeing killer, was now in the hands of PC Long. On further investigation of the immediate surroundings, the policeman found what was to prove a controversial piece of evidence. On the black dado of the staircase wall in the model dwellings was a chalked message. Written in a rounded schoolboy hand in inch-high lettering in five lines were the words:

The Juwes are
The men That
Will not
be Blamed
for nothing

The writing on the wall.

PC Long reported his discoveries at Leman Street Police Station, handing over the bloodstained piece of apron which he claimed had not been in the street when he passed through at 2.20 a.m. Detectives were sent to Goulston Street and a detailed search was mounted. Nothing further came to light and the message on the wall remained the focus of attention. Daniel Halse, a detective with the City Police, stood guard over the message pending the arrival of Inspector James MacWilliam, head of the City CID, who instructed that the writing should be photographed as quickly as possible. The difficulty that emerged was one of jurisdiction. As Goulston Street was in the Metropolitan Police district, the man immediately responsible was Superintendent J. Arnold who inclined to the view that the message should be erased as it might inflame prejudice against the local Jewish population.

Arnold was not, however, prepared to give the order to remove the words until directed by higher authority. This came from Sir Charles Warren, the Metropolitan Police Commissioner, when he arrived on the scene at about 5 a.m. The City Police tried to talk him out of his decision but he was adamant. He would not even defer the erasure for an hour until there was sufficient light to take a photograph, nor would he allow only the single most offending word to be erased. According to Major Smith, once the words had been copied down, Warren himself rubbed out the message. He justified this action to the Home Office by saying he feared that if he had waited any longer, with street traders about to set up their stalls, a riot would ensue. He had some difficulty persuading Inspector MacWilliam of the correctness of his action and the City Police CID chief told him bluntly that he had made a bad mistake.

One further discovery was made before tired officers of both the City and Metropolitan forces were able to stand down. Detectives searching Dorset Street found blood in a public sink which stood in a recess where the murderer had, in all probability, washed his hands. Traces of the bloodstained water were still present in the sink when Major Smith was called to the scene.

The sequence of the night's events appeared to be that the killer had first murdered in Berner Street at about 1 a.m. when he was disturbed and then moved eastwards to Mitre Square, a walk of about fifteen minutes, where he murdered again between 1.30 and 1.45 a.m. Having completed his night's fiendish work, he made off, probably via Aldgate, and then turned northwards into Goulston Street at some time between 2.20 and 2.55, dropping a bloodied piece of apron as he went and lingering long enough to write his controversial message on the wall. Finally, still heading north, he stopped to wash his hands in Dorset Street and from there the trail ran cold. This would have been the

58

logical escape route, progressively distancing the murderer from the scene of the second murder.

On Monday 1 October, Mr Wynne Baxter, fresh from the criticism he had suffered from the legal fraternity over his disclosures in the Chapman case, opened the inquest on the Berner Street victim. This took place at the Vestry Hall, Cable Street, St George's-in-the-East where the room was of sufficient size to accommodate jury, press and public. After the jury had been sworn, they went with the coroner to view the body in the mortuary. Following his instructions, the body had not been stripped and washed so the jury were able to see it in much the same way as its discoverer at Berner Street. Sven Ollsen, pastor of the Swedish church in Prince's Square, identified the dead woman as Elizabeth Stride, born at Gothenburg, Sweden, in 1843 and named Elizabeth Gustaafsdotter. She had arrived in England in 1866 and married John Thomas Stride, a carpenter from Sheerness. He was supposed to have drowned, together with two of their nine children, when the *Princess Alice* sank in the Thames in 1878 with great loss of life. Stride's death was not corroborated by the records of the ship disaster and it was believed his wife put out this story to hide the fact that they had separated.

For the last three years of her life Elizabeth Stride had lived with Michael Kidney at 35 Dorset Street, Spitalfields. Their relationship was more or less regular but Stride took to drink and when life between them became strained, she would take herself off for a time but invariably returned. She had walked out on him a few days before she was murdered and Kidney did not see her again until she was in her coffin.

Dr Blackwell, the first doctor to arrive at the murder scene, stated that except for the extremities, the body was still warm when he examined it. The right hand, smeared with blood on the palm and back, lay on the chest; the left hand, partially closed, gripped a packet of cachous and lay on the ground. The woman's clothes had not been disturbed although a silk scarf round her neck had been frayed by the sweep of the knife across her throat, which was the only incision found on the body. The cut began on the left side, two and a half inches below the angle of the jaw and almost in direct line with it. The vessels on the left side had nearly been severed and the windpipe had been cut through. The cut terminated on the opposite side of the neck about one and a half inches below the angle of the right jaw but without severing the vessels on that side.

The doctor thought the murderer might have dragged his victim backwards by the scarf, the knot of which had been tightly pulled to the left side. He could not say if she had been standing or lying down when her throat was cut although, from the nature of the cut, he believed she probably bled to death inside a minute and a half. Dr Phillips who attended the post-mortem was more sure in his opinion regarding the murderer's mode of attack. He said, 'There was bruising over both shoulders and under the collar bone on the front of the chest indicating that she had been seized by the shoulders and forced down onto the ground. From the bloodstains it was obvious that her throat wasn't cut until she was lying down.'

Both doctors had examined a knife which had been found on the night of the murder in Whitechapel Road at about 12.30 a.m. Thomas Coram discovered it in the doorway of a laundry shop. The knife was nine to ten inches long with a bloodstained handkerchief wrapped round the handle. The blade was rounded at the end and its edge had been blunted as though turned up by continuous rubbing on a stone. Neither medical man thought this was the murder weapon – it was a slicing knife used in a joiner's shop and not the sharp pointed weapon used by the killer.

Evidence was given by William Marshall who lived at 64 Berner Street to the effect that he had seen Elizabeth Stride on the evening she was murdered talking to a man on the pavement at about 11.45 p.m. He recognized Stride both facially and also by the clothes she was wearing but the man's face was turned away from him. He described him as middle-aged and of rather stout build. He was about five feet six inches tall and wore a black cut-away coat and dark trousers with a round, peaked cap on his head; he had the appearance of a clerk. Marshall heard the man say to Stride, 'You could say anything but your prayers.' Two other witnesses saw a man and a woman talking together in Berner Street late that fateful night. Police Constable William Smith saw a couple at 12.30 a.m. and James Brown who was working late in a chandler's shop in Berner Street saw a man and a woman standing near the board school. Descriptions of the man given by the policeman and Brown were sufficiently similar in some respects to encourage the police to publish two descriptions in the *Police Gazette*:

At 12.35 a.m. 30th September, with Elizabeth Stride found murdered on the same date in Berner Street at 1 a.m., a man, age 28, height 5 feet 8 inches, complexion dark, small dark moustache; dress, black diagonal coat, hard felt hat, collar and tie, respectable appearance, carried a parcel wrapped up in newspaper.

At 12.45 a.m., 30th, with the same woman in Berner Street, a man, age about 30, height 5 feet 5 inches; complexion fair, hair dark, small brown moustache, full face, broad shoulders; dress, dark jacket and trousers, black cap with peak.

Mr Baxter's summing-up on this occasion was devoid of the dramatic revelations he had engaged in at the inquest on Annie Chapman. He gave a factual account of the evidence and agreed with Dr Phillips that the victim's throat had been cut while she lay on the ground. Despite the lack of mutilation in this instance which distinguished the crime from its predecessors, the coroner said 'there had been the same skill exhibited in the way in which the victim had been entrapped and the injuries inflicted so as to cause instant death and prevent blood from soiling the operator, and the same daring defiance of immediate detection which – unfortunately for the peace of the inhabitants and trade of the neighbourhood – had hitherto been only too successful'.

'Like a prowling tiger seeking its prey,' wrote Harold Furniss in the police budget edition of *Famous Crimes*, the killer 'when he vanished from Berner Street stole silently into the City, with his soul athirst for blood, and his long knife adrip, seeking for another victim on whom he might glut his fiendish appetite'. That victim was Catherine Eddowes, or Kate Kelly as she was known to some, and her mutilated remains reposed in the Golden Lane mortuary when Dr F. Gordon Brown arrived on Sunday afternoon to carry out the post-mortem examination. He was assisted by Dr Sequiera and Dr Saunders; Dr Phillips was also in attendance.

The doctors witnessed the removal of the clothing from the body which was quite cold, with *rigor mortis* well established. The corpse was washed and carefully examined. A bruise the size of a sixpence was observed on the back of the left hand and there were a few older bruises on the right shin. The hands and arms were tanned from exposure to the sun, but there were no bruises elsewhere on the body, which tended to support the view that, like Stride, she too had been murdered where she lay and had not struggled. The face was mutilated with several cuts. Both eyelids were nicked and the skin below the left eye had been cut through. There was a clean cut over the bridge of the nose, extending from the left border of the nasal bone down to the angle of the jaw on the right side across the chin. This cut went into the nasal bone and divided all the tissues of the cheek, with the exception of the mucous membrane of the mouth. The tip of the nose was quite detached by an oblique cut from the bottom of the nasal bone, and a further cut divided the upper lip and extended through the gums. About half an inch from the tip of the nose was another cut and there was also one in the angle of the mouth. The upper lip had been divided for a distance of about one and a half inches and slashes on each cheek had left triangular flaps of skin.

The throat was cut for about six inches, starting about one and a half inches behind the left ear and about two and a half inches below it, extending across the neck and finishing some three inches below the lobe of the right ear. All the vessels in the left side of the neck were severed and all the deeper structures in the throat were divided down to the backbone, the knife leaving a mark on the vertebral cartilage. Both the left carotid artery and jugular vein were opened, death being caused by haemorrhage from the cut artery. The other injuries were inflicted after death. Dr Brown recorded:

> The front walls of the abdomen were laid open from the sternum to the pubes, and the incision went upward. It was a rip. The cut commenced opposite the ensiform cartilage and ran up without penetrating the skin that was over the sternum or breast bone. The knife must have been held so that the point was towards the left side and the handle to the right. Behind this the liver was stabbed, as if by the point of the knife. Below was another incision into the liver 2½ in. deep, and below this again the left lobe of the liver was cut through some 3 in. to 4 in. The cuts were shown by the jagging of the skin, as if the knife had been withdrawn and stabbed in again. The abdominal walls were divided vertically in the middle line within ¼ in. of the navel on the left side, and made a parallel incision to the former horizontal one, leaving the navel on a tongue of skin. The incision then took an oblique course to the right. It divided the lower part of the abdomen and went down to ½ in. behind the rectum. There was little or no bleeding from the abdominal wounds, showing that they were inflicted after death. The cuts were probably made by one kneeling between the middle of the body.

When the doctors came to examine the contents of the abdomen they discovered what they had perhaps feared from the start – that there were organs missing from the body. Again Dr Brown gave his account:

> The left kidney was completely cut out and taken away. The renal artery was cut through ¾ in. This must have been done by someone who knew the position of the kidney and how to take it out. The membrane over the uterus was cut through, and the womb abstracted, leaving a stump about ¾ in. The rest of the womb was absent – taken completely away from the body, together with some of the ligaments.

The inquest on Catherine Eddowes opened at the Golden Lane mortuary on Thursday 4 October. The City coroner, Mr S.F. Langham, presided over a crowded court which included several senior figures. Major Smith, Acting Commissioner of the City Police, was present, together with Inspector MacWilliam, head of CID, and Mr Crawford, the City solicitor.

One of the first witnesses was Eliza Gold, sister of the dead woman, who gave evidence of identification. She said that Eddowes, who was aged forty-three, was not married but had lived with a man named Conway for several years and had two children by him. More recently, she had been living with John Kelly who had lodgings at 55 Flower and Dean Street. Kelly, who had seen the body in the mortuary, confirmed the identification and said he had lived with Eddowes for seven years. He explained that he earned a living as a street hawker and last saw her on Saturday afternoon in Houndsditch when she told him she intended visiting her daughter in Bermondsey. He heard later that she had spent part of the night in the police cells.

The keeper of the lodging house in Flower and Dean Street gave his former resident a good character. She was never violent and seldom drank to excess. In fact she was a jolly woman and was much liked by her fellow lodgers. She earned money by hawking and cleaning and Kelly paid their rent fairly regularly. He had never heard of Kate walking the streets for immoral purposes. When Kelly paid for his bed on Saturday, the keeper asked, 'Where's Kate?' 'I hear she's locked up,' he replied and paid fourpence for a single bed.

The police officers called to Mitre Square next gave evidence of the night's events. Inspector Collard confirmed that no money had been found on the dead woman and he produced her apron which he said corresponded with the piece found in Goulston Street. Then came the medical evidence with the horrifying catalogue of injuries noted by the doctors at the post-mortem examination. Dr Brown was cross-examined at some length by Mr Crawford who asked what conclusion could be drawn from the lack of abdominal bleeding. He answered, 'That the cut in the abdomen was made after death, and that there would not be much blood left to escape on the hands of the murderer. The way in which the mutilation had been effected showed that the perpetrator of the crime possessed some anatomical knowledge.' Mr Crawford went on to ask about the kind of weapon used to inflict the injuries and Dr Brown replied, 'With a sharp knife, and it must have been pointed. And from the cut in the abdomen I should say the knife was at least six inches long.' The cross-examination continued:

Solicitor: Would you consider that the person who inflicted the wounds possessed great anatomical skill?
Doctor: A great deal of knowledge as to the position of the organs in the abdominal cavity and the way of removing them.
Solicitor: Could the organs removed be used for any professional purpose?
Doctor: They would be of no use for a professional purpose.
Solicitor: You have spoken of the extraction of the left kidney. Would it require great skill and knowledge to remove it?
Doctor: It would require a great deal of knowledge as

to its position to remove it. It is easily overlooked. It is covered by a membrane.

Solicitor: Would not such a knowledge be likely to be possessed by one accustomed to cutting up animals?

Doctor: Yes.

Solicitor: Can you as a professional man assign any reason for the removal of certain organs from the body?

Doctor: I cannot.

In answer to other questions, Dr Brown thought that the murder had been committed by one person only and that there had been no struggle. He believed that the injuries inflicted on the body would have taken at least five minutes to perform. The doctor was specifically questioned about the disposition of the intestines. He replied, 'The abdomen was all exposed; the intestines were drawn out to a large extent and placed over the right shoulder; a piece of the intestine was quite detached from the body and placed between the left arm and the body.' 'By "placed",' asked the City solicitor, 'do you mean put there by design?' 'Yes,' was the reply. This exchange was to be accorded considerable significance at a much later date when Masonic influence was considered as the motive behind the murders (see Chapter 6, 'Royal Jack').

When the inquest resumed on 12 October, PC Alfred Long gave evidence about his discoveries in Goulston Street. Of the message on the wall, he said it read, 'The Jews are the men that will not be blamed for nothing.' The City solicitor asked him, 'Have you not put the word "not" in the wrong place? Is it not "The Jews are not the men that will be blamed for nothing"?' The policeman repeated the words as before and was then taxed about his spelling of the word 'Jews'. '. . .was it not on the wall "J-u-w-e-s"? Is it not possible you are wrong?' 'I may be as to the spelling,' replied PC Long. The circumstances which led to the message being obliterated were related to the jury. Long said he left the scene some time after 3 a.m. and when he returned at about 5 a.m. the writing was still intact. It was still not quite daylight when the chalked writing was finally and irretrievably erased at 5.30.

Joseph Lawende, who, in the company of two friends, had been in the Imperial Club at Duke Street close to Mitre Square on the night of the murder, observed a man and woman at one of the entrances to the square at 1.30 a.m. The three men were leaving the club when they noticed the couple standing at Church Passage. Lawende could not see the woman's face but from the clothing he had been shown in the mortuary thought it was the same that she had been wearing. The woman had her hand on the man's chest. He was taller than she and wore a peaked cloth cap. Mr Langham, the coroner, intervened at this point, saying, 'Unless the jury wish it I have a special reason why no further description of this man should be given now.' The jury agreed and Mr Langham summed up, suggesting the inevitable verdict of wilful murder against some person or persons unknown. The jury duly complied.

The description of the man seen in the vicinity of Mitre Square a matter of minutes before Eddowes was murdered was subsequently published in the *Police Gazette*:

At 1.35 a.m., 30 September, with Catherine Eddowes, in Church Passage, leading to Mitre Square, where she was found murdered at 1.45 a.m. same date, a man, age 30, height 5 feet 7 inches or 8 inches; complexion fair, medium build; dress: pepper and salt colour loose jacket, grey cloth cap with peak of same material, reddish neckerchief tied in knot; appearance of a sailor. Information respecting this man to be forwarded to Inspector MacWilliam, 26 Old Jewry, London, E.4.

Following the double murder, the climate of the East End of London reached a state close to hysteria. The murders were bad enough in themselves but a number of subsequent events screwed up the tension still further. Shortly before

67

the killings, the Central News Agency in London received a letter dated 25 September and postmarked 27 September 1888. Its chilling contents appeared to have been written by the murderer, who signed himself 'Jack the Ripper'. This letter gave the murders their unique title and, if genuinely written by the perpetrator, he christened himself.

Dear Boss

I keep on hearing the police have caught me but they won't fix me just yet. I have laughed when they look so clever and talk about being on the right track. That joke about Leather Apron gave me real fits. I am down on whores and I shan't quit ripping them till I do get bucked. Grand work the last job was. I gave the lady no time to squeal. How can they catch me now. I love my work and want to start again. You will soon hear of me with my funny little games. I saved some of the proper red stuff in a ginger beer bottle over the last job to write with but it went thick like glue and I can't use it. Red ink is fit enough I hope *ha ha*. The next job I do I shall clip the lady's ears off and send to the police officers just for jolly wouldn't you. Keep this letter back till I do a bit more work, then give it out straight. My knife is nice and sharp I want to get to work right away if I get a chance. Good luck.

Yours truly

JACK THE RIPPER

Don't mind me giving the trade name.

Wasn't good enough to post this before I got all the red ink off my hands curse it.

No luck yet they say I am a doctor now *ha ha*.

The reference in this taunting epistle to 'the last job' was to the Chapman murder but, bearing in mind the date of the letter, the reference to 'The next job I do I shall clip the lady's ears off' appeared to be a threat. Indeed the mutilations inflicted on Catherine Eddowes included a slashed ear although it was not severed from the head.

A second, shorter communication, postmarked 1 October 1888 and written on a postcard, was also received by the Central News Agency. The writer had not dated it.

> I was not codding dear old Boss when I gave you the tip. You'll hear about Saucy Jack's work tomorrow. Double event this time. Number one squealed a bit. Couldn't finish straight off. Had not time to get ears for police. Thanks for keeping last letter back till I got to work again.
>
> ## JACK THE RIPPER

According to *The Times*, the letter was received at the Central News Agency on Thursday 27 September and the postcard on Monday 1 October. The contents of neither communication were made known until 2 October. Details of the 'double event' appeared in the newspapers on Monday 1 October, thereby making it possible for someone other than the murderer to have written the postcard. The fact that the writer used the same unique name as in the letter and that there is the repetition of the desire to get the victim's ears upholds the common authorship of the two items. That they were written by the murderer appears to be borne out by the reference to failure regarding the first victim and also the expression of appreciation for keeping the first letter back, which was not known publicly until 2 October.

On 16 October, Mr George Lusk, Chairman of the Whitechapel Vigilance Committee, received a postal delivery at his home in Alderney Road off Globe Road, Mile End. There was a letter accompanied by a small cardboard box. The letter, addressed to Mr Lusk, 'From Hell' read:

> Sir,
> I send you half the Kidne I took from one woman prasarved it for you tother piece I fried and ate it was

very nise. I may send you the bloody knif that took it
out if you only wate a whil longer

Catch me when

you can

Mishter Lusk

Mr Lusk, already the recipient of several letters purporting
to come from the Whitechapel murderer, thought this latest
gruesome offer was another hoax. Nevertheless, he and
some of his fellow committee members took the cardboard
box and its revolting contents to a local doctor. The physician thought it was half of a human kidney which had been
divided longitudinally and he advised Lusk to show it to a
specialist. It was public knowledge by this time that a
kidney had been removed from the body of Catherine
Eddowes and there was at least a strong possibility that the
missing organ had now reappeared.

Major Smith was consulted in the matter and he requested the City of London Police surgeon, Dr Frederick Brown, to confer with the London Hospital. There, Dr Thomas Openshaw, the Pathological Curator of the Hospital Museum, examined the object and declared it to be a 'ginny' kidney from a woman aged about forty-five years who suffered from Bright's disease. He thought that it had been removed within the last three weeks and one of his colleagues was strongly of the opinion that the remains of the organ had been put in spirits within a few hours of being removed from the body. According to Major Smith the kidney remaining in Eddowes' body was also 'ginny'. Of the renal artery, which is about three inches long, two inches remained in the body while one inch was still attached to the kidney.

Following this episode, officers of the Metropolitan Police engaged in a few jibes at their City Police colleagues with references to the kidney having come either from a dog or from the dissecting room. For his part in the affair, Dr Openshaw received a mocking letter signed 'Jack the Ripper':

Old boss you was rite it was the left kidny i was goin to hoperate again close to your ospitle just as i was going to dror mi nife along of er bloomin throte them cusses of coppers spoilt the game but i guess i wil be on the job soon and will send you another bit of innerds

Jack the ripper

O have you seen the devle with his mikerscope and scalpul a-lookin at a kidney with a slide cocked up.

Letter-writers of all kinds were busy after the 'double event'. Frederick Wellesley wrote to *The Times* as follows: 'Sir – I beg to suggest the organization of a small force of plain-clothes constables mounted on bicycles for the rapid and noiseless patrolling of streets and roads by night.' In a similar vein, Mr L.R. Thomson wrote to the same newspaper: 'Sir – Will you allow me to recommend that all the police boots should be furnished with a noiseless sole and heel, of india rubber or other material, to prevent the sound of their measured tread being heard at night, which would enable them to get close to a criminal before he would be aware of their approach?'

The police were naturally under enormous pressure to halt the series of murders, the ferocity of which increased with every killing, and to capture the perpetrator who now mocked them in his letters. The Metropolitan force on whom the greater burden fell was in a state of some disarray and disillusion under its Commissioner, Sir Charles Warren. A serving army general, Sir Charles had been summoned from his military command in Africa in March 1886 to take over as Metropolitan Police Commissioner. This move was initiated by the Home Secretary, Henry Matthews, in order to improve public confidence in the police. Unfortunately, Warren's appointment achieved the opposite effect.

His first action was to reorganize the police on military lines, which did not endear him to the professional policemen who served under him, including his deputy and head of the CID, James Monro. During the 'work or bread' riots staged by the unemployed in 1887, Warren called out a squadron of Life Guards to disperse protesters in Hyde Park. This was an act which alienated the public and also made him unpopular with members of the government and civil servants. He was constantly at war with the Home Office over matters unconcerned with policing the capital. He disputed the Home Secretary's right to apply the Official Secrets Act to the Police Commissioner, and his annual reports, while neglecting to refer to criminal matters, were full of discussion about such matters as the provision of boots and saddles.

Sir Charles Warren's running battle with James Monro over the independence of the CID came to a head in August 1888 when he forced his deputy's resignation. Monro left on 31 August, the day that the mutilated body of Mary Ann Nichols was found in Bucks Row. Monro, widely regarded as the only man likely to catch the Whitechapel murderer, was replaced by Sir Robert Anderson who, for health reasons, was immediately sent on two months' sick leave. The night before he crossed the English Channel heading for Switzerland, the murderer struck down Annie Chapman in Hanbury Street.

Senior detectives already demoralized by Monro's enforced departure were now without leadership. Worse still, they were held up to criticism and ridicule. Even the coroner at Chapman's inquest asked if it was 'too much even yet to hope that the ingenuity of our detective force would succeed in unearthing the monster?' and *The Times* blamed the general lawlessness in the East End on 'the inability of the police to properly cover the whole of the ground within their jurisdiction'. Moreover, the very existence of the various vigilance committees was a reminder to the police that the public's confidence in them as custodians of the law had diminished.

Among the numerous innovations that Sir Charles Warren was urged to try was the use of bloodhounds. Writing in *The Times*, Percy Lindley offered some advice: 'Sir – With regard to the suggestion that bloodhounds might assist in tracking the East End murderer, as a breeder of bloodhounds and knowing their power, I have little doubt that, had a hound been put upon the scent of the murderer while fresh, it might have done what the police have failed in. There are doubtless owners of bloodhounds willing to lend them if any of the police – which, I fear, is improbable – know how to use them.'

The Times followed this up on 6 October 1888 by reporting that Sir Charles Warren had been making enquiries regarding the use of bloodhounds in the streets of London. Later it was rumoured that instructions had been issued to the police that in the event of any person being found murdered under circumstances similar to those of recent crimes, the body of the victim was not to be touched until bloodhounds were brought and put on the scent.

Sir Charles, who by now was virtually under seige by

the press and the public, ordered a private demonstration of the tracking powers of bloodhounds to be staged in Regents Park. On 8 October at 7 a.m. when the hoarfrost was still thick on the ground he was present when two champion dogs belonging to Edwin Brough of Scarborough, Yorkshire, were put through their paces. Barnaby and Burgho hunted a man for a mile after he had been given a head start of fifteen minutes. The Commissioner himself acted as the hunted man on two occasions when the tests were repeated the following morning in Hyde Park.

Sir Charles was made the subject of derision over the bloodhounds when it was reported that the dogs had become lost. This was due to a misunderstanding on an assignment completely unassociated with the trials, but so low was the Commissioner's stock that he was the universal scapegoat. *The Times* reported that Barnaby and Burgho had been bought by Sir Charles for use by the police, although this was refuted the following day by their owner, Edwin Brough.

Public interest in the murders remained highly tuned, indeed it appeared that there were no other newsworthy events in London. The women of the East End organized a petition to the Queen which was circulated in Whitechapel and the surrounding boroughs within days of the double event.

To Our Most Gracious Sovereign Lady Queen Victoria.
Madam:
We, the women of East London, feel horror at the dreadful sins that have been lately in our midst and grief because of the shame that has befallen the neighbourhood. By the facts which have come out in the inquests, we have learned much of the lives of those of our sisters who have lost a firm hold on goodness and who are living sad and degraded lives. We call on your servants in authority and bid them put the law which already exists in motion to close bad houses

within whose walls such wickedness is done, and men and women ruined in body and soul.

We are, Madam, your loyal and humble subjects.

Suggestions and offers of help poured into Scotland Yard – letters came in at the rate of 1,200 a day. One correspondent suggested that a body of strong, reliable and active women should be enrolled as special policewomen, and another put forward the idea of sending out on patrol policemen disguised as women. Among those with special skills which might have been helpful to the police was Dr L. Forbes Winslow, a specialist in mental disorders. On the advice of a friend, he placed himself in communication with Scotland Yard and shortly afterwards gave a lengthy interview to one of the evening newspapers. The doctor's modest boast was that he could capture the Whitechapel murderer inside a fortnight provided he was given a free hand.

His first plan was to set up a dozen decoys around London dressed in female clothing. Candidates for this risky task would be drawn from the ranks of wardens at mental hospitals. Dr Winslow believed the killer was suffering from incurable homicidal mania and men equipped by their training to deal with such maniacs would obviously stand the best chance of recognizing and apprehending him. He suggested to Scotland Yard that they contact every private and public lunatic asylum close to London, possibly even nationwide, and draw up a list of lunatics who had either escaped or been pronounced cured. His considered view was that the murderer of Annie Chapman was a lunatic at large, likely to be well-to-do and probably living in the West End. The doctor was thinking in terms of someone killing while in the grip of an epileptic attack who would subsequently have no recollection of his act.

Other medical men wrote to the newspapers giving their opinions – some supported Forbes Winslow, others preferred to put their trust in more conventional methods. A correspondent signing himself 'Medicus' made the point that a homicidal maniac would not seek privacy but would slay where he found his victim. It was therefore quite probable that the murderer's intention in seeking out-of-the-way places was nothing else than to commit an immoral act, and being on the point of committing this act, his excitement became epileptic with homicidal impulses.

A steady stream of letters purporting to come from the murderer was received by the police. The nation's hoaxers and jokers had a field day with prose and verse. Their tone ranged from the threatening to the humorous and occasionally bordered on prophecy. A scribe from Glasgow jested: 'Think I'll quit using my nice sharp knife. Too good for whores. Have come here to buy a Scotch dirk. Ha! Ha! That will tickle up their ovaries.'

One of the rhymes which secured a place in the history of the Jack the Ripper murders was the following:

> I'm not a butcher
> I'm not a Yid,
> Nor yet a foreign skipper,
> But I'm your own light-hearted friend,
> Yours truly, Jack the Ripper.

Another rhyme which had a sting in the tail in light of subsequent events was:

> Eight little whores, with no hope of heaven,
> Gladstone may save one, then there'll be seven.
> Seven little whores begging for a shilling,
> One stays in Henage Court, then there's a killing.

> Six little whores, glad to be alive.
> One sidles up to Jack, then there are five.
> Four and whore rhyme aright,
> So do three and me,
> I'll set the town alight
> Ere there are two.

> Two little whores, shivering with fright,
> Seek a cosy doorway in the middle of the night.
> Jack's knife flashes, then there's but one,
> And the last one's the ripest for Jack's idea of fun.

An alarmingly prophetic letter was received by Dr Forbes Winslow. Dated 19 October and signed P.S.R. Lunigi, the message informed the doctor that a murder would take place on 8 or 9 November. The correspondent added that the location would not be in Whitechapel but perhaps in Clapham or the West End.

Lord Mayor's Day fell on 9 November and the East End lodging houses were fuller than usual as hawkers and costermongers came into the area in the expectation of rich pickings. John M'Carthy, a Whitechapel lodging-house keeper who lived at 27 Dorset Street where he kept a grocer's shop, chose the morning of 9 November to chase up some of his outstanding rents. At about 10.45, he sent his shop assistant, Thomas Bowyer, to 'Mary Jane's' room to collect the thirty-five shillings that she owed. Mary Jane Kelly, a 24-year-old prostitute, occupied a single room which was really part of a larger house but had been partitioned off to provide ground-floor accommodation. It had a door leading to a narrow court and its address was 13 Miller's Court. A narrow arch led from Dorset Street into the court and the room was on the right-hand side. Further along the court were other houses, the rooms of which were mostly used by prostitutes. Like many of her kind Mary Kelly had had, until recently, a regular man living with her, Joseph Barnett, who worked as a labourer and had shared her accommodation for about eighteen months.

Bowyer walked into the grubby little court and went up to number 13. He knocked on the door and waited. When there was no reply he moved round to the window, one of the lower panes of which was broken. He pushed back the muslin curtain and peered into the dingy interior. His gaze alighted on two lumps of flesh on the table by the bed. Then his vision tracked across to the bed, where he saw a butchered corpse, and to the floor, which was covered with blood. Horror-struck, Bowyer ran back to M'Carthy and blurted out his discovery. The shopkeeper and his assistant ran back to Miller's Court and M'Carthy looked through the broken window at the bloody scene inside.

The remains of a barely recognizable human body lay on the bed in a welter of blood; the contents of the abdomen had been strewn about and one leg, bent grotesquely, showed white where the thigh had been stripped to the bone. M'Carthy sent his assistant to Commercial Street Police Station to fetch help while he remained outside 13 Miller's Court. Inspector Beck quickly arrived and after one look through the window sent a telegram summoning Divisional Superintendent Arnold. Inspector Abberline was notified at Scotland Yard and Dr Phillips was also sent for.

Abberline arrived on the scene at about 11.30 and gave orders that Miller's Court should be sealed off. The door to number 13 was locked and the results of this latest crime were viewed through the broken window. Dr Phillips's assessment was that the victim was obviously beyond any help. 'Having satisfied myself,' he said later, 'that there was no one else in view to whom I could render medical assistance, I thought it advisable in the public interest that no entrance should be made at the time.' He and Abberline decided that here was a chance to make use of bloodhounds and a telegram was sent to Sir Charles Warren requesting permission to fetch dogs to the scene immediately. What neither man knew at the time was that Warren had resigned the previous day, leaving the higher echelons of the Metropolitan Police in some disarray.

The police officers and doctor at Miller's Court waited for a decision to be given about the use of dogs, and they waited and waited. Finally, at 1.30 p.m., Superintendent Arnold decided to take matters in hand. First he had the window removed so that the room could be surveyed properly and photographs taken. When this was completed, John M'Carthy broke the door down with a pick axe. The appalling nature of the mutilation apparent through the window was considerably heightened by the proximity afforded by stepping into the room itself. The room was about twelve feet square and contained a bed, two tables and a chair. Dr Phillips, when he pushed back the broken door, knocked it against the bedside table on which was set a mound of red flesh hacked from the body.

The body, naked save for a linen chemise, was lying on the edge of the bed nearest the door; the other side of the bed was hard up against the partition wall of the room. The bedclothes had been pulled back and judging by the amount of blood on the sheets nearest the partition, Dr Phillips thought the body had been moved after the throat was cut. 'The large quantity of blood under the bedstead, the saturated condition of the palliasse and pillow at the corner of the bedstead nearest the partition led me to the conclusion', he said, 'that the severance of the right carotid artery, which was the immediate cause of death, was inflicted while the deceased was lying at the right side of the bedstead, with her head and neck at the top right-hand corner.'

The horrific details of the injuries were published in the *Illustrated Police News*:

> The throat had been cut right across with a knife, nearly severing the head from the body. The abdomen had been partially ripped open, and both of the breasts had been cut from the body, the left arm, like the head, hung to the body by the skin only. The nose had been cut off, the forehead skinned, and the thighs, down to the feet, stripped of the flesh. The abdomen had been slashed with a knife across downwards, and the liver and entrails wrenched away. The entrails and other portions of the frame were missing, but the liver, etc, it is said, were found placed between the feet of the poor victim. The flesh from the thighs and legs, together with the breasts and nose, had been placed by the murderer on the table, and one of the hands of the dead woman had been pushed in her stomach.

Among the carnage there were a few signs of order: the victim's clothes were neatly folded on the chair and still-warm ashes lay in the fire grate. Apart from the greatest mystery of all – identifying the murderer – the room at Miller's Court provided its own particular puzzles. The fire was one of them. A fierce fire had burned in the little grate and the sifted ashes produced traces of female clothing. Parts of a woman's skirt and the rim of a hat remained. Who the garments had belonged to, bearing in mind that the dead woman's clothes were still in the room, and why they were burned were questions that pundits would debate in later years. Abberline believed the clothes had been burned to provide illumination for the murderer's ghastly work. Another puzzle was that of the locked door. The popular view was that the murderer had locked the door when he departed, taking the key with him. Inspector Abberline's enquiries led him to the conclusion that the key had been missing for some time. Apparently Kelly and Barnett had been in the habit of fastening and unfastening the door by putting an arm through the broken lower pane of the window to operate the door bolt. Yet, if the door had to be forced to allow the police to enter after the murder, it appeared that someone did have a key.

The authorities contrived their own little mystery by having the eyes of the dead woman photographed. This resulted from the suggestion that in cases of violent death, the last impressions recorded by the retina remained fixed in the eye and could be retrieved photographically. Beyond the official statement that the eyes had been photographed, there was no further information on the subject either at the time or subsequently. Another non-event was the use of bloodhounds. After delaying their investigation of a brutal murder for over two and a half hours waiting for a decision, officers at the scene carried on without the benefit of the canine sleuths. It turned out that as Sir Charles Warren could not make up his mind whether or not to buy the dogs for the police, the animals had been detailed for other duties, Burgho to compete in a dog show and Barnaby to provide unofficial assistance in connection with a robbery enquiry.

As the Lord Mayor's Show proceeded towards St Paul's

Cathedral, the jollity of the annual occasion was broken by the cries of newsboys shouting that another murder had been committed in Whitechapel. Tension crackled among the spectators who were eager for details yet anxious for the safety of their womenfolk. The fact that the murder victims had been selected from the East End's band of prostitutes did not really impinge on the public until after the panic had subsided. The feeling was that every woman was at risk and respectable citizens no longer frequented the streets after darkness, much to the disappointment and financial loss of shopkeepers and especially pub owners.

As the day progressed, the news of Sir Charles Warren's resignation the day before was publicized. Having shifted Monro, he had still failed to exert the hold over the CID that he wanted and he was aware as the Whitechapel murders investigation progressed that the CID chiefs conferred under the auspices of the Home Office with minimal reporting back to the Commissioner. In his anger, Warren wrote an article for *Murray's Magazine* on 'The Police of the Metropolis' in which he stressed the need for the CID to be subordinate to the Commissioner. This was an unacceptable way for the Commissioner of the Metropolitan Police to discuss a grievance and Warren was told as much. He responded by offering his resignation to the Home Secretary who accepted it, probably in the knowledge that James Monro would succeed his former superior, which he did in the following month.

One of the unhappy Commissioner's last tasks was to issue an official pardon before he left office on 12 November:

MURDER – PARDON. Whereas, on November 8 or 9 in Millers Court, Dorset Street, Spitalfields, Mary Jane Kelly was murdered by some person or persons unknown, the Secretary of State will advise the grant of her Majesty's pardon to any accomplice not being a person who contrived or actually committed the murder who shall give such information and evidence as shall lead to the discovery and conviction of the person or persons who committed the murder.

This set the seal on a demoralizing phase in the fortunes of the Metropolitan Police and the press were quick to applaud Warren's departure. *Punch* ran a parody piece entitled 'Who Killed Cock Warren?'

Who chased COCK WARREN?
'I,' said the Home Sparrow,
'With my views cramped and narrow,
I chased COCK WARREN.'

And who'll fill his place?
'I,' said Monro,
'I'm the right man, I know,
And I'll fill his place.'

There were two more verses in similar vein, but *Punch* had adequately caught the public mood. Warren, the army general, returned to military affairs and Monro, the policeman, returned to his rightful place wherein he did a great deal to restore the status of the Metropolitan force.

An anxious and weary day for the officials at Miller's Court drew to a close when Dr Phillips gave instructions for the victim's remains to be removed to Shoreditch mortuary for post-mortem examination. At about 3.45 p.m. a battered coffin was brought to the Dorset Street entrance to Miller's Court on a horse-drawn cart. News that the murder victim's body was about to be removed caused a surge of public interest and people from adjoining streets came hurrying to the scene. The police held them back and their curiosity turned to something like respect as the mutilated remains of one of their number were driven away. Heads were bared and a few tears were shed as Mary Kelly made her last journey along Dorset Street. The door of 13 Miller's Court was secured with a padlock and the window boarded up. A police constable was stationed at the entrance to the court to deter curiosity seekers and the other officers returned to their stations. One of the detectives who had been present was Walter Dew who later gained fame as the officer who arrested Dr Crippen.

A deepening sense of fear and doom gripped the streets of the East End as news unfolded of the latest atrocity. A few of its densely packed inhabitants had something relevant to add concerning the last days and hours of the murdered woman but most could only pass on garbled tales of horror. Mary Ann Cox, one of the little clique of prostitutes who lived in Miller's Court, saw Mary Kelly with a male companion about 11.45 p.m. on the night she was murdered. Kelly had spent most of the evening drinking in and around Commercial Street and when she was seen by Cox entering Miller's Court she was very drunk and her man friend was carrying a pail of beer. He was described as a short, stout man, shabbily dressed and wearing a round billycock hat; he had a blotchy face and a carroty moustache. Cox followed the couple into the narrow court and called out 'Goodnight, Mary' as they entered number 13. Kelly called back, 'Goodnight, I'm going to have a sing.' This was followed by strains of 'Only a violet I plucked from my Mother's Grave when a boy'. Cox went to her room at number 5 where she stayed for about fifteen minutes before going out again. When she returned at 1 a.m. Kelly could still be heard singing, but after her final sortie for the night, at about 3.10 a.m., Cox reported that it was raining, the court was quiet and number 13 was in darkness. There were people living in the court who worked in the markets and Mrs Cox heard some of them moving about early in the morning. She distinctly heard footsteps at 6.15 a.m. which she thought was late for a man going to work at one of the markets.

The person who occupied the room above Kelly's was Elizabeth Prater, a married woman living apart from her husband and probably earning a living by prostitution. Mrs Prater returned to her room, which was designated 20 Miller's Court, at about 1.30 a.m. She was very tired and

MARY KELLY'S MOVEMENTS ON 8/9 NOVEMBER 1888 RECONSTRUCTED FROM WITNESSES' STATEMENTS

1 MARY COX
Lived at 5 Miller's Court; saw Kelly with man at 11.45 p.m.; followed them to Miller's Court; heard Kelly singing at 1 a.m.; all quiet at 3.10 a.m.

2 ELIZABETH PRATER
Sleeping in room above Kelly's; between 3.30 and 4 a.m. heard cry of 'Oh! Murder'.

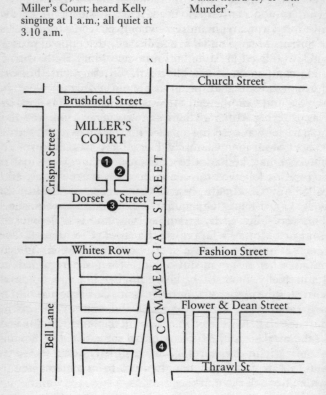

3 SARAH LEWIS
Visitor at 2 Miller's Court; at 2.30 a.m. saw a man standing at court entrance in Dorset Street. Just before 4 a.m. heard cry of 'Murder'.

4 GEORGE HUTCHINSON
Saw Kelly and companion at 2 a.m. in Commercial Street. Followed them to Miller's Court, waited and then left about 3 a.m.

lay on her bed fully clothed; she fell asleep almost immediately. She was disturbed at some time between 3.30 and 4 a.m. by her cat and, thus awakened, heard a low cry of 'Oh! Murder' in a woman's voice which appeared to come from the court below. Prater took no notice of what was a fairly commonplace cry in that district and went back to sleep.

Another person also heard a cry in the night. This was Sarah Lewis, a laundress who lived at 24 Great Pearl Street, and who called at 2 Miller's Court, opposite number 13, at about 2.30 a.m. on Friday morning. She saw a man standing at the door of the nearby lodging house in Dorset Street and described him as a stout individual wearing a black wide-awake hat. He was looking into the court as if waiting for someone. Sarah Lewis stayed at number 2 for nearly three hours. She dozed for a time in a chair and, a little before 4 a.m. heard a loud cry of 'Murder!' Like Elizabeth Prater she took no notice although she said she would have been alarmed if the cry had been repeated.

It was known that Kelly, aged twenty-five and unusually young for a victim of the Whitechapel murderer, was badly in arrears with her rent and was desperate to raise money. She had taken the room at 13 Miller's Court earlier in the year at a rent of four shillings a week and shared the accommodation with Joseph Barnett until 30 October. On that day, there had been a violent quarrel which resulted in a broken window and Barnett moved out and went to a lodging house in Bishopsgate. When Barnett was interviewed by the police he explained that he had fallen out with Mary Kelly when she insisted on bringing home a fellow prostitute, Maria Harvey, whom she invited to share their room. After attempting to make this arrangement work for two or three nights, a violent argument took place during which objects were thrown about, one of which smashed a window. By this time, Harvey had installed herself with some of her belongings, and Barnett, fed up with the whole business, left for other pastures. He last saw Kelly alive during the early evening of Wednesday

7 November when she was conversing with Maria Harvey.

Barnett was able to provide background information about Mary Kelly which at least helped to establish her antecedents. She was born in Ireland at Limerick, one of a family of seven, and moved to Wales where her father gained employment at an ironworks in Carmarthenshire. She married a Welsh miner when she was only sixteen and suffered a tragedy in her young life when he was killed in a pit explosion. According to Barnett's account of what Kelly told him, she took to prostitution while still a teenager because of the delay in payment of compensation due after her husband's death. She moved to London in 1884 where she was supposed to have lived in the West End before going to France with a gentleman friend. It was there that she acquired the habit of calling herself Marie Jeannette. In due course, she returned to England and to the East End of London where, still in her early twenties, she degenerated into the life of a common prostitute with an addiction to drink.

The inquest opened at Shoreditch Town Hall on 12 November before Dr Roderick Macdonald, coroner for North-East Middlesex. The expectation was that like previous inquests the proceedings would extend over several days. To the surprise of everyone, Dr Macdonald concluded the affair in half a day, and thereby handed down a subject of controversy for later generations to debate. Some critics claimed that the inquest was wrongfully taken away from Mr Wynne Baxter and that Dr Macdonald misdirected proceedings and withheld information. One of the Shoreditch parishioners called for jury service asked the coroner why the inquest was being held in his district when the murder had taken place in Whitechapel. Dr Macdonald's high-handed answer to this question was, 'Do you think that we do not know what we are doing here? The jury are summoned in the ordinary way, and they have no business to object. If they persist in their objection I shall know how to deal with them. Does any juror persist in objecting?' The original questioner did persist. 'We are summoned for the Shoreditch district,' he said. 'This affair happened in Spitalfields.' Another juror added moral support by saying, 'This is not my district. I come from Whitechapel, and Mr Baxter is my coroner.' Plainly irritated by the puzzlement of the jurors, Dr Macdonald declared, 'It happened within *my* district.' Later, however, he explained that 'jurisdiction lies where the body lies, not where it was found' which seemed to contradict his previous statement.

As no satisfactory answers were forthcoming, the jurors proceeded to the grim business of viewing the body in the mortuary. The mutilated corpse was covered to the neck so that only the head was visible. The face had been savagely disfigured and the only semblance of humanity was in the eyes of a once attractive woman. The jurors were then taken to the scene of the crime at 13 Miller's Court before returning to Shoreditch to hear the evidence of witnesses.

Joseph Barnett and the women who thought they had seen or heard things of significance – Mary Ann Cox, Sarah Lewis and Elizabeth Prater – gave their evidence. This suggested that time of death lay somewhere between 3.30 and 4 a.m. although this was contradicted by Caroline Maxwell, wife of the lodging-house keeper at 14 Dorset Street. She claimed to have seen Mary Kelly at the entry to Miller's Court between 8 and 8.30 a.m. on Friday morning, several hours after she was thought to have been killed. Mrs Maxwell said she spoke to Kelly saying, 'Why Mary, what brings you out so early?' Kelly said she felt unwell and indicated that she had just bought a drink at the nearby Britannia public house. Mrs Maxwell went about her business and when she returned half an hour later, she saw Kelly talking to a man at the same spot. She described the clothes she was wearing as consisting of a dark skirt, velvet bodice and maroon shawl but, unusually, she wore no bonnet. The man was taller than Kelly and wore dark clothes and a plaid coat.

The last witnesses at the inquest included Dr Phillips and Inspector Abberline. Advised by the coroner that he did not propose to go into all the medical details at that stage and that more detailed evidence could be given later, Phillips contented himself with stating that the immediate cause of death was due to severance of the carotid artery. This truncated form of medical evidence took no account of the time of death, the likely murder weapon or whether any parts of the body were missing. Inspector Abberline gave an account of the condition of the murder room, especially of the fire which had burned in the grate and which he believed had enabled the murderer to see what he was doing.

As far as Dr Macdonald was concerned, the proceedings had come to an end. To the amazement of most of those present he said that he did not propose to take any more evidence and enquired of the jury whether they were ready to reach a verdict. If they were satisfied that Mary Kelly had died as a result of the cut carotid artery, he advised them to bring in a verdict to this effect and leave the rest of the affair in the hands of the police. The foreman announced that they had heard sufficient evidence to return a verdict of wilful murder against some person or persons unknown.

The speed with which the inquest was concluded prompted comment by several newspapers. The *Daily Telegraph* expressed surprise 'that the inquest should have been closed before an opportunity was given to the relatives of the deceased to identify the body'. Referring to the possibility of 'rejection of evidence, irregularity of proceedings, or insufficiency of inquiry', the newspaper pointed out that the Attorney General could apply to the High Court of Justice to hold a new inquest. It was further observed that the failure to record witnesses' statements while their minds were still fresh might seriously disadvantage the prosecution in the event that this worst murder in the series resulted in a criminal trial.

The 'indecent haste', as it was described in some quarters, with which the inquest was drawn to a close meant that an important witness was not heard. This was

George Hutchinson, a labourer who lived at the Victoria Home in Commercial Street. He claimed to have seen Mary Kelly in the company of a man in Whitechapel within two hours of the estimated time of the murder. Hutchinson walked into Commercial Street Police Station at 6 p.m. on 12 November 1888 and made the following statement which was witnessed by Superintendent Arnold and two other police officers:

About 2 a.m. 9th I was coming by Thrawl Street, Commercial Street, and just before I got to Flower and Dean Street, I met the murdered woman Kelly and she said to me, Hutchinson will you lend me sixpence. I said I can't I have spent all my money going down to Romford, she said good morning I must go and find some money. She went away towards Thrawl Street. A man coming in the opposite direction to Kelly tapped her on the shoulder and said something to her, they both burst out laughing. I heard her say alright to him and the man said you will be alright for what I have told you. He then placed his right hand around her shoulders. He also had a kind of small parcel in his left hand with a kind of strap round it. I stood against the lamp of the Queen's Head Public House and watched him. They both then came past me and the man hung down his head with his hat over his eyes. I stooped down and looked him the face. He looked at me very stern. They both went into Dorset Street I followed them. They both stood at the corner of the court for about 3 minutes. He said something to her. She said alright my dear come along you will be comfortable. He then placed his arm on her shoulder and gave her a kiss. She said she had lost her handkerchief. He then pulled his handkerchief a red one out and gave it to her. They both then went up the Court together. I then went to the court to see if I could see them but could not. I stood there for about three quarters of an hour to see if they came out. They did not so I went away. Description, age about 34 or 35, height 5 ft 6, complexion pale. Dark eyes and eye lashes. Slight moustache curled up each end and hair dark. Very surly looking. Dress, long dark coat, collar and cuffs trimmed astrakhan and a dark jacket under, light waistcoat, dark trousers, dark felt hat turned down in the middle, button boots and gaiters with white buttons, wore a very thick gold chain white linen collar, black tie with horseshoe pin, respectable appearance, walked very sharp, Jewish appearance. Can be identified.

The statement was signed by George Hutchinson and bore the signatures of E. Badham (Sergeant), E. Lisson (Inspector) and J. Arnold (Superintendent) as witnesses. The description was annotated 'Circulated to A.S. [all stations]' and when Chief Inspector Abberline submitted the statement to his superiors, he reported, 'I have interrogated him [Hutchinson] this evening and I am of the opinion that his statement is true.'

The Times in its edition of 10 November carried an account of a suspicious character seen in the East End on the day of the murder. Mrs Paumier, a seller of roasted chestnuts, reported that at about midday on the day the murder was discovered 'a man dressed like a gentleman' asked her if she had heard about the murder in Dorset Street. When she said she had, the man grinned and, staring intently at her, remarked, 'I know more about it than you.' With that, he walked from her pitch at Widegate Street, which was about two minutes' walk from Miller's Court, down Sandy's Row. He looked back at her once before he disappeared in the crowded streets. Mrs Paumier described the man as about five feet six inches tall with a black moustache. He was wearing a black silk hat, a black coat and speckled trousers and carried a shiny black bag. She claimed that the same man had accosted three young women on Thursday night (8 November) and they chaffed him about the contents of his bag. His reply was that it was 'Something that the ladies don't like'.

Not surprisingly, after the various descriptions of Jack the Ripper suspects were published, anyone wearing a hat similar to those described or carrying a black bag was liable to be menaced by members of the public. A plainclothes policeman, unfortunate enough to be wearing a broad-brimmed hat, was pursued by a crowd of people in Commercial Road on 14 November. It only required some-one to point a finger and shout 'Jack the Ripper' and the curiosity of the mob turned to threatening behaviour. The detective was rescued by uniformed officers before he came to any harm. Doctors going to and fro at the London Hospital in Commercial Road had to be protected from the menace of crowds hanging about the entrance. Almost overnight, the black bag, traditional accoutrement of the visiting physician, had become a badge of murder.

Mary Kelly's remains were buried on 18 November at Leytonstone Cemetery. At least, the mutilated body found at 13 Miller's Court was buried on that day. The room was rented by her and the corpse, unclothed, facially disfigured beyond recognition and unseen by her family, was pre-sumed to be hers. She was not put in her grave until nine days after falling to the murderer's knife because the authorities feared that the awful circumstances of her death, hurriedly glossed over at the inquest, would inflame the population of the East End to riot. Several thousand people attended the funeral service at Shoreditch Church and among the coachloads of mourners was Joseph Barnett, her common-law husband. The coffin, which bore three ostentatious wreaths, was interred in a grave unmar-ked by a headstone. The cost of the burial was met by the clerk of the church who invited the public to contribute to the expense on the understanding that any excess would be used to erect a headstone.

The tense excitement in the East End gradually subsided although there was a panic on 21 November when rumour had it that another prostitute had been murdered.

The victim was Annie Farmer, a woman of the same type as the Ripper victims, who had been attacked by a male client in her lodgings at 19 George Street. She appeared in the lodging-house kitchen bleeding profusely from a wound in the throat. Several men there went to intercept her attacker but he had escaped. This incident, however, had the stamp of a prostitute's quarrel with her client over money. Farmer was found to have some coins concealed in her mouth and the injury to her throat had not been made with a knife. Happily, she recovered from her frightening experience.

The Autumn of Terror slid into winter, and 1888, perhaps the worst year in the fortunes of the Metropolitan Police, drew to a close. With Sir Charles Warren's return to soldiering, the way was clear for James Monro's appointment to the office of Commissioner. The prostitute population of the East End, reduced by five poor souls, would never be quite the same again. Reform was in the air; Jack the Ripper had seen to that with his brutal murders which had highlighted the social degradation which Victorians had perpetuated in England's capital city. The instigator of reform, perhaps even the scourge of the country's conscience, melted into the history books. Jack the Ripper would be a touchstone for retired police officers to write about in their memoirs and generations of crime writers would turn the reality of those grim days in 1888 into a legend. On the very last day of that fateful year, M.J. Druitt, a young barrister tired of life, committed suicide in the River Thames and added his own chapter to the story, either by coincidence or by design.

CHAPTER TWO
Interlude

The dying embers of the Ripper sensation were suddenly
fanned into life again in 1889. On 17 July, at about 1 a.m.,
PC Walter Andrew patrolling the streets of Whitechapel
found the body of a woman lying in Castle Alley, a long,
narrow passage which ran parallel to Goulston Street and
gave access to Whitechapel High Street. The constable
blew his whistle and his sergeant, to whom he had been
speaking only minutes before, came running. The two men
knelt down by the body which was still warm despite the
light rainfall. The woman's stockinged legs emerged from
her skirts which had been bunched up about her waist,
indicating a sexual attack, and there was a pool of blood by
her head.

A clay pipe found under the dead woman's body enabled the police to establish her identity as Alice McKenzie,
whose nickname was 'Claypipe Alice'. She lived at 52 Gun
Street with a labourer, John McCormac, who said he had
returned to their lodgings about 4 p.m. on 16 July and had
given Alice some money. He went to sleep and, when he
awakened, found that she had gone. That was at some time

between 10 and 11 p.m. and the next time he saw her was when he identified her body in the mortuary. McCormac described his former companion as a respectable woman who made a living by cleaning and tailoring jobs. The police had other ideas about her true vocation but everyone agreed that she was a heavy drinker. It was thought that she had originally come from Peterborough and that she had children from whom she was separated.

Dr Bagster Phillips was present at the scene within ten minutes of being called and his detailed report is still in existence. He described finding the woman, 'lying on back, face turned sharply to right . . . right arm enveloped with shawl which extended to end of fingers; forearm flexed over chest. Left arm not covered by shawl was flexed and hand rested on shoulder . . . left side of neck incised, wound jagged and exposed . . . clothes turned up exposing genitals . . . wound of wall of abdomen apparently not opening the cavity.' Later that day the doctor, accompanied by Dr Gordon Brown (City Police surgeon), performed a full post-mortem examination. The throat had been stabbed rather than cut. There were two wounds each about two inches deep made by knife thrusts directed from above probably while the victim lay on the ground. Dr Phillips concluded that these wounds, which had been 'caused by a sharp cutting instrument . . . by someone who knew the position of the vessels, at any rate where to cut' were the cause of death.

Bruises on the upper part of the chest suggested that the murderer held the woman down with one hand while stabbing her with the other. A jagged incision in the abdomen extended down the right side from the chest to navel. This wound, which pierced the skin and subcutaneous tissues without opening the abdominal cavity, had been made by a series of cuts. There were other superficial cuts around the genital region which, together with the main abdominal wound, had been made after death. Dr Phillips believed 'the instrument used was smaller than the one used in most of the cases that have come under my observation in the

"Whitechapel Murders" '. He noted in his report that 'Dr Gordon Brown has been good enough to express his concurrence in the foregoing conclusions.'

It seems clear that this murder was not committed by the Ripper, the strongest indication of this lying in the neck wound which was a stab and not a cut. For reasons which were not explained, Sir Robert Anderson, head of CID, decided to obtain another medical opinion – it was not really a second opinion, for Dr Brown had already given that – and asked Dr Thomas Bond to consider the post-mortem findings. On 18 July, in the presence of Dr Brown, Phillips discussed the post-mortem appearances with Dr Bond. By this time, the wounds had been sutured and the decomposition process had begun. In his report Dr Phillips noted: 'I believe I satisfied him [Dr Bond] of the correctness of the appearances. This must be so as he has since signified generally his assent to this report.' It later emerged that while Dr Phillips discounted Alice McKenzie as a Ripper victim, Dr Bond took a contrary view, stating, 'I see in this murder evidence of similar design to the former Whitechapel murders . . . I am of the opinion that the murder was performed by the same person . . .'

Thoughts of another spate of Ripper murders were overtaken by events of a different kind which drew in some of the participants of the Ripper story. In July 1889, news of the Cleveland Street scandal began to break. The existence of a male brothel in the West End of London shocked Victorian England to its moral roots and rumours that homosexual activities had been unearthed involving 'the highest in the land' appealed to the lascivious-minded public. The name of the Queen's grandson, Prince Albert Victor (later the Duke of Clarence), was linked with the scandal at the time as it would be, posthumously, to the Ripper murders. Chief Inspector Abberline was the CID investigating officer, acting under instructions from the new Commissioner of Police, James Monro. The Cleveland Street scandal finished with trials for gross indecency, criminal libel and conspiracy to defeat the ends of justice.

The police came out of the affair rather well. The *North London Press* told its readers that 'Mr Monro has spared neither himself nor his staff in his efforts to detect and punish.' Not that such praise was sufficient to prevent Monro's resignation over the matter of police pensions in June 1890.

The following year saw another resurgence in popular belief that Jack the Ripper was at work in his old killing grounds. On 13 February 1891, PC Benjamin Leeson, who, several years later, in 1911, distinguished himself at the seige of Sidney Street, answered the unmistakable whistle call from a colleague summoning assistance. It was a bitterly cold night that had emptied most of the streets of their teeming humanity. Perhaps glad to have the opportunity to warm himself, Leeson ran from his beat in the neighbourhood of the Mint towards Swallow Gardens, a railway arch spanning Royal Mint Street and Chambers Street. In Swallow Gardens he found a Metropolitan Police colleague, PC Ernest Thompson, and two nightwatchmen. 'What's up?' asked Leeson. 'Murder,' answered Thompson. 'A Jack the Ripper job.' Thompson, who had only been in the police service for six weeks, was clearly shaken and Leeson understood the reason when he saw the body. 'The form lying in the roadway,' he wrote later, 'was that of a young woman. Her clothing was disarranged, and there could be no doubt that she had been brutally murdered. Apart from the fearful wound in the throat there were other terrible injuries about the lower part of the trunk.'

Leeson recognized the victim as a local woman known as 'Carroty Nell' whose real name was Frances Coles. She was still breathing although she could not speak and it was plain that she was dying. PC Thompson walked his beat in rubber-soled boots and it was thought that his unheralded approach had very nearly surprised the murderer. Hundreds of police were drafted into the area in the hope of cutting off the murderer's escape and a full-scale house-to-house search was mounted. Dr Phillips, who by this time must have been England's busiest police surgeon, was called to the police station where the body had been taken.

In the gutter close to the murder spot a new crepe hat was found, which Frances Coles had obviously only recently acquired as her old hat was pinned to her shawl. The police pursued the clue with vigour and their persistent enquiries were rewarded when a shopkeeper in Bakers' Row, Spitalfields, identified the hat and stated that it had been bought for five shillings by Frances Coles on the previous afternoon. Apparently, earlier in the day Coles had made a down payment for the hat, promising to pay the rest later. The shopkeeper noticed a man standing outside the shop while they were talking. She was unable to observe him clearly but described him as thick-set, middle-aged and fairly well-dressed. Having bought the hat, Coles placed it on her head and pinned the old one to her shawl. She rejoined her companion and the pair walked away.

The police were obviously keen to question this man and were about to organize a search for him when further information came to light. Apparently, a man asking for Frances Coles had called at her lodgings in Thrawl Street on the night of the murder. One of the man's hands was bleeding and, by way of explanation, he said that he had been attacked and robbed. He stayed with Coles for about an hour and left at 1 a.m. Half an hour later, Coles left her lodgings bound for Swallow Gardens where she was later found dying from knife wounds. At about 3 a.m., the man returned to the lodging house covered with blood and in a highly excited state. His explanation, once again, was that he had been assaulted and robbed. The lodging-house keeper, not yet knowing that Frances Coles was dead but deeply suspecting the man's story, refused him lodgings and advised him to seek treatment at the London Hospital.

As Benjamin Leeson wrote later, 'There was tremendous excitement now among the police engaged on the case, as it really looked as though they were hot on the trail of the Terror.' The crowds gathered outside Leman Street Police Station went wild when they heard that a man had been arrested in Whitechapel – it was taken for granted that Jack the Ripper had been caught at last. There were scuffles when the man was taken into the police station and, if they had laid hands on him, there would surely have been a lynching. The arrested man was a seaman by the name of James Saddler who gave his occupation as ship's fireman aboard the SS *Fez* berthed in London docks. He protested his innocence of any involvement in the death of Frances Coles but was nevertheless charged with her murder.

Saddler freely admitted having been in her company from the evening of 11 February when he had been discharged from his ship. They had known each other on and off for a period of eighteen months since he had first picked her up while on shore leave. The couple's movements on the eve of her murder were readily plotted – they had lurched from one public house to another and, in between, she bought a hat and he was mugged. Saddler was quite emphatic that after leaving Coles at her lodgings at 12.40 a.m. he had not seen her again. Convinced of his guilt, the authorities held Saddler in Holloway Prison while the most prejudicial stories of his behaviour were allowed to circulate. So outrageous were some of these reports that the Home Secretary was obliged to offer his regrets in Parliament that the newspapers sought to gratify public curiosity in this way.

None of this, of course, helped Saddler, who, still protesting his innocence, knew only that everyone was against him. In his despair, he appealed to the Stokers' Union for help. 'What a godsend my case will be to the police,' he wrote, 'if they can only conduct me, innocent as I am, to the bitter end – the scaffold!' His case was taken up by Harry Wilson who began to construct a powerful defence for his client. For a start, he obtained glowing references from three ship's captains who upheld Saddler's character and conduct. Then he proved satisfactorily that the seaman had been attacked in the street on two separate occasions on the eve of Frances Coles' murder. The police were reluctant to let go of their best prospect to date of securing a conviction but after the magistrate had consulted the Attorney General it was decided there was insufficient evidence on which to base a prosecution. Saddler was duly discharged and the *Spectator* reported, 'It is almost beyond doubt that, black as the evidence against Saddler looked, he did not kill the woman; and it is more than possible, it is almost probable, that she was killed by 'Jack the Ripper', as the populace have nicknamed the systematic murderer of prostitutes in Whitechapel.'

The murder of Frances Coles was the last killing in England to be even remotely attributed to Jack the Ripper. Her death and that of Alice McKenzie have been generally ruled out of the Ripper series, being designated 'copy murders' because the *modus operandi*, although similar, indicated the killings had been carried out by another hand.

Monro's departure from the office of Metropolitan Police Commissioner in June 1890 brought promotion for Colonel Sir Edward Bradford, and Sir Charles Howard came in as Assistant Commissioner. Two years later, Chief Inspector Frederick Abberline retired to Bournemouth on his pension of £206 13s 4d a year. Unlike some of his contemporaries, he kept his memories to himself, resisting any temptation he may have had to put pen to paper. Poor Ernest Thompson, the constable who found Frances Coles' body, was himself killed in the course of duty. He was fatally stabbed by a man called Abrahams during a coffee-stall brawl in Commercial Road. Although mortally wounded, he clung so tightly to the collar of his attacker's coat that it required two men to loosen his grip.

Thus did the reality and first-hand memories of the Ripper murders and related events begin to diminish as the old century ran its course through the 1890s. Major Arthur Griffiths, one of Her Majesty's Prison Inspectors, and not a man directly involved with the Ripper murder investigations, nevertheless wrote extensively about his knowledge of police matters in his three-volume work, *Mysteries of Police and Crime*, published in 1898. It may be supposed that he knew many of the senior men in the police service and he certainly spoke in warm terms of Sir Melville Macnaghten whom Major Griffiths described as 'A man of presence . . . well built with a military air', who was 'more intimately acquainted, perhaps, with the details of recent celebrated crimes than anyone else at New Scotland Yard'.

It is also fair to assume that Griffiths was in the know as far as police thinking was concerned on the Ripper murders. Such insights as he did possess were doubtless included in his remarks on the subject published in his book. Under the comprehensive heading of 'A General Survey of Crime and its Detection', he wrote that 'the police, after the last murder, had brought their investigations to the point of strongly suspecting several persons, all of them known to be homicidal lunatics, and against three of these they held very plausible and reasonable grounds of suspicion'. The case against two of them was admittedly weak. These were a Polish Jew, a known lunatic who frequented the Whitechapel district and ended up in a lunatic asylum, and an insane Russian doctor who was in the habit of carrying surgical knives and instruments about with him and whose fate was unknown. The third individual offered stronger grounds for suspicion, according to Griffiths who wrote, '. . .there was every reason to believe that his own friends entertained grave doubts about him. He also was a doctor in the prime of life, was believed to be insane or on the borderland of insanity, and he disappeared immediately after the last murder, that in Miller's Court on the 9th of November 1888. On the last day of that year, seven weeks later, his body was found floating in the Thames and was said to have been in the water a month. The theory in this case was that after his last exploit, which was the most fiendish of all, his brain entirely gave way, and he became furiously insane and committed suicide. It is at least a strong presumption that "Jack the Ripper" died or was put under restraint after the Miller's Court affair, which ended this series of crimes.'

This account, although omitting any names, has the same general tenor and similar use of words as the notes written by Sir Melville Macnaghten in 1894, which did name names but did not see the light of publication until 1965. At some time during the early part of that long interlude, Sir Melville no doubt discussed his views with numerous contemporaries including Major Griffiths who used the ex-CID chief's overall conclusions in his book. Interestingly, Griffiths refers to his prime suspect as a doctor, repeating the mistake made by Macnaghten himself in describing the profession of M.J. Druitt, the barrister who the records showed drowned himself in the Thames at the end of 1888 and whose name appears in Sir Melville's notes as being that of one of three main suspects. The same error has been perpetuated in numerous accounts of the crimes, such as Canon J.A.R. Brookes' reference in his book *Murder in Fact and Fiction*, published in 1925. This author also referred to the murders being the work of a doctor on account of the skill used to perform 'the amputations'!

A decent interval elapsed before some of the leading figures in the Ripper murder investigation retired and published their memoirs which inevitably included reference to the events of 1888. Readers of such autobiography enjoyed a bumper year in 1910 with the publication of books by Sir Robert Anderson who succeeded Monro as head of the CID, Lieutenant Colonel Sir Henry Smith who was Acting Commissioner of the City Police in 1888, and Dr L. Forbes Winslow, a specialist in mental disorders. These three authors were all very certain about what they knew and, since over twenty years had passed since those terrible autumn days in Whitechapel, they doubtless felt beyond the range of serious challenge. 'I am almost tempted to disclose the identity of the murderer,' declared Anderson. 'There is no man living who knows as much of these murders as I do,' boasted Smith. '. . .it was I and not the detectives of Scotland Yard who reasoned out an accurate scientific mental picture of the Whitechapel murderer,' claimed the learned doctor. It was to be hoped that this combination of forensic talent, not to mention their various boasts, would result in a solution to the mystery.

Sir Robert Anderson, KCB, LLD, entitled his memoirs *The Lighter Side of My Official Life* and devoted part of a chapter to the Whitechapel murders. He explained how he was recalled to London from sick leave in Switzerland to be told by the Home Secretary, 'We hold you responsible to find the murderer.' Sir Robert's response was to decline the challenge in the way that it was put to him although he offered to 'hold myself responsible to take all legitimate means to find him'. He told the Home Secretary and the Metropolitan Police Commissioner that the measures he found in operation were 'wholly indefensible and scandalous; for these wretched women were plying their trade under definite Police protection'. Sir Robert was both a gentleman and a Christian who was offended by the low moral tone of the East End and conceived it as a practical instruction to have the police 'arrest every known "street woman" found on the prowl after midnight, or else let us warn them that the police will not protect them'. He admitted that the first course was too drastic and proposed to implement the second which seemed hard luck on the prostitute community who might have argued that they received scant police protection anyway.

Anderson seemed to take some credit for this measure which was put into effect after the 'double event' on 30 September. '. . .it is a fact', he wrote, 'that no other street murder occurred in the "Jack the Ripper" series. The last and most horrible of that maniac's crimes was committed in a house in Miller's Court . . .' This seemed a somewhat hollow victory for police strategy. He went on to say that 'One did not need to be Sherlock Holmes to discover that the criminal was a sexual maniac of a virulent type; that he was living in the immediate vicinity of the scenes of the murders; and that, if he was not living absolutely alone, his people knew of his guilt, and refused to give him up to justice.' Perhaps, at last, the secrets of police thinking at the highest level were about to be made public. 'During my absence abroad,' continued Sir Robert, 'the Police had made a house-to-house search for him, investigating the case of every man in the district whose circumstances were such that he could go and come and get rid of his bloodstains in secret. And the conclusion we came to was that he and his people were certain low class Polish Jews; for it is a remarkable fact that people of that class in the East End will not give up one of their number to Gentile justice.'

No supporting evidence was offered for this statement beyond the assertion that 'the result proved that our diagnosis was right on every point'. Conscious perhaps that he was asking his readers simply to accept this conclusion on his authority, Anderson rather lamely added that 'Scotland Yard can boast that not even the subordinate officers of the department will tell tales out of school, and it would ill become me to violate the unwritten rule of the service.'

He went on to refer to the Jack the Ripper letter which is preserved in the Police Museum as 'the creation of an enterprising London journalist' and, still aware of the credibility gap which widened with his every statement, wrote, 'I am almost tempted to disclose the identity of the murderer and of the pressman who wrote the letter . . .' Again, he drew back, saying, 'But no public benefit would result from such a course, and the traditions of my old department would suffer.' Sir Robert could not resist playing cat and mouse with his readers for he then proceeded to state, 'I will merely add that the only person who had ever had a good view of the murderer unhesitatingly identified the suspect the instant he was confronted with him; but he refused to give evidence against him.'

Aware of the possibly biased overtones of his pronouncement on Jack the Ripper's background, Anderson felt the need for further explanation: 'In saying that he was a Polish Jew I am merely stating a definitely ascertained fact. And my words are meant to specify race not religion. For it would outrage all religious sentiment to talk of the religion of a loathsome creature whose utterly unmentionable vices reduced him to a lower level than that of the brute.' Having told his readers at the outset that enough nonsense had been talked and written about the Ripper murders to sink a dreadnought, Sir Robert, far from adding enlightenment to the subject, merely fired a few blank salvoes.

If Sir Robert Anderson's revelations had been both few and disappointing, would the seeker after insights into the Ripper story learn anything from Sir Henry Smith, KCB? Sir Henry's memoirs, entitled *From Constable to Commissioner*, were also published in 1910 but, earlier that year, Anderson's theories about the identity of the Whitechapel murderer had appeared in an article in *Blackwood's Magazine*, thereby giving Sir Henry a chance to comment on them. He made full use of the opportunity to criticise what he termed as Sir Robert's 'reckless accusation'. It was the City Police Commissioner's boast that no one living knew more about the murders than he did and he claimed to have been 'within five minutes of the perpetrator one night'. Of course he was forced to concede that only one of the murders, that of Catherine Eddowes on 29 September, came within his jurisdiction. 'In August 1888,' he wrote, 'when I was desperately keen to lay my hands on the murderer, I made such arrangements as I thought would ensure success.' Sir Henry put nearly a third of his men into plain clothes and imagined, probably correctly, that 'they thoroughly enjoyed themselves, sitting on door-steps, smoking their pipes, hanging about public-houses, and gossiping with all and sundry'.

He claimed to have visited every butcher's shop in the city and 'every nook and corner which might, by any possibility, be the murderer's place of concealment'. The excitement in the East End had subsided after the murder of Annie Chapman and the night of Saturday 29 September found Sir Henry Smith sleeping fitfully in his bed at Cloak Lane Police Station close to Southwark Bridge. Suddenly the bell at his bedside jangled. 'What is it?' he asked the officer at the other end of the speaking tube. 'Another murder, sir, this time in the City,' came the reply. Dressing quickly, Sir Henry leapt into a hansom and with a superintendent sharing the double seat and three detectives hanging on the outside, he was driven to Aldgate. 'Although we rolled like a "seventy-four" in a gale, we got to our destination – Mitre Square – without an upset . . .' he recorded.

'I was convinced then, and I am convinced now', wrote Sir Henry in his memoirs, 'that had my orders been carried out in the spirit – they may have been to the letter – the reign of terror would have ceased that night.' What caused the Commissioner's indignation was the knowledge that the murdered woman had been in police custody a short time before she was attacked. Catherine Eddowes had been put into the cells at Bishopsgate Police Station for drunkenness earlier that night and had been discharged at about 1 a.m.; three-quarters of an hour later (Sir Henry claimed it was twenty minutes) she was found murdered. His instructions were to account for every man and woman seen together. 'It may be', he said, 'that the man and woman, having made an appointment, went separately to meet in the Square.' He added, 'That does not exonerate the officers of the City Police . . . Had she been followed, and men called to guard the approaches, the murderer would to a certainty have been taken red-handed.'

Sir Henry was critical of Sir Charles Warren's part in the night's activity. Of the Metropolitan Police Commissioner's instruction to erase the message on the wall at Goulston Street, Sir Henry wrote, 'This was, I thought, a fatal mistake.' He believed that the message, if photographed, might have provided an important clue. Its loss, like the bloodstained water washed from the killer's hands which he saw disappearing down the plug hole of a public sink in Dorset Street, added up to a night of frustration for Sir Henry. 'I wandered round my station-houses, hoping I might find someone brought in and finally got to bed at 6 a.m., after a very harassing night, completely defeated.'

The kidney incident was not designed to improve the City Police Commissioner's humour, not least on account of the ribbing he received from his Metropolitan Police colleagues. There were other distractions too, such as the letter addressed to Sir Henry, but unstamped, whose writer sought an appointment to pass on information about the murders. As Smith put it, the man's only reservation was that, as he was on ticket of leave from a prison and had not reported to the authorities, he was afraid the detectives at Old Jewry (City Police headquarters) would arrest him as soon as he made an appearance. He said that he could be contacted by means of a letter sent to an address in Hoxton.

Sir Henry took advice as to the course of action he should adopt and decided to write to the man at the address given. This he did, making an appointment to meet him alone in a West End square at night. 'Shortly before the hour named,' wrote Sir Henry, 'I took up my position on the pavement opposite. Punctual almost to the minute I saw a man advance from the north, and halt under the lamp. Crossing the road at once, I walked quickly up to him and looked him over steadily. The man confronting me could not have been more than five feet two or three inches in height. He was stoutly built, black-bearded, and of an ugly and forbidding countenance. "Have you come to meet anyone my man?" I said. "No, I haven't," he replied, in a civil tone. "Well, I have," I said, "and I mean to wait a bit longer to see if he keeps his appointment." ' Sir Henry decided that the most sensible action was to retreat to his former position and wait. 'There we stood,' he wrote, 'facing one another for five or six minutes, when the man turned and walked leisurely away.' After this inconclusive encounter, Sir Henry received another note declaring, 'Now I know I can trust you, I'll be at the Old Jewry as soon as I can.' Yet another disappointment ensued for there was neither a visit nor a further letter. The promised 'startling revelations' never materialized and Sir Henry, who believed 'at last I was on the right scent', was thwarted.

Not surprisingly, the City Commissioner believed 'the Ripper had all the luck'. He referred in such terms to the sighting made of a man supposed to be the Ripper in Mitre Square. A person he described as 'a sort of hybrid German' (Joseph Lawende, a commercial traveller) was leaving a club near Mitre Square when he noticed a man and woman standing close together. He was not sure of the time but said he saw the couple clearly in bright moonlight; 'without doubt,' wrote Sir Henry, this was 'the murderer and his victim'. The man was described as 'Young, about the middle height, with a small fair moustache, dressed in something like navy serge, and with a deerstalker's cap . . .' Sir Henry was quite certain this was the Ripper: 'The enquiries I made at Berner Street, the evidence of the constable in whose beat the Square was, and my own movements, of which I had kept careful notes, proved this conclusively,' he wrote.

Sir Henry was quite scathing about Sir Robert Anderson's declaration that the Ripper was a low-class Jew. 'Surely,' he said, 'Sir Robert cannot believe that while the Jews, as he asserts, were entering into this conspiracy to defeat the ends of justice, there was no one among them with sufficient knowledge of the criminal law to warn them of the risks they were running.' He pointed out that in murder cases at that time accessories after the fact were liable to penal servitude for life, adding, 'thus the Jews in the East End, against whom Sir Robert Anderson made his reckless accusation, come under that category'. He also took Sir Robert to task for studiously avoiding reference to the writing on the wall episode and the 'unpardonable blunder of his superior officer'. No doubt some old scores were being settled here and Sir Henry advised Sir Robert to refer to his Bible wherein Daniel interpreted the writing on the wall which brought matters to a crisis at Belshazzar's feast. 'Sir Robert is fortunate to live in times like the present,' he commented, 'but I fear the King of the Chaldeans would have made short work of him.'

While Sir Henry was a little more forthcoming than Sir Robert in his memoirs about the Whitechapel murders, his chief contribution was to plead the 'If only . . .' principle; if only his men had carried out his instructions, Jack the Ripper would have been captured. Apart from his criticism of the actions of the senior men at Scotland Yard, he had nothing new to offer his readers. At least it can be said in his favour that he did not pretend he had. The result was as disappointing to his readers as the frustrations of that night in September 1888 were to Sir Henry.

Dr L. Forbes Winslow MB, DCL, LLD, was a specialist in mental disorders who believed in giving his opinions 'straight out from the shoulder, as every true-born Englishman should do without fear of consequences'. Dr Winslow was not officially concerned with the investigation of the Ripper murders but there is no doubt that he would have liked to be. In his autobiography, *Recollections of Forty Years*, published in 1910, he wrote, 'I became intensely interested in the field of research before me, and gave my whole heart and soul to the study of the mystery . . . Day after day and night after night I spent in the Whitechapel slums.' While there is no doubting the doctor's enthusiasm for unravelling the Whitechapel murders, it is pertinent to enquire as to his qualifications in order that proper weight may be attached to his opinions.

His father was a medical practitioner who specialised in treating the mentally ill and founded an asylum at Hammersmith. Young Winslow was thus acquainted with mental illness from an early age and also appreciated that his father argued forcibly for recognition of the plea of insanity in criminal cases. He graduated in medicine from Cambridge in 1869 and joined his father whom he described as enjoying 'the largest practice in lunacy in England'. After his father's death in 1874 he ran the practice himself from consulting rooms in Cavendish Square. He earned subsequent degrees from both Oxford and Cambridge for dissertations on 'The History of Lunacy Legislation' and 'On the Criminal Responsibility of the Insane'. He gave expert evidence in a number of criminal cases including the Bravo poisoning case in 1876, the trial of Mary Pearcey who murdered Phoebe Hogg and her child in 1890, and the trial of Amelia Dyer who drowned several babies at Reading in 1896. Even when his advice was not sought Dr Winslow insisted on giving it, usually by means of the newspapers. As late as 1911, he was still campaigning on behalf of Florence Maybrick who was convicted of murdering her husband in 1889. His opinions usually ran counter to prevailing views. He believed Mrs Maybrick was wrongfully imprisoned, that Mrs Pearcey was epileptic and should not have been convicted and that Mrs Dyer suffered under a prejudiced judge. James Berry, the public hangman from 1884 to 1892, who would probably have despatched Jack the Ripper had he been caught and convicted, told Winslow, 'You've always got something to say.'

Not surprisingly in view of his professional interest in criminal lunacy and his undoubtedly strong views on related matters, Dr Winslow was keen to be consulted about the Ripper killings. His overtures to Scotland Yard were mostly rebuffed, which no doubt led to his remark that the police were incompetent and foolish not to take others into their confidence. 'Surely,' he wrote, 'in this case it would have been far better to have admitted the inability of the police to trace the murderer, and allowed others, who were apparently more able to deal with the matter, to assert themselves.'

Condemned to the pursuit of amateur sleuthdom, Dr Winslow threw himself energetically into his self-appointed task. 'I was at once a medical theorist and a practical detective,' he proclaimed. As a result of his visits to Whitechapel both by day and night, 'The detectives knew me, the lodging-house keepers knew me, and at last the poor creatures of the streets came to know me. In terror they rushed to me with every scrap of information which might to my mind be of value. To me the frightened women looked for hope. In my presence they felt reassured, and welcomed me to their dens and obeyed my commands eagerly, and found bits of information I wanted,' he told his readers.

According to the crusading doctor, Jack the Ripper claimed eight victims, the first being an unknown woman murdered in July 1887. Winslow believed all the crimes were committed by one and the same person who was a homicidal monomaniac of religious views labouring under the morbid belief that he had a destiny to fulfil. He chose prostitutes as the victims of his vengeance on society. As the murders progressed, so Dr Winslow refined his theory and he came to believe that the murderer was in all probability 'a man of good position and perhaps living in the West End of London. When the paroxysm which prompted him to his fearful deeds had passed off, he most likely returned to the bosom of his family.'

After the fifth and sixth murders (that is the 'double event' which claimed Stride and Eddowes as victims), he further modified his views. Mindful of the frightful mutilation performed on Eddowes, he wrote, 'I concluded that the perpetrator was a homicidal lunatic goaded on to his dreadful work by a sense of duty. Religious monomania was evidently closely allied with his homicidal instincts, because his efforts were solely directed against fallen women, whose extermination he probably considered his mission. Many homicidal lunatics consider murder to be their duty. Jack the Ripper possibly imagined that he received his commands from God.'

This kind of analysis was advanced for its day although later generations of murderers have borne out its correctness, for example Peter Sutcliffe, the Yorkshire Ripper. The psychological portrait of the killer is now a regular part of the investigation of murder but in Dr Winslow's time it was not an approach which had a place in the police repertoire. 'I communicated my ideas to the authorities at Scotland Yard,' wrote the doctor, 'and expressed my opinion that I would run down the murderer with the co-operation of the police.' He proposed to place a prominent advertisement in all the newspapers designed to tempt the murderer into the open. 'A gentleman who is strongly opposed to the presence of fallen women in the streets of London would like to co-operate with someone with a view to their suppression', was his suggested wording. His plan was to have detectives lurking at the place of appointment who would immediately arrest anyone who answered the advertisement. The proposal had to be abandoned as Scotland Yard, to use the doctor's words, 'refused to entertain the idea'.

Because of his interest in the murders, Winslow became the target for letters allegedly penned by Jack the Ripper. One of these, written on 19 October, was uncannily prophetic in declaring that a murder would occur on 8 or 9 November. This was the murder of Mary Kelly at 13 Miller's Court, generally acknowledged to be the last Ripper killing, although the doctor believed Alice McKenzie, killed on 17 July 1889, was the final victim. He accounted for the long interval 'by the fact that the lunatic had undoubtedly had a "lucid interval", during which he was quite unconscious of the horrible crimes he had previously committed'. Winslow again provided useful insights into the murderer's likely mental picture. He believed that his well-to-do killer suffering from religious mania was a 'quiet man with a perfect knowledge of what he was, oblivious of the past' when not in the grip of his mania. 'Jack the Ripper, however, in his lucid intervals,' he wrote, 'was a man whom no one would suspect of the fearful crimes he had committed.' Again this is consistent with the understanding gained by modern psychiatrists of the psychopathic mind.

Winslow believed he had achieved a breakthrough in his private investigation in August 1889, 'when a woman with whom I was in communication (for I had never stopped working on the murders) came to me'. She told him that a man had tried to pick her up in Worship Street, Finsbury, but she refused. Spurred by curiosity, she watched him enter a house in the yard of which she saw him washing blood from his hands after the murder of McKenzie. When the house was searched, the man had disappeared but a lodging-house keeper (another of the doctor's informants), told him that he had let a room to a man of the same description. That was in April 1888 when a gentlemanly-looking man called at the house in Sun Street, Finsbury Square, in answer to an advertisement. He rented a large bed-sitting room and said that he was on business which might necessitate a stay of a few months or perhaps a year. He told his new landlord that he had previously occupied rooms near St Paul's Cathedral.

The lodging-house proprietor and his wife noticed that their lodger changed his clothes frequently, often as many as three or four times a day. He kept very late hours and his return to the house was always completely noiseless, no doubt due to the fact that he liked to wear rubber overboots or galoshes, three pairs of which he had in his room. On 7 August, the night of Martha Turner's murder, the lodging-house proprietor stayed up late waiting for his wife to return from a visit to the country. About 4 a.m. his lodger turned up looking rather the worse for wear; he explained that he had been robbed of his watch in Bishopsgate and reported the incident to the police. This statement turned out to be false and when the maid went into his room the next day she found things not entirely to her satisfaction. There was a large bloodstain on the bed and a shirt with recently washed cuffs had been hung up to dry in the room.

A few days later, the lodger left the house explaining that he was going to Canada. Whatever his real intentions were, he was spotted boarding a tram in London several months later in September. This man was regarded by all who encountered him as a person of unsound mind. He often passed critical remarks about the number of prostitutes on the streets and, if anyone would listen, harangued them with his views on immorality. He filled his free time by writing vast tracts on religious subjects which he occasionally recited to his landlord – they were full of hatred and violence directed towards the prostitute community.

Dr Winslow assiduously gathered all this information together. 'As soon as I heard the description of the habits of his man, I said instantly: "That's the man".' He wrote in his memoirs that if he had constructed an imaginary person from his experience of people suffering from homicidal mania, 'his habits would have corresponded almost exactly with those told me by the lodging-house keeper'. Excited by his discovery and armed with a pair of rubber galoshes covered with dried blood left behind in the man's room, the doctor went straight to the police. 'To my great surprise,' he said, 'the police refused to co-operate.'

A record exists in Scotland Yard's files of an interview which took place with Dr Winslow at 70 Wimpole Street on 23 September 1889. Having been spurned yet again by the police, the doctor passed his information on to the *New York Herald* who published it in their London edition. 'I was severely criticized,' he wrote, but added with satisfaction, 'No more murders were committed after the news of my researches.' Chief Inspector Donald Swanson reported the interview to his superiors, including Winslow's explanation that his views had been misrepresented by the newspaper. It emerged that the lodging-house keeper who suspected one of his tenants was Mr E. Callaghan who subsequently moved to 20 Gainsborough Square, Victoria Park. The suspect was named as G. Wentworth Bell Smith, 'whose business was to raise money for the Toronto Trust Society'. Apparently he was in the habit of talking and moaning to himself and, on one occasion, told Callaghan, 'Physically I am a very weak man, but the amount of my will power is so great that I am able to outwork several men.' This statement bears an interesting comparison to the Yorkshire Ripper's reference to his 'latent genius' and 'dynamic energy'.

G. Wentworth Bell Smith had been the subject of police enquiries in August 1888 when detectives called at Mr Callaghan's house. It is not known what conclusions were reached, although it was alleged that Bell Smith kept loaded revolvers in his room. The Toronto fund-raiser was described in Chief Inspector Swanson's document as 'about 5 ft 10 in. in height, walks very peculiarly with his feet wide apart, knees weak and rather bending in. Hair dark, complexion the same, moustache and beard closely cut giving the idea of being unshaven. Nice looking teeth probably false, he appeared well-conducted, was well-dressed and resembled a foreigner speaking several languages; entertains strong religious delusions about women and stated that he had done some wonderful operations. His manner and habits were peculiar. Without doubt this man is the perpetrator of these crimes.'

Dr Winslow claimed that several months after the publication of his discoveries 'a young man was arrested for attempted suicide, and when examined by the police surgeon was proved to be hopelessly insane. He was committed to a Government asylum . . . the asylum authorities noticed that his description tallied with that of Jack the Ripper in my published statements.' The matter was investigated but it was found that the asylum inmate was not Jack the Ripper. 'In my opinion,' wrote Winslow, 'there was no doubt the murderer was the one who, on quitting his lodgings in Finsbury, left behind him a pair of silent rubber shoes, stained with blood, which I had in my possession for a considerable period.' The good doctor had also acquired three pairs of women's shoes and 'a quantity of bows, feathers and flowers, such as are usually worn by women of the lower class'. He added that some of the latter were stained with blood. It seemed that Dr Winslow's reward for all his investigative zeal was a motley collection of shoes.

The old adage that eavesdroppers rarely hear other than ill spoken about them was not true in the case of Winslow, at least according to his memoirs. He wrote about a train journey some time after these momentous events when he overheard two strangers discussing the Whitechapel murders. Oblivious of their travelling companion's identity, one said, 'At all events, if Dr Forbes Winslow did not actually catch Jack the Ripper he stopped the murders by publishing his clue.' The two men alighted at the next station and the doctor had to restrain himself from saying 'Hear, hear!' He wrote, 'I felt that what they said was the general opinion in England expressed by everyone except the Scotland Yard authorities, who would have deemed such an expression of gratitude towards me as unworthy of the great dignity of their office. I should like, in conclusion, to ask them one question, and that is: "If I did not arrest the murderous hand of Jack the Ripper, who did, and what part did they play in the transaction?" '

There is no doubting the part that Dr Forbes Winslow believed he had played in the affair – he is quite unequivocal about that. It is unfortunate that the sensible and, perhaps, far-reaching comments he made about the personality of the Whitechapel murderer were diluted by a desire for publicity which, in the end, gained the upper hand. He certainly never gave up his quest and reported receipt of a letter in July 1910 forwarded to him by the Postmaster General. Postmarked GPO Melbourne 10/6/1910, and signed by an unnamed woman, the gist of the letter was to confirm the doctor in the correctness of his views. He quoted the epistle in full in his memoirs, having considered it sufficiently important to pass on to the police because 'It seems in every way to corroborate my views on the matter, and may possibly lead to an arrest of the right man.'

Winslow's correspondent told him that he had frightened Jack the Ripper to the extent that he fled to Australia on board the *Munambidgee*. This man, who gained his medical knowledge from the family doctor who had allowed him to attend post-mortem examinations, confessed that he was Jack the Ripper. He said that he committed the crimes for revenge and research. The letter-writer claimed to have written to Sir Robert Anderson about her discovery and also to have approached the police in Melbourne, but no one seemed interested in what she had to say. After several years in Australia, Jack decided to move to South Africa where he was employed on the railways.

The anonymous lady correspondent seemed keen to have her man brought to justice if only to exonerate 'that poor demented Irish student' who had suffered in his place. In characteristic manner, Winslow set about righting this wrong and established that one William Grant, an Irish medical student, had apparently been charged with stabbing a woman in Whitechapel in 1895. As the case proceeded, the man was also accused of being Jack the Ripper, but protested that he had been accidentally involved in a skirmish with a gang of hooligans who had wounded the woman in question. Grant's solicitor had abandoned his client during the course of the police-court proceedings, claiming that Grant was indeed Jack the Ripper. Grant received a sentence of ten years' penal servitude for illegal wounding. Convinced that the real Jack the Ripper was in South Africa and that William Grant had been wrongfully convicted, Winslow pursued the case through the courts. The good doctor's final word on Jack the Ripper was his hope that 'I shall be the means of bringing his capture about'. If persistence and single-mindedness reaped their due reward, Dr Forbes Winslow's earnest wish would have been realized. Sadly, these qualities were not sufficient to solve the Ripper mystery. Winslow's sense of frustration still comes through in the pages of his memoirs and he could never reconcile himself to the thought that logic alone might not be enough to win him the criminal scalp he so badly desired.

A number of lean years followed the bumper recollections published in 1910, but the appearance of Sir Melville Macnaghten's autobiography, *Days of My Years*, in 1914 aroused expectations that new evidence might come to light.

Sir Melville started his chapter entitled 'Laying the Ghost of Jack the Ripper' by writing, '. . . I shall endeavour to show . . . the Whitechapel murderer, in all probability, put an end to himself soon after the Dorset Street affair in November 1888, certain facts, pointing to this conclusion, were not in the possession of the police till some years after I became a detective officer'. Macnaghten became Assistant Chief Constable at Scotland Yard on 1 June 1889 when, as he put it, 'police and public were still agog over the tragedies of the previous autumn'. He was quite emphatic in dismissing some of the murders attributed to Jack the Ripper and said that there were five murders only.

He lost little time in firing a salvo at 'a book of police reminiscences (not by a Metropolitan officer), in which the author stated that he knew more of the "Ripper murders" than any man living'. He was referring, of course, to his former City Police colleague, Sir Henry Smith, whom he described as 'a prophetic soul' as he claimed to have been looking for the murderer even before the first murder occurred. Sir Melville pointed out that the first real Whitechapel murder took place on 31 August and he briefly outlined the course of subsequent events.

Of the letter signed 'Jack the Ripper' and sent to the Central News Agency, he wrote, 'In this ghastly production I have always thought that I could discern the stained forefinger of the journalist – indeed, a year later, I had shrewd suspicions as to the actual author! But whoever did pen the gruesome stuff, it is certain to my mind that it was not the mad miscreant who had committed the murders.' Of the writing on the wall, written after the 'double event', the wording of which he gave as, 'the Jews are the men who will not be blamed for nothing', Sir Melville commented only that the 'chalk writing was obliterated by the order of a high police official, who was seemingly afraid that a riot against the Jews might be the outcome . . .' Macnaghten drew attention to the fact that the murderer's indulgence in mutilation increased on every occasion and that at Miller's Court he reached his crescendo. '. . . after his awful glut on this occasion,' he wrote, 'his brain gave way altogether and he committed suicide; otherwise the murders would not have ceased'. He was disinclined to accept the fictional thesis put forward by Mrs Belloc Lowndes in her novel *The Lodger*, published in 1913. This centred on a religious maniac, after the style of Dr Forbes Winslow's suspect, obsessed with the idea that he was predestined to kill prostitutes. Sir Melville did not subscribe to the view that the Whitechapel murderer had escaped from a criminal lunatic asylum, rather he was inclined to believe 'that the individual who held up London in terror resided with his own people; that he absented himself from home at certain times, and that he committed suicide on or about the 10th of November, 1888, after he had knocked out a Commissioner of Police and very nearly settled the hash of one of Her Majesty's principal Secretaries of State'.

Sir Melville Macnaghten shared with Dr Forbes Winslow the doubtful privilege of meeting Mary Pearcey the murderess, but the two men had little in common as far as their ideas on Jack the Ripper were concerned. Indeed Macnaghten thought so little of the doctor's theories that he did not even mention them. Nor did he mention any of his other contemporaries apart from the jocular reference to Sir Henry Smith. His conclusions were disappointing in their lack of detail and supporting evidence but he lent his weight to the theory that the murders ended because Jack the Ripper committed suicide.

Macnaghten was the last of the senior men of the day to go into print with accounts which might be expected to show insight or special knowledge. Many years after him came some of his more junior contemporaries who might have been heir to factual details about the murders but would not have been privy to the thinking of the top men. Frederick Porter Wensley, for example, was a young constable in his first year with the Metropolitan Police in 1888. He was appointed Chief Constable of the CID at Scotland Yard in 1924 and published his memoirs in 1931 after completing forty-two years' service. He would certainly have had access to the file on the Ripper investigation but his book, *Detective Days*, insofar as it deals with this subject, touches mainly on side issues. He wrote of being drafted to Whitechapel during his first year of service and of patrolling the streets without, as he put it, 'any tangible result'. At least his unsuccessful patrols were silent, for he said that beat policemen of the day nailed strips of old bicycle tyres to their boots in order not to give away their approach. He gave the official murder count as five victims but noted the striking similarity in method used to kill Frances Coles in 1891. Wensley's description of the East End of London made it clear how difficult it was to maintain law and order. He wrote that 'murder was probably more common than the official statistics showed; for bodies of people, who it is likely had been knocked on the head, were frequently found in the streets . . .'

Ex-Superintendent Neil who, as a detective sergeant in 1903, played a part in the capture of the poisoner George

Chapman, believed that his man was also Jack the Ripper. In his memoirs, *Forty Years of Manhunting*, published in 1932, Neil wrote, 'We were never able to secure definite proof that Chapman was the Ripper . . . In any case, it is the most fitting and sensible solution to the possible identity of the murderer in one of the world's greatest crime mysteries.' This view, which was said to have been shared by Inspector Abberline, is discussed in Chapter 3. Another detective sergeant who wrote about his police career was Benjamin Leeson who served under Wensley, a man he described as the 'World's Greatest Detective'. Leeson had a story to tell, for he became caught up in the momentous events of the seige of Sidney Street, but he also reserved a chapter for Jack the Ripper in his book, *Lost London*, published in 1934. He wrote about his experience of being called to the scene of Frances Coles' murder in 1891 which has already been related. Leeson also commented on the idea that George Chapman was the Ripper, giving a balanced account of the arguments for and against, concluding, '. . . nobody knows and nobody ever will know the true story of "Jack the Ripper" '.

A man who thought he did know the true story was Sir Basil Thomson, Assistant Commissioner of Police from 1913 to 1921. In his book, *The Story of Scotland Yard*, published in 1935, he wrote about 'the belief of the police' as far as Jack the Ripper was concerned. This was a reiteration of the suicide theory: '. . . he was a man who committed suicide in the Thames at the end of 1888,' wrote Sir Basil. He dismissed the later murders as 'imitative crimes' and regarded the famous letters as bogus documents. He went on to say that 'the belief of the CID officers at the time was that they [the murders] were the work of an insane Russian doctor and that the man escaped arrest by committing suicide at the end of 1888'. Thomson was mildly critical of Sir Charles Warren but otherwise had little to add to what he understood was the official view held by the police. Bearing in mind his senior rank and the fact that he succeeded Sir Melville Macnaghten, it is reasonable to conclude that he had access to all the available information. Even as late as the 1960s it was said that most incoming senior officers at Scotland Yard used their authority to send for the Ripper file if only to satisfy their curiosity.

Memories were fading fast by the time Chief Inspector Walter Dew went to print with his reminiscences of police service. He was one of the young policemen present at Miller's Court on 9 November 1888 and was destined to make his name as the man who arrested Dr Crippen. In his book, *I Caught Crippen*, published in 1938, Dew naturally devoted a few pages to his Ripper experiences – after all, he had been there. 'I was the first police officer on the scene of that ghastly crime in Miller's Court . . . What I saw when I pushed back an old coat and peeped through a broken pane of glass into the sordid little room which Kelly called her home, was too harrowing to be described. It remains with me – and always will remain – as the most gruesome memory of the whole of my police career.'

It was Dew's opinion that Emma Smith was the Ripper's first victim and he agreed with Sir Robert Anderson that the murderer enjoyed protection. 'Someone, somewhere, shared Jack the Ripper's guilty secret,' he wrote. 'Of this I am tolerably certain.' He was also inclined to dismiss the Ripper letter which 'did not deceive me for one moment. I was ready to stake my reputation that it was never penned by the man whom the signature was supposed to represent.' Of the suggestion that the murderer was a doctor, Dew commented, 'I did not see all the murdered women, but I saw most of them, and all I can say is that if the wounds they sustained are representative of a doctor's skill with the knife, it is a very simple matter to become a surgeon.' This is an understandable reaction but, of course, Dew was not qualified to give an opinion and, in any case, his view was at variance with those expressed by some of the doctors at the time.

He added a little to the collected wisdom on the murders by his remarks about the type of person the Ripper must have been. 'It will never be known just what were the powers of fascination Jack the Ripper held over women,' he wrote. 'There must have been something about him which inspired confidence in those he selected as his victims . . .' He asked if the explanation was that 'the man in appearance and conduct was entirely different from the popular conception of him?' As he pointed out, even after the horror of Annie Chapman's murder, the women caught up in the 'double event', aware of the dangers to their personal safety, still allowed themselves to be lured to their deaths. 'Is it feasible,' asked Dew, 'that there was something about him which placed him above suspicion?' The answer was probably the killer's ordinary appearance and behaviour but Dew did not answer his own question.

He thought it could be safely said that 'The man at times must have been quite mad', adding, 'There can be no other explanation of those wicked mutilations. It may have been sex mania, blood lust, or some other forms of insanity, but madness there certainly was.' He did not agree with the theories of Dr Forbes Winslow though. 'There is a big stumbling block to the acceptance of his theory,' wrote Dew. 'It is that the man who committed the Whitechapel murders had with him when he met his victims the weapon – and no ordinary weapon – with which the deeds were done. This surely suggests premeditation and indicates when he set out on his evil excursions it was his deliberate intent.'

By the time Walter Dew ventured into print with his memories of fifty years previously, the Ripper story had already been taken over by the new theorists, the first of whom was Leonard Matters in 1929. The memoirs of those who lived close to the events of 1888 and had first-hand knowledge and experiences promised more than they delivered. The senior police officers, knowing that they were expected to tell all, failed any reasonable credibility test by their hints of secrets they were not at liberty to divulge. Dr Forbes Winslow, for all his craving of official recognition, probably came as close as anyone to defining the persona of the Ripper. Perhaps unhappily for posterity, the doctors who attended the victims at the scenes of crimes maintained their silence and, with it, their professional dignity. The junior policemen gave their often vivid experiences of murder and mayhem in London's East End and repeated theories handed down from more senior echelons.

The strongest thread to emerge was the idea first put forward by Major Griffiths and subsequently reiterated by Sir Melville Macnaghten and Sir Basil Thomson, that the police believed the Ripper committed suicide in the Thames in 1888. Sir Melville commented that 'certain facts, pointing to this conclusion, were not in the possession of the police till some years after I became a detective officer'. His appointment as Assistant Chief Constable at Scotland Yard started on 1 June 1889, a year after he returned from India where he managed his father's property. A reasonable interpretation of 'some years' would be more than three, perhaps five, which leads up to 1894, the year that Macnaghten wrote his famous notes. Whatever credence may have been placed on the suicide theory, it was not a strongly held view, for, apart from the point made above by Macnaghten, there was irrefutable evidence of vigorous police investigation of Ripper-like activities as late as 1891. Of course there might have been an official cover-up in progress. But that is another story which is dealt with in Chapter 6. In the meantime, the field was open for the first of the armchair theorists.

CHAPTER THREE
Doctor Ripper

It was perhaps natural that Victorians, unfamiliar with the mutilating excesses of sex crimes, should think in terms of Jack the Ripper being a doctor. A surgeon or physician, his mind unhinged for some reason which sent him on the rampage with his operating knives, at least seemed to the man in the street a plausible explanation of those terrible murders. There is no doubt that this was the trend of public opinion from the time it was rumoured that the Whitechapel murderer carried his murder weapons in the type of black bag so universally associated with the visiting doctor. The close proximity of London Hospital to the district in which the murders occurred fuelled the flames of speculation.

The emotive and largely uninformed public view was, to some extent, strengthened by the statements made by some of the medical men who examined the victims. None of them suggested that a fellow professional was guilty of the murders but there were several positive references to surgical skill and knowledge. Dr Ralph Llewellyn noted the 'deftly and skilfully performed' incisions on the body of

Mary Ann Nichols; Dr Gordon Brown spoke of Catherine Eddowes' killer having 'a good deal of knowledge as to the position of the organs', and Dr Bagster Phillips, who examined four of the five victims, referred in the case of Annie Chapman to the Ripper as 'an expert' at least to the extent of his anatomical knowledge. Not that there was unanimity of views on the subject but the balance of opinion among those doctors who actually examined the victims was in favour of some skill having been demonstrated by the murderer.

At the time, the idea that Jack the Ripper might be a medical man went no further than an irrational prejudice against black bags. There was also the occasional eccentric suggestion such as a newspaper advertisement devised to trap the murderer:

> Medical Man or Assistant wanted in London, aged between 25 and 40. Must not object to assist in occasional post-mortem. Liberal terms. Address stating antecedents.

Replies stating name and address were optimistically requested.

There were suspicions too in the ranks of the police. Detective Sergeant Leeson, one of the officers called to the scene of the murder of Frances Coles in 1891, wrote of the Ripper murders: 'Amongst the police who were most concerned in the case there was a general feeling that a certain doctor, known to me, could have thrown quite a lot of light on the subject. This particular doctor was never far away when the crimes were committed, and it is certain that the injuries inflicted on the victims could only have been done by one skilled in the use of the knife.'

In a history of Scotland Yard, Sir Basil Thomson, Assistant Commissioner of the CID in 1913, wrote about the 'Jack the Ripper outrages' and of the victims 'who were ripped up by what appeared to be surgical knives of extreme sharpness'. He went on to say that it was the belief of CID officers at the time that the murderer was 'an insane Russian doctor and that the man escaped arrest by committing suicide at the end of 1888'. Later in his narrative, Sir Basil elaborated on this opinion: 'The only clue was the fact that the man . . . had probably been at some time a medical student.' Perhaps there was a thought that to ennoble the fiendish mutilator with the title of doctor was to denigrate a respected profession, whereas a medical student might be more acceptable while still possessing the necessary skill.

One of the milestones in publishing theories about Jack the Ripper's identity was the appearance of *The Mystery of Jack the Ripper* in 1929. This book, written by Leonard Matters, an Australian journalist who became an MP, is the first of what have come to be known as the classic theories. It is perhaps surprising that it took over forty years for the first full-length book to appear on the subject, but Matters perceived a gap in the readership market which has been heavily exploited ever since. In his introduction, the author asked the question, 'How could this mystery ever be solved when nobody seemed to be careful about the facts before attempting to suggest a solution?' In light of the explanation he proposed, Leonard Matters' regard for the facts of the case has been found wanting.

'I do not pretend that I shall determine exactly who "Jack the Ripper" was,' wrote Matters, 'but I shall indicate as closely as it may ever be possible for anyone to do so.' His candidate for the supreme criminal accolade was a Harley Street surgeon whom he introduced in a chapter intriguingly entitled 'The Satanic Dr Stanley'. This man was a doctor whose early brilliance had furnished him with a considerable reputation in London's exclusive medical circles. He was admired by the medical students at the great hospitals and commanded large fees for the practice of his skills.

Having reached the pinnacle of an outstanding career, Dr Stanley suffered the first of two bitter personal tragedies which were to alter his whole life. The first was the loss of his wife which left him lonely and embittered save for the devotion he lavished on his son. The second blow was the loss of that son whose illness and death medical science was powerless to prevent. It was the loss of his son which turned the suave West End surgeon into the 'satanic Dr Stanley'.

After his wife's death, Stanley was consumed by the desire to give his son every conceivable advantage to succeed in life. His dream was that the boy should become a great surgeon and a saviour of humanity. He was prepared to sacrifice his own career to bring this about and his friends found him a changed man. Single-mindedness became a neurotic obsession and the morose and unapproachable nature he showed in his hospital work was only lifted when he was in the presence of his son.

The young man with the devoted father had all the advantages of good looks and a keen mind. He embarked on a brilliant university career and the right doors were opened for him by his father's money. But this clever son of a clever father had a singular flaw – he had an unhealthy appetite for drinking, gambling and womanizing. Herbert Stanley appeared on the social circuit that his father had long since abandoned. He was welcomed everywhere as a prince of good fellows distinguished by his dash and looking for a good time.

But all this gaiety and brilliance was to come to a sordid end. On boat race night in 1886, young Stanley met attractive Marie Jeannette in the Café Monico where he was celebrating with friends. He found her a compelling personality and asked her to join his party. After an evening of laughter and carousing, Stanley and his newly-found girl friend slipped away to spend the remainder of the night together. Had he been more sober and more a man of the world Stanley would have realized that his chance companion was a member of the oldest profession in the world. Marie Jeannette and her friends knew they would secure rich pickings from well-heeled, semi-inebriated students celebrating the boat race. Their clients, throwing all caution to the winds, ran the risk of contracting venereal disease. Stanley was to be such a luckless victim.

When he realized the nature of the girl's background, Stanley finished with her but by then it was too late. The awful revelation that he had contracted syphilis dawned on him and he eventually admitted his plight to his father. Dr Stanley resolved at once to pit all his medical skill and experience against the disease. Despite his own efforts and those of the top medical men of the day, Stanley was powerless to halt the progress of the syphilis which was inexorably eroding his son's health. The point was reached when both father and son realized the hopelessness of the struggle. Dr Stanley quizzed his son about the woman who had brought him so low. 'Who was this woman? . . . Where did she live?' Young Stanley's eyes flickered with light: 'She calls herself Kelly.' Dr Stanley registered the full name – Marie Jeannette Kelly.

After his son died, Dr Stanley stood by his bed and vowed to find the woman whom he held responsible for his death. 'I will find the woman. When I find her, I will kill her; by God, I will!' This brooding bitter man started his search the very next day. He did not return home after he had completed his hospital duties but went up to London's West End where he mingled with the crowds and took a particular interest in the streetwalkers. His objective was to be able to tell at a glance whether a girl was respectable or not. He quickly acquired a knowledge of the appearance, behaviour and background of London's prostitutes. He also learned a great deal about the methods of the police and how they organized their street patrols. After a month's self-imposed familiarization course, Dr Stanley felt equipped to begin his task of looking for Marie Jeannette Kelly.

He began his search in Wardour Street, Soho, at an address he had been told was used by his quarry. This first enquiry proved disappointing, for Stanley soon learned that Marie had moved out and now lived in the less salubrious East End of London. The woman from whom he gleaned this information found him menacing, and declared, 'My God! I'm glad I'm not Marie. If I was that man would kill me.' Armed with nothing more than

Marie's name and his knowledge of her occupation. Stanley ventured into the slums of Whitechapel and Spitalfields. He decided that the quickest way of finding her would be to question other prostitutes and, regardless of the answer he received, despatch them to the death he felt sure they deserved. He realized that he might need to approach several women before he acquired the answer to his question, but he was prepared to take the risk. He justified his plan on the grounds that 'All such women should be killed' because they were 'a curse on civilisation – a menace to society and public health'.

On the night of Bank Holiday, 6 August 1888, armed with a dagger and a long surgical knife, Dr Stanley became transformed into Jack the Ripper. Wearing a long, shabby black coat, he walked the dimly-lit streets and lanes that led off from Commercial Road. In Brick Lane, Flower and Dean Street and then Fashion Street, he observed the raucous behaviour of the denizens of Whitechapel as they downed their ale and quarrelled drunkenly in the road. Then, turning into Osborne Street, he spotted a lone prostitute. He engaged her in conversation and they walked into the shadows of a nearby alley. He asked her about Marie Jeannette Kelly but, no, she did not know the girl. No sooner was the denial on her lips than Stanley's knife was at her throat. She collapsed silently to the ground – the first of Jack the Ripper's victims.

When this act of murder was not followed by sensational headlines in the newspapers, Stanley realized how easy it was to rid the world of these worthless women who plagued mankind with disease. But he also felt that he had acted wildly on his first excursion on the murder trail and resolved in future to use more of the skill and precision for which he had been trained. On 31 August, he encountered a streetwalker in Bucks Row. She was unable to help him with his question and he left her dying on the pavement with a cut throat. A few days later, on 8 September, he tried again, this time in Hanbury Street. The result was the same – another murdered prostitute but no answer to his question regarding the whereabouts of Marie Jeannette Kelly.

By this time, the deaths of several prostitutes in London's East End had attracted newspaper coverage but Stanley entertained no fears. It was obvious that the police had no idea as to the identity or purpose of the killer and he was confident in the knowledge that no one shared his secret. He had even been bold enough to open up his last victim and remove the uterus which he wanted for his collection of anatomical specimens. He afforded himself the luxury of private humour at the confusion which prevailed among the authorities and their tales of a madman's mutilations.

In the early hours of 30 September, Dr Stanley once again donned his long black coat of death and made for Whitechapel. He followed a streetwalker into a yard in Berner Street and quickly despatched her when it was obvious she could not provide him with the information he so earnestly needed. Frustrated, he hurried from the scene and quickly encountered another prostitute who had been ejected from police custody for being drunk. His pulse quickened when he learned that her name was Kate Kelly but he could not conceive that this broken-down old hag was the woman who had caused his son's misfortune. She explained that her real name was Eddowes but she confirmed that she knew a Mary Kelly who lived in Dorset Street. Stanley's excitement was immediately rekindled and he drew back into the shadows with his companion as a patrolling police constable walked by.

When the policeman passed the same spot some fifteen minutes later, he found the body of a dead woman lying sprawled on the pavement. Jack the Ripper had struck again. Following the double murder, Dr Stanley waited before homing in on his final victim. Two murders on the same night had created a sensation in London and the whole city was tense with anxiety. He was excited at the prospect of finally confronting Marie Jeannette Kelly but decided to wait for the clamour to die down before seeking her out.

He let a few weeks pass and then made a reconnaissance trip to Whitechapel to spy out the ground. He knew that she had a room at Miller's Court off Dorset Street and he observed her return on one occasion with a man friend. Patiently biding his moment over several night-time visits, the opportunity eventually arrived on the eve of the Lord Mayor's Show, 9 November 1888. When Mary Kelly arrived at Miller's Court late at night and slightly tipsy, death stalked her in the shadows. Stanley waited for her drunken singing to subside and then, as the woman lay asleep, he entered her room. Standing beside the bed, he felt for her throat. 'Wake up!' he commanded. 'Don't shout or scream. I'll kill you if you do. You are Marie Jeannette Kelly?' Her affirmation came in a hoarse, frightened whisper. 'I am "Jack the Ripper". I have come to kill you . . .' he said, after accusing her of ruining his son. The woman emitted the solitary shout of 'Murder' before Stanley's knife sliced through her throat. Alone with his helpless victim, Stanley exacted his mutilating vengeance on her body as he had sworn to do at his son's deathbed. His revenge completed, Dr Stanley disappeared into the night leaving his handiwork for a frightened world to discover on the day of the Lord Mayor's Show.

That was the way Leonard Matters reconstructed the events of 1888 and the part that Dr Stanley played in their execution. He contended that the only fictitious aspect of his account was the use of the name Dr Stanley. He was certain that such a person existed. 'To me there is no alternative consistent with the theory which I am developing but to believe that such a man as Dr Stanley was a resident of the West End of London when "Jack the Ripper" amazed the world . . ."' Matters concluded his story with a South American flourish, claiming that after murdering Mary Kelly, Dr Stanley fled to Argentina. When Matters was in the city of Buenos Aires working as editor of an English language newspaper, he claimed to have discovered the confession of Dr Stanley published in one of the local Spanish papers.

A surgeon who lived in the Argentine capital and who claimed to have been trained in London by Dr Stanley, was called to his former teacher's hospital bed. He received a message which read:

Dear Sir – At the request of a patient who says you will remember him as Dr Stanley, I write to inform you that he is lying in this hospital in a dangerous condition. He is suffering from cancer, and though an operation has been performed successfully, complications have arisen which make the end inevitable. Dr Stanley would like to see you. Instructions have been given to the reception room to waive all regulations in your case and admit you at once to Ward V, where the patient is lying in Bed No. 28.

Yours truly.
Jose Riche
Senior House Surgeon

Shocked by the news, the doctor rushed to the hospital to visit Dr Stanley. The sick man welcomed his visitor and told him that he wanted to clear his conscience before he died. 'Have you ever heard of "Jack the Ripper"?' he asked. 'Yes.' 'Well – I am he!' The doctor recoiled in shock but the dying man begged him not to interrupt his confession. He explained that his son died a hopeless wreck, 'A victim of the night life of London – ruined by a woman. Science could do nothing for him. He died an idiot, and all my hopes died with him. Yes, perhaps I went mad. I swore to avenge him. I murdered all those women!' With the promise that he would be given a decent funeral and with his conscience unburdened, Dr Stanley passed away.

Leonard Matters' theory as to Jack the Ripper's identity has been fairly harshly treated over the years. Edwin T. Woodhall, in his *Jack the Ripper – or When London Walked in Terror*, published in 1937, repeated the story of Dr Stanley without any acknowledgement to the author. While he embraced the theory warmly as 'the most plausible account ever given', he was highly inaccurate in his telling of it and has the downfall of Stanley's son whom he calls 'Angus' beginning on boat race night 1887. Of the later Ripperologists, Daniel Farson wrote that Matters' story probably began as a novel and was 'unacceptable in the context of a documentary' and Donald Rumbelow decided that he 'almost certainly invented his Dr Stanley theory', while Stephen Knight described Matters as 'a romancer' and declared his account to be 'based on unsupported and palpably false statements'. In his book, *More Studies in Murder*, Edmund Pearson, the distinguished American crime writer, referred to Dr Stanley's 'deathbed confession' as bearing 'about the same relation to the facts of criminology as the exploits of Peter Rabbit and Jerry Muskrat do to zoology'.

An interesting aside on the Dr Stanley affair came along in April 1972 after Colin Wilson had interviewed two Ripper authors on television about their views on the murderer's identity. A letter subsequently arrived from Mr A.L. Lee of Torquay whose father had worked at the City of London Mortuary in Golden Lane at the time of the murders. Mr Lee said he believed he knew Jack the Ripper's identity. Colin Wilson's interest inspired another letter from Mr Lee:

In 1888 Dad was employed by the City of London Corporation at the City Mortuary. Among his duties was to collect all bodies of persons who died in the City of London and bring them to the City Mortuary: when an inquest was necessary he prepared them for postmortem by Mr Spilsbury (father of Sir Bernard Spilsbury). His immediate superior was Dr Cedric Saunders, the Coroner of the City.

Dr Saunders had a very special friend, a Dr Stanley who used to visit the mortuary once a week. Whenever he saw Dad he always gave him a cigar.

One day Dr Stanley arrived, and passing Dad, said to Dr Saunders, 'The cows have got my son. I'll get even with them!'

Very soon afterwards the murders started. Dr Stanley still visited the mortuary during this time, but as soon as the murders stopped, he was never seen again.

Dad asked Dr Saunders whether Dr Stanley would be coming again. The answer was no. When pressed by Dad, Dr Saunders said 'Yes, I believe he was Jack the Ripper'.

A tailpiece to this. In the early 1920s I read in the *People* one Sunday a paragraph which read 'A Dr Stanley, believed to have been Jack the Ripper, has died in South America'.

A real Dr Stanley may well have been suspected by the City coroner and, in turn, by Mr Lee, and Leonard Matters might have heard this suggestion and used it as the basis for his theory. The fact is that no surgeon from Harley Street is recorded having forsaken his practice in 1888 for a position in Buenos Aires. But the Dr Stanley theory does not hold water for other reasons which Donald McCormick referred to in his account of Jack the Ripper's identity published in 1959.

Firstly, the syphilis theory is flawed in the way it is applied to Dr Stanley's son and, secondly, Mary Kelly, the object of the doctor's vengeance was proved at post-mortem not to be suffering from syphilis. In its early stages syphilis is a mild disease. The savage, chronic effects usually take several years to appear, and the duration of the disease is marked by years rather than by months. The first signs of syphilis normally occur about a month after infection. These die away, even without treatment, and re-emerge some weeks later before the symptoms recede and the disease becomes quiescent. It may stay dormant for any period between three and twenty years before the third stage errupts. General paralysis of the insane (GPI) is one of the grim features of late syphilis, which may appear many years after the original infection. Death usually occurs within three to four years of the symptoms of GPI becoming manifest.

Viewed against this background, the illness from which Dr Stanley's son suffered and died does not appear to be syphilis. Herbert Stanley was supposed to have contracted the disease on or around boat race night, 1886, and to have died, 'the victim of his own folly', at the beginning of 1888, 'a hopeless wreck for whom medical skill, had, at that time, no sure aid to offer'. Death from syphilitic paresis is extremely unlikely on that timescale, especially as Dr Stanley allegedly obtained the best available treatment for his son right from the outset.

There was no sure treatment for syphilis in 1888 and the organism which caused the disease, *Treponema pallidum*, was not discovered until 1905. The Wasserman diagnostic test for syphilis was devised in 1907 and, two years later, Ehrlich announced his discovery that arsphenamine, an organic arsenic compound, was an effective treatment for the disease. In Stanley's day the only remotely effective syphilitic treatments were mercury which had been used for centuries and potassium iodide which came into use in 1834.

The thesis of the vengeful father of the syphilitic victim does not hold up against the facts and Dr Bagster Phillips' post-mortem finding that Mary Kelly was 'in the early stages of pregnancy and that she was healthy and suffering from no other disease except alcoholism' rules her out as the purveyor of Herbert Stanley's misfortune. The least that can be said is that she was a wrongfully selected victim. The concept of a revenge motive against prostitutes as carriers of venereal disease has been a popular view of Jack the Ripper's murderous inclinations. It is not without a certain logic but Leonard Matters' weaving of theory and fantasy simply does not work.

Three years after Jack the Ripper completed his murderous exploits, Dr Thomas Neill Cream made his contribution to ridding London's streets of prostitutes. He was a dyed-in-the-wool villain who murdered on both sides of the Atlantic and who some believed was also the Ripper. Cream kept an appointment with the hangman at Newgate on 15 November 1892. While he was standing on the scaffold, just as the bolt was drawn to send him to perdition, he is reported to have exclaimed, 'I am Jack the . . .!' The hangman, James Billington, is said to have sworn to the authenticity of the condemned man's last utterance which gave rise to speculation that Cream was Jack the Ripper. Cream's dying words can best be described as muffled, bearing in mind that it was the practice for prisoners to be hooded before being hanged. Nigel Morland, crime writer and publisher of *The Criminologist*, recorded a footnote in an article on Jack the Ripper in 1974 to the effect that a relative, a retired prison doctor, received a letter from James Bellington four years before his death in 1901. In this letter, the former hangman recollected of the Cream incident, 'I heard the condemned man cry "I am Jack the –" just as the trap fell.'

Beyond mentioning the incident, Ripperologists have taken little note of this claim, although Sir Edward Marshall Hall who unknowingly defended Cream on a bigamy charge before he achieved notoriety, believed the man had a double. In light of what he regarded as overwhelming evidence, the advocate advised his client to plead guilty. This he refused to do, declaring it was all a case of mistaken identity and claiming to be in prison in Sydney, Australia, at the time the alleged bigamous offences were committed. The name and full description of Marshall Hall's client were cabled to Australia and, to the surprise of everyone but the defendant, the reply confirmed his alibi. Several years later, Marshall Hall saw Thomas Neill Cream, the 'Lambeth Poisoner', in the dock and was amazed to find that he was none other than his acquitted bigamist. This led Marshall Hall to the conclusion, recorded by his biographer, Edward Marjoribanks, that Cream had a double who helped him out in his confrontations with the law.

Unfortunately, the date of Marshall Hall's defence of Cream the bigamist is not given by his biographer. The facts suggest this was during Cream's first visit to England in 1876/8 but a report carried in the *Guardian* newspaper of 1 March 1979 suggested the encounter might have been later. A University of Columbia professor, Tony Barrett, was reported as stating that 'an English barrister of the time' (presumably Marshall Hall) defended Cream 'on a charge of bigamy during the crucial murder year' (presumably 1888). This was taken to indicate that Cream had earlier bribed his way out of prison in the USA.

According to official records, Cream was serving a life sentence for murder in the Illinois State Penitentiary at Joliet, some thirty miles from Chicago, from November 1881 to June 1891. This of course, rules him out as a candidate for Jack the Ripper unless, as suggested, his double stood in for him to serve the prison sentence. The *Chicago Tribune* in its edition of 18 October 1881 was quite clear in its reporting of the outcome of the trial: 'Sheriff Ames will start for Joliet tomorrow with "Dr" Thomas Neill Cream, yesterday sentenced by Judge Kellum to confinement in the penitentiary for life for the murder of Daniel Stott. . .'

Cream had a varied if unglamorous career. He was born in Glasgow in 1850 and emigrated with his parents to Canada in 1854. In 1872, he enrolled as a medical student at McGill University and graduated in March 1876. He immediately embarked on a career that was distinguished principally by his professional misconduct. He was suspected of burning down his lodgings while still a student in order to obtain money through the insurance. Soon after his graduation he quite literally celebrated a shotgun wedding. He met and subsequently made pregnant a young woman named Flora Eliza Brooks of Waterloo, Ontario. After he had attempted an abortion on the girl he fled to Montreal where he was cornered in a hotel by Mr Brooks who pointed a shotgun at him and demanded he marry his daughter. The wedding was solemnized in September 1876 but, less than a years later, Cream's wife died of 'consumption'. In later year there were suspicions that she had been poisoned but this was never substantiated.

Cream first came to London in October 1876 to pursue his studies at St Thomas's Hospital where he showed a special interest in obstetrics. In March 1878, he returned to Canada to practise in London, Ontario, but he was soon in trouble. In May 1879, a girl died in mysterious circumstances at his surgery. The official verdict, that the girl had 'died of chloroform administered by some persons unknown', was especially significant bearing in mind that Cream's thesis at McGill had been on the subject of chloroform. Following this encounter with the law, Cream moved to Chicago where he set up a practice in West Madison Avenue. He practised his arts on some of the inhabitants of the city's red-light district and developed a taste for the low life.

In 1880 Cream performed an abortion on a young Canadian girl, Mary Anne Faulkner, who died as a result of his treatment. Cream was tried for murder but found not guilty. Undeterred by this close shave with the law, he next murdered an elderly epileptic, Daniel Stott, the husband of his mistress at the time. Two days after Stott was buried, supposedly of natural causes, Cream sent a telegram to the Coroner. 'Suspect Foul Play. Will write immediately. Dr Cream.' This was followed by the explanation that he believed Stott's death was due to a mistake on the part of the pharmacist who made up his medicine. The dead man's corpse was exhumed and found to contain a large amount of strychnine. By this time, the instigator of the enquiry had disappeared. Cream was quickly tracked down and put on trial for murder. This time he was convicted and sent to prison 'for the term of your natural life and one day of each year to be spent in solitary confinement'.

Ten years later, on 12 June 1891, Dr Cream was released from Joliet prison, receiving a pardon from the Governor of Illinois, Joseph W. Fifer. This was duly reported in the Joliet *Daily News*, but the release of one of Chicago's most notorious murderers made no impact elsewhere. On 1 October 1891 he landed at Liverpool and a few days later was in London. He had inherited a legacy of

$16,000 from his recently deceased father and had more than adequate funds to finance his travels.

Within two weeks of reaching England, Cream had claimed his first victim by poison. A nineteen-year-old prostitute, Ellen Donworth, accepted the 'Lambeth Poisoner's' gift of strychnine in the guise of medicine and collapsed in Waterloo Road. Before she died she gave a graphic description of her murderer: 'A tall gentleman with cross eyes, a silk hat and bushy whiskers . . .' Following his success in self-advertisment in Chicago, Cream wrote two remarkable letters. The first was sent to the deputy coroner of East Surrey informing him that he had evidence which would lead to the arrest of Miss Donworth's assassin. There was a catch though, for the writer, who signed himself 'A. O'Brien, Detective', added, 'provided your government is willing to pay me £300,000 for my services'. The second letter was addressed to Frederick W.D. Smith, a partner in the firm of W.H. Smith and Son at 186, Strand. The writer, 'H. Bayne', stated that he had proof that Mr Smith was Ellen Donworth's murderer and, claiming to be a barrister, offered his services to defend Mr Smith. He suggested that a notice requesting Mr Bayne to call should be pasted in one of the windows of the firm's office. Mr Smith wisely informed the police of this development and a paper asking Mr Bayne to call was posted and a strict watch maintained. Dr Cream, who was later proved to be the author of the letter, did not appear.

On 20 October 1891, Cream again singled out a prostitute as his murder victim. Matilda Clover was seen in the company of Cream, silk-hatted and wearing a large coat, entering the house in which she lived at 27 Lambeth Road. In the early hours of the morning, the woman was taken ill and died. The doctor who attended her gave the cause of death as drinking a mixture of sedatives and brandy. Murder was not suspected. As before, Cream now set about drawing suspicion to himself. First he wrote to Countess Russell who was resident at that time in the Savoy Hotel, accusing her husband of poisoning the dead prostitute.

Next, he wrote to Dr William Henry Broadbent, a distinguished London physician, informing him that Matilda Clover had died of strychnine poisoning. He declared that the doctor was guilty of the crime, the proof of which he was prepared to sell for £2,500. The letter was signed 'M. Malone'.

Dr Broadbent told the police about this extraordinary epistle and an advertisement was placed in the *Daily Chronicle* inviting Malone to call at the doctor's home. Detectives lay in wait hoping to trap the letter writer but they waited in vain.

By this time, Cream was making other plans and on 7 January 1892 he sailed from Liverpool on board the *Samia* bound for Canada. It is known that the itinerant doctor stayed for a while in Quebec where he wrote and had printed a circular referring to the death of Ellen Donworth and warning guests at the Metropole Hotel, London, to be on guard against the murderer who was employed at the hotel. This perfectly amazing document was dated 'April 1892' and signed 'W.H. Murray'. In March, Cream was in New York and making ready to return to England where he landed at Liverpool on 1 April. By 9 April he was in residence at 103 Lambeth Palace Road and the 'Lambeth Poisoner' was poised to strike again.

On 11 April, a tall man with a moustache and wearing a dark overcoat and silk hat was seen at the lodging house in Stamford Street. In the early hours of the morning, awakened by screams, the landlady went upstairs to find two of her lodgers writhing in agony. Alice Marsh, aged twenty-one, and eighteen-year-old Emma Shrivell, both prostitutes, were taken to hospital where they died of strychnine poisoning. Cream was arrested on a blackmailing charge and on 21 July was charged with murder. He was tried at the Central Criminal Court and found guilty. While in the condemned cell he seems to have provided his warders with numerous diversions. He told them he had murdered many other women and it is recorded by Daniel Farson in his book *Jack the Ripper* published in 1972 that the son of one of Cream's gaolers told him, 'Cream declared several times to my father that he was Jack the Ripper.'

Sir Edward Marshall Hall, commenting on Cream's alleged utterance on the scaffold, said he thought this was a manifestation of vanity, 'an inherent disease in murderers'. He added that if Cream had been allowed by the hangman to complete the statement to the effect that he was Jack the Ripper he would not have believed him, 'I should have regarded it as another exhibition of the murderer's vanity'. In his comments on this episode, Don Rumbelow in his *The Complete Jack the Ripper* (1975) noted a suggestion that while Cream was serving his life sentence at Joliet, his double was busy with the Whitechapel murders. In return for his double providing him with the bigamy alibi, Cream sought to honour his debt by declaring on the scaffold that he was Jack the Ripper.

The argument in favour of Dr Cream being the Ripper was revived in 1974 with the publication in *The Criminologist* (vol. 9 no. 33) of an article entitled 'Jack the Ripper – The Final Solution?' The author, Donald Bell, a Canadian newspaper man, set out a thesis which sought to overcome the two principal objections to Cream's candidature. Firstly there were the undoubted differences in *modus operandi* and, secondly, the apparent truth that Cream was incarcerated in America at the time of the Whitechapel murders.

On the first point it was argued that Cream's character was intrinsically criminal and that he harboured a strong sadistic impulse. A man who could perform abortions, conduct fatal experiments with chloroform, commit arson, blackmail and murder by strychnine poisoning was surely capable of anything. That both the Ripper and Cream favoured prostitutes as their victims, there is no doubt. But if they were one and the same person, the switch of *modus* from poison to knife and back again is hard to explain. It is certainly unusual and difficult to imagine a killer who has traded so successfully in the swift delights of the knife changing to the slower method of poison. Admittedly strychnine is fast-acting but, as the 'Lambeth Poisoner', Cream was not even present to witness his victims' dying moments. His satisfaction was remote, designedly so in the attempt on Lou Harvey's life on 21 October 1891. Cream met the girl at Charing Cross and gave her some of his lethal capsules, together with money to buy a ticket to the Oxford Music Hall. As Donald Bell remarks, this was 'to have been a remote-control killing. Possibly in full view of many people.' Fortunately, when out of sight of her cross-eyed companion, the girl threw away the capsules and saved herself from almost certain death. This was not the Ripper's style at all.

On the matter of Cream's imprisonment in Joliet, it is argued that he may not have been in prison at all. In Chicago at that time, criminal chicanery was rife at all levels of bureaucracy and it was known for penitentiary inmates to buy their way out. The fact that Cream's release in 1891 received so little publicity, bearing in mind his previous notoriety, suggested a possible cover-up by prison officials who knew their man had already absconded to England. Interestingly enough, while the official date of his release in 1891 was given as 12 June, Cream himself told Scotland Yard officers that it was 31 July. It is possible, after he inherited a considerable sum from his father, that Cream was able to bribe his way to freedom, or he may simply have escaped. There is no documentary evidence for either assertion; the Illinois State Penitentiary archives apparently do not go back that far.

An entirely new point which Donald Bell makes is to connect one of the supposed descriptions of Jack the Ripper with Cream's known appearance. On 12 November 1888, as we have seen, a labourer named George Hutchinson made a statement to the Metropolitan Police at Commercial Street. He stated that in the early hours of 9 November he saw and spoke to Mary Kelly, the Ripper's last victim, in the vicinity of Flower and Dean Street. When she walked away towards Thrawl Street he saw her meet a man and converse with him briefly. The couple then turned and slowly walked past Hutchinson on their way to Dorset Street and Kelly's room at Miller's Court. He heard the man proposition the woman and heard her accept. Hutchinson's statement was widely held to be one of the few reliable descriptions of Jack the Ripper. He described the man as aged about 34 or 35, height 5 ft 6 in., surly looking with a curled moustache. He was well dressed for that area in a long, dark coat trimmed with astrakhan and wearing a dark felt hat. His coat was open, revealing a thick gold watch chain and a black tie with a horseshoe pin. Inspector Abberline himself questioned Hutchinson and reported to his superiors, '. . . I am of the opinion that this statement is true'.

It was the last element of this description – the reference to the horseshoe tiepin – which attracted Donald Bell, although the extracts he uses from Hutchinson's statement are badly misquoted. He goes on to show that a photograph of Cream taken when he was studying at McGill depicts him wearing a neat cravat fastened with a horseshoe tiepin. Cream had a reputation as a stylish dresser and a liking for jewellery. The horseshoe tiepin was said to be one of his favourite adornments and he was known to wear it in later years. An attempt is made to strengthen the jewellery connection by reference to Lou Harvey's description of Dr Cream which she gave to the magistrates. She wrote in a letter to the court that he was wearing 'an Old fashioned Gold Watch, with an Hair or silk fob Chain and seal'. This is related to Hutchinson's statement wherein it is claimed that the man he saw with Mary Kelly wore a watch chain 'having a seal and red stone'. Donald Bell refers to Hutchinson making this particular statement 'elsewhere'; certainly it does not appear in the authenticated statement he made to the police on 12 November 1888.*

---

* Until 1975 most Ripper authors used the version of Hutchinson's statement published by Leonard Matters in 1929. This noted that 'The man had a massive gold watch chain which had a big seal attached.' Donald Rumbelow used the first authentic version of the Hutchinson text in 1975 and, in the following year, Stephen Knight published a facsimile of the document. It will be seen from the correct version of the statement that Hutchinson did not describe the watch chain as 'massive' but as 'thick' and made no mention at all of any seal attached. See pp. 62–3.

Lou Harvey's evidence given at Cream's trial contained several interesting points of comparison. She described Cream's approach: 'He came up and touched my shoulder', and his appearance: 'He had a flat-topped hard felt hat, a black overcoat, and a black suit of clothes.' These descriptions are strikingly similar to Hutchinson's.

In the same issue of *The Criminologist*, Derek Davis, a handwriting examiner, contributed an article entitled ' "Jack the Ripper" – The Handwriting Analysis'. The starting point is to compare two documents regarded as 'genuine' Ripper letters. The first was that sent 'From Hell' to Mr George Lusk accompanying the unsolicited gift of a kidney purporting to have come from one of the Ripper victims. The second letter signed 'Jack the Ripper' is the one sent to Dr Openshaw, examiner of the kidney at the London Hospital, although this is not stated. These letters, previously thought to be the work of different authors, are considered by Derek Davis to have been written by the same hand. They indicate movement of the pen in unaccustomed directions (i.e. contrary to the writer's normal practice), over-emphasis, and hesitation before mis-spelling. All this indicates an attempt by the writer to modify his natural writing habits.

Next, the known handwriting of Dr Cream was examined. There are many authenticated examples of this as the doctor liked nothing better than to send baffling epistles to all and sundry. He had a small, neat and fairly rounded hand which the handwriting analyst compared with the Ripper writing. After due consideration of all the necessary calculations the conclusion is reached that Cream also wrote the two Ripper letters, 'using as much disguise as possible on each occasion'. Or, as Alexander Kelly observed in his *Jack the Ripper Bibliography* published in 1984, '. . . someone else using not quite as much disguise as possible?' As a matter of further interest, Patricia Marne, a journalist specializing in graphology, in her book *Crime and Sex in Handwriting* published in 1981, refers to the same two Ripper letters as Mr Davis. She describes the writing as

143

'smudgy' or 'dirty' and observes that it is completely chaotic in form and erratic in rhythm. It suggests aggression, and emotional instability leading to violent mood variation. The jumble of lines is interpreted as inability to control intense emotion. No reference is made to any evidence indicating disguise of the writer's normal handwriting technique.

As to whether the case is made for proving that Jack the Ripper and Dr Thomas Neill Cream were the same person, readers may judge for themselves. Some of the proposed arguments are tenuous and lacking in real supporting evidence. The key issue – Cream's official term of imprisonment at the crucial time – has not so far been adequately surmounted. The other components of the argument remain unconvincing. Certainly, Cream was capable of practically anything and his addiction to cocaine and morphine no doubt accounted at least in part for his extremes of behaviour. His detailed knowledge of the powers of chloroform could have provided him, in his alleged role as Ripper, with a technique to silence his victims before cutting their throats. But all this falls short of any kind of proof. Interestingly, both Cream and Jack the Ripper indulged in 'double events', the former with his murders of Alice Marsh and Emma Shrivell on 11 April 1892, and the latter with his killings of Elizabeth Stride and Catherine Eddowes on 30 September 1888. Even 'double events' are more coincidence than proof!

Another theory attributing a doctor's identity to Jack the Ripper was that propounded in 1959 by Donald McCormick in his book, *The Identity of Jack the Ripper*. It is a highly convoluted story and ranks as the first book arguing a named identity for the murderer (Dr Stanley was simply another way of saying Dr 'X'). The story also embraces the activities of George Chapman, a well authenticated character who, like Cream, was a transatlantic traveller and poisoner. There were many who believed that Chapman was the Ripper and no less a person than Chief Inspector

Abberline said as much to the arresting officer in 1903 when Chapman the poisoner was brought to book.

Donald McCormick's account of Jack the Ripper's identity began with Chapman, a Pole whose real name was Severin Antoniovitch Klosowski. He took the name Chapman from one of his mistresses on the grounds that it was a more English-sounding name than his own. Chief Inspector Abberline, leaving no stone unturned in his hunt for the Ripper, overheard an assistant in a Whitechapel barber shop called by the name of 'Ludwig'. The man bore a striking resemblance to a German of that name who had been arrested as a Ripper suspect but subsequently released. Abberline decided to pursue this connection and discovered that the barber shop assistant's real name was 'Schloski', or something similar, and that he was Polish. He traced 'Schloski' to another barber shop in West Green Road, South Tottenham, where he learned that his real name was Klosowski.

A central figure in the unfolding of this story is Dr Thomas Dutton who, among other things, was Chief Inspector Abberline's mentor. He advised the detective to keep a special watch for Russians or Poles on the grounds that they could pass for Englishmen at a pinch, were fundamentally barbarous by nature and tended to have scant respect for the female sex. Moreover, the doctor suggested that a larger number of Poles and Russians had a smattering of surgery and anatomy than almost any other nationality.

Abberline thought he might well be on the right track when he had Klosowski in his sights. The Pole was born in 1865 and his parents intended their son to follow a medical career. Their aspirations did not fully materialize, for after serving as an assistant surgeon at Praga, Klosowski entered the Russian army as a *feldscher* or unqualified assistant. A *feldscher* had an elementary knowledge of medicine, pharmacy and surgery and was commonly known as a barber's surgeon. In those days, barbers performed services other than cutting the hair

145

and shaving the chins of their customers. Many employed assistants to carry out minor surgical operations such as cupping, bleeding and removing warts. The barber was very often the ordinary man's physician and the significance of the barber's red and white pole lies in this trade. It was in his capacity as a barber-surgeon that Severin Klosowski, or 'Schloski', first found employment when he came to England some time in 1888.

In the course of his enquiries, Abberline came across a traveller in hairdressers' appliances named Wolff Levisohn who knew Klosowski and was familiar with his background. Perhaps sensing that the policeman suspected Klosowski of involvement in the Ripper murders, Levison told him he was wasting his time because the Pole was more interested in settling down and buying a business. In May 1890, having acquired a barber in High Road Tottenham which failed, Klosowski married and went to America. His bride was Lucy Baderski, the sister of a Polish tailor who lived at Walthamstow. They lived in Jersey City where Klosowski opened a barber shop but, apparently, his flirtations with other women caused Lucy to return to England in 1891. Her husband followed the next year and in 1893 he met Annie Chapman* and changed his name.

The change of name marked a change in behaviour, for the former barber-surgeon became a publican and resorted to murder by poison. This has been well documented, and outstandingly so in the 'Notable British Trials' series in the volume on Chapman edited by Hargrave L. Adam. On returning to England, Chapman went to live with a married woman, Isabella Spink. He used her money to set up as landlord of a public house in City Road. Mrs Spink died in December 1897 following a brief illness. The following year, Chapman employed a young barmaid, Bessie Taylor, who also became ill and died. Doctors expressed surprise but not suspicion. In 1901, Chapman engaged Maud

---

* This is not the Annie Chapman who was the second victim.

Marsh as a barmaid and, like her predecessors, she developed a fatal illness. Miss Marsh's mother suspected Chapman of foul play and talked to the police. Maud Marsh was found to have died of antimony poisoning, as were the two previous women. George Chapman, real name Severin Klosowski, was found guilty of murder and was hanged in April 1903.

Chief Inspector Abberline's remark, 'You've got Jack the Ripper at last!' lent some weight to the idea that Chapman had taken up poisoning when his Ripper-style murders made him too vulnerable to detection. The arguments for considering Chapman and the Ripper to be the same person were weighed by Hargrave Adam. He came to no definite conclusion beyond stating that, 'It is quite certain that nobody ever did know for certain who Jack the Ripper was.' The factors favouring joint identity were Chapman's vaguely medical background and the fact that the Ripper murders ceased when he went to America. The evidence against was the familiar problem of reconciling the propensity to kill with the knife and the change to murder by poison. This was a re-run of the Dr Cream discussion with the difference that Chapman, if he were the Ripper, also changed his type of victim.

But it is not the possibility of Chapman and the Ripper being the same person that is the foundation of Donald McCormick's theory. It is his contention that Klosowski/Chapman had a double and that the double was Jack the Ripper. From this point, the story becomes a little convoluted, with Abberline and his mentor, Dr Thomas Dutton, still much in evidence. During 1888, Dr Dutton lived in Bayswater, London, and consequently was readily accessible to Abberline. The Chief Inspector persisted for a while in thinking that Chapman was the Ripper but was finally convinced to the contrary by his discovery, recorded by Dr Dutton, that the Pole had a double, also a barber-surgeon, who sometimes posed as Chapman for reasons that were not apparent.

Taking up this amazing revelation, Donald McCormick

questioned whether this man might be the Russian surgeon hinted at by Sir Basil Thomson and others and named by William Le Queux, or Quex*, as Dr Alexander Pedachenko? William Le Queux, politely described as a journalist and amateur spy, but more critically as 'a pathological liar', published his autobiography, *Things I Know about Kings, Celebrities and Crooks*, in 1923. This was a collation of name dropping – the illustrations include Princess Luisa of Saxony, King Nicholas of Montenegro and Tewfik Pasha – and the idle chitchat of those who had not quite made the heights of high society. Le Queux, whose recreations included pistol shooting and wireless research, claimed to have forecast the advent of the First World War and to have disclosed for the first time the 'actual identity of Jack the Ripper'.

He claimed that following the murder of the Russian monk, Grigori Rasputin, the Kerensky government 'handed to me, in confidence, a great quantity of documents which had been found in the safe in the cellar of his house, in order that I might write an account of the scoundrel's amazing career'. Among the mass of documents, Le Queux found the greater part of a manuscript written in French by the monk which, 'to my amazement', contained 'the actual truth concerning the "Jack the Ripper" crimes!' He claimed that he did not include it in his book *Rasputin* because he had not at the time been able to verify the facts. However, before he returned the manuscript to the revolutionary government he copied down its text. 'The mysterious assassin was Doctor Alexander Pedachenko, who had been on the staff of the Maternity Hospital at Tver, and lived on the second floor in the Millionnaya but had gone to London, where he lived with his sister in Westmoreland Road, Walworth. From there he sallied forth at night, took an omnibus across London Bridge and walked to Whitechapel, where he committed his secret crimes.'

* Pronounced Le Queue.

This confident piece of information was disclosed by a Russian secret police spy, Nideroest, who was working in London. He was a member of the Jubilee Street Club, the anarchist centre in the East End, when the Ripper's identity was revealed to him by Nicholas Zverieff, a Russian anarchist. According to Zverieff, Dr Pedachenko was aided by a friend named Levitski and a young tailoress called Winberg. The girl approached the victim and engaged her in conversation until Pedachenko pounced from the shadows with his knife. Levitski kept a watch out for the police and it was he who sent the Ripper postcard to the press and who told the story to Zverieff. The motive for the murders was explained as a desire on the part of the Russian secret police to show up the shortcomings of the English system. 'It was, indeed, for that reason that Pedachenko, the greatest and boldest of all Russian criminal lunatics, was encouraged to go to London and commit that series of atrocious crimes, in which agents of our police aided him.' In due course, Pedachenko was spirited out of England, landing in Belgium under the name Count Luiskovo, from whence he was whisked off to Moscow. The murderous doctor was sent to an asylum where he died in 1908 and his accomplices were exiled to Yakutsk. This then was what Le Queux purported to know about Jack the Ripper.

Before moving on to Donald McCormick's next revelation, it is worth referring to the spy Nideroest and a comment on his role made by Donald Rumbelow who has written authoritatively about the Sidney Street seige and the anarchist scene in London in his *The Houndsditch Murders*, published in 1973. The presence of Nideroest in the capital is a matter of record. He featured in news stories in January 1909 when he used a false name to gain access to the hospital where one of the anarchist group involved in an attempted wages snatch in Tottenham lay wounded. He was arrested in the attempt and the *Daily Mirror* of 27 January 1909 carried his photograph. Twenty-four-year-old Nideroest, who was well known to the police, was discharged by the magistrates with a reprimand. He was not commended for his veracity by those who knew him and, as Donald Rumbelow has pointed out, Nideroest, the budding secret agent, was three years old at the time of the Ripper murders. Moreover, as the Anarchist Club in Jubilee Street, Whitechapel, was not opened until 1906, it must have been after that date that Nideroest had his meeting with Zverieff – this being some eighteen years after the Ripper murders.

Now the plot thickens further when Donald McCormick attempts to confirm proof of Dr Pedachenko's existence using Russian source material. Prince Serge Belloselski, a Russian exile who spent the latter part of his life in Britain, corresponded with many of the principal figures in the Czarist government and apparently kept a scrapbook in which he stored newspaper accounts of pre-1914 Russian political affairs, to which he added his own handwritten comments. The prince cast doubt on Le Queux's interpretation of Rasputin's manuscript which he maintained would not have been dictated by the monk in French for he was not sufficiently fluent in the language. It was more probably dictated in Russian, then translated into French and subsequently rendered in English, by which time its meaning had been changed. Alternatively, the prince suggested that the original text might have been altered by the Kerensky government in order to portray the Czarist regime in the worst light. Prince Belloselski claimed to know nothing of Zverieff but believed the person who could shed most light on the subject was Peter Straume, a Latvian living in the East End of London, and believed by Sir Basil Thomson to be Peter the Painter. Straume escaped from the house in Sidney Street before the seige began and made his way to Australia. It was Straume who allegedly reported to Myednikov, head of the Ochrana, Russia's secret police, that Dr Pedachenko, whose real name was Konovalov, was operating in London.

Donald McCormick claimed to have learned all this from Prince Belloselski himself who told him that his information came from Myednikov. The Ochrana chief had given the prince of copy of the *Ochrana Gazette*, dated January 1909, which featured an item on Pedachenko. This bulletin was issued fortnightly to heads of section in the Ochrana to keep them up-to-date on developments in revolutionary Russia. Donald McCormick quoted from the entry:

KONOVALOV, Vasilly, alias PEDACHENKO, Alexey, alias LUISKOVO, Andrey, formerly of Tver, is now officially declared to be dead. Any files or information concerning him from district sections should be sent to the Moscow Central District of Ochrana. Such information, photographs, or identification details as may still exist might refer to KONOVALOV, PEDACHENKO or LUISKOVO either individually or collectively. If documents held by you do not contain these names, they should also be examined for any information concerning a man answering to the description of the above, who was wanted for the murder of a woman in Paris in 1886, of the murder of five women in the East Quarter of London in 1888 and again of the murder of a woman in Petrograd in 1891.

KONOVALOV's description is as follows: Born 1857 at Torshok, Tver. Height medium. Eyes, dark blue. Profession, junior surgeon. General description: usually wore black moustache curled and waxed at ends. Heavy black eye-brows. Broad-shouldered, but slight build. Known to disguise himself as a woman on occasions and was arrested when in woman's clothes in Petrograd before his detention in the asylum where he died.

These sources supporting the Dr Pedachenko theory can hardly be described as impeccable. William Le Queux's contribution was severely dented by J. Hall Richardson in his book, *From the City to Fleet Street*. He observed that in any case Nideroest was not Russian but Swiss and that in previous dealings with the police he had proved himself to be an unscrupulous liar. 'The fact that Mr Le Queux's theory rests on his testimony,' wrote Richardson, 'is sufficient for us to regard it as fiction . . .' The manuscript said to have been written by Rasputin and identifying Jack the Ripper as Dr Pedachenko is also suspect, not least for Prince Belloselski's reservations about its language of origin. More importantly, A.T. Vassilyev, the former Czarist police chief, in his book *The Ochrana* published in 1930 mentioned that a thorough search was made of Rasputin's apartment immediately after the monk's death. The police were looking for any compromising documents but Vassilyev reported that none were found. Donald Rumbelow recorded that the journalist, C.W. Shepherd, who ghosted three of Queux's books, recounted to him the story of a visit he made to the south coast to see Le Queux. During their meeting, Le Queux produced an impressive envelope bearing seals and other devices in which the Rasputin documents were said to be enclosed. The visitor, his interest aroused, was not allowed to see the contents of the envelope.

Despite several shortcomings in the status of his Russian sources, Donald McCormick ploughed on with his theory. When the threads threatened to break, he calls in Dr Dutton to provide support. The good doctor, a much-travelled man, had a well-developed interest in criminology and compiled three handwritten volumes, never published, but accorded the title of *Chronicle of Crime*. This work, written over a period of three years, was either lost or destroyed after Dutton's death in 1935, but not before Donald McCormick had seen it at sufficient leisure to take extensive notes. These notes, many years later, were to form Donald McCormick's principal reference source in expounding his theory of Jack the Ripper's identity. As it is impossible to corroborate any of the statements made by Dr Dutton, their value as supporting evidence is considerably weakened.

Nevertheless, it is Dr Dutton, friend of Chief Inspector Abberline, who comes to the rescue. It was he, according to Donald McCormick, who criticized Le Queux for taking the Rasputin manuscript too seriously and for failing to realize that Pedachenko worked as a barber-surgeon in 1888 for a hairdresser named William Delhaye in Westmoreland Road, Walworth, London. 'And for once,' wrote McCormick, 'a careful check of this statement leads one to something more than a negative conclusion.' He had discovered a listing for Delhaye at that address in the *London Post Office Directory* of 1889.

Not unreasonably, Dr Dutton had advised Abberline to follow up this line of enquiry which was in keeping with the belief that while Jack the Ripper may not have lived in the East End, he must have been within easy reach. Wolff Levisohn had hinted at a domicile south of the river and Dr Dutton made the amazing discovery that four of the Ripper's victims had attended a clinic in Walworth right up to the time of their deaths. He had gleaned this from Dr J. F. Williams who had a surgery at St Saviour's Infirmary in Westmoreland Road. Dr Williams also divulged to his fellow medic that he was assisted at the clinic from time to time by Dr Pedachenko, a Russian barber-surgeon. The doctor found the Russian intelligent and conscientious and believed he lived locally although he did not know his address. He also thought the man worked for various hairdressers, including William Delhaye.

Chief Inspector Abberline apparently thought that Pedachenko and Klosowski/Chapman were one and the same person whereas Dr Dutton contended that the Russian posed as the Pole's double. Throughout the Ripper murders, Klosowski worked at various hairdressers' establishments in the East End and was said to lodge in a building in George Yard. Joseph Lave, an east European member of the International Workers' Education Club in Berner Street, was quoted as telling the police that there was a stranger in the club earlier on the night that Elizabeth Stride fell victim to the Ripper. The man, who claimed to be

Polish but was clearly a Russian, said he was a barber and that he had a basement in George Yard. Lave's description was of a man 'between thirty and thirty-five years of age, with a dark moustache and dark suit. I also remember that he had a rather heavy gold watch-chain with some sort of stone set in a seal. Oddly enough, he wore a peaked hat, rather like a sailor's.'

When the police followed up Lave's statement by rushing round to George Yard, they found no Russian but only Klosowski. Lave cleared Klosowski straight away by saying he was not the man he had seen in the club. Donald McCormick posed the question as to whether the man found at George Yard was not Dr Pedachenko in his role as Klosowski's double. He also asked if the two men knew each other and whether the basement lodging was really Jack the Ripper's nocturnal bolt hole, although he admitted 'There is no complete answer to all these questions'. Detective Sergeant Leeson confirmed in his memoirs, *Lost London* (1934), that Chapman/Klosowski 'carried on a hairdresser's business in a sort of "dive" under a public house at the corner of George Yard . . .' No wonder that Abberline believed Chapman was the Ripper, but his considered view of the Pedachenko double theory is unrecorded.

Donald McCormick in his reconstruction of the murder of Mary Kelly has the woman attending the clinic at St Saviour's Infirmary (although no reason is given) where she encountered Dr Pedachenko. The junior surgeon would have appeared a respectable catch for Kelly and, presumably, she would have had little compunction about arranging to meet him and take him back to her room. It is pointed out that George Hutchinson's description of the person he saw with Mary Kelly tallied with that of the man Joseph Lave saw, even down to the ' "big gold watch chain" with a seal', although it is known that Hutchinson in fact made no mention of any seal. It is surmised that Pedachenko carried a getaway disguise in the shape of female clothing in the 'American-cloth parcel' described by

Hutchinson. Dressed as a woman and having stopped to shave off his moustache, Pedachenko, who was known to the Russians for his use of female disguise, slipped away from his butchery at Miller's Court. Not surprisingly, confirmation of the feasibility of this ploy comes from Dr Dutton who recalled Dr Williams telling him that Pedachenko had a soft, low voice like a woman's. Dr Williams also told Dutton that their man 'wore a large gold watch with a heavy and unusual seal of foreign pattern'. This is taken to strengthen 'the most convincing proof of identity'.

Donald McCormick's elaborate theorizing is weakened by his use of uncorroborated reference sources, particularly those attributed to Dr Dutton. As Donald Rumbelow pointed out, it seems significant that Dutton made no reference to Pedachenko until 1923, the year that William Le Queux first published the Russian doctor's name. Daniel Farson felt that the Pedachenko theory 'fell to pieces' with McCormick's use of Sir Melville Macnaghten's notes. The former CID chief's notes,* written in 1894, came to light in 1959 when they were made available to Farson and the text was subsequently published for the first time (with numerous errors) by Tom Cullen in 1965 in his book, *Autumn of Terror*. Sir Melville named his now famous three suspects: M.J. Druitt, an English barrister who committed suicide; Kosminski, a Polish Jew who was committed to an asylum in 1889; and Michael Ostrog, a mad Russian doctor who was a homicidal maniac.

The appearance of some real documentary evidence, written by a senior policeman in his own hand, a mere six years after the Ripper murders occurred, caused a flurry of excitement. The notes stimulated two books arguing the case for identifying M.J. Druitt as the Ripper and caused the Russian doctor theoreticians to think hard. Confusion was introduced where none existed when Donald McCormick

---

* See Chapter 5.

in the second edition of his book, published in 1970, suggested that Kosminski was a misspelling for Karminski and that Michael Ostrog should have been Mikhail. This has no relevance except to impute that Sir Melville Macnaghten's notes were inaccurate. Strangely, for one who relied so heavily on note-taking and hearsay as a means of collecting evidence, McCormick criticizes Macnaghten whose work was 'compiled from memory after having had conversations with men engaged in the case' and also described the notes as 'minimal and lacking in detail'. Of course, Macnaghten's suspicions did nothing to further the case for Dr Pedachenko and, if anything, ruled out that theory of identity at least as far as the police were concerned.

As mentioned earlier, Major Arthur Griffiths, in his *Mysteries of Police and Crime*, published in 1898, mentioned three Ripper suspects. One was a lunatic Polish Jew, the second 'a Russian doctor, also insane, who had been a convict in both England and Siberia', and the third 'a doctor in the prime of life', who committed suicide in the Thames. In his book *The Story of Scotland Yard*, Sir Basil Thomson, Assistant Commissioner of Police, also referred to 'an insane Russian doctor' who escaped arrest by committing suicide. It is highly probable that these authors were talking with some knowledge of the views held by Sir Melville Macnaghten whom Griffiths referred to as 'more intimately acquainted, perhaps, with the details of the most recent celebrated crimes than anyone else in New Scotland Yard'. Is it not likely that two men such as Macnaghten, head of CID in Scotland Yard, and Griffiths, an HM Inspector of Prisons, with a professional interest in criminal matters, not to mention a healthy curiosity, discussed the Ripper murders and perhaps even looked together at the photographs of the victims which the policeman kept under lock and key? Griffiths probably discovered in confidence all there was to know about police suspicions of the Ripper's identity and included oblique references in his book.

Perhaps Kosminski was really Klosowski alias

Chapman, Pedachenko, Konovalov and, possibly, Ostrog as well. The best that can be said is that the case for Dr Alexander Pedachenko is far from proven, resting as it does on unsupported and frequently third-hand information, albeit the story is ingeniously argued by Donald McCormick in the face of some formidable obstacles.

'I Caught Jack the Ripper' was the eye-catching headline of an article which appeared in the *Daily Express* on 16 March 1931. The claim was made in a letter sent to the newspaper by Robert Clifford Spicer, a former member of the Metropolitan Police. As a uniformed beat constable in his early twenties, Spicer was on patrol in the East End during the early hours of 30 September 1888 – the night of the Ripper's 'double event'. In keeping with police tactics at the time, he worked his beat back to front in order to make his patrol less predictable. Coming out of Brick Lane and into Henage Street, he spotted a man and a woman sitting on a brick-built dustbin. The woman was a local prostitute called Rosy who was clutching a two-shilling piece in her hand. Her companion was well dressed and carried a Gladstone bag – the cuffs of his shirt were stained with blood.

Spicer said later, 'As soon as I saw the man in that dark alleyway in the early hours of the morning, I felt sure he was the Ripper.' The man evaded the policeman's questions when he was challenged, telling the officer that it was no business of his to ask what he was doing. Spicer promptly took the man into custody and, with Rosy trailing behind, marched him along to Commercial Street Police Station. No doubt in a state of some excitement, Spicer took the man before the duty inspector and asked that he be charged on suspicion of being Jack the Ripper. 'There were about eight or nine inspectors at the station at the time – all taking part in the hunt for the criminal. Imagine how I felt when I got into trouble for making the arrest,' said Spicer. 'The station inspector asked me what I meant by arresting a man who had proved to be a respectable doctor.'

The doctor, who gave the police a Brixton address, was allowed to leave the station, his bloody shirt cuffs unexplained and his Gladstone bag unexamined. 'I was so disappointed when the man was allowed to go,' said Spicer, 'that I no longer had my heart in police work.' He saw the man several times after this incident, usually accosting women in the street, and the policeman worked off his earlier disappointment by asking, 'Hello, Jack! Still after them?' Not surprisingly, the man invariably fled. He was described as wearing a 'high hat, black suit with silk facings, and a gold watch and chain. He was about 5 feet 8 or 9 inches and about 12 stone, fair moustache, high forehead and rosy cheeks.'

In 1972, B.E. Reilly wrote in the *Journal of the City of London Police* about his follow-up of the Spicer story. He set out to investigate the careers of doctors resident in Brixton at the time of the Ripper murders as a means of identifying the man arrested by Spicer. In a shortlist of such doctors who disappeared from the *Medical Register* within a year or two of 1888 was a practitioner whom he called 'Dr Merchant'. This man aroused curiosity because he had a connection with Liverpool, the city from which one of the apparently genuine Ripper letters had been posted. Reilly found that 'Dr Merchant' died in December 1888, a few weeks after the murder of Mary Kelly. The death certificate indicated the cause as a septic abscess of tubercular origin.

Apparently 'Dr Merchant' had a common surname which made it difficult to trace his family background. However, the enterprising Mr Reilly discovered that his suspect was born in India in 1851 and came to London from a practice in the provinces about 1886. It appears that the doctor might have been ill for some time and had run down his savings. He left no will and letters of administration granted to his widow in 1892 valued his estate at £93. The fact that the occupation of the deceased had been filled in on the Death Certificate by the medical signatory as 'unknown to informant' was taken to indicate that 'Dr Merchant' was not admitted to hospital by his wife.

Mr Reilly finds it significant that the man seen by Robert Spicer was described as having rosy cheeks, a characteristic which he points out is a sign of tuberculosis. He suggested that the risks taken by Jack the Ripper were so bold as to be the acts of a desperate person. Perhaps a man knowing that he was terminally ill, such as 'Dr Merchant', ran amok and exacted a price from society by dealing out death to its outcasts. In conclusion, Mr Reilly wrote that his doctor 'may have sought a frantic outlet for his skill in these murders, characterized as they were by expert mutilations'. 'Dr Merchant', be he in reality Smith, Brown or Jones, was buried in a pauper's grave and joined the host of Ripper might-have-beens.

The reason so many have thought Jack the Ripper was a doctor was that he was supposed to have shown skill in the way he killed and mutilated his victims. A number of modern commentators have argued against this, including Professor Francis Camps, the eminent pathologist who took a great deal of professional interest in the murders. In April 1966, the national press announced a verdict on Jack the Ripper which was that new evidence showed the murderer was not a doctor: 'Skill theory rejected' reported the *Daily Telegraph*, and 'Jack the Ripper not a medical man' ran the *Guardian*. The new evidence was the discovery in a basement at London Hospital of sketches pertaining to one of the Ripper's 'double event' victims. There were pencil sketches of the body of Catherine Eddowes and a plan of Mitre Square where she was killed on 30 September 1888.

Professor Camps published these finds in *The London Hospital Gazette* in an article called 'More About Jack the Ripper'. In a report in the *Medical News*, the professor gave his assessment that 'the cuts shown on the body could not have been done by an expert'. To the layman, the sketch of Catherine Eddowes' mutilated body bears out this view although it should be remembered that the murderer's objective on this occasion appeared to have been the removal of the woman's left kidney and uterus. It was the way this had been achieved that led Dr Frederick Gordon Brown, surgeon of the City of London Police, to conclude that the murderer possessed some skill. At the inquest on Eddowes, Dr Brown gave a detailed account of the dead woman's injuries and then answered questions under cross-examination. He stated that 'The way in which the mutilation had been effected showed that the perpetrator of the crime possessed some anatomical knowledge.' To the question, 'Would you consider that the person who inflicted the wounds possessed great anatomical skill?' the doctor replied, 'A good deal of knowledge as to the position of the organs in the abdominal cavity and the way of removing them.'

While Dr Brown's colleagues did not endorse his opinions – believing that the degree of anatomical knowledge demonstrated by the murderer was such as might be expected of a professional butcher or meat cutter – Dr George William Sequeira added a significant rider. After assisting at the postmortem, he told a newspaper reporter that the murderer was 'No stranger to the knife'. The strong point that can be made regarding these doctors' statements is that they derived from direct examination of the body and observations of its injuries. In his report on the Eddowes' murder, dated 6 November 1888, Chief Inspector Donald Swanson of the Metropolitan Police drew on the essentials of the case being investigated by his colleagues in the City of London Police. He wrote the following with reference to the medical aspects:

The surgeon, Dr Brown, called by the City Police, and Dr Phillips who had been called by the Metropolitan Police in the cases of Hanbury Street and Berner Street, having made a post-mortem examination of the body reported that there were missing the left kidney and the uterus, and that the mutilation so far gave no evidence of anatomical knowledge in the sense that it evidenced the hand of a qualified surgeon, so that the police could narrow their

160

enquiries into certain classes of persons. On the other hand as in the Metropolitan Police cases, the medical evidence shewed that the murder could have been committed by a person who had been a hunter, a butcher, a slaughterman, as well as a student in surgery or a properly qualified surgeon.

This report, published for the first time by Stephen Knight in his *Jack the Ripper: The Final Solution*, shows the doctors making guardedly helpful statements in confidence to a senior police officer.

An opponent of the skill theory was Dr Thomas Bond, lecturer in forensic medicine at Westminster Hospital, who had given evidence at the trial of Kate Webster in 1879. He was present at the post-mortem examination on Mary Kelly and on 10 November 1888 submitted his report. His findings were based on taking part in the one post-mortem and on reading the notes pertaining to the other four murder victims. Dr Bond's conclusion is quite unequivocal. 'In each case,' he wrote, 'the mutilation was implicated by a person who had no scientific or anatomical knowledge. In my opinion he does not even possess the technical knowledge of a butcher or horse slaughterman or any person accustomed to cut up dead animals.' In view of the gross destruction performed on Kelly's body, this was an understandable view although it may be argued for that reason that her case was the least favourable on which to judge any question of skill. As Dr Bond himself said, 'Owing to the extensive mutilation it is impossible to say in what direction the fatal cut was made . . .'

Apart from the gruesome photograph taken of the shredded remains of Mary Kelly there is little documentary evidence to guide the independent commentator seeking to analyse the medical aspects. The inquest was abruptly terminated by the coroner Dr Roderick Macdonald after Dr Phillips had given evidence as to cause of death. The jury were asked if they would return a verdict and obligingly did so leaving the public with little fact and a great deal to imagine concerning London's, if not England's, most notorious murder case. The *Daily Telegraph* was quick to criticize this action, pointing out that an opportunity had been lost to take statements from witnesses while events were still clear in their minds. Commenting on this in his *A Casebook on Jack the Ripper* (1975), Richard Whittington-Egan wrote, 'I do not think . . . it was the question of Kelly's alleged pregnancy which exercised Macdonald's cautionary discretion. I believe that the real clue is to be found in that statement made by Roslyn D'Onston Stephenson* that semen had been discovered in the dead woman's rectum.' He reasoned that if Kelly had been sodomized, here was a firm fact about the Ripper's behaviour which the police may have held back for fear of putting him on his guard. Consequently, 'the authorities decided in 1888 to keep what they knew to themselves'.

Surely, the person best placed to give an overall professional opinion on the matter of skill was Dr George Bagster Phillips. He was a man of considerable experience, having been involved in police work for twenty years, and, most importantly, of all the doctors called in to examine the Whitechapel murder victims, Phillips saw more of the Ripper's work at first hand than anyone. He was present at the scene of the crime examination in three cases and conducted three out of the five post-mortems.

Because the Eddowes' murder was a City Police matter, Dr Phillips was not involved at the crime scene but attended the post-mortem examination. The evidence he gave at the Chapman inquest found its way into *The Lancet*. Details of the victim's injuries included his opinion that, 'Obviously the work was that of an expert – or one, at least, who had such knowledge of anatomical or pathological examinations as to be enabled to secure the pelvic organs with one sweep of the knife.'

Donald Rumbelow attested to Dr Phillips' thorough-

---

* See Chapter 7, 'Black Jack', for a full account of Dr Roslyn D'Onston Stephenson's statement to the police.

Victim	Crime Scene Examination	Post-Mortem Examination
Nichols	Dr Ralph Llewellyn	Dr Ralph Llewellyn
Chapman	Dr G.B. Phillips	Dr G.B. Phillips
Stride	Dr G.B. Phillips	Dr G.B. Phillips
	Dr F. Blackwell	Dr F. Blackwell
Eddowes	Dr F.G. Brown	Dr F.G. Brown
	Dr G. Sequeira	Dr G. Sequeira
		Dr W.G. Saunders
		Dr G.B. Phillips
Kelly	Dr G.B. Phillips	Dr G.B. Phillips
	Dr F.G. Brown	Dr T. Bond
	Dr D. Duke	

ness noting that he 'ignored all evidence which he hadn't had at first hand'. An example of this highly professional approach to his work is to be found in the doctor's post-mortem report, dated 22 July 1889, on Alice McKenzie whose still warm body was found in Castle Alley, Whitechapel, on 17 July. He ended the report, 'Holding it as my duty to report on the PM appearances and express an opinion solely on professional grounds based on my own observations. For this purpose I have ignored all evidence not coming under my observation.'

Dr Phillips' hand-written report on nine foolscap sheets survived the rigorous vetting of official documents, perhaps indicating that the authorities were certain Alice McKenzie was not a Ripper victim. This report is interesting in the model it offers for what is missing in the documentation of the Whitechapel murder victims. When writing it, Dr Phillips was clearly conscious of making comparisons and it emerges that the police thought it necessary to obtain a second opinion. The doctor invited to give this was Thomas Bond, who had given his views of the sequence of Ripper murders on the strength of taking part in the post-mortem on Mary Kelly. It was clear that the two medical men did not see eye to eye.

Phillips noted in his report, 'On Thursday (18 July 1889) about 6 p.m. I accompanied Dr Bond to view the body of the decd. and as far as I was able explained the appearances to him.' This matter-of-fact statement hid a fundamental disagreement which was that Bond was of the opinion 'that the murder was performed by the same person who committed the former series of Whitechapel murders'. This was an assessment that Phillips did not share. Moreover, he indicated that he did not believe all the Whitechapel murders had been the work of one man. He concluded his report on McKenzie: 'After careful and long deliberation I cannot satisfy myself on purely anatomical and professional grounds that the Perpetrator of all the "Whitechapel Murders" is one man. I am on the contrary impelled to a contrary conclusion – this noting the mode of procedure and the character of the mutilations and forgoing of motive in connection with the latter.'

As Donald Rumbelow remarked in his discussion of these points, Phillips' evidence on this matter, taking into consideration his experience, 'must carry a lot of weight'.

Professional rivalry between Bond and Phillips might set the former's opinions into a different perspective. But the question of skill does not rest on Phillips's assessment alone. Of the six medical opinions expressed at the time on the subject of the murderer's skill, five were in favour of some skill having been used while only one (Bond) was totally against. Of the five positive opinions, three were strongly in favour and two might be described as lukewarm. There is a consensus here which cannot be easily dismissed – it argues favourably for a view that the Ripper was familiar with the use of knives and knew something about cutting. This may have fallen short of a surgeon's skill but there was something about the murderer's *modus operandi* which several doctors believed set him above a no-skill level.

The removal of a kidney from the body of Catherine Eddowes provided a clue as to the evidence which persuaded Dr Brown to state at the inquest, 'It would require a great deal of knowledge as to its position to remove it. It is easily overlooked. It is covered by a membrane.' Set against the accurate timetable provided by PC Watkins, the killing of Eddowes was swift indeed and the theft of the kidney was carried out with remarkable speed. The policeman was quite sure that when he passed through Mitre Square at 1.30 a.m. and cast the light from his bull's-eye lantern into its recesses, there was nothing untoward visible. When he next passed through the square, fourteen minutes later at 1.44 a.m. he found a woman's body ripped up like 'a pig in the market'.

Jack the Ripper was undeniably a fast worker. Within fourteen minutes he manoeuvred his victim silently to the corner of the square where he rendered her unconscious and laid her on the pavement to cut her throat. (She may already have been dead from strangulation, of course, with Ripper and limp victim cloaked in the darkness of the square as the footfalls of the patrolling policeman drew nearer.) When it was safe, he raised her clothing and made a massive incision from groin to breastbone, pulling out great loops of intestine to locate a kidney and remove it. Then, still working in the dark, he had time to make several comparatively delicate cuts to the face before slithering away to safety as PC Watkins returned to discover his handiwork. As Don Rumbelow says, the Ripper would only have had between seven and eight minutes in which to kill the woman and do his work. Dr Brown said the act of mutilation would have taken at least five minutes, but then he was an advocate of a skilled murderer. Of course, if the removal of the kidney was not a deliberate act but simply a chance occurrence, the theories become idle speculation. But if the murderer had the intention to secure the organ there can be little doubt that he had sufficient knowledge of human anatomy to find it and remove it with great speed.

This train of thought led Robin Odell in his *Jack the Ripper in Fact and Fiction*, published in 1965, to develop the slaughterman as an identity type for the Ripper. The slaughterman angle was by no means new and the general idea had been well aired at the time of the murders and was thought to make sense out of the chaotic incident of the crimes. Following their occupational calling, slaughtermen could reasonably be expected to own and indeed to carry about sharp knives; bloodstained clothing was simply an occupational hazard. The meat market was one of Whitechapel's regular trades and the district abounded with abattoirs. Butchers' Row, Aldgate, E3, was known as 'Blood Alley' and when trade was brisk, slaughtermen often worked through the night. At times, animals were even slaughtered in the streets, a practice which caused the vicar of St Jude's, Whitechapel, to write a letter to *The Times*. He protested that the sight of butchers in their bloodstained aprons tended to brutalize persons of gentle nature.

Queen Victoria had taken sufficient interest in the Ripper murders to ask if the cattle boats coming into London had been searched. The *Star* took this up, commenting, 'An opinion has been formed among some of the detectives that the murderer is a drover or butcher employed on one of these boats – of which there are many – and that he periodically appears and disappears with one of the steamers.' It had certainly not escaped the attention of the City of London Police that the East End abounded in slaughterhouses and Major Smith claimed to have 'visited every butcher's shop in the city'.

There were slaughterhouses near two of the murder sites and, in the case of the Bucks Row killing, there was an abattoir within a hundred and fifty yards of the spot where Mary Nichols was slain. Men were working in the abattoir at Winthrop Street that very night. They were questioned by detectives investigating the murder, but what could they expect to discover except a few men with blood on their clothes and knives in their hands? Following the 'double event', Chief Inspector Donald Swanson reported on 19 October 1888 that 'Seventy-six butchers and slaughterers have been visited and the characters of the men employed enquired into . . .' A slaughterman would have enjoyed the perfect alibi even on the street in broad daylight and he would have fitted Dr Sequiera's description of the Ripper as 'no stranger to the knife.'

Professor Camps, using contemporary reports of the murders in *The Lancet*, suggested that in all probability the Ripper strangled his victims before touching them with the knife. This would have accounted for the lack of any cries or screams on the part of the victims and also for the relatively small spillage of blood, for, with the heart ceasing to pump, cut arteries would spurt less blood. In each case, the Ripper laid his victim flat on the ground before cutting her throat; with his victim already dead, this was something of a ritualistic mutilation.

This technique was used daily by Jewish slaughtermen, called *shochim*, to provide kosher meat for the large Jewish population of the East End, estimated in 1889 as 60,000. This number was due to an influx of Polish and Russian Jews fleeing their own countries and entering Britain, often without check by the authorities, where they set up businesses and shops. The mode of slaughter, known as *shechita*, was designed to drain the meat of blood which, as the means of atonement, is sacred to God. The rules of the ritual are believed to have been given by God to Moses and are set out in the *Talmud*, the primary compilation of Jewish law and tradition. Meat prepared according to ancient custom is an essential part of Orthodox Jewish life and it is forbidden to eat meat that has not been so prepared.

The methods of *shechita* have changed little over the centuries except for the introduction of more hygienic and humane methods during the last fifty years. A glance into a Jewish abattoir in Aldgate High Street in the 1880s would have revealed a scene that had its origins in the Holy Land of the Old Testament.

The *shochet* used a long steel knife, honed to perfection, called the *khalef*, which was a central feature of the ritual. The ceremonial knife not only had to be sharp but its blade was required to be free of the slightest imperfection. Its fitness for use was tested by rules laid down in the *Talmud*, for to kill with an imperfect knife would render the meat unfit to eat and lead to censure of the slaughterman. Holding the knife in his right hand, the *shochet* slowly drew its blade at right angles over the finger nail and fleshy tip of the index finger of his other hand. Backwards and forwards, inclining the blade this way and that, he searched for the slightest imperfection through the sensitivity of his fingertip. When he was satisfied that the knife had been satisfactorily tested according to religious law, the *shochet* signalled to his assistants who had prepared the animal for slaughter by hobbling its legs with a rope and, forcing its head on the ground, 'cast' its throat ready for the knife. As the beast was restrained by means of ropes, the Benediction was spoken, 'Blessed art thou who sanctified us with His commandments and commanded us concerning slaughtering.' Silence reigned as the *shochet* stepped forward and drew his razor-sharp knife across the prescribed area of the animal's throat. A quick stroke, forward and backward, and the throat was cut through to the bone. Death was immediate, and as the slaughterman stepped back, the animal's life blood gushed onto the ground from its severed vessels.

The responsibility of the *shochet* was paramount during this ritual for he had to observe the five laws of *shechita* which God had handed down to Moses. In performing the act of slaughter he had to take care not to delay, press, deviate, slip or tear in his use of the knife. Any contravention of these rigid rules would invalidate the whole ritual, rendering the meat unfit and making the slaughterman liable for punishment. Having skilfully observed these requirements, the *shochet* next inspected the wound. According to law he ensured that the throat had been correctly cut between the thyroid cartilage and that portion of the windpipe which was level with the upper part of the lungs. He also needed to check that both the windpipe and gullet had been properly cut through by the knife.

After satisfying himself on these matters, the *shochet* proceeded to make a thorough post-mortem, or *bedikah*, of the dead animal. Making an incision in the chest, he examined the heart and lungs for any sign of injury or disease. Being vital for life, these organs had to be found in a perfectly healthy state. Any perforations or adhesions of the lungs were quickly noted and would rule the animal as unfit for consumption and *trefah*, or forbidden. Similarly, the abdomen was opened and the internal organs examined for any defects; stomach, intestines, gallbladder, liver, kidneys, blood vessels and spinal cord were all closely inspected. Any pathological defects or injuries in these organs was diagnosed according to Talmudic law and the *shochet* decided whether or not they ruled the animal as kosher.

The fat lying on the intestines and kidneys was carefully removed with a special knife. Jews were forbidden to eat the fat of a slaughtered animal and the *shochet* was penalized if he allowed tainted meat to go for consumption. The sciatic nerve was expressly forbidden by the Old Testament and its removal from the animal's hindquarters was an especially skilful task. Certain veins in the rump were also regarded as fat and these were drawn out of the flesh of the still warm body. After completing these duties and being satisfied that the slaughtering was valid, the *shochet* gave the signal for the carcass to be butchered. Every portion of meat, before delivery to the butchers' shops, was marked with a lead seal bearing the date and the stamp, *kosher*, meaning 'fit'.

From the earliest times, and certainly since the Middle Ages, *shochims* were specially selected and subjected to the stern principles of an honourable profession. Those selected were of high moral character, steady religious faith and well-versed in Talmudic learning. To qualify for a licence or *kabbalah*, the prospective *shochet* had to demonstrate a thorough knowledge of the rules governing *shechita* and of the associated anatomical and pathological principles. *Shochim* were ordained priests because their profession was primarily a religious one and, being minor clerics, were often given the title of reverend. They held positions of esteem in the Jewish communities on account of their importance in maintaining the orthodoxy of the faith. Their degree of learning also earned them places as readers and writers for the great mass of their fellows who lacked these attributes.

Shochim were trained in London and other European capitals with courses of instruction and apprenticeship sometimes lasting seven years. Their profession was strict and they were expected to observe the ethics and rules of conduct of their calling. Rabbis frequently made surprise visits to Jewish slaughterhouses to observe the *shochim's* knives and to be reassured that proper standards were being maintained. The practice of *shechita* in London was strictly controlled as early as 1804. *Shechita* boards regulated standards of slaughtering and licensed the *shochim*, with emphasis on good procedure and skill.

There can be no question that a Jewish slaughterman trained as a *shochet* would have possessed that better than layman's anatomical knowledge which was attributed to the Ripper. Moreover, such a man combined elements of training and circumstance that fitted the *modus operandi* of the Whitechapel murderer. He was an accomplished user of the knife especially for the purpose of throat-cutting and he had been taught to be swift and decisive. His knowledge of anatomy was more than adequate to the task of finding and removing a kidney, even at speed and in the dark. The *shochet's* position in the community was such as to make his appearance in the streets of the East End whether in daylight or at night quite unexceptional. The proximity of slaughterhouses to the murder district meant that he could emerge onto the streets and disappear from them with ease. Should he be stopped and questioned, he would have a perfect explanation for being in possession of a knife or having bloodstains on his hands and clothing.

Statements made during two of the murder enquiries support the slaughterman thesis. The coroner enquiring into the death of Annie Chapman commented on her injuries. 'There were no meaningless cuts,' he said, adding that had the post-mortem examination been less thorough the missing uterus might not have been noticed. 'An unskilled person could not have performed such a deed,' he said. He made light of the suggestion that a mere slaughterer of animals could have performed such deeds, preferring 'someone accustomed to the post-mortem room'. Perhaps he was ignorant of the particular skills possessed by a Jewish ritual slaughterman. Dr Phillips thought the murder weapon must have been 'a very sharp knife with a thin, narrow blade, at least six inches to eight inches long'. Questioned by the coroner he thought that the knives normally used by slaughtermen, which were well ground down, might have been used.

In the case of Catherine Eddowes, Dr Brown told the inquest that the injuries were caused by a 'a sharp knife, and it must have been pointed; and from the cut in the abdomen I should say the knife was at least six inches long'. Asked by the coroner if the knowledge shown by the murderer in removing the kidney would 'be likely to be possessed by one accustomed to cutting up animals', the doctor answered simply and unequivocally, 'Yes'. Stephen Knight, writing in 1975, marvelled at the removal of the kidney, 'one of the most difficult organs to locate, as it is secreted deep inside the body and concealed in a mass of fatty tissue.' He declared that 'No theorist has yet been able to explain how the Ripper worked with such silent skill and swiftness, his efficiency unimpaired by the impenetrable gloom.' Dr Brown, of course, had long since put a considered view on record.

In his book, *The Lighter Side of My Official Life*, Sir Robert Anderson wrote that the police had reached the conclusion that the Ripper and his people were certain low-class Polish Jews. He stated it as 'a remarkable fact that people of that class in the East End will not give up one of their number to Gentile justice'. It would have been more fair if he had added that they frequently dealt out their own justice in keeping within their strict moral discipline. Sir Robert continued by declaring that the only person who had ever had a good view of the murderer unhesitatingly identified his suspect, but refused to give evidence against him. If this was the basis of his claim that Jews were intent on shielding their people from justice, it is rather strange that the witness should have 'unhesitantly identified' the suspect in the first place! Sir Robert did not elaborate and it is possible that he had in mind the Polish Jew, known as 'Leather Apron' whose name was John Pizer and whose occupation was that of a boot-finisher. Pizer came under suspicion following the murder of Annie Chapman. When he was put on an identity parade, several women who claimed to know 'Leather Apron' failed to recognize him and he was

Broadsheet: capture of John Pizer, known as 'Leather Apron'.

released. Don Rumbelow's thorough researches identified Sir Robert Anderson's Polish Jew as Pizer from an account in *The Times* dated 12 September 1888, which also recorded the name of the witness as Emanuel Violenia. This an, who was residing in the East End prior to emigrating to Australia, witnessed a street quarrel when a man threatened to kill a woman whom he subsequently took to be Annie Chapman. Violenia identified John Pizer as the man but failed to recognize Chapman in the mortuary.

The ritual slaughterman theory of the Ripper's identity set out only to match the known characteristics of the murderer with the most likely analogue. There was never any intention of seeking to name a London-based *shochet* which, in any case, it would have been impossible to verify as the records of the London Board of Shechita were destroyed by enemy action in 1940. The theory has the considerable advantage that it is not necessary to go to extraordinary lengths to adapt the facts to fit it.

Don Rumbelow criticized the *shochet* theory on two main counts. Firstly, that many ordinary butchers or slaughtermen had skills similar to those of a *shochet* and that the fact the Ripper strangled his victims before cutting their throats invalidates the theory. He quotes at length a letter from a London slaughterman written to the police in October 1888 pointing out the skills possessed by an expert butcher which would qualify him as the Ripper. A graphic account is given of the likely throat-cutting technique used by the Ripper that was completely in harmony with contemporary slaughtering technique. If anything, this tends to strengthen the slaughterman theory. Don Rumbelow's man was talking about the dexterity of 'a good slaughterman' at the peak of his craft – an 'expert butcher' with experience enough to kill at a speed which would surprise the medical fraternity. This adequately defines the *shochet*'s skill with the addition of the ritual throat-cutting – there can be little doubt this was the Ripper's hallmark.

Whether or not the Ripper strangled his victims has little bearing on the *shochet*'s standing, although Rumbelow suggests it 'falls to the ground completely'. The balance of evidence favours the suggestion that the victims were rendered senseless, thus preventing them crying out and also, as Professor Camps has observed, thereby accounting for the lack of blood. Interestingly, Dr Bond's letter which Don Rumbelow terms a major document on which to some extent hinges 'the arguments for or against the respective theories', makes no mention of the possibility of strangulation although he goes into the murderer's *modus operandi* at some length. There was nothing to prevent the *shochet* silencing the women by strangulation, indeed it would have been an expeditious way of restraining the sacrificial victim in the absence of abattoir assistants to 'cast' up the throat ready for the knife. But, more significantly, strangulation was one of the Talmudic punishments for harlotry.

The most valid criticism of the *shochet* theory came from Chaim Bermant in his book, *Point of Arrival*, published in 1975. He touched on the Jacob the Ripper idea and noted that the police took the ritual slaughterman idea sufficiently seriously at the time to make visits to Jewish abattoirs. Apparently, two *shochim* were detained but later released. The concept of a slaughterman, steeped in Old Testament law and driven by the harsh punishments for harlotry prescribed in the *Talmud* to kill prostitutes in London's streets, was not without credibility it seems. But when Dr Brown was asked to examine a *shochet*'s ceremonial knife, the *khalef*, to see if he judged it capable of inflicting the sort of injuries he had found on Eddowes' body, his conclusion was that the *khalef*, single-edged and lacking a point, was not the type of cutting instrument used by the Ripper. The correctness of Dr Brown's conclusion cannot be doubted, as several doctors who had examined Ripper victims described the weapon as pointed. That this was so does not, however, rule out the possibility that a *shochet* carried out the Ripper murders. He may not have used his ceremonial *khalef* for he had at his routine disposal other types of knives which were used for different parts of the ritual slaughter.

Sir Charles Warren's view that anti-Semitic feelings in

174

the East End might erupt if the reference to the Jews in the famous message on the wall were made public was supported by the *Jewish Chronicle*. Chaim Bermant observed that its edition of 14 September 1888 reported, 'Without doubt the foreign Jews in the East End have been in some peril during the past week owning to the sensationalism of which the district has been a centre.' It could not have helped the police working in the East End to read in *The Times* of 2 October 1888 that a Jew had been arrested in the Polish city of Cracow charged with the ritual murder of a Christian woman. He was accused of having sexual intercourse with the woman after which he killed her in the belief that this was necessary to conform with Jewish law. The man was acquitted and the Chief Rabbi of England, Dr Herman Adler, protested in a letter to *The Times* that Jewish law made no such barbaric reference. Another piece of mischief-making was a report from central Europe to the effect that candles made from the uterus emitted fumes which had the effect of making people unconscious. It was believed in parts of Germany that criminals used such devices to render their victims helpless. This report appeared two days after it became known that the uterus had been removed from the body of Catherine Eddowes.

The idea that Jack the Ripper was a doctor was probably kindled in the public mind by the thought that no other person would find it easy to cut open bodies and remove their internal organs. It seemed like surgery gone mad and therefore the work of a mad surgeon. Understandably this was not a view the doctors themsleves were keen to embrace but, generally speaking, they did not allow it to cloud their professional judgement. The opinions expressed at the time by first-hand, professional observers of the Ripper's handiwork were clear and forthright. Although there were dissenters, there was, as we have seen, a majority view in favour of anatomical skill having been demonstrated by the murderer.

Extending Dr Thomas Neill Cream's terms of reference to include murder by the knife or similarly converting

VICTIMS	MURDER BACKGROUND			SCENE OF THE MURDER				
	Date	Time	Location	Throat cut	Loss of blood	Signs of struggle	Doctor called	Nature of throat cut
NICHOLS, Mary Ann, 42. Separated from husband. Five children. Lived at Thrawl Street, Spitalfields	Friday 31 Aug. 1888	Approx 3 a.m.	Bucks Row	Yes	Small amount of blood considering extent of injuries (police at scene)	Residents close by heard no cries	Llewellyn	Left to right
CHAPMAN, Annie, 47. Separated from husband. Two children. Lived in Dorset Street, Spitalfields	Saturday 8 Sep. 1888	Between 5 and 6 a.m.	29 Hanbury Street	Yes	Large clots of blood around body	No evidence of a struggle (police at scene)	Phillips	Left to right
STRIDE, Elizabeth, 45. Separated from husband. Nine children. Lived in Flower and Dean Street, Spitalfields	Sunday 30 Sep. 1888	Between 12.35 and 12.55 a.m.	40 Berner Street	Yes			Blackwell	Left to right
EDDOWES, Catherine, 43. Separated from husband. Three children. Lived variously in Dorset Street and Thrawl Street, Spitalfields	Sunday 30 Sep. 1888	Between 1.30 and 1.45 a.m.	Mitre Square	Yes		'I feel sure there was no struggle' (Dr Brown)	Sequiera and Brown	Left to right while victim lay on ground
KELLY, Mary, 25. Husband dead. Two children. Lived at 13 Miller's Court	Friday 9 Nov. 1888	Between 3.30 and 4 a.m.	13 Miller's Court	Yes	Heavy loss of blood	None. Clothes lay neatly folded on a chair	Phillips	Left to right

Bruising	Mutilations	Doctors in attendance	Likely murder weapon	Doctors' Remarks
	Disembowelled.	Llewellyn	'Exceptionally long-bladed knife' (Dr Llewellyn).	The mutilations were 'deftly and skilfully performed' (Dr Llewellyn).
Bruise on right side of head, also on the face and chin; tongue swollen.	'The abdomen had been entirely laid open and the intestines severed from their mesenteric attachments' (Dr Phillips). The uterus was missing.	Phillips	'Very sharp knife with a thin narrow blade' (Dr Phillips).	'Obviously the work was that of an expert – or one, at least, who had such knowledge of anatomical or pathological examinations as to be enabled to secure the pelvic organs with one sweep of the knife' (Dr Phillips).
Bruising on both shoulders and chest, but no facial contusions.	No mutilations; murderer thought to have been disturbed.	Blackwell and Phillips		
	'The walls of the abdomen were laid open' (Dr Brown). The left kidney and the uterus had been removed. There were cuts to the face.	Sequiera Brown Phillips Saunders	'A sharp knife, and it must have been pointed' (Dr Brown).	'The way in which the mutilation had been effected showed that the perpetrator of the crime possessed some anatomical knowledge' (Dr Brown). 'No evidence of any anatomical knowledge other than that which could be expected of a professional butcher . . ' (Drs Sequiera and Brown). 'No stranger to the knife' (Dr Sequiera).
	Gross mutilation. Some organs had been cut out of the body (including uterus).	Phillips, Bond and Brown	'A strong knife at least six inches long, very sharp, pointed at the top and about an inch wide. It may have been a clasp knife, a butcher's knife or a surgeon's knife' (Dr Bond).	'No scientific or anatomical knowledge' (Dr Bond).

George Chapman from barber-surgeon to poisoner would be a neat solution. The murderer would be doubly damned and the public would find its prejudices confirmed. But there are powerful arguments for rejecting such theses, as there are too for eschewing those identities based on barber-surgeons with Russian pedigrees, mysterious doubles and numerous aliases.

The obsession to name the Ripper, to be able to say who he was, to root him firmly in an historical background, has led to contortions and conjuring tricks that have obscured simpler explanations. Contemporary senior police officers found it difficult to live with public expectations that they had privileged and secret knowledge of the Ripper's identity. Their memoirs hint at that special knowledge but their conclusions are as disappointing as they are different. On the other hand, the doctors of the day who were also expected to know and who quietly expressed their opinions as part of the public record have been largely ignored. The weight given by these contemporary medical opinions, although not unanimous, favours the view that Jack the Ripper demonstrated some anatomical knowledge. This consensus cannot be lightly dismissed.

The skills exhibited by the murderer had more in common with those of the slaughterman than with the technique of a medical man. There is no necessity for too intricate theorizing – the known facts and informed contemporary opinions fit the slaughterman model readily enough. Such a conclusion has the powerful constraint of failing to produce a named identity for the Ripper but, ultimately, it may do more justice to the known facts of the case.

Of course, the unthinkable can happen. A *bona fide* doctor, perhaps even Queen Victoria's own physician, might have been Jack the Ripper. No less a person than Sir William Gull, MD, FRCP, FRS, one-time lecturer in physiology and comparative anatomy and Physician-in-Ordinary to the Queen, has been nominated for that role. Certainly, he was eminently qualified but that is another story and it is told in Chapter 6.

CHAPTER FOUR
Jill the Ripper

The idea that the Whitechapel murderer might be not Jack but Jill the Ripper was current at the time of the killings: Inspector Abberline himself is credited by Donald McCormick with discussing the possibility with Dr Dutton. This came about after the murder of Mary Kelly and related to the evidence given by Caroline Maxwell, the wife of a Dorset Street lodging-house keeper.

Mrs Maxwell claimed to have seen Kelly on two occasions during the early morning of Friday 9 November 1888, several hours *after* doctors believed the prostitute had met her death. The first time was between 8 and 8.30 at the corner of Miller's Court. The witness was sure of the time because her husband finished work at eight o'clock. She thought Kelly looked ill and offered her some rum, observing privately that it was unusual for her to be about so early. The second time she saw Kelly was about an hour later talking to a man outside the Britannia public house.

Mrs Maxwell described the clothes Kelly was wearing as consisting of a dark skirt, velvet bodice and a maroon-coloured shawl. Asked if she had seen Kelly in these clothes before, she replied that she had definitely seen her in the shawl. Mrs Maxwell was adamant both as to her identification and timing when she was cross-examined by Abberline. The policeman was so perplexed that he dashed off to Dr Dutton to try out a theory on him.

'Do you think', he asked, 'it could be a case not of Jack the Ripper but Jill the Ripper?' He recounted Mrs Maxwell's statement and wondered if the killer was not a woman who had escaped from Miller's Court wearing her victim's clothes. Dr Dutton apparently thought this was a doubtful suggestion but said the only sort of woman capable of committing such a murder would be a midwife.

The concept of a midwife Ripper had several facets to commend it. The universal assumption that the Ripper was a man meant that a woman could move about the East End with impunity even at the height of the terror. She would not have the same urgency to quit the streets and, indeed, as a midwife would have the perfect excuse for being abroad at a late hour. Her calling would explain the presence of any bloodstains on her clothing and she could reasonably be expected to have a basic knowledge of anatomy. In this respect, the theory was an extension of the idea that the Ripper was a doctor or at least a member of an allied profession.

Victorians were quite used to the idea of the female murderer following several sensational murder trials involving members of the fair sex. Young Constance Kent pleaded guilty in 1864 to cutting the throat of her half-brother four years earlier, Mary Ann Cotton was hanged at Durham in 1873, suspected of fourteen or fifteen murders by poisoning, and teenaged Madeleine Smith won a not-proven verdict from an Edinburgh court in 1857. Murderesses were supposed to use poison and they mostly did. The exception was Kate Webster, the thirty-year-old Irish servant hanged in 1897 for killing her employer with a cleaver. She subsequently dismembered the corpse, an act which she described graphically in her eve of execution statement. 'I chopped the head from the body with the assistance of a razor which I used to cut through the flesh afterwards. I also used the meat saw and the carving knife to cut the body up with.' The Kate Websters of Victorian England were obviously capable of the most violent blood-letting. Elliott O'Donnell in his *Confessions of a Ghost Hunter*, published in 1928, recorded that one of the theories current in 1888 was that the Ripper was a woman. 'Numbers of the men and women whom I met in the East End,' he wrote, 'steadfastly adhered to this theory, and, moreover, saw nothing remarkable in it.'

The first serious thesis arguing that the Ripper was a woman was proposed by William Stewart in his book, *Jack the Ripper: A New Theory*, published in 1939. He began by asking four of the questions which every student of the murders has asked: 1. What sort of person could have safely roamed the streets of Whitechapel at night without exciting the suspicions of the local populace who were on edge because of the murders? 2. What sort of person wearing bloodstained clothing could have passed through the streets without raising any suspicion? 3. What sort of person would have had sufficient medical knowledge to inflict mutilations on a victim's body in such a way as to suggest that a doctor was responsible? And, 4. What sort of person could have risked being found near a murder victim and yet have a good alibi? It is clear from the way the questions are formed that William Stewart's intention was to provide a murderer type rather than a named identity for the Ripper.

The answer to each question, according to Stewart, was a midwife. He argued that a person of such a calling would attract the least suspicion. In all probability she lived in the East End and would be well known to many people, including her victims. As far as the mutilations were concerned, he believed they were inflicted not by the practised hand of a surgeon but by someone who had a little anatomical knowledge and manual dexterity. After slashing her first victim for the sheer pleasure of it, the midwife mutilated subsequent victims according to the cue given by the press in suggesting the murders were committed by a doctor.

181

Stewart explained that 'mutilation is the supreme expression of spitefulness and spitefulness is a vice to which female criminals are addicts'.

The difficulties of avoiding detection by a blood-spattered killer fleeing the scene of the crime presented no problem at all to a midwife. Wearing the voluminous skirt and cloak of the times she could easily have reversed these garments to hide any blood stains. It would have been equally easy to have hidden a knife underneath such heavy clothing. On this count alone Stewart believed the murderer could not have been a man. Donald Rumbelow in his assessment of the midwife theory suggested that Stewart was somewhat obsessed with bloodstained clothing and seemed not to have considered the possibility of prior strangulation of the victims. Stewart did say that the Ripper seized her victims 'in a certain way which rapidly produced unconsciousness'. He did not elaborate on this other than to say the method was also used by midwives who practised among the extremely poor.

On the question of the Ripper's habit of removing organs from his victims' bodies and with particular reference to the uterus in the Chapman case, Stewart argued that a midwife 'had just as much knowledge as any surgeon as to the exact position of that organ, and this, together with a manipulative skill inculcated by her calling, would make its removal an easy matter'. The reason for this visceral theft, at least as far as the removal of the kidney from Eddowes' body was concerned, was attributed to an attempt to divert attention from the real purpose behind the murders. Stewart believed that this ploy contribution more than anything else to ensure that the Ripper's identity remained a mystery. Somewhat dramatically he declared that 'the particular mutilations practised by the killer held a psychological fascination and horror for all women, and as a result physiological reactions took place among women and in places remote from the scenes of the murders'.

What then was the purpose of the murders if they were committed by a woman? Stewart theorized that the murderess 'may at some time or other have practised those operations which in those days were more severely punished by law than they are today'. In other words, she was an abortionist. He went on to argue that people who implore others for help frequently end up by denouncing their saviour. On this reckoning the midwife and obliging abortionist may have been betrayed to the police and ended up serving a prison sentence. When she was released, seething with resentment, the midwife became Jill the Ripper, an avenging abortionist seeking out as victims some of her former patients. Stewart might have argued that the womb which was the physiological focus of the caring midwife became the psychological target of her eventual hatred.

William Stewart paid particular attention to the circumstances of Mary Kelly's death. Especially significant is the knowledge that the Ripper's last victim was three months pregnant, a fact which was withheld at the time by the coroner. Having a child would have involved Kelly in loss of earnings and probable eviction from her accommodation – a situation which she would hardly look on with pleasure. She decided therefore to call in the professional assistance of a midwife who was known to respond favourably to requests for abortion.

The midwife called at Miller's Court in the early hours of 9 November ostensibly to consider terminating Kelly's pregnancy. The prostitute stripped for what she imagined would be a thorough medical examination, carefully folding her clothes and piling them on a chair. With her unsuspecting victim, naked and prostrate before her, the midwife produced her knife and cut Kelly's throat. After jamming a piece of furniture against the door to ensure that she would not be disturbed, she set about her frightful dissection of the body.

According to William Stewart's account, this macabre activity was carried out in darkness. For when she realized that her clothes were heavily bloodstained, the midwife decided to swop hers for Kelly's and lit a candle in order to find them. This accounted for the momentary light which

Sarah Lewis, a Spitalfields laundress, claimed to have seen when she passed Kelly's room at about 3.30 a.m. The murderess removed her bodice, skirt and hat and put them in the fire grate where she destroyed them in a fire started with some rubbish. The ashes found in the grate by the police when they eventually gained entry to the room contained remnants of clothes which had not belonged to the murdered woman. Putting on Kelly's hat, bodice and skirt, the murderess escaped through the window, leaving the door blocked on the inside. She was the person mistakenly thought to be Kelly who was seen by Caroline Maxwell about 8 a.m. on Friday morning.

That was Jill the Ripper's last murder escapade for she realized that the sudden cessation of police enquiries after the Miller's Court killing indicated a new approach was being adopted. In the knowledge that this last victim had been pregnant, the police now thought the murderer might be a midwife and hence for Jill to continue her activities would be too dangerous. Stewart suggested that Scotland Yard believed the Ripper was a woman but continued to arrest male suspects in order not to upset their quarry's confidence.

Stewart concluded that 'Not Jack but "Jill the Ripper" can be the only satisfactory answer to the mystery', and he went on to suggest that Mrs Pearcey might have been the killer as her *modus operandi* was similar. Mary Pearcey hacked her lover's wife and child to death in her kitchen and cut their throats. She then wheeled their bodies in a perambulator from her home at Priory Street in Camden Town to Hampstead. She dumped the woman's body in the street and abandoned the dead child in Finchley. Twenty-four-year-old Mary Pearcey committed these crimes in October 1890 and Stewart found two significant points of comparison with the earlier Ripper murders. Firstly, there was the savage throat-cutting and, secondly, the technique of killing in private and then conveying the bodies by means of a perambulator to the places where they were found. This latter point would explain the odd silence that accompanied the Ripper murders – no one living nearby heard anything suspicious.

Sir Melville Macnaghten recalled in his memoirs meeting Mary Pearcey. 'I have never seen a woman of stronger physique,' he wrote, '. . . her nerves were as ironcast as her body.' He described the amazing scene at her house in Priory Street when it was being searched by police officers: 'she sat herself down at the piano and strummed away at popular tunes'. When a bloodstained poker and knife were found, Mrs Pearcey was questioned about the use to which the implements had been put. 'Killing mice, killing mice, killing mice,' was the treble reply. Mary Pearcey remained an enigma to the end which, for her, was achieved on the scaffold at Newgate Prison on 23 December 1890.

Before her execution, Mary Pearcey had arranged with her solicitor to have an advertisement placed in the Madrid newspapers. This duly appeared and read, 'M.E.C.P. last wish of M.E.W. Have not betrayed.' M.E.W. was Mary Eleanor Pearcey but the intended recipient of this message remains unknown. William Stewart suggested that she might have confessed her crimes to someone who could have been prosecuted for being an accessory and the message was to make it known that she had not repeated the admission.

Stewart discounted Martha Turner as a Ripper victim and made the interesting point that her death at the hands of another killer showed the ease with which such women could be murdered. He also excluded Elizabeth Stride from the reckoning on the grounds that her death was mere coincidence and 'both Press and public jumped to the conclusion that both this murder and that of Eddowes, which took place an hour later, was the work of the Ripper'. His reason was that Stride's throat had not been cut in the left to right direction which he took as the Ripper's hallmark. This was an erroneous view, as Dr Blackwell who examined the body at the crime scene reported that 'the incision in the neck commenced on the left side . . .' Nevertheless, Stewart had the distinction of trying to reduce the number of Ripper victims rather than add to it as others have done.

This left him with four victims which he listed in tabular form in order to demonstrate the curiosity that the murders occurred at the ends of different weeks:

Victim	Day of Murder	Date
Nichols	Friday	31 August
Chapman	Saturday	8 September
Eddowes	Sunday	30 September
Kelly	Friday	9 November

This phenomenon was noted at the time and many commentators linked it with the arrival of cattle boats in the Thames on Thursdays and their departure on Mondays. Having demonstrated this link, Stewart then demolished it with the patently weak argument that no cattle-hand would have been able 'to leave his ship to commit the crimes and return without exciting suspicion'.

With some modesty, Stewart concluded that his theory was but a theory and that he would continue the search in order to substantiate it. He acknowledged, even in 1939, that 'The East End murders have become almost legendary and in doing so have been surrounded with romance and fable.' The fables have increased in the years since the advent of the 'Jill the Ripper' theory to a degree that would have astounded his pursuit of 'strict examination in conjunction with the known facts'.

Although invariably included in the shortlist of serious contenders as a Ripper identity type, Stewart's theory is generally regarded as lightweight. Donald McCormick thought he 'argued his case logically and presented it convincingly' although he faulted it on the grounds that there was no evidence of a woman having been seen in the company of any of the victims prior to their murder, whereas there was overwhelming evidence in at least four of the cases that the victim had been seen with a male companion.

Don Rumbelow pointed out a major flaw which was that, with the exception of Mary Kelly, none of the other victims was known to be pregnant. He observed that in view of their age and hard-drinking life style, the likelihood of becoming pregnant was not strong. Dan Farson took a similar view, saying, 'It is in relation to the other victims that the theory falls to pieces.' There is no convincing reason, he argued, why these women should have accompanied a midwife into the back yards of Whitechapel.

Tom Cullen thought that Stewart had missed a more plausible line of enquiry by overlooking the hint dropped by Joseph Barnett that Kelly was a lesbian. Barnett, himself a latter-day Ripper suspect, lived with Kelly but lost her affection to one Maria Harvey. Having been ousted from her bed, he moved to other accommodation. The possibility of murder by a vengeful female was suggested as a more rewarding path for Stewart to have followed. In his book, *Autumn of Terror*, Cullen recorded that Arthur Conan Doyle, who in 1888 was on the first rung of his success as creator of Sherlock Holmes, believed that Jack the Ripper disguised himself as a woman to avoid detection. Conan Doyle's son apparently wrote to Cullen telling him that his famous father believed the Ripper was a man with a rough knowledge of surgery who dressed in female clothing in order to facilitate his approach to his victims. Interestingly, in the story Conan Doyle wrote about the Ripper, called *Jack the Harlot Killer*, the murderer is unmasked as a Scotland Yard inspector, and it is Sherlock Holmes who played the decoy dressed as a prostitute.

In *The Michaelmas Girls*, a work of fiction by John Brooks Barry, published in 1975, the Ripper story received a novel treatment. Despite its fictional status, the story is set against the historic background of the murders whose victims are called the Michaelmas Girls because two of them were murdered on or about Michaelmas Day, 29 September. The Feast of St Michael and All Angels is one of the English quarter days when leases began, rents became due and servants were hired; it also marks the start of the last term of the law courts and universities. Perhaps with appropriate symbolism, St Michael, the prince of all the angels, is depicted in the final judgement holding scales in which he weighs the souls of the risen dead.

John Brooks Barry structured his story along the lines of a journal written by a young man who worked as a volunteer at Toynbee Hall in the East End during the period of the Ripper murders. By this means, the author created a vivid picture of Whitechapel in the 1880s in which he set the factual elements of the murders and drew his readers to the intriguing conclusion that there was not one Ripper, but two – one male and one female working in concert.

The number of victims is taken as six and includes Martha Turner, otherwise it is the familiar roll call until the final murder occurs at Miller's Court. The female half of the killing duo proves to be none other than Kelly herself who is depicted as a lady of lesbian inclinations or what the Victorians liked to call Sapphic desires. Part of her psychology is to maintain a secret relationship with a man outside the sphere of her prostitution and she uses him to avenge herself on her own kind.

The man, who nurses a morbid fear of women, finds the sadist's pleasure in inflicting cruelty on them. He chooses prostitutes because their very calling involves sexual pleasures which mock his inhibitions. These two twisted souls, the lesbian prostitute and the male sadist, are attracted to each other to combine their lust in killing and mutilation – 'their shared ecstasy is the ecstasy of murder'. Acting as one, they can attribute their violence to a third party – Jack the Ripper. The murderous instrument is the knife, a phallic device used to attack the sexuality of their victims. The knife – the 'penis knife', as John Brooks Barry calls it – binds the couple together 'in a new sexual unity as if it were a wedding band'.

The murders themselves become ritual killings performed by the Ripper for the benefit of his companion. What he could never do alone is possible in the presence of a third party; Mary Kelly's chief role is to complete the gratification simply by being on hand. Ultimately, though 'the madness is shared'. There is an element of display in the way some of the victims' corpses were arranged with their legs placed together lying on their backs in 'supplicating poses'.

The killers obviously knew the environs of Whitechapel intimately and Kelly's room off Dorset Street placed her at the very centre of the web of murder. The murdering duo plotted their violent excursions from 13 Miller's Court and quickly returned there afterwards. As the ferocity and daring of the murders increased, so the clues were more strongly associated with Dorset Street. On the night of the double murder, the killers fled from Mitre Square travelling north into the heart of Whitechapel, probably via Aldgate and along Goulston Street where a torn, bloodied piece of Catherine Eddowes' apron was discarded in a passageway. Close by, scrawled across the black dado of a staircase wall, was the infamous message, 'The Juwes are the men that will not be blamed for nothing.' Further on, in Dorset Street itself, the killer washed the blood from his hands at a public sink situated in a narrow close. These acts of daring were committed within a few minutes' reach of Kelly's room at 13 Miller's Court. Within fifteen minutes or so of completing their act of mutilation in Mitre Square, the murderers had reached a haven within the very heart of their territory.

The murder committed at Miller's Court was the final act of fantasy and deception. In his reconstruction of the event, John Brooks Barry suggested Kelly wanted to be seen on the streets in the early hours of 9 November in the company of her partner who was dressed 'in an outfit difficult to overlook'. They made no attempt to avoid the attention of George Hutchinson who, afterwards, gave a detailed description of the man and his dress. Hutchinson told the police that he saw Kelly and her companion enter Miller's Court and he hung about for forty-five minutes hoping they would emerge. When they did not he became tired of waiting and left. Hutchinson's watchful presence constrained the murder plan, for the victim was not at that time inside 13 Miller's Court. Only when Hutchinson left at about 2.45 a.m. were the murderous duo able to leave, procure their victim and walk her back to the room where she was murdered.

The idea was to murder the final victim in Kelly's room and to mutilate the corpse beyond description so that the world would believe Kelly herself was the victim. The unfortunate sacrificial victim of this plot was one of the homeless, destitute denizens of the East End whose numbers were swollen by an influx of vagrants hoping to make something out of the Lord Mayor's Show. The woman who succumbed to the Ripper's blandishments was subjected to the horror of the knife and literally hacked to pieces. The act of deception was completed by Mary Kelly leaving her own clothes behind; the murder victim's garments, stripped from her body before the carnage began, were burned in the fire grate. As the new day dawned, the Ripper melted away while Mary Kelly allowed herself to be seen on the street before disappearing herself.

John Brooks Barry's fictional account of the Ripper murders provides an intriguing idea which, because it is not forced into a factual mould, has a curious consonance with reality. The killer's psyche is well observed with the notion that the murders are a form of self-mutilation for a man incapable of satisfying normal desire. The mental conflict between Jekyll and Hyde, the higher and lower man, is resolved when brute lust harnesses the faculties of the higher man to evolve a plan. Part of that plan develops a sort of Bonnie and Clyde partnership with a lesbian who makes possible his blood lust by helping him prepare for the act of murder and also by witnessing it. On a practical level, she acted as lookout and it was she, with her prostitute's knowledge, who set the trap for the victims. It was she who chose the secluded place at the right time, and it was she who laid the false trails – the letters, the torn apron, the message on the wall – and it was she too who by being the killer's companion made his apprehension by the police less likely because they were on the lookout for an unaccompanied man.

The final intrigue concerned the delay in burying the corpse of the Miller's Court victim; the funeral of Mary Kelly took place at St Leonard's, Shoreditch, on 18 November, nine days after the murder. Was this, enquired John Brooks Barry, because the police were trying to find the real identity of the victim? Perhaps, too, by not revealing their knowledge of the final deception they still hoped to trace the murderous duo?

Another Jack and Jill partnership was suggested in a series of articles which appeared in *The Sun* newspaper in August 1972. 'Ex-Yard Chief Arthur Butler dramatically re-opens a case that horrified London 84 years ago' was the announcement made to *Sun* readers. Former Detective Chief Superintendent Butler, credited with having solved eight murder cases during his career, proposed that Jack the Ripper was a female abortionist aided by a male assistant. This was the conclusion he came to after 'years of patient research' and beginning at a point which most Ripper observers have rejected – the death of Emma Smith on 3 April 1888. Unlike the later victims, Smith died in hospital after receiving a brutal beating. She was set upon and robbed outside Whitechapel Church by several men believed at the time to be members of one of the gangs which terrorized East End residents. According to Arthur Butler, the 45-year-old prostitute died 'because she knew too much'. His thesis was that her 'continued existence constituted a threat to the person who was later responsible for London's autumn of terror – a female abortionist'.

Claiming to have uncovered 'facts unknown to the police at the time', Butler argues that four of the six women generally accepted as victims of Jack the Ripper were not murdered at all – they were the victims of bungled abortion attempts. By mutilating and then dumping the bodies of the already dead women, the abortionist hoped to divert police attention down fruitless paths of enquiry. Her male accomplice murdered the other women to make sure they did not talk and played an essential part in helping to transport the bodies from the room near Brick Lane where the abortions were carried out to the locations where they were discovered. A cart or perambulator was used for this purpose and the useful point made that a woman pushing a pram accompanied by a man was not likely to excite suspicion.

Arthur Butler acknowledged that for an abortionist to resort to murder and mutilation to preserve her secret seemed 'somewhat drastic'. Nevertheless, he believed that the life imprisonment which would have been the undoubted punishment for a person convicted of performing illegal abortions in the 1880s was sufficient of a spectre to drive a bungling practitioner to desperate measures. There was also the added incentive of retaining the good livelihood to be earned by a shady midwife working in the East End's prostitute community. 'By piecing together hitherto unknown and unconnected items of information, I established that this woman had dealings with each of the dead prostitutes,' wrote Butler. He also talked of 'my informants' but, unfortunately, neither these nor the other sources of information were identified.

The claim was made that Emma Smith acted as a go-between for such a midwife who carried out a profitable abortion sideline. The reason for the prostitute's death was tied in with hearsay evidence that she had been unwise enough to mention in a public bar that she reckoned on being in the money again soon with funds from a female benefactor. Smith's regular consort, a street conjurer and pickpocket, was seen in the district with a well-dressed man who was a stranger. He was presumed to be the abortionist's accomplice looking for Emma Smith and intent on silencing her.

Montague John Druitt: the case of the drowned barrister (*Reproduced with the permission of the Warden and Scholars of Winchester College*)

The Duke of Clarence: did he create a constitutional crisis? (*The BBC Hulton Picture Library*)

Sir William Gull: healer turned destroyer? (*The BBC Hulton Picture Library*)

Lord Salisbury:
supposed instigator of a
conspiracy at high level
(*The BBC Hulton
Picture Library*)

Sir Charles Warren:
ordered erasure of the
famous 'message on the
wall' (*The BBC Hulton
Picture Library*)

THE DISCOVERY OF THE SIXTH "RIPPER" MURDER.

Police News and *Famous Crimes:* How the contemporary press covered the murders (*The BBC Hulton Picture Library*)

POLICE THE ILLUSTRATED NEWS

LAW COURTS AND WEEKLY RECORD.

No. 1,282.   SATURDAY, SEPTEMBER 8, 1888.   Price One Penny.

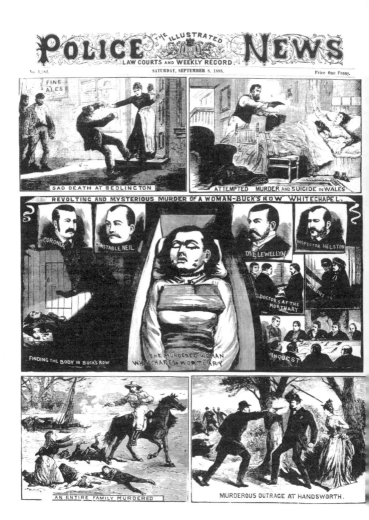

SAD DEATH AT BEDLINGTON

ATTEMPTED MURDER AND SUICIDE IN WALES

REVOLTING AND MYSTERIOUS MURDER OF A WOMAN—BUCK'S ROW, WHITECHAPEL.

CORONER

CONSTABLE NEIL

DR. L. LEWELLYN

INSPECTOR HELSTON

WITNESSES

DOCTORS AT THE MORTUARY

FINDING THE BODY IN BUCK'S ROW

THE MURDERED WOMAN WHITECHAPEL MORTUARY

INQUEST

AN ENTIRE FAMILY MURDERED

MURDEROUS OUTRAGE AT HANDSWORTH.

THE ILLUSTRATED POLICE NEWS
LAW COURTS AND WEEKLY RECORD.

FIFTH VICTIM

MORTUARY

THE BERNER ST VICTIM.

INSPECTOR REID

INQUEST ON FIFTH VICTIM AT ST GEORGES IN THE EAST

TWO MORE WHITECHAPEL HORRORS. WHEN WILL THE MURDERER BE CAPTURED?

BACK of BERNER STREET

THE DISCOVERY of the CRIME

POLICE CONSTABLE WATKINS SIGNALLING FOR ASSISTANCE

MITRE SQUARE ALDGATE

THE FATAL SPOT

GOING TO HER DOOM

FINDING THE BODY IN MITRE SQUARE.

THE SCENE ON SUNDAY IN BERNER STREET

THE FIFTH VICTIM OF THE WHITECHAPEL FIEND.

FINDING THE MUTILATED BODY IN MITRE SQARE.

POLICE · BUDGET · EDITION   EDITED · BY · HAROLD · FURNISS

FAMOUS CRIMES

PAST AND PRESENT

ONE · PENNY

HOW THE "RIPPER'S" VICTIMS WENT TO THEIR DEATH.

Vol. II.—No. 17.

Sir Melville MacNaghten: his notes fuelled suspicion about Druitt
(*The BBC Hulton Picture Library*)

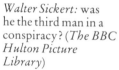

Walter Sickert: was he the third man in a conspiracy? (*The BBC Hulton Picture Library*)

Aleister Crowley: suggested the Ripper was a Black Magician (*The BBC Hulton Picture Library*)

The next victim was Martha Turner who, like Emma Smith, has been rejected as a genuine Ripper victim by the majority of Ripperologists. She died of multiple stab wounds following an attack at George Yard Buildings on 7 August 1888. Her death was attributed by the police to the street violence that was so prevalent in the East End, but Arthur Butler perceived greater significance in her death. He contended that in the days preceding her murder, Turner had been involved with an abortionist on behalf of a friend. Rosie Johnson had confided in Turner that she was pregnant and that she knew 'someone who'll get rid of it'. The two women paid a visit to the abortionist at her premises near Brick Lane and Rosie remained for treatment.

When Turner called back the following day, she was told that her friend had left. She searched unsuccessfully for Rosie and eventually returned to the abortionist. There was an argument and, hours later, Turner, who had proved to be a persistent nuisance, was found dead, the victim of an apparently motiveless attack. It is possible that she was lured into the dark entry of George Yard Buildings by the abortionist's accomplice on the pretext of giving her information about her missing friend. Whatever the motive, she ended up on the mortuary slab.

Mary Nichols, of whom Butler wrote, 'I do know that she visited an abortionist', was, he believed, killed in the lair near Brick Lane and her mutilated body dumped where it was found in Bucks Row. He pointed out that there was very little blood around the body and believed the medical and police evidence strongly indicated that the victims were not killed where they were found. He argued that this was certainly true of the killing of Annie Chapman in the back yard at Hanbury Street where there was no sign of any struggle and little blood. In this case the victim's pockets had been turned out, probably in a search for a scrap of paper bearing the name and address of the abortionist which would have been highly incriminating if found by the police.

Arthur Butler had surprisingly little to say about the 'double event' beyond discounting Elizabeth Stride's unmutilated death as being in the same category as the other murders. 'I cannot believe,' he wrote, 'that the same hand which struck down Elizabeth Stride would have gone on to kill or mutilate again in such a short space of time – knowing that a hue and cry had begun only a little distance away.' She was just another East End murder victim, he concluded. Of Catherine Eddowes, he only remarked that 'Her corpse bore the now familiar signs of grotesque mutilation'. In his concluding article, Butler dealt with 'The Fiend Who Butchered Jolly Mary Jane'. The key is the fact that Mary Jane Kelly was three months pregnant; 'I know,' wrote Butler, 'that Mary told acquaintances that she was getting rid of the pregnancy – and that there was an abortionist living near who had connections with other prostitutes who had been in similar straits.'

Unlike her fellow victims, Mary Kelly had a room which she could claim as her own. The abortionist called on her to carry out an illegal operation which went wrong. After performing her mutilating excesses to cover up her bungled work, the abortionist discovered she was heavily bloodstained. She therefore burned her outer clothing and left 13 Miller's Court wearing some of her victim's garments. She waited until daylight to make good her escape, thus avoiding the police night patrols. The fact that the murderess was wearing some of Kelly's clothes accounted for the apparent sighting of Kelly after she was known to be dead. Thus the killings ended and the abortionist was persuaded 'to pack in her risky business' because new lines of enquiry were being pursued by the police following the resignation of Sir Charles Warren. This, claimed Arthur Butler, may be deduced from 'a close study of police records at the time'.

In many ways Butler's theory is really an update of William Stewart's but, as Don Rumbelow remarked, without knowing the precise nature of his sources it is impossible to know how much weight can be given to it. 'Mr

Butler', he wrote, 'would put everyone in his debt if he committed his sources to paper and so ensured that his theory be not dismissed as just another story.' Apart from being the world's most bungling abortionist, Butler's Jill the Ripper left a great number of loose ends. For instance, what was her purpose in removing organs from some of her victims? With reference to the dumping of Annie Chapman's body, Butler wrote that it was necessary to move the corpse complete with near-severed head but 'with the exception of certain organs'. No further explanation is given, nor is the phenomenon of the Ripper letters explained.

There is nothing far-fetched about the idea of using a perambulator to transport a murder victim's body – Mrs Pearcey, referred to earlier, demonstrated the technique to good effect in 1890. But the crucial aspect of these manoeuvres was that the blood-letting occurred in the abortionist's den with the consequence that very little blood was evident at the places where the victims were discovered. While this was commented on at the time by police officers investigating the death of Mary Nichols, the pattern is by no means consistent. Certainly there were large clots of blood around the body of Annie Chapman when it was discovered and it is self-evident from the contemporary medical drawing of Catherine Eddowes that there were considerable pools of blood either side of her heart. As discussed in the previous chapter, some experts who regarded this loss of blood as relatively slight accounted for the phenomenon by suggesting that the Ripper's victims were first strangled. Arthur Butler appeared not to have considered this possibility.

It is difficult to believe that the world's worst abortionist, after a murder spree lasting (according to Butler) for some eight months, simply gave up because she believed the police were adopting new tactics. Also, as Don Rumbelow observed, it is surprising that the abortionist, having found a foolproof method of disposing of Martha Turner's friend Rosie, did not use the same method of disposal for her other 'failures'. And why, if it was just a matter of covering up a bungled abortion, was the butchery in the case of Mary Kelly so gross? Arthur Douglas, commenting on the abortionist theory in his book *Will the Real Jack the Ripper*, published in 1979, described ex-Detective Chief Superintendent Butler's assertions as 'models of what a policeman could never expect to say in court without being acutely challenged'.

'Was it *Jill* the Ripper?' was the title of an article which appeared in the *Evening News* on 8 September 1955. Introduced by Richard Herd, the story itself purported to be 'The Secret of Ex-Convict SYF45'. The ex-convict was a forger whose prison record went back to 1896 and who in the 1950s was 'spending the last few years of his life in a bungalow near the sea'. The story he told began in Parkhurst Prison, years after the sensational murders had ceased. He found himself in the prison hospital next to an old lag who wanted to unburden his conscience. The old lag revealed that his wife had committed the Ripper murders.

The storyteller related how, when he was a teenager, he saw one of the Ripper victims. His uncle was a special constable and when he was out with him one night, they responded to a nearby policeman's whistle call and came across a murder victim in an alleyway. 'If only I'd known then what I honestly believe to be the truth now we might have prevented the rest of the Ripper murders,' he said. The police were instructed to apprehend every man seen in the vicinity of each murder but women, of course, were unchecked.

The old lag in the hospital asked the forger if he was a Roman Catholic. Receiving an affirmative answer, the next question was whether one Catholic could make a confession to another and whether it would be treated with the same confidentiality as if made to a priest. A bargain was struck to the effect that if the old lag unburdened his conscience, his confidant would not repeat what he was told unless his informant died in prison.

While serving as a steward on board a ship returning from Australia in the autumn of 1887, the old lag fell ill and, on reaching England, was admitted to hospital. He fell in love with one of his nurses and they were married before he set off for his next seafaring trip. This was to be his last trip and when he returned, the plan was that he and his wife would settle down in their home at Forest Gate. After three months at sea, the wanderer returned and, in the best tradition of paid-off seamen, stopped at a dockside hotel for a few drinks with his shipmates before going home. The carousing men were joined by some streetwalkers and the old lag was tempted to go off with one of them.

When he was reunited with his wife, she informed him that it would not be possible for them to live together as man and wife. No explanation was given for this strange welcome but one night after he returned from his job as a hospital porter he saw in the kitchen sink a bloodstained carving knife. It was one of a set which the hospital staff had given them as a wedding present. Two or three days later, he found a pair of his trousers hanging out to dry – they had been washed but there were still bloodstains on them.

When he questioned his wife, she broke down and confessed that she was responsible for murdering the East End prostitutes. 'And I'll go on killing them,' she declared. 'Both our lives have been ruined by women of that class – and I'll see they don't wreck other people's lives!' She recalled that on one occasion she had been called to attend one of the victims at the very time she was hurrying from the murder scene. Her *modus operandi* was to dress as a man – as a sailor – but carrying a nurse's cloak and bonnet in a bag. Once she had despatched her victims with her carving knife, she dressed in her nurse's garb and calmly walked away.

It was not uncommon to see a nurse or a midwife in the street late at night and she knew that she could walk away from her crimes unchallenged. Her ex-sailor husband was astonished at her revelations and could hardly believe what he heard. Then she told him that one of her intended victims was Mary Kelly, the prostitute with whom he had consorted when he returned from his last sea trip. After Kelly had been murdered by the anonymous killer known to the public as Jack the Ripper, a man was arrested and it was widely believed he would be charged with murder. The avenging wife apparently declared that if the man detained was charged she would give herself up. In the event, the suspect was released but the possibility of an innocent person being condemned was sufficient shock to make her end her murderous exploits. Kelly was the last Whitechapel murder victim and Jill the Ripper, the vengeful nurse, was never discovered.

Richard Herd said that he had spent 'a great deal of time checking the facts and matching dates, times and places'. He concluded that 'No one other than a Roman Catholic priest to whom the old lag's last confession was made a few weeks after the meeting in the garden will ever know for certain whether his story was true.' He added, 'After my researches, I too believe his story.' In his comments on the story Donald McCormick thought it had an authentic ring about it – 'the ring of a typical old lag's tale'.

Another woman who wore the trousers was Olga Tchkersoff, Edwin Woodhall's avenging angel in *Jack the Ripper – or When London Walked in Terror*. According to his account, published in 1937, the original story was written by an American for a New York newspaper just before the war. The writer was said to be related to the Russian family at the centre of the story. Ivan Tchkersoff with his wife and two daughters fled from Vilma in Russia to escape capture by the Czarist secret police at a time of political tyranny. The Tchkersoffs arrived in England as refugees on 22 February 1887.

The family stayed with fellow Russian refugees in London's East End until they were able to plan a new life. The eldest daughter Olga, aged twenty-four, was a skilled needlewoman and aimed to put her craft to good use. She was also blessed with a practical view of life and had managed to smuggle a quantity of valuable jewellery out of Russia. This was sold to raise funds with the aim of setting up in the garment trade. Her intention was to buy a property which could be used both as accommodation for her family and also as a garment workshop. She had already secured promises of work from the Jewish community in the East End and was keen to start the enterprise which would give her and her family a future.

A semi-dilapidated house was found in Spitalfields and Ivan Tchkersoff negotiated a two-year tenancy agreement with rent in advance which made him sole landlord with an option to sub-let if he wished. Olga's joy was quickly dashed when she realized that her parents had different plans to her own. Their earnest desire was to make as much money as quickly as possible by turning their accommodation into a lodging house. Olga strongly contested what she regarded as a wrong-headed decision which opposed her more constructive plans to establish a tailoring and dressmaking business. But her parents were adamant in their refusal to alter their decision and Olga's nineteen-year-old sister Vera supported them.

From this moment, the fortunes of the Tchkersoff family began to slide downhill. The offer of low-priced accommodation attracted the worst elements of the East End, including prostitutes, and the income which they received was frittered away by Ivan and his wife on drink. But the worst aspect of the whole unsatisfactory business was that Olga could see her impressionable sister being pulled into the orbit of the district's prostitute community. Olga remonstrated with her sister but the lure of easy money and the bright lights had cast its spell and, to all intents and purposes, she was irretrievable.

In due course, Vera slipped her family bonds completely and placed herself beyond any sisterly influence by not returning home. She sent word to her parents announcing that she was working as housekeeper for 'a very influential gentleman'. Tchkersoff and his wife regarded this as a minor kind of triumph and seemed undisturbed that their younger daughter had become a whore. Olga, on the other hand, was furious and during a heated argument struck her mother. She stormed out of the house declaring that if she had her way with the women who had brought Vera to her ruin 'she would hack them to pieces'.

In the spring of 1888, Ivan Tchkersoff died of pneumonia and his wife drowned her sorrows in alcohol. While in a drunken state she fell heavily into the stone-flagged basement of a warehouse and broke her neck. Suddenly deprived of both parents, Olga resolved to put her original plan into action. She cleared the house of its numerous tenants, save an elderly Russian couple who were family friends, and began to establish her tailoring and dressmaking business.

One night in July 1888, Olga had an unexpected visitor in the form of her sister Vera. While she was pleased to see her, it was immediately apparent that Vera was ill. She was deathly pale and collapsed in her arms. Despite receiving medical attention, Vera died in her sister's care on 28 July 1888. Cause of death was due to sepsis resulting from an abortion. Olga was distraught, having lost all her family in a few months. Her sorrow eventually gave way to anger and she decided to exact revenge against the prostitutes whom she believed had caused her sister's downfall and death. 'All women of that type were her enemies, innocent or otherwise', was how Edwin Woodhall described her intentions.

Olga Tchkersoff became Jill the Ripper and, after her reign of terror in London's East End, disappeared. The house which she had mistakenly hoped would be the base for a family business was kept on for a while by the old Russian couple who acted as caretakers but when the lease ran out, it was demolished as part of a slum clearance policy. The Russian couple went to live with their son in America, where, eventually, they related their mysterious tale of crime in the Old World.

Immediately after her sister died Olga became something of a recluse, locking herself up in a remote part of the house. After about a month of this withdrawn behaviour, Olga appeared at the door of the basement flat occupied by the Russian caretakers. She told them that she planned to go away and advised them to take up their son's offer of living in America. They were shocked at her appearance: 'Her large black eyes glittered with a kind of strange, wild, unalterable stare – the kind observed in people just on the border line of sanity and madness.' She gave them twenty pounds in order that they should have adequate funds and then departed.

Some time later, during the early hours of 9 November 1888, the caretaker who had risen early in order to fetch a drink for his wife who was unwell noticed someone moving in the yard. The slim figure of a man appeared in the yard and went into the house. The entrance to the yard was by means of the street door which Olga had expressly asked should be kept unfastened. Convinced that an intruder had entered the house, the old man armed himself with a stick and went to investigate.

He paused on the landing outside Olga's room and could see from the light emerging under the door that the room was illuminated. He could also hear movement and sounds of water being used. He knocked timidly on the door and elicited her undoubted response. He explained that he believed an intruder had entered the house whereupon, without opening the door, she told him there was nothing to worry about. She explained that she had been secretly trying out some new fashions. Knowing Olga to be a forward-looking tailoress and also a woman of advanced ideas, the caretaker felt reassured and returned to his own quarters. This was the last time he spoke to Olga Tchkersoff.

Two months later, when the elderly Russians were due to set out across the Atlantic, they were concerned because Olga was absent and they were unable to take their leave properly. They were advised by the landlord to lock up the house and to leave the keys with him. Two days before they sailed to America, the elderly caretaker, weighing the keys in his hand, decided to take a peek into Olga's rooms. Everything appeared to be in good order except that the remnants of a large fire lay in the fireplace. Among the ashes were recognizable portions of towels and clothing – including the remains of a man's jacket and trousers. Overcome with curiosity, the old man decided to look into a few drawers and cupboards. He pulled out a drawer and to his astonishment found a bloodstained towel within the folds of which was a knife. It was a sharp sheath knife, the blade and hilt of which were encrusted with dried blood.

Putting all the clues and circumstances together, the old Russian realized that Olga Tchkersoff was the murderer that the whole of England was seeking – Jack the Ripper. Notwithstanding the fact that she had committed dreadful crimes, he decided to protect her – after all she had been kind to him and his wife and she was Russian. Collecting together the incriminating fragments of clothing, he made sure that they were thoroughly combusted. Two days later in mid-Atlantic during the hours of darkness, he dropped the bloodstained knife into the ocean from the ship which bore him and his secret to America.

Edwin Woodhall in the introduction to his book wrote, 'To the best of my knowledge, I believe it is the first effort of its kind to appear in popular cheap edition form.' On this point he was probably right, although his conclusions regarding the Ripper's identity may be regarded as unreliable and inaccurate. Olga Tchkersoff was the figment of someone's fevered imagination with the trousers routine providing a novel twist.

Arthur Butler's abortionist is too much of a bungler to be believable and it is disappointing that the ex-policeman did not identify his new sources of information. As various Ripperologists have pointed out, Butler's dismissal of Elizabeth Stride as a Ripper victim revealed his lack of understanding of the type of killer typified by the Ripper. Dan Farson remarked in an article published in *Men Only* in

June 1973 that 'As there is no question of a bungled abortion with Stride, it helps his theory to say that she was murdered by someone else . . .' The stated grounds on which he excluded her were that the killer would not have gone on to kill again (as he did with the murder of Catherine Eddowes) in so short a time. This is where the lack of understanding comes in, for as Farson remarked, 'Imagine the Ripper's frustration: a sexual murderer deprived of his climax!' It was precisely because he failed to practice mutilation on his first victim on the night of 30 September 1888 that the Ripper selected another target.

William Stewart's midwife satisfied some of the criteria defining a rational identity for Jack the Ripper but failed the most crucial test. To necessitate a visit from the avenging midwife, her victims were required to be pregnant. Unfortunately for the theory, only one was. The concept of Jill the Ripper was perhaps best summed up by the *Spectator* in its edition of 7 May 1891: 'Whoever he is – we reject the theory that the murderer is a woman, for no woman could deceive so many of her own sex . . .'

CHAPTER FIVE
Gentleman Jack

Sir Melville Macnaghten was appointed Assistant Chief Constable at Scotland Yard in June 1889. He became head of CID in 1903 and retired due to ill health in 1913. In his memoirs, published in 1914, Sir Melville bemoaned the fact that he became 'a detective officer six months after the so-called "Jack the Ripper" committed suicide' and, consequently, 'never had a go at that fascinating individual'.

Although prevented from having a go at the time, Sir Melville did make an important, although perhaps unwitting, contribution to the Ripper legend. On 23 February 1894, he made some handwritten notes, the purpose of which was to exonerate a man named Thomas Cutbush from allegations that he was the Ripper. Cutbush was found to be insane and was sentenced to be detained during Her Majesty's pleasure following a charge of attacking two girls intent on wounding them. In the course of writing this seven-page document, Macnaghten referred to the Ripper murders and mentioned three men, 'any one of whom would have been more likely than Cutbush to have committed this series of murders'. The first of these was 'A Mr

M.J. Druitt, said to be a doctor & of good family – who disappeared at the time of the Miller's Court murder, & whose body (which was said to have been upward of a month in the water) was found in the Thames on 31st December – or about 7 weeks after the murder. He was sexually insane and from private information I have little doubt but that his own family believed him to have been the murderer.'

Sir Melville made no mention of Druitt's name in his published memoirs. He simply referred to the 'Whitechapel murderer', who, 'in all probability, put an end to himself after the Dorset Street affair in November 1888'. Later in the same chapter, he wrote that 'the individual who held up London in terror, resided with his own people; that he absented himself from home at certain times, and that he committed suicide on or about the 10th of November 1888 . . .' Many years later, the former CID chief's notes came to light and the name of M.J. Druitt was extracted and promulgated as the true identity of Jack the Ripper. Sir Melville's notes, one of the relatively few authentic documents relating to the events of 1888, have since been quoted and misquoted, their content construed and misconstrued and their author unfairly blamed for lapses of memory and accuracy.

First on the scent of M.J. Druitt was the writer and television interviewer, Dan Farson. In 1959, while visiting Lady Rose McLaren in North Wales, he mentioned his interest in Jack the Ripper. It transpired that her mother-in-law, the Dowager Lady Aberconway, was Sir Melville Macnaghten's daughter. As Farson put it, 'she was kind enough to give me her father's private notes which she had copied out soon after his death. At the time I hardly realized the discovery that lay in my hands . . .' These *typewritten* notes included reference to M.J. Druitt as a possible Ripper suspect. Farson included this new discovery in one of his television programmes although, respecting Lady Aberconway's wishes, he referred to the suspect only by his initials, M.J.D. Subsequently, M.J.

Druitt has been the subject of at least two major books and is well established as one of the mainstream identities for Jack the Ripper. With his mortal remains lying in a grave at Wimborne, Dorset, bearing the epitaph, 'In memory of Montague John Druitt, who died 4 December 1888. Aged 31', there can be no doubt that he once existed.

Montague John Druitt was born on 15 August 1857 at Wimborne in Dorset. His father was a doctor and he was one of seven children. At the age of thirteen, Montague won a scholarship to Winchester where he distinguished himself at sport, playing cricket at Lords in 1876 as a member of the school first eleven. In the same year he was awarded a scholarship to New College, Oxford. He went up to university and read Classics, graduating with a Bachelor of Arts degree in 1880.

The new graduate decided on a career in the law, a choice in which he might have been encouraged by his success in the College Debating Society at Winchester. He was admitted to the Inner Temple in May 1882 and found studying for the Bar an expensive business. He borrowed money from his father in the form of an advance deducted from a legacy of £500 contained in a codicil to Druitt senior's will. Montague was called to the Bar in March 1885 and suffered the loss of his father who died of a heart attack in the autumn of that year. He did not benefit from his father's estate which was worth £16,579 although his three sisters and elder brother each gained a legacy.

Druitt rented chambers at 9 King's Bench Walk and joined the Western Circuit and Winchester Sessions. It appeared that his services were not required and no record exists of his having received any brief. The 1880s were acknowledged to be difficult times for the legal profession and as few as one in eight barristers reckoned to make a living by practising law. Before being called to the Bar, Druitt had taken a teaching post in order to pay for his tuition and, faced with no offers of briefs and lacking a private income, he was obliged to continue as a teacher. He was an assistant at a private boys' school in Blackheath run by George Valentine. It was a school with at least one distinguished former pupil, as Benjamin Disraeli had been taught there. In Druitt's time, its forty-two boys, all boarders, were there to be 'crammed' by their three teachers. Druitt occasionally lightened an otherwise dull life by playing cricket for Kingston Park and Dorset County Cricket Club and also for other south of England clubs.

At the end of Michaelmas term (autumn) 1888, Montague John Druitt was dismissed from his teaching post for reasons which are unknown. There was an unsubstantiated suggestion that he was homosexual but the cause was more likely to be found in a growing anxiety that he was going mad. In July his mother had been confined in a private mental home at Chiswick and it later became apparent that he too was psychologically disturbed. Not that this prevented him from playing cricket, for he turned out on numerous occasions during August and September. He was last seen alive on 3 December 1888, and on the last day of the year his body was found floating in the River Thames.

The *County of Middlesex Independent* on 2 January 1889, under the heading 'Found in the River', reported that 'The body of a well-dressed man was discovered on Monday in the river off Thorneycroft's torpedo works, by a waterman named Winslow. The police were communicated with and the deceased was conveyed to the mortuary. The body, which is that of a man about 40 years of age, has been in the water about a month. From certain papers found on the body friends at Bournemouth have been telegraphed to. An inquest will be held today.'

The body, which was beginning to decompose, was fully clothed; the coat pockets contained four large stones. At the inquest held at the Lamb and Tap in Chiswick, PC George Mouson testified that he had searched the body. In addition to the stones, he found £2 10s 0d in gold, 7s in silver and 2s in bronze. There were two cheques drawn on the London and Provincial Bank, one for £50 and the other for £16. The simple explanation regarding the source of these was that they represented his final salary payment from the school at Blackheath. The speculative explanation was that they were payments demanded by a blackmailer. The dead man's other possessions included two rail tickets: a first-class season ticket from Blackheath to London and the second half of a return from Hammersmith to Charing Cross (dated 1 December). In addition there were a silver watch, a gold chain and adornment, a pair of gloves and a white handkerchief.

At the inquest, William Druitt, the dead man's brother who was a solicitor in Bournemouth, said that he had last seen Montague some time at the end of October. He heard from a friend on 11 December that his brother had been missing from his chambers for over a week. On receiving this news, he travelled to London to make enquiries and learned that Montague had been dismissed from his teaching post. When he sorted through his brother's possessions he found a note addressed to him. Its message was sadly unequivocal: 'Since Friday I felt I was going to be like mother and the best thing for me was to die.' The coroner's jury returned a verdict of 'Suicide whilst of unsound mind'.

The *Southern Guardian* in its edition of 5 January 1889 carried the inquest verdict and a short tribute to Druitt under the heading, 'Sad Death of a local Barrister'. 'The deceased gentleman was well known and much respected in this neighbourhood. He was a barrister of bright talent, he had a promising future before him and his untimely end is deeply deplored.' Montague John Druitt was buried at Wimborne Cemetery on 3 January 1889. Many years later the cemetery superintendent told newspaper men, 'There is something odd about the burial. At that time the usual price for a grave was around 8s. Yet this one cost £5 11s and it was most unusual for a suicide to be buried in consecrated ground in those days.'

So much for the short life and tragic end of Montague John Druitt. What was missing, as Don Rumbelow observed, 'is any shred of evidence that Montague John Druitt was Jack the Ripper'. Of speculation and justification there has been no end and the Druittites, as Arthur Douglas described the supporters of the Druitt for Ripper school, have used arguments akin to 'landing on the moon without benefit of rocket propulsion'. Dan Farson admitted that nothing of what was known to this point proved that Druitt was Jack the Ripper for he acknowledged that Sir Melville Macnaghten's notes which referred to Druitt by name lacked corroboration. Nevertheless there was evidence to suggest that among the higher echelons of the police there was a view that the Ripper had become insane and committed suicide.

Following Dan Farson's coverage of the Ripper murders in his television series, *Farson's Guide to the British*, in which he made an appeal for information, he received a great many letters. Anyone who has taken an interest in the Ripper murders knows that the lunatic fringe is only too willing to impart the information that Uncle Henry was the Ripper or that Nazi memorabilia may be readily obtained at a price. Mr Farson had his share of 'junk mail', but the obvious public fascination for the subject caused him to remember that he had received a possibly vital clue *before* he had access to the copy of Macnaghten's notes. A Mr Knowles had written to him from Australia concerning a document entitled 'The East End Murderer – I knew him' written by Lionel Druitt or Drewett and 'printed privately by a Mr Fell of Dandenong in 1890'. The knowledge that Montague John Druitt's cousin was Dr Lionel Druitt who was listed in the *Medical Register* until 1887 when he was reported to have left England for Australia caused a great deal of excitement.

The problem for Dan Farson at this juncture was that he no longer had the letter from Mr Knowles. Together with other material on the Ripper murders it disappeared from his desk in Television House and was never returned. He was philosophical about this and realized that he could not keep to himself the information he had about Druitt – after all, the death certificate with the name blacked out had been shown on television with cause of death given as

'Found dead drowned by his own act whilst of unsound mind'. With this information, it would not have taken a diligent researcher long to find out the name of the deceased. Undaunted, Farson decided to follow up the clue given in Knowles's letter at source: he was, in any event, planning to visit Australia on other business.

From an independent source, an amateur criminologist who had helped him during the preparation of his television programme, Farson learned more about the Australian connection. Maurice Gould had lived in Australia during the period 1925 to 1932 and encountered two persons who claimed to know the identity of Jack the Ripper. The source of this information was papers belonging to W.G. Fell of Dandenong who died in 1935. One of Gould's informants, a freelance journalist, claimed to be acquainted with Fell and knew that the man from Dandenong had provided accommodation for a person called Druitt who had left him papers proving the identity of Jack the Ripper. Apparently, Fell was willing to part with the papers for the then princely sum of £500 which the journalist was not able to find. On the face of it, it looked very much as if Maurice Gould had provided corroboration of the existence of a Mr Fell who, thousands of miles from the locus of Jack the Ripper's activities, had once held in his hands the clue to the killer's identity.

Farson travelled to Australia in 1961 and visited Dandenong, only to suffer disappointment at the lack of any useful information to be gleaned there. At nearby Drovin, he met an elderly lady who remembered Dr Lionel Druitt as a doctor practising in the town in 1903. Dr Druitt had a daughter named Dorothy whose birth in 1899 was later confirmed through family records. It was also possible to confirm that Lionel Druitt practised at Cooma, New South Wales, in 1887, at Koroit, Victoria, in 1897, later at Drovin and that he died in Mentone, Victoria, in 1908. But of the crucial document supposedly written by Dr Druitt, 'The East End Murderer – I knew him', there was no trace. Australian television and newspapers carried news of

Farson's search but if anyone knew anything of value, they were keeping it to themselves.

The news that Montague John Druitt was now the chief suspect as Jack the Ripper had filtered through to many with an interest in the subject. While Dan Farson was pursuing his researches in Australia, others were following their own Druitt leads. In 1965, Tom Cullen published his book, *Autumn of Terror*, in the introduction of which he claimed, 'I shall reveal for the first time the names of three men against whom Scotland Yard held "very strong suspicion". In particular, I shall identify the individual to whom police suspicion finally narrowed.' That individual was, of course, Montague John Druitt and the source, once again, was Sir Melville Macnaghten's notes. It was not immediately clear which version of the notes Tom Cullen had used, but Don Rumbelow eventually confirmed from Cullen himself that he had referred to the typewritten notes belonging to Lady Aberconway. It was later to emerge that there were at least two slightly different renderings of these.

Meanwhile, Cullen made out his thesis for Druitt as the Ripper although he admitted that the suicide left a trail of questions. In tackling the reason which lay behind the 'strong suspicion' of the police that Druitt was the Ripper, he cited a statement made by Albert Backert, a member of the Whitechapel Vigilance Committee. After the Miller's Court murder, Backert apparently went to the police to express his concern at the way their patrols had been reduced. In March 1889, he complained of complacency which had entered police practice simply because there had been no murders during recent months. According to Donald McCormick, Backert agreed to be sworn to secrecy if he was given certain information. He was told that the police were quite sure the Ripper was dead, having been fished out of the Thames two months previously. Whether he believed it or not, Backert was left with the clear impression that a poor view would be taken of his behaviour if he broke his pledge.

Tom Cullen believed the key to the mystery rested in

Macnaghten's notes and the statement in which he referred to 'private information' which led him to conclude that Druitt's family suspected him of being the Whitechapel murderer. He suggested that at some time between 3 December when he was last seen alive and 31 December when his body was found in the Thames, Druitt's family must have reported him missing. 'Did one of the Druitts seize the occasion', he asked, 'to confide to the police the family's private fears concerning Montague John?' He conjectured that this was more than likely and that it was possible the family had decided before 3 December to commit Druitt to an insane asylum and to request assistance from the police for this purpose. There is certainly the evidence of Druitt's suicide note to underline his own fear that he was going mad: his mother died in a Chiswick mental home in December 1890 of 'melancholia' and 'brain disease'.

Establishing the existence of Montague John Druitt proved to be the easiest part of Cullen's equation – fitting the gentleman barrister into the Ripper mould was more difficult. The argument was strong on conjecture and Cullen recognized that the obstacles were formidable. For example, what was a man of Druitt's background and standing doing in the slums of the East End? It was suggested that he embraced the urge that a few Victorians nurtured to visit the slums for a little 'do-gooding'. There were certainly ample precedents, not least in the form of Prime Minister William Gladstone who went on the occasional East End foray to redeem fallen women. There were also true reforming pioneers such as the Reverend Samuel Barnett who established Toynbee Hall in 1885 as a residential settlement from which university undergraduates could perform useful social work. 'It would be natural', suggested Cullen, 'that Druitt should turn to Toynbee Hall not only as a means of recreation, but as an opportunity to do good.'

Having established that his candidate had a reason for being in the East End, Cullen proceeded to make something out of his admittedly weak mental state. 'Might not someone of Druitt's education and refinement whose mind was delicately balanced, at best, have been pushed to the edge of insanity by the sights around him in London's East End?' he asked. Overwhelmed by the grim spectacle of women selling themselves for mere coppers, such a man's sensitivities might have been crushed by a sense of hopelessness and futility, contended Cullen. He might too have considered it his mission to focus attention on these evils by committing murder.

A picture was painted of Montague John Druitt, impelled by a sense of 'the mercy which can be angry as well as pitiful', striking down Whitechapel's lowliest prostitutes until he finally subsided after the Miller's Court bloodbath. The Ripper's elusive character could have been accounted for by Montague John Druitt's association with the school at Blackheath, south of the river. This would help to explain the murderer's 'seemingly miraculous ability to elude the police; it would have been easy for him to slip in and out of Whitechapel by means of the underground railway via Cannon Street station'. Cullen himself helped to refute this as a means of escape from the scenes of the murders by reference to *Bradshaw's Guide* for 1888. All the Ripper murders occurred between the hours of 12.35 and 4 a.m., after the last train had left Cannon Street for Blackheath. But, it was suggested, with his chambers at 9 King's Bench Walk, the murderous barrister would have had no need to catch a train – he would only need to take a short walk to safety through near deserted streets to the cloistered haven of the Inner Temple.

Having confronted the problems posed by Druitt's presence in and escape from the East End, Tom Cullen turned to the vexed question of the murderer's surgical skill. He acknowledged the variety of professional opinions on this subject and quoted Donald McCormick's mentor, Dr Thomas Dutton: 'Speed was the substitute for skill . . . And, without doubt, the Ripper was a fast operator, much faster than the average British surgeon could possibly have been.' Erring on the side of accepting the possibility that

214

the Ripper possessed some anatomical skill, he leaned for support on the strong medical background of the Druitt family. Druitt's father, grandfather, uncle and cousin were all doctors: 'It is more than possible, indeed it is probable, that Druitt, as an interested spectator, sat in a surgical amphitheatre and watched his father practise his art. He would thus have gained some knowledge of surgery even though that knowledge was rudimentary.'

When Tom Cullen's book identifying Montague John Druitt as the Ripper was published, a *Sunday Express* reporter interviewed one of the family, Dr Robert Druitt, in Christchurch, Dorset. 'This will make my patients sit up,' said the doctor who goodnaturedly received the news of the allegedly black character of one of his relatives. The doctor, who declared, 'I'm not like Jack the Ripper – my form of surgery is much less ambitious,' acknowledged Montague John as a distant cousin. 'It is much better to have someone like Jack the Ripper as an ancestor than a dull old parson,' he told the newspaper reporter, and went on to deny that there was any actual history of mental illness in the family, although he added, 'Let's face it, there were some eccentrics.'

The book reviewers treated Cullen's thesis cautiously and generally regarded it as intriguing. 'Was Jack the Ripper a Gentleman?' asked the *Daily Mail*; 'So *that's* who Jack the Ripper was', ran the *Daily Express*, adding, 'Or was it?' The general feeling was that the solution offered was not too convincing: 'We are indeed no nearer the identification of the Ripper', concluded *The Daily Telegraph*. The fraternity of Ripperologists naturally probed more deeply, defending their own theses as much as attacking Cullen's. Donald McCormick, referring to the Druitt theory in the revised edition of his *The Identity of Jack the Ripper*, published in 1970, believed that Cullen 'offers no evidence at all, only surmise' and particularly faulted him for not giving any evidence as to the state of Druitt's mind or any mention at all that the suspect had been seen in the vicinity of the crimes. Indeed, McCormick contended that on two occasions, at the material times, Druitt was not even in London, but residing in Bournemouth. His authority for this is an unnamed London doctor who knew Walter Sickert the painter and was aware of his interest in the Ripper murders. The doctor, whose father was at Oxford with Montague John Druitt, related the story that at the time Mary Ann Nichols and Annie Chapman were murdered, Druitt was living in Bournemouth. This information was elaborated, suggesting that Druitt was being blackmailed by an unnamed person who threatened to denounce him as Jack the Ripper to the Blackheath school where he worked. This accounted for the money found on Druitt's body which was intended to pay off the blackmailer.

According to McCormick, the Oxford doctor was quite convinced that Druitt was not the Ripper and was equally certain that the unfortunate barrister told his mother of his plight and that she in turn informed the police when she reported her son missing in December 1888. Walter Sickert, who appears elsewhere in the Ripper saga, is supposed to have told his London doctor friend that this tied in with another piece of independent information. When Sickert took rooms, some years after the Whitechapel murders, at a house in Mornington Crescent, his landlady asked him one day if he knew who had occupied his room before him. When he said he had no idea, she replied simply, 'Jack the Ripper'. This episode, which was recounted by Osbert Sitwell in his book *Free House: Being the Writings of Walter Richard Sickert*, concerned a young veterinary student whose comings and goings were observed by his landlady. He occasionally stayed out all night, returning at about 6 a.m. when he paced his room before leaving the house to buy an early morning newspaper. He then retired to bed and his astute landlord noticed when he called his lodger that he had burned the clothes he had worn the previous night in the fireplace.

The young man was consumptive and his health worsened to the point where it was necessary for his mother to come up from Bournemouth to take him away. The murders stopped from that moment and the young man died three months later. Walter Sickert mentioned that the man's name was something like Drewett or Hewitt and that he told the story to Sir Melville Macnaghten one day when they met at the Garrick Club. Sir Melville, allegedly, was convinced that the man in question was Druitt because he knew that he had relatives living in Bournemouth. It is at least imaginable that someone with an artist's intellect does not habitually use deductive reasoning but for a senior police officer to forgo the fundamentals of investigative enquiry is unbelievable. As Richard Whittington-Egan remarked of Tom Cullen's exposition of the Druitt thesis, 'It won't do. It simply won't do.'

The uncorroborated and undocumented suggestion from an unnamed source that Druitt was located in Bournemouth at the times when two of the murders occurred in the East End of London was sufficient for Donald McCormick to close the file on the hapless barrister. With an air of finality, he wrote, 'This seems finally to dispose of the case that Druitt had any connection with the crimes.' This was not a view shared by Dan Farson, for in 1972, seven years after Montague John Druitt was declared a candidate for Jack the Ripper's identity, he published his book entitled simply *Jack the Ripper* in which he developed the thesis further. Professor Francis Camps who contributed the foreword wrote, 'I feel that we are getting very near the truth.' With his Australian researches behind him, and despite the disappointment of not being able to track down the document, 'The East End Murderer – I knew him', Farson felt that he had strengthened the link with its author Dr Lionel Druitt.

Considering the basis on which Dr Druitt might have accused his cousin Montague of being the Ripper, Farson believed he had found a crucial piece of evidence. He discovered from the *Medical Register* that Dr Druitt had a surgery at 140 the Minories in 1879 and declared that this provided the first link between Druitt and the East End, the lack of which had hitherto been a stumbling block. Montague was poised to leave Oxford about this time and, wrote

Farson, 'There is every reason to believe that Montague and Lionel knew each other.' He argued that the other man might well have considered it his responsibility to look after his younger cousin and thought it reasonable to assume that Montague visited the surgery. It was even possible that he lived there after the doctor had left and thereby certainly acquired a knowledge of the area.

Apart from its position relative to the East End, the Minories had significance on account of one of the Ripper letters posted from Liverpool on 29 September 1888. In this epistle, signed 'Jack the Ripper', the writer declared, 'Beware, I shall be at work on the 1st and 2nd Inst in Minories at twelve midnight, and I give the authorities a good chance, but there is never a policeman near when I am at work.' In what Donald Rumbelow described as 'a chance in a million, *while it was still in the post*, Eddowes was murdered at about 1.30 a.m. on 30 September'. Mitre Square was only a minute's walk from the Minories and a second taunting letter sent from Liverpool after the murder read, 'What fools the police are. I even give them the name of the street where I am living.'

Farson believed that 'Montague Druitt kept in touch with the Minories and possibly rented a room there himself'. Don Rumbelow is not in accord with this conclusion for he pointed out that while Dr Lionel Druitt was listed as practising at the Minories in the 1879 edition of the *Medical Register*, the *Medical Directory* for the same year does not list him at all although he is referenced in the 1878 and 1880 editions. According to the 1879 edition, the doctors practising at 140 the Minories were J.O. Taylor and T. Thyne, and in 1880 only Dr Thyne is listed. Both the *Medical Register* and the *Medical Directory* for 1880 published Dr Lionel Druitt's address as 8 Strathmore Gardens, as in the 1878 editions. It would appear that Dr Druitt's period of residence at the Minories was brief and the temptation to build too much on it should be avoided. Rumbelow's suggestion is that Dr Druitt worked briefly as Dr Taylor's *locum tenens* in 1879.

In considering Druitt's state of mind, Farson brought out three points for which he acknowledged the help of David Anderson, an amateur criminologist. The background is one in which Druitt's life was clearly in decline after he left Oxford. His failure to secure the legal work for which he had trained and being forced to take up teaching in the unrewarding climate of a 'cramming' school was demoralizing. Then there was his mother's lapse into insanity which Farson claimed occurred in July, shortly before the Ripper murders began, and his own fear of going the same way. Montague Druitt's dismissal from the school at Blackheath for reasons which can only be speculated about must have been a severe blow.

Farson wrote, '. . . at the very point where the evidence might seem weakest, I can see its strength'. He was referring to Montague's brother William who testified at the coroner's inquest and who 'must have suspected Montague because he had proof'. It was argued that William had nothing to gain and was not searching for notoriety when he drew the attention of the police to his suspicions. Moreover, the police would not have accepted his statement without proof. After all, the authorities suffered a deluge of accusations and confessions from all quarters so that a suicide in the Thames would mean little unless they knew there was more to it. Indeed, Druitt, with his particular background, would have been the last person to be suspected. As Farson put it, 'the very "innocence" of such a man suggests he must have been guilty to be suspected in the first place'. So, the thesis is that William Druitt sowed the seed in official quarters that his brother Montague was as Sir Melville Macnaghten phrased it, 'sexually insane'.

In support of the contention that the official search for Jack the Ripper ended with the discovery of Druitt's body in the Thames, Farson quoted a number of opinions, some of them highly placed. Major Arthur Griffiths in his *Mysteries of Police and Crime* wrote of the suspect that his friends 'entertained grave doubts about him' and he perpetuated the idea that he was 'a doctor in the prime of life', an erroneous remark for which Sir Melville Macnaghten has been widely criticized. Griffiths also said the man was insane and disappeared after the last murder, being found dead in the River Thames about a month later. Sir Charles Warren's grandson, Watkin Williams, believed his grandfather's view was that the murderer was 'a sex maniac who committed suicide after the Miller's Court murder – possibly the young doctor whose body was found in the Thames on 31 December 1888'. Sir John Moylan, Assistant Undersecretary at the Home Office, and Sir Basil Thomson, Assistant Commissioner of the CID both record their belief that the culprit committed suicide at the end of 1888. Added to these views was that of Albert Backert and his claim that Scotland Yard had sworn him to secrecy in the knowledge that the Ripper was dead.

In resting his case, Dan Farson wrote, 'I gather that the official files in Scotland Yard, which are not open to the public until 1992, confirm my conclusions and have little else to add.' Unfortunately, the emergence of an authentic signed copy of Sir Melville Macnaghten's famous notes weakened rather than strengthened the Druitt theory. Part of the undoubtedly authentic version of these notes was published for the first time in 1966 by Robin Odell in a revised edition of his *Jack the Ripper in Fact and Fiction* and they were subsequently published for the first time in full in Don Rumbelow's *The Complete Jack the Ripper* (1975). What was immediately apparent was the differences in wording and interpretation between this version of the notes and those used by Tom Cullen and Dan Farson. Both authors had access to Lady Aberconway's typewritten copies but the eventual references in their respective books differ in some details. The differences in wording and the nuances of interpretation may at first seem trivial but they become important in light of the emphasis placed on them.

Consider first Sir Melville's preamble to naming his three suspects, which, according to Tom Cullen, ran as follows:

A much more rational and workable theory, to my way of thinking, is that the Ripper's brain gave way altogether after his awful glut in Miller's Court, and that he then committed suicide, or, as a less likely alternative, was found to be hopelessly insane by his relatives, that they, suspecting the worst, had him confined in a lunatic asylum . . . I enumerate the case of three men against whom the police held very reasonable suspicion. Personally, and after much careful and deliberate consideration, I am inclined to exonerate the last two, *but I have always held strong opinions regarding No. 1 and the more I think the matter over, the stronger do these opinions become.* The truth, however, will never be known, and did, indeed, at one time lie at the bottom of the Thames, if my conjectures be correct. (No. 1 is M.J. Druitt and the italics are Cullen's.)

According to Dan Farson, the preamble ran slightly differently:

No one ever saw the Whitechapel murderer (unless possibly it was the City PC who was on a beat near Mitre Square) and no proof could in any way ever be brought against anyone, although very many homicidal maniacs were at one time or another suspected. I enumerate the cases of three men against whom the police held very reasonable suspicion. Personally, and after much careful and deliberate consideration, I am inclined to exonerate two of them.

Sir Melville's signed notes, written clearly in his own hand and without emphasis, read as follows:

A much more rational theory is that the murderer's brain gave way altogether after his awful glut in Miller's Court, and that he immediately committed suicide, or as a possible alternative, was found to be so hopelessly mad by his relations, that he was by them confined in some asylum.

No one ever saw the Whitechapel Murderer, many homicidal maniacs were suspected, but no shadow of proof could be thrown on anyone. I may mention the cases of three men, any one of whom would have been more likely than Cutbush to have committed this series of murders.

It is quite clear that Macnaghten referred to the suicide idea as a 'theory' rather than a fact and went on to suggest a 'possible alternative'. The certainty which others have construed from his notes is simply not evident. Nor did he single out Druitt for greater suspicion than the other two names mentioned – he was at pains, as he quite clearly recorded, to absolve Cutbush from the allegations made against him.

Then there are the three names, and particularly the entry for Druitt. Both Cullen and Farson use substantially the same text in this instance:

No. 1 Mr M.J. Druitt, a doctor of about 41 years of age and of fairly good family, who disappeared at the time of the Miller's Court murder, and whose body was found floating in the Thames on 3rd December, i.e. seven weeks after the said murder. The body was said to have been in the water for a month, or more – on it was found a season ticket between Blackheath and London. From private information I have little doubt but that his own family suspected this man of being the Whitechapel murderer; and it was alleged that he was sexually insane.

Interestingly, Farson omitted the use of the opening designation, 'No. 1', and in any case listed Druitt after the other suspects. Cullen's order of precedence is the same as Macnaghten's, but the former CID chief's text ran as follows:

(1) A Mr M.J. Druitt, said to be a doctor and of good family who disappeared at the time of the Miller's

Court murder, and whose body (which was said to have been upwards of a month in the water) was found in the Thames on 31st Dec. – or about 7 weeks after that murder. He was sexually insane and from private info I have little doubt that his own family believed him to have been the murderer.

Macnaghten had already indicated in his preamble that he cast no special suspicion on any of the three names and, in what he wrote about M.J. Druitt, made it clear that it was the dead man's family, rather than the police, who believed him to be the murderer. Interestingly, in their versions of the statement on Druitt, both Cullen and Farson gave the date of discovery of the body as 3 December when it should have been 31 December, as correctly given by Macnaghten himself. Of course, Sir Melville has been taken to task for incorrectly describing Druitt as a doctor which Donald McCormick ascribed to a failure of memory, bearing in mind that the former CID chief boasted that he 'never kept a diary, or even possessed a notebook'.

The only sensible conclusion to be drawn from all this, especially in view of the pivotal importance of Sir Melville's notes, is to regard his signed and dated version which resides in Scotland Yard's files as the definitive version. By that standard, other accounts of what he wrote are in default and their use to support the Druitt theory is, in large measure, miscalculated. Careful reading of the authentic notes (included in full in the Appendices) makes the writer's intentions perfectly clear and, if the Queen's English means anything, it cannot be construed that Sir Melville was out to condemn Montague John Druitt as Jack the Ripper.

Commenting on the publication of Dan Farson's book, Philip Loftus, in an article published in the *Guardian* on 7 October 1972, added his own contribution to the Druitt story. He recalled an occasion in 1950 when he was staying with an old school friend, Gerald Melville Donner, Sir Melville Macnaghten's grandson, and saw what he took to be a copy of the famous Jack the Ripper letter written in red ink framed as a picture on the wall. Donner claimed that it was the original and when the two men went on to discuss the murders, Loftus was shown some of Sir Melville's handwritten notes, 'on official paper, rather untidy and in the nature of rough jottings'. As he remembered them, three suspects were noted: 'a Polish tanner or cobbler; a man who went round stabbing young girls in the bottom with nail scissors; and M.J. Druitt, a doctor of 41 years of age'.

Gerald Donner died in 1968 and no one knows what became of these particular papers. From Loftus's description of them it is virtually certain that they were not the same notes which are in the Scotland Yard files. The authentic version is a succinct text, carefully and tidily written with neither hestitation nor blemish. So neat are they that Don Rumbelow presumed them to have been written up from a rough draft or jottings – perhaps from the jottings in the possession of his grandson.

In the wake of his book, which was serialized in the London *Evening News*, Dan Farson received a considerable number of letters. Some of these were included as a postscript in a revised edition published in 1973. One of them was from a Mr Edhouse of Kentish Town who had made an interesting discovery. Reading the death certificate of Druitt's mother he noticed the entry, 'Emily Knowles present at death, Manor House, Chiswick'. Knowles, of course, was the name of the person who had written to Farson telling him about the paper 'The East End Murderer – I knew him', supposedly written by Dr Lionel Druitt. If Emily Knowles had looked after Mrs Anne Druitt and was privy to information about Montague John, she might have passed this on to another member of the family who, in due course, communicated with Lionel in Australia. Interestingly, Edward Druitt, Montague's younger brother who became an army officer, went to Australia in 1889 to join the Queensland Defence Forces. Farson's correspondent managed to track down a man called Arthur Knowles who died in Hackney in 1959. That was the year in which Farson received the famous letter that went missing. Somewhat exaggeratingly, he wrote, 'The combination of these facts make it more evident than ever that such a document as "The East End Murderer" really did exist.'

The January 1973 issue of *The Cricketer* contained an article by Irving Rosenwater entitled, 'Jack the Ripper – Sort of a Cricket Person?' which reviewed Montague John Druitt's sporting career. During 1882 and 1883 when he played for the Incogniti, he proved himself no mean bowler, taking eleven wickets in a match at Dorchester, and five wickets in each innings in a game at Plymouth. It appeared that Druitt turned out as usual in 1888 for Blackheath for whom he was the principal bowler and was highly regarded as a 'keen and enthusiastic cricketer'. Despite his personal problems, he had a busy season. During the critical months of that year, July, August and September, his known cricket engagements have been reconstructed as follows.

Date	Match	Venue
21 July	Blackheath v. Beckenham	Blackheath
3 and 4 Aug	Gentlemen of Bournemouth v. Parsees Touring Side	Bournemouth
10 and 11 Aug	Gentlemen of Dorset	Bournemouth
1 Sept	Canford v. Wimborne	Canford, Dorset
8 Sept	Blackheath v. Brothers Christopherson	Blackheath

The last two matches are the most relevant in terms of Druitt combining his passion for cricket with other possibly more violent urges. Mary Ann Nichols was murdered on 31

August, the day before Druitt's match at Canford, Dorset, and Annie Chapman was murdered on 8 September, the very day that he played at Blackheath. Irving Rosenwater pointed out in his article that Chapman's body was found at 5.55 a.m. with the evidence suggesting the murder took place at about 5.30 a.m. Later that morning, at 11.30, Druitt, clad in his cricketing whites, took the field at Blackheath. Rosenwater, an advocate of Druitt as the Ripper, wrote, 'It was an easy task to make the comparatively short journey from Spitalfields to Blackheath.' Hence, Druitt was available both to play cricket and to commit murder and the conclusion is reached that '. . . on the evidence now disclosed, it will require a courageous and learned man to say that the Whitechapel murderer was not Montague John Druitt, cricketer'.

This is a bold assertion based on a narrow piece of argument. Paving the way for Druitt to be in separate places at different times engaged in markedly different pursuits does not make out a case for him being Jack the Ripper. Indeed, using Mr Rosenwater's terminology, it would be a courageous person who said it did. The evidence in favour of 'Montague of the Minories', as Arthur Douglas dubbed Druitt, is slender indeed. The proper use of Sir Melville Macnaghten's notes weakens the argument. 'Far from implicating Druitt,' wrote Douglas in his assessment of the theory, the notes indicate 'the absolute absence of evidence against Druitt. . .'

Another gentleman and barrister whom tragedy overtook at an early age was identified as Jack the Ripper in 1972. In *Clarence: The Life of the Duke of Clarence and Avondale KG 1864–1892*, Michael Harrison nominated James Kenneth Stephen, the duke's friend and tutor, as the infamous murderer. This followed suggestions made over the years that the Ripper was a member of the royal family and which came to a climax in November 1970 with the publication of an article by Dr T.E.A. Stowell in *The Criminologist*. Although the author, on that occasion, studiously avoided naming his suspect (he gave him the designation 'S'), the public widely interpreted the story as referring to the Duke of Clarence. Stowell's article and its aftermath are discussed in Chapter 6, 'Royal Jack'.

Michael Harrison was at pains to defend the duke from the charges made against him and to point the finger of suspicion at J.K. Stephen. The duke's exoneration lay in the Court Circular which Harrison explained provided an alibi for one of the murders and, hence, for the whole series. Unfortunately, he chose an example that most students of the Whitechapel murders do not consider to have been a Ripper victim. Alice McKenzie was murdered on the night of 16 July 1889 in Castle Alley, Whitechapel, when the Duke of Clarence was engaged on royal duties in connection with a visit to England by the Shah of Persia. This particular victim was important to Harrison for reasons which emerged later.

J.K. Stephen was the son of Sir James Fitzjames Stephen, the judge who tried Florence Maybrick for murder in 1889 and was heavily criticized for his conduct of the proceedings. He resigned from the bench in 1891 because of mental illness and died three years later. His uncle was Sir Leslie Stephen, editor of the *Dictionary of National Biography* and father of Virginia Woolf. J.K. Stephen was a handsome man and was acknowledged to be among 'the ablest of the younger generation'. A scholar at Eton and Cambridge with a keen intellect and privileged background, he came to the notice of the Prince and Princess of Wales when they were looking for a tutor to prepare their son Edward, the Duke of Clarence, to enter Cambridge University.

Stephen was appointed tutor in the spring of 1883. He became a controlling influence in Clarence's life, determining who should or should not join his circle of student associates, even down to deciding his partners for whist. It was a closed circle of friends and intimates and it has been suggested that the relationship which developed between Stephen and Clarence was a homosexual one, at least on the intellectual plane. It was feelings of jealousy arising out of the severance of this close tie which allegedly drove Stephen to violence.

After a brilliant career at Cambridge, Stephen was called to the Bar in 1884, but, like Montague John Druitt, he never took a brief. When Clarence completed his university studies, he went off to pursue a military career and attend to his royal duties. The close-knit student group broke up and the maturing young men went their separate ways. In 1886, Stephen sustained an accidental blow to the head while out riding in Suffolk. His horse shied and backed its rider into the path of a windmill. He was knocked unconscious but after he was examined in London by Sir William Gull he apparently made a perfect recovery. Sir Leslie Stephen, his uncle, remarked later this accidental blow 'inflicted injuries not perceived at the time'. There were those who believed that this injury was the seat of his subsequent insanity or, as Michael Harrison put it, his 'homicidal mania'.

Again, in parallel with Montague John Druitt, Stephen kept chambers but, despite his academic brilliance and his illustrious background, he received no legal work. He lived with his parents in De Vere Gardens, Kensington, and after his accident lapsed into a generally lethargic state which was lightened by occasional bursts of activity when he took up his pen in pursuit of literature. He told his father at about this time that he wished 'to dedicate himself entirely to literature'. Sir James Fitzjames Stephen, who was not well himself although still in office, appointed his son to a vacant clerkship on the South Wales Assize Circuit towards the end of 1888. He never effectively took up the appointment, for he was overtaken by ill health and resigned the position in 1890.

Sadly, the men of the Stephen family sank into the pit of mental breakdown. Sir James's conduct of the Maybrick case was regarded as incompetent and he was heavily criticized for misdirecting the jury and giving a biased summing-up. Sir Leslie Stephen collapsed in 1889; according to Harrison this occurred when he was told that his nephew was Jack the Ripper. Shortly after this he gave up his editorship of the *Dictionary of National Biography*. In October 1890, J.K. Stephen was committed to an asylum or, as it was tactfully put at the time, he decided 'to settle in Cambridge'. He was receiving treatment from Sir William Gull, the acknowledged authority of the day on diseases of the brain and spinal cord. When not under constraint and when his condition allowed, Stephen wrote poetry and in 1891 published two small volumes of verse, *Lapsus Calami* and *Quo Musa Tendis*. Later that year he deteriorated suddenly and was admitted to St Andrew's Hospital, Northampton, where he died on 3 February 1892.

Michael Harrison became convinced that Dr Stowell's Ripper, whom the doctor designated by the letter 'S', was not the Duke of Clarence, as commonly supposed, but was J.K. Stephen. He contended that, having demonstrated Clarence's innocence of the charge, the only person who fitted the requirements of 'S' was Stephen. It had to be someone close to the duke, a contemporary and an intimate whose identification would create a scandal. Unable to pursue Dr Stowell's tantalizing revelations because the doctor's papers were burned after he died, Harrison looked for other evidence to support his theory. 'His explanations are elaborate, ingenious and often amusing,' wrote Don Rumbelow, 'but they cannot be taken too seriously.'

Michael Harrison suggested there was a link both of style and of sentiment between Jack the Ripper's letters and Stephen's verse. For example, the Ripper's 'Up and *down* this goddam *town*' was compared with Stephen's 'will not *effect* the least *neglect*' and secret allusions in the latter's verse were taken to be meaningful in relation to the murders. There is no doubt that both scribes harboured a hatred of women; the sentiment was clearly expressed by thc Ripper in the line, 'I am down on whores' in the 'Dear Boss' letter dated 25 September 1888. Stephen, in a verse entitled 'A Thought' published in February 1891, wrote:

> If all the harm that women have done
> Were put in a bundle and rolled into one,
> Earth would not hold it,
> The Sky would not enfold it
> It could not be lighted nor warmed by the sun . . .

Harrison swooped on Stephen's 'thought', exclaiming that it was written in the very month in which Frances Coles was 'offered up as the "final sacrifice"'.

Frances Coles, like Alice McKenzie, was another luckless victim of an unidentified murderer but few commentators have attributed her death to the Ripper. Her inclusion in the story is nevertheless central to Harrison's thesis, for he argued that Stephen's association with the bawdy ballad, *Kaphoozelum*, provided a rationale for the murders. The twenty-four stanzas of this work called up the 'ten harlots of Jerusalem' who meet their poetic doom in the lines:

> For though he paid his women well,
> This syphilitic spawn of hell,
> Struck down each year and tolled the bell
> For ten harlots of Jerusalem

Kaphoozelum was quoted in Stephen's book of verse, *Lapsus Calami*, and it is suggested that when his mind turned to revenge against his friend Clarence he conceived the idea of creating a massive scandal by murdering ten prostitutes.

Faced with the difficulty that one of the Ripper letters referred only to 'eight little whores', Michael Harrison made some adjustments to the arithmetic of the Ripper's tally of victims. To the five universally recognized victims he added two (Emma Smith and Martha Turner) who had been occasionally considered and then mostly rejected, two (Alice McKenzie and Frances Cole) generally regarded as copy murders, and two (Annie Farmer and a woman called Mallet) who have never previously been thought of as Ripper murders. By counting Stride and Eddowes as one, the magic figure of ten is reached and Harrison went on to suggest that in order to maximize the embarrassment he was causing, Stephen chose to commit his murders on important anniversaries.

	Victim	Date of murder	Anniversary
1	Smith	3 April 1888	Feast of Cybele, the Earth Mother
2	Turner	6 August 1888	Birthday of the Duke of Edinburgh (Clarence's uncle)
3	Nichols	31 August 1889	Birthday of Princess Wilhelmina of the Netherlands
4	Chapman	8 September 1888	—
* 5	Stride Eddowes	30 September 1888	—
6	Kelly	9 November 1888	Birthday of Prince of Wales
** 7	Farmer	21 November 1888	Birthday of the Empress Frederick
8	Mallet	28 December 1888	The Feast of the Holy Innocents
9	McKenzie	16 July 1889	Anniversary of Clarence's nomination as a Freeman of London
10	Coles	13 February 1891	The Ides of February

* 'obviously counted as one' noted Harrison!
** Don Rumbelow pointed out that according to *The Times*, 22 November 1888, Amelia Farmer was not murdered at all but was 'slightly injured and was at once able to furnish the detectives with a full description of her assailant'.

If Stephen was bent on creating the maximum sensation, he missed an obvious trick by not scheduling one of his victims to be despatched on 24 May – Queen Victoria's birthday. Harrison attached particular significance to the symbolism of the last victim who, according to his reckoning, was Frances Coles. She met her death on 13 February, the Ides of February and the Roman Feast of Terminalia celebrated in honour of the god Terminus, patron of limits, boundaries, treaties and of endings. It was also the Roman custom to make a blood sacrifice on this anniversary.

The Duke of Clarence was not directly involved in the Ripper murders, maintained Harrison, 'although his reputation would have suffered if it had been disclosed that the murderer was none other than his former tutor, J.K. Stephen. For this reason, careful steps were taken to ensure that the truth never leaked out.' In concluding his thesis, he showed that nine of the ten harlots were murdered during term time when Stephen should have been attending his duties at Cambridge and living in at his college. Nevertheless, it would have been easy for him to travel by train down to London where he had the choice of two bases – his parents' house in De Vere Gardens or his chambers at 3 Stone Buildings, Lincoln's Inn.

The year following publication of his book on the Duke of Clarence in which he named J.K. Stephen as the Ripper, Michael Harrison published *The World of Sherlock Holmes* which included some additional information. He had discovered that Professor Quentin Bell, in his biography of Virginia Woolf, the daughter of Sir Leslie Stephen who committed suicide, states that J.K. Stephen was in the habit of arming himself with a sword stick when walking the streets of London or Cambridge. An incident was recalled when Stephen burst into his cousin's house at Hyde Park Gate and thrust his sword into a loaf of bread. Drawing as heavily on symbolism as on credulity, Harrison suggested that the shape of the cottage loaf represented the female figure and that by plunging his sword into the symbolic female breast Stephen demonstrated his desire to kill females which he had openly expressed in his poetry.

'And that is not all,' commented Richard Whittington-

Egan in his account of this bizarre information in *A Casebook on Jack the Ripper*. In addition to being a misogynist, Stephen was also a homosexual, which provided a further explanation of his sword play. In the arcane world of the homosexual in the 1880s, a 'cottage' was a public urinal and a 'cottage loaf', a male prostitute. The attack on the loaf may consequently be interpreted with another layer of symbolism. Whittington-Egan concluded that 'male prostitutes of the East End in the old Queen's reign had a lucky escape'.

Don Rumbelow criticized Harrison's theory and 'elaborate conjecturing' insofar as he failed to make a detailed comparison of Stephen and Dr Stowell's suspect, 'S', to determine whether or not they were the same person. When this comparison is made it can readily be shown that they are not one and the same. 'S' went on a round-the-world cruise at the age of sixteen and held a commission in the army; Stephen had neither of these experiences.

At least two of Harrison's strolling players – Clarence and Sir William Gull – featured prominently in Stephen Knight's theory, expounded in his book, *Jack the Ripper: The Final Solution* (1976), which is considered in Chapter 6, 'Royal Jack'. Knight believed from his researches at Scotland Yard that only one of the many letters purportedly penned by Jack the Ripper had any credence. On this basis alone he dismissed that part of Harrison's argument which compared the styles of the Ripper and J.K. Stephen. He also felt that misogyny was weak as a motive, for the Scotland Yard suspects file was full of lunatics, sexual lunatics and women haters who 'were almost two a penny'. Joseph Sickert, son of Walter Sickert, the painter who featured in Stephen Knight's own elaborate theorizing, contributed an Afterword to his book. He suggested that the families of many named Ripper suspects, the Druitts and Stephens included, 'owe a debt of gratitude to Stephen Knight' for removing the stain of suspicion. The last word might be left with Arthur Douglas who observed, 'Clearly James Kenneth Stephen did not much like the ladies, but whether he loathed them – and himself – so much that he degenerated into an albeit uncommon murderer is extremely doubtful.'

Another candidate for Gentleman Jack was proposed by Thomas Toughill of Glasgow and aired briefly in Colin Wilson's introduction to *The Complete Jack the Ripper* by Don Rumbelow. His nomination was Frank Miles, a homosexual artist and friend of Oscar Wilde. At the beginning of the 1880s Wilde had rooms in a house at Salisbury Street, a turning off the Strand which ran down towards the river. The accommodation above Wilde's was occupied by Frank Miles, an Oxford acquaintance who had begun to establish himself as an artist. His speciality was pencil drawings of beautiful women which sold well in stationery shops of the day.

According to Hesketh Pearson, Wilde's biographer, Miles's great 'find' was Lillie Langtry, whom he sketched many times and helped to promote as the most talked-of beauty in London. Miles was credited with saying, 'I with my pencil, Oscar with his pen, will make her the Jaconde and the Laura of this century.' Miles took part in the weekly gatherings of celebrities which Wilde held in his rooms and Lillie Langtry was a regular visitor. When hard times came along early in 1881, Wilde was forced to leave his luxurious accommodation for the more modest surroundings provided by Keats House at 3 Tite Street, Chelsea. Frank Miles moved with him and they shared rooms.

A certain amount of mystery surrounds Miles but apparently he had a predilection for exposing himself to small girls, which eventually landed him in trouble. He was a popular figure at Wilde's parties which continued at Tite Street with celebrities such as the Prince of Wales often in attendance. The tea parties given by Wilde and Miles were highly regarded and a young girl named Sally whom Miles had discovered selling flowers outside Victoria Station was installed to preside over the tea cups. Miles also used her as a model, as did other artists of the time.

There was an occasion at Tite Street when the police

called enquiring after Miles, and Wilde entertained them at the door in conversation while his friend escaped over the roof to an adjoining house. When the officers eventually gained entry, they threatened to arrest Wilde for obstructing them in the course of their duty. Meanwhile, the bird had flown and Wilde apologized, explaining that he thought their arrival was a joke on the part of some of his friends. He charmed away their anger and the police left empty-handed.

Shortly after this incident, Wilde and Miles ended their close friendship following a quarrel. Miles began to lose his popularity as an artist and also suffered a mental decline. He entered Brislington Asylum near Bristol and there were conflicting reports of his death; he was said to have died insane but other accounts recorded his death by suicide. *Magazine of Art* announced his death in March 1888, which appeared to be premature, for Thomas Toughill established that he died of general paralysis of the insane on 15 July 1891.

This seemed to clear away a major obstacle by proving that Miles was at least alive during the period of the Ripper murders. Richard Whittington-Egan though, in his *A Casebook on Jack the Ripper*, noted that Miles spent the last four years of his life in the asylum near Bristol; this would have clearly ruled him out as a Ripper candidate. Nevertheless, Thomas Toughill believed that Oscar Wilde thought Miles was Jack the Ripper and dropped several hints to that effect in his novel, *The Picture of Dorian Gray*, which was published in *Lippincott's Monthly Magazine* the year before Miles died. Miles was well known for picking up young women from the street whom he used as models for his sketching but, unless he was searching for local character, the type of women who fell to the Ripper's knife were not cast in the mould of artists' models. Toughill, who proposes to publish a full account of his researches, discovered some interesting, if inconsequential, links between Frank Miles and other personalities who have loomed on the Ripper horizon. Sir Melville Macnaghten, for example, was at one time a neighbour of Wilde's at Tite Street and Miles's cousin was an equerry to the Duke of Clarence; Miles himself served in the same regiment as Montague John Druitt's brother Edward.

Fact and fiction are so difficult to disentangle in the Ripper epic that it came as no surprise when, in December 1965, the BBC Home Service perpetrated the ultimate sacrilege in the field of accusation by naming Sherlock Holmes as Jack the Ripper! In 'The Case of the Unmentioned Case', L.W. Bailey suggested that the gentleman detective was the evil miscreant who had escaped the ends of justice all these years. He pointed out the curious circumstances that with Holmes at the height of his powers during the Autumn of Terror in 1888, with the entire police force at its wits end, the Home Office not knowing which way to turn and Queen Victoria complaining about the efficiency of some of her loyal servants, the world's greatest detective was not called in. 'Surely,' he said, it is, 'impossible to conceive that Holmes would not have been consulted in the case of Jack the Ripper unless there was some compelling reason why he could not be . . .'

Certainly in the case of Annie Chapman who was murdered on 8 September 1888, several witnesses claimed to have seen a man in her company wearing a deerstalker's hat. It cannot be doubted that Holmes regularly wore such headgear but, as L.W. Bailey pointed out, 'to have seen a man in a deerstalker's hat in the vicinity of the crime proves nothing. It is merely a straw in the wind that can set our minds working in a certain direction.' If, for the sake of argument, the idea can be entertained that Holmes was in the Whitechapel area in the early hours of the morning, the question must be asked what was he doing there if he was not actually involved in the investigation of the crimes?

The evidence showed that Jack the Ripper was probably the most cunning criminal ever to have foxed the police. He had an intimate knowledge of the geography of the East End and was able to elude even the most intensive police searches. Moreover, he used disguises and may even on one occasion have passed himself off as a woman. To complete the picture, the nature of his crimes showed that he had a knowledge of anatomy and his choice of victims was based on a dislike of the female sex and an 'ascetic distaste for sexual relationships carried to the extreme of madness'.

How then did Sherlock Holmes compare with this master criminal? To start with, Holmes was a man of genius with an ice-cold brain who lived at such a peak of tension that he needed drugs to help him relax. Despite the fact that they provided him with a great deal of his work, he regarded the police with contempt. Certainly he was familiar with the environs of London's East End and was an undisputed master of disguise. On the question of 'knowledge of anatomy', Dr Watson noted that he was 'accurate but unsystematic'. Holmes, of course, was a complete ascetic and there is no record of his ever having any kind of sexual relationships. His attitude to women was not overtly one of dislike but he tended to dismiss the idea of passion with a sneer.

It is possible that his immense intellectual labours and the physical exertion required by long and detailed criminal investigations built up stresses that he sometimes found unbearable. He was known to suffer dark moods from which he sought refuge in tobacco smoking, violin playing and drug taking. He suffered a breakdown in health in the early part of 1887 and it is possible that he was not fully recovered when he resumed a taxing backlog of cases in the following year. L.W. Bailey recalled that the great detective solved cases as far apart as Russia and Ceylon during the first three months of 1888.

If Holmes's breakdown precipitated some kind of insanity, it is possible that an outlet might have taken the form of violent crime. Applying a mind warped from its customary logical path, he might have decided to remove from the streets of London the women whose degenerate way of life was responsible for so much crime. Free from the surveillance of Dr Watson, who in 1888 was living the life of a married man, he took to wandering the streets at night, probably in disguise. The deerstalker hat worn at the time he encountered Annie Chapman might have been sheer bravado and constituted a clue which even Inspector Lestrade at Scotland Yard could not ignore.

Wrestling with the knowledge that their chief crime consultant was in fact Jack the Ripper, the Yard might have reasoned that his continued availability to deal with Professor Moriarty was more important than the lives of a few worthless prostitutes. Consequently, it was decided to keep a watch on Holmes's movements and try to contain his violent outbursts. This ploy worked with moderate success until 1891 when Holmes was faced with the challenge of confronting Moriarty at the Reichenbach Falls. Holmes and the Ripper who were one and the same apparently disappeared into the swirling waters. But he survived the ordeal and lived for three years in Switzerland where it is believed his brother Mycroft arranged for him to enter a clinic anonymously to be treated for his mental affliction. Cured, he returned to London in due course to resume his crime-solving partnership with Dr Watson.

As L.W. Bailey remarked, 'At this distance of time no theory about Jack the Ripper can have absolute proof. The one I have put forward is tentative, and will, I fear, cause pain to many worthy devotees of the great detective.' He was quite correct in his fear, for a correspondent to the *Listener* referred to the 'shameful thesis that Sherlock Holmes was Jack the Ripper' and called it too improbable to be credible. Inspector Lestrade was regarded as an ambitious officer who would have regarded the discovery of Jack the Ripper's identity, even if he proved to be Sherlock Holmes, as the pinnacle of his career. It was suggested that Holmes did not discuss the Ripper case with Watson because brutal assault interested him less than cases dignified with more subtle features. L.W. Bailey refuted these points and drew attention to Holmes's most celebrated dictum which was that 'when you have eliminated the impossible, what remains, however improbable, must be the truth'. Generations of Ripperologists have certainly subscribed to that view.

It is perhaps surprising, with all the duplicity and complicity which have been brought to bear on the Ripper murders, that no one has seriously suggested that the perpetrator was a police officer. Despite 'The Case of the Unmentioned Case', Sherlock Holmes inevitably became involved in the murder investigation as chronicled by W.S. Baring-Gould in his biography of the great detective, *Sherlock Holmes*, published in 1962. In 'Jack the Harlot Killer: Friday, 9 – Sunday, 11 November 1888', Holmes unmasked the Ripper as a Scotland Yard police inspector.

After the murder of Mary Kelly, so the story went, Inspector Athelney Jones was instructed by Sir Melville Macnaghten to call in the great detective who was given *carte blanche* to solve the murders. After receiving a briefing from the inspector and expressly forbidding Dr Watson to accompany him, Holmes ventured into the East End. He had disguised himself as a harlot in order to set himself up as a potential victim. He was not disappointed. Quickly attracting the attention of a man in a public house he was followed to a darkened court where he maintained the pretence until his companion produced a knife.

With incredible speed the drab had a glittering sword in her hand and growled, 'Drop your knife, Jack.' Trapped by Sherlock Holmes, one of Europe's most accomplished swordsmen, the Ripper backed off and appeared to yield. But then he lunged forward, and knocked Holmes off his feet so that he finished up lying unconscious on the cobbled street. At that moment, with the ace detective lying helpless, a heavy figure emerged from the shadows and felled the Ripper with a mighty blow. 'My dear Watson,' breathed Holmes struggling to regain his senses.

The Ripper was unmasked as none other than Inspector Athelney Jones whom, of course, Holmes had suspected from the start. He discovered that the policeman had attended lectures on surgery as part of his training in detective work and was particularly impressed by his office at Commercial Street Police Station. This had a separate door which gave access to an adjacent alleyway – obviously the perfect lair for a killer who wanted to get off the streets quickly. 'Extraordinary, my dear Watson,' said Holmes; 'Elementary, my dear Holmes,' replied the doctor.

Of the senior police officers involved in the Ripper murder investigations, the worst that could be said of some of them was that they were bunglers. That damning assessment did not apply to James Monro, who was appointed chief of CID at Scotland Yard and Assistant Commissioner of the Metropolitan Police in 1884. He was a highly-rated officer and regarded by Tom Cullen as 'possibly the only man at Scotland Yard who was capable of tracking down, the killer. . .' Monro, whose proudest boast was that he was 'born, bred and educated in Edinburgh', had served in India for twenty-six years and was Inspector General of the Bengal Police when he was snapped up for the vacancy at Scotland Yard left by the departure of Sir Howard Vincent. Regrettably, the able Monro was forced to resign after only four years in his post as a result of a clash with his superior, Sir Charles Warren, Commissioner of Police for the Metropolis. George Dilnot, in his book, *The Story of Scotland Yard*, wrote, 'It is sufficient to say that an arrogant Commissioner and niggling Home Office caused him to resign the post. . .' Then, on 8 November, the day before the Ripper's final blood bath at Miller's Court, Sir Charles Warren himself resigned.

'Warren's place,' wrote Sir John Moylan, 'was filled by the return of Mr Monro, an expert on crime and the creator of the Special Branch.' Sir Robert Anderson, who thereby became junior to Monro, said his appointment 'marked an epoch in police administration in London'.

James Monro took up his appointment as Commissioner on 3 December 1888 and began to put through a number of long-needed reforms. He raised the status of the policeman and established the police service as a respected professional career. He was particularly, even passionately, associated with police pensions and this was to be the issue which led to his eventual resignation. Sir John Moylan recorded that 'Mr Monro was impatient and unfortunately allowed his sympathy with the men's claim to drive him into unnecessary antagonism to his parliamentary chief. . . he eventually resigned in June 1890, mainly because he thought the Pensions Bill which the Secretary of State was about to introduce into Parliament did not meet the just claims of his men.'

There was a belief in the force that Monro had been pushed out of office because he too readily identified with his men's grievances. As *Punch*, keeper of the public conscience on such occasions, asked on behalf of the Home Secretary:

> Why *did* Monro resign?
> Was it any fault of mine?
> If you want to know the truth –
> Ask the p'liceman.

Sir John Moylan noted in addition that Monro also intended to resign 'as a protest against the Secretary of State's private secretary who had no police, military or legal training, becoming an Assistant Commissioner. . .'

James Monro thus sacrificed his career while still in his prime, for the sake of principle. Perhaps he was too naïve for the political rough and tumble or, possibly, his strong religious outlook caused him to be too outspoken where his masters were concerned. One of his final decisions concerned the move of police officers from Great Scotland Yard to premises on the embankment which he called New Scotland Yard.

Unlike his predecessors and contemporaries, Monro was not honoured with a knighthood. He became a missionary and returned to India where he used his own money to found the Medical Mission at Ranaghat, some forty miles from Calcutta. The mission was well attended and thousands came to receive medical attention at the settlement he called Dayabari – 'Abode of Mercy'. The condition of receiving treatment was attendance at a religious service. After twelve years of undoubted labour and service, Monro returned, in 1905, not to his beloved Scotland, but to England and settled at Cheltenham. He died, aged eighty-one, in 1920. His Death Notice published in *The Times* referred only to his service in India and his founding of a medical mission – no reference was made to his appointments at Scotland Yard.

Following publication of his book, *Jack the Ripper in Fact and Fiction*, Robin Odell received a letter from a retired company secretary in Australia hinting at a new theory as to the identity of the Whitechapel murderer. The correspondence developed over several months and it emerged that the chief suspect was James Monro, who spent nearly half his life in India and only six years of his working career in England. Of those six years, he was out of office, although not out of London, during the crucial period of the Ripper murders. He resigned on the eve of the first murder and was reinstated after the last one.

There was no doubt that Monro was a strong personality and had a fierce sense of mission. His obituary in *The Times*, 30 January 1920, described him as a person of unquestionable efficiency but 'perhaps lacking in tact and diplomacy'. He resigned high office twice on grounds of principle and the second time went into virtual exile. The suggestion made by the retired company secretary, in an unpublished thesis compiled in Australia, is that Monro had a pathological hatred of Sir Charles Warren with a basis which perhaps went beyond the departmental disagreements. Certainly the atmosphere at Scotland Yard was highly charged in the period which led up to the climax of the forced resignation.

This would have been a burden for a temperate personality but for a man with a mission who had been thwarted by what he regarded as a conspiracy, the desire for revenge might run strong. A person obsessed with grandiose ideas of reform, as Monro undoubtedly was, might have been temporarily pushed over the edge of reason by the trauma

242

of rejection. In a controlled psychopathic state, he plotted a campaign to draw attention to the inadequacies of Scotland Yard, the unsuitability of Sir Charles Warren and the shocking conditions then prevailing in the East End. Whether or not Monro had anything to do with the Whitechapel murders, it can be fairly said that all those objectives were achieved. And, in their wake, Monro was recalled, doubtless to his great pleasure, to replace Warren.

Monro was highly regarded by Sir Robert Anderson, his one time successor who ended up working under him and rated him a personal friend. But more than a hint of the rancour which existed between Monro and Sir Charles Warren emerged in the biography of Sir Charles written by his grandson. Of Monro's resignation, he wrote, 'After throwing a good many obstacles in Warren's way, Monro at last resigned . . . and the news of his resignation was received in Parliament before Warren had any suspicion that he intended to resign. . .' Of Warren's resignation, he noted the outgoing Commissioner's understandable bitterness at the 'appointment of Monro as his successor – a man who, as a subordinate, had been instrumental in throwing obstacles in his way. . .' Those must have been acriminous days for both men but perhaps more difficult for Monro who went into virtual obscurity, whereas Warren continued in a distinguished military career.

James Monro married in 1863 and, presumably, his wife accompanied him during his service in India where he was described as 'a veritable terror to the criminal classes of Bengal'. His religious inclinations were those of Second Adventism and it was his faith which guided his work after he left Scotland Yard. If he was a man with a secret, he left no hint of it – there were no papers, no memoirs, only brief mentions in official histories. Nevertheless there was an air of mystery about the man whom fate plucked out of the centre of action and placed on the sidelines when the terror of 1888 broke loose in London. If he was responsible for the terror, there is little coherent evidence to support it beyond a possible bitter motive.

CHAPTER SIX
Royal Jack

The Criminologist was a small quarterly magazine whose circulation was restricted largely to policemen and members of the legal profession. The issue for November 1970 contained an article modestly entitled 'Jack the Ripper – A Solution?' by T.E.A. Stowell, CBE, MD. The article did not actually name a suspect as Jack the Ripper; it spoke of him simply as 'S', and explained that 'he was an heir to power and wealth', and that 'his family had for fifty years earned the love and admiration of large numbers of people by its devotion to public service . . .'

A few days later, on Sunday, 1 November 1970, the *Sunday Times* carried an article by Magnus Linklater entitled: 'Did Jack the Ripper have royal blood?' and it speculated that the suspect named by Dr Stowell was Queen Victoria's grandson, the Duke of Clarence. The story was picked up by Associated Press and within hours had been telegraphed all over the world – one writer estimates that it appeared on the front pages of two thousand newspapers. Dr Stowell became an overnight celebrity – or perhaps it would be more accurate to say that he acquired overnight notoriety. The following evening, interviewed on BBC television by journalist Kenneth Allsop, Stowell declined to name his suspect, but made no objection when Allsop made the assumption that they were talking about the Duke of Clarence. But six days later, his nerve broke, and he wrote a letter to *The Times* flatly denying that 'S' was the duke. By the time the letter appeared, Stowell was dead – the furore created by his article had been too much for him.

Stowell was not telling the truth when he denied that his suspect was Clarence, as I was in a position to know. Stowell had told me his theory ten years earlier, in August 1960, over lunch at the Athenaeum club; we had been in touch ever since, and I (C.W.) was aware that he had not changed his mind.

I made Stowell's acquaintance as a result of a series of articles I wrote in the London *Evening Standard* ·(8–12 August 1960) collectively entitled 'My Search for Jack the Ripper'. I described how the Ripper murders had fascinated me ever since, as a small boy, my grandfather had told me stories of how his parents would not allow him to go out after dark at the time of the murders, and how, when I came to live in London in the early 1950s, I had spent days wandering around the murder sites, and reading about the Ripper crimes in the British Museum's bound copies of *The Times* for 1888. The motive was not simply morbid curiosity; I used the murders as the background of my first novel *Ritual in the Dark*, which appeared in the autumn of 1960.

As a result of the articles, I received a great many letters. One of these came from Dr Thomas Stowell, and he remarked that I obviously knew a great deal more about the murders than I was willing to admit. The remark intrigued me; I wrote back to say that he was mistaken, and asking what comment in my articles had led him to this conclusion. The result was an invitation to lunch at the Athenaeum, one of London's more sedate and impressive clubs.

Stowell proved to be a friendly man in his early seventies. He told me he was a surgeon, although when I noticed the way his hand shook as he cut his steak I concluded that he would soon be obliged to retire from this profession.

He came quickly to the point – that I had described one man observed near the scene of a Ripper murder as a 'gentleman', and that I had mentioned this more than once. I said I was merely quoting the account of witnesses. In that case, he said, my instinct had led me to the correct solution. Jack the Ripper was the Duke of Clarence.

He must have been disappointed by my reaction. My knowledge of the royal family was minimal, and the only Duke of Clarence I had ever heard of was drowned in a butt of malmsey. But as he talked on, I gathered that *this* Duke of Clarence was Queen Victoria's grandson, son of Edward VII and heir to the throne of England.

He had learned this, he said, when Caroline Acland, daughter of the royal physician, Sir William Gull, had asked him to examine her father's papers in the 1930s. Stowell had studied medicine at St Thomas's under Theodore Dyke Acland, Caroline's husband. The papers contained 'certain confidential matters', and she wanted Stowell's advice. Apparently they revealed that the Duke of Clarence had not died in the 'flu epidemic, as the history books state, but in a mental home near Sandringham, of softening of the brain due to syphilis. There was also mention of the famous Cleveland Street scandal in 1886, in which various members of the upper classes were accused of sodomizing telegraph boys. The Duke of Clarence – known to the newspapers as Eddie, or 'collar and cuffs' – was, according to Stowell, among those questioned about telegraph boys, and he inferred that Clarence was homosexual. And, associated with Clarence, there were mysterious hints about the Ripper.

There was also the peculiar story about the 'spirit medium' R.J. Lees who, according to a persistent legend, was responsible for the capture of Jack the Ripper – a story that had been told to my first wife by Lees' daughter. It was claimed that Lees had, on a number of occasions, had dreams – or visions – of the murders, and that one day, travelling on a bus along the Bayswater Road, he suddenly recognized the man sitting opposite him as the Ripper. He followed him home, to a mansion in the West End, then notified the police. They told Lees that he must be mistaken, because the man was an eminent surgeon whose patients included royalty. But when the doctor's wife was questioned, she admitted that she had fears for her husband's sanity, and that he had been absent from home on the nights of the murders. The police kept watch, and took the surgeon into custody one evening as he was leaving the house with a black bag – this proved to contain a very sharp knife of the type used in the murders. The doctor was incarcerated in a mental home. Stowell told me that Gull's notes had contained mysterious references to Clarence, and the fact that he had blood on his shirt after one of the murders – I think he told me that the duke had come to his home. Gull lived in 74 Brook Street, Grosvenor Square, so his home would fit the description of a mansion in the West End.

There was evidence, said Stowell, that Queen Victoria had sent for Lees, and also that she was interested in the Ripper murders – she had even made suggestions about how he might be caught. If she suspected that her grandson was the murderer, then she would have a good reason for asking Lees to the palace.

So the story about Lees and Jack the Ripper was not quite accurate. Gull was not the Ripper. But he had known the Ripper's identity and guarded his secret, and Lees may have learned this through the 'spirits'.

According to Stowell, Clarence's story was roughly as follows. He was born in 1864, and named Albert Victor. On a world cruise at the age of sixteen, he contracted syphilis from a male partner. After the Cleveland Street scandal (when he was twenty-two) he was sent on another sea voyage. It was after his return that he began killing prostitutes. Stowell thought that he had been caught after the 'double event' but had escaped from his keepers and committed the final murder in Miller's Court. He was then treated by Gull – so successfully that he was able to go on a five-month cruise. But he finally died of syphilis in 1892.

Stowell told me that he had another interesting piece of evidence from Caroline Acland. At the time of the murders, her mother, Lady Gull, was annoyed when one evening a police inspector called, accompanied by a medium, and asked 'impertinent questions'. She also told Stowell that she had seen in her father's diary an entry: 'Informed Blank that his son was dying of syphilis of the brain.'

At the time of this meeting with Dr Stowell, I was planning an encyclopedia of murder, and looked forward to including the Clarence theory in it. Stowell made no attempt to swear me to secrecy, or even to suggest discretion. The result was that when, later that day, I met the German newspaper editor Frank Lynder, I told him the story, and agreed to write it for his newspapers. But when I rang Stowell to ask him if I could quote him, he told me that 'it might upset Her Majesty', and that he would prefer that I should not publish it. Yet I had an odd feeling that he rather hoped I would. He had been sitting on it for thirty years, and wanted to see what kind of impact it would make. He certainly showed no kind of reticence in discussing it – we exchanged several letters, and a few years later I had a long telephone conversation with him about it and made notes on a telephone directory.

I also recounted the story to a number of friends, including Dan Farson, Kenneth Allsop, Nigel Morland and Donald McCormick. Nigel contacted Stowell, and an early issue of *The Criminologist* contained an article by Stowell on the bones of Edward the Martyr. Then, apparently, Nigel persuaded Stowell to tell his story of the Duke of Clarence, disguising his identity; and Stowell, tired of sitting on his secret, agreed. I am inclined to wonder if he would have refused if he could have foreseen the furore it caused. Perhaps not; I suspect that, like most of us, he had a craving to 'become known'.

Oddly enough, he died on the eighty-second anniversary of the last of the Ripper murders – that of Mary Kelly.

Frank Lynder told me that he had checked the Court Circular for 1888, and that the Duke of Clarence had been in London at the time of all the murders. In fact, he proved to be mistaken. At the time of the Mary Kelly murder, Clarence was celebrating his father's birthday at Sandringham. And, as a correspondent in *The Times* pointed out, he had been with a hunting party at Balmoral on the morning after the 'double event'. This does not quite exclude the possibility that he was the Ripper; he could have slipped away from Sandringham in order to be in London by the early hours of the morning, and there was in those days an excellent train service to Scotland that would have had him there by midday. But I suspect that Stowell himself would not have been convinced by all this, and might have abandoned his theory. . .

A *Times* report shortly after Stowell's death stated that his son had burnt all his papers unread. (This, apparently, is not entirely true – some were in the possession of Nigel Morland.) So by way of preserving what I could remember, I wrote the story for the weekly newspaper of my home town, *The Leicester Chronicle*; it was subsequently printed as an appendix in my book *Order of Assassins* (1972). And that, presumably, should have been the end of the matter. But it was not, quite. About a year after Stowell's death, I received a letter from an old friend, Michael Harrison, who asked me if he could quote my Clarence article in a book he was writing about the duke. He also mentioned that he had now established the Ripper's identity, and that he had a letter from him at present lying on his desk. I had to wait six months or so before I saw a proof copy of the book, and learned the identity of Michael's suspect. It was James Kenneth Stephen – a close friend of the duke, and possibly his lover. This theory has already been discussed in the preceding chapter, 'Gentleman Jack'; nevertheless, it is necessary briefly to summarize the facts here.

As he had read Stowell's account of his suspect's life in the *Criminologist* article, it had struck Michael Harrison that, in fact, the career of Stowell's suspect (whom he called

'S') was *not* that of the Duke of Clarence. For example, Stowell says that 'S' resigned his commission at the age of twenty-four; but Clarence never resigned his commission. Stowell says that 'S' had another relapse in 1889, then slid into the final stage of syphilis; but Clarence went to India in 1889, and later made three public appearances, making speeches on each occasion – which would seem to argue against softening of the brain.

And *why* did Stowell call his suspect 'S'? Could it have been because Gull himself made mysterious references to 'S' as Jack the Ripper? And that Stowell, finding also references to Clarence, decided that *he* was Jack the Ripper?

Was it possible that Eddie, Duke of Clarence, had a friend or close associate whose name began with 'S' – and could this explain the confusion?

Harrison discovered that there *was* such a person – J.K. Stephen (known as Jim or Jem) who had become Clarence's tutor and friend in 1883 when Clarence was at Cambridge. Eddie did not take to university life, nor did he like some of Stephen's effete literary friends, like the homosexual Oscar Browning. Jim Stephen was ambitious; he hoped to become the 'power behind the throne'. But it was not to be; Eddie left Cambridge after only two years. During that time, Harrison theorizes, Clarence and Stephen became lovers. But they saw little of each other thereafter.

In 1886, riding near Felixstowe, Stephen rode his horse up to a windmill on a slight rise; something startled his horse, which backed into the descending vane; Stephen was knocked unconscious. Under the care of Sir William Gull, he apparently made a perfect recovery. But the accident left injuries which – as his father Sir James Stephen commented – 'were not perceived for some time'. He became a barrister, but was overtaken by a 'strange lethargy'. In 1888, he was appointed to a Clerkship of Assizes in South Wales. Michael Harrison discovered that the dates when Stephen was in Wales were those that fell between Ripper murders. In 1890, Stephen resigned his Clerkship, and was confined to a mental home for two years, dying in 1892. During his last years he became increasingly 'odd'. One of Michael Harrison's most convincing pieces of evidence is a poem written by Stephen in the year before his death and printed in *The Cambridge Review*. It is, as Harrison comments, 'a perfectly appalling poem', which begins: 'As I was strolling lonely in the Backs,/I met a women whom I did not like.' It goes on to describe her general ugliness and slovenliness, and concludes:

> I did not like her: and I should not mind
> If she were done away with, killed, or
> ploughed.
> She did not seem to serve a useful end:
> And certainly she was not beautiful.

All this certainly amounts to circumstantial evidence that Jim Stephen might have been the Ripper. Yet there is still no positive link between Stephen and the Ripper killings. To judge whether Gull might have had Stephen in mind, we would have to see his papers; and these, Stowell told me, were destroyed on his advice.

In 1978, an American, Frank Spiering, produced a book called *Prince Jack, The True Story of Jack the Ripper*. It is an excellent summary of the murders, and of Stowell's theory; but in the last analysis, it is basically as unconvincing as Stowell's original article in *The Criminologist*. But in a letter to me (13 March 1980), Spiering mentioned at least one interesting piece of evidence. He told me that in November 1977 he visited the archives of the New York Academy of Medicine, where he was able to study Gull's medical papers. There was a printed volume of Gull's writings, and a brown leather volume with nothing on the spine; this, he said, contained Gull's handwritten notes. And thirty or so pages into these notes, he came upon the comment: 'On 3 October I informed the Prince of Wales that his son was dying of syphilis of the brain. Under suggestion, using the Nancy method, my patient admitted to the details.' So it would seem that at least some of Gull's original material still survives. But it is not quite clear why Gull should have been obliged to use the 'Nancy method' – a kind of waking hypnosis – to lead the Duke of Clarence to admit to syphilis; presumably an ordinary physical examination would be all that was required.

In 1973, the year after the publication of Michael Harrison's biography of the duke, *Clarence*, I received a letter from a BBC producer, Paul Bonner, asking me if I would be willing to act as consultant on a series of programmes on Jack the Ripper. Apparently these would be semi-fictionalized, and would star two popular television policemen, Barlow and Watt of *Z Cars*. Donald Rumbelow, the policeman who had rediscovered the original morgue photographs of the Ripper's victims, had also been consulted.

A few days later I happened to be delivering a lecture at Scotland Yard, so I arranged to meet Paul Bonner in the pub next door. He explained that what he now intended to tell me must be treated as a secret. The BBC research team had apparently uncovered a completely new theory of the murders. Its origin, it seemed, was Joseph Sickert – known as 'Hobo' – son of the famous Victorian painter Walter Sickert.

Sickert's story was as follows. In the mid-1880s, Walter Sickert, who was then a Bohemian young painter living in Cleveland Street, Soho, became acquainted with Eddie, the Duke of Clarence, a young man who loved wine, women and song (Sickert apparently rejected the notion that Eddie was homosexual). In Sickert's studio, Eddie met a young shop girl who modelled for him; her name was Annie Elizabeth Crook. Annie was a Catholic. She became Eddie's mistress, and on 18 April 1885 she gave birth to Eddie's child, a girl who was named Alice Margaret. Soon after this, Eddie and Annie Crook went through a ceremony of marriage at a private chapel, with Sickert as a witness. The other witness was an Irish Catholic girl named Marie Jeannette Kelly, who was the child's nanny.

Inevitably, the secret leaked back to the palace. The

Prime Minister, Lord Salisbury, was horrified. What was to be done? Eddie had married a woman who was not only a commoner but a Catholic. One day, early in 1888, a carriage drove up to the house at 6 Cleveland Street where Annie lived, and she and Eddie were hustled away. Annie was certified insane, and confined in a mental home. Eddie was presumably given a good talking to by his grandmother and had to promise never to see Annie again.

The child, Alice Margaret, was taken away to the East End to live with Mary Kelly. She found her way back to Sickert, who took her to Dieppe. When she grew up she became his mistress, and Joseph Sickert was born to them.

Mary Kelly made the mistake of telling the story to some gin-sodden prostitutes, and decided to blackmail the royal family. This was her downfall and, according to Joseph Sickert, Sir William Gull was given the task of eliminating Kelly and her friends. He did this with the aid of a coach driver named Netley, who took him to and from Whitechapel. Sir William Gull was the Ripper, and Mary Kelly's fellow blackmailers – Mary Nichols, Annie Chapman and Elizabeth Stride – were his victims. (Catherine Eddowes was killed by mistake because she was also known as Mary Ann Kelly.) So, finally, was Marie Jeanette Kelly.

This was the story on which Bonner wanted my opinion. I said it was obvious nonsense. I was not aware then that Gull had had a stroke in 1887, and was almost totally incapacitated (or if I was, I had forgotten about it). But surely it was obvious that if a group of blackmailers are murdered one by one, they would begin to suspect an organized plot long before the Ripper completed his task, and would hasten to the nearest police station to tell their story. Besides, no theory of the Ripper's identity makes sense that fails to recognize that he was a sadistic maniac; no other motivation could account for the disembowelling of the victims and for the final dismemberment of Mary Kelly. There is no evidence whatever that Gull was a sadist. And the notion of driving around the East End at 4 a.m. in a carriage looking for prostitutes is grotesque.

Nevertheless, said Paul Bonner, there *was* a certain amount of evidence for the story. They had checked at the Cleveland Street address – number 6 – and a woman called Elizabeth Cook – obviously a careless misprint for Crook – had lived in the basement in 1888, as the rate book showed. They had located the birth certificate of Alice Margaret Crook, and no father's name was given. They had even discovered that there had been a 'driver' named John Netley who had been born in May 1860 and had died in 1903 when thrown from his van as it went over a stone. Bonner also mentioned Stowell's story about the police inspector who called on Lady Gull, together with a medium, and quoted Stowell's comment that Gull had been seen in the Whitechapel area around the times of the murders, and his admission that he had been suffering from lapses of memory and had once found blood on his shirt . . .

The story still sounded absurd to me. Nevertheless, it was duly told in a BBC television serial in six parts, *The Ripper File*, in July and August 1973, and Joseph Sickert took part in the final episode and repeated his rather unlikely story.

A young north London journalist named Stephen Knight, who had been conducting his own investigation into the Ripper case, decided to write a book about Sickert's theory. This appeared in 1976 with the optimistic title *Jack the Ripper, The Final Solution*. I reviewed it in *Books and Bookmen*, and the central paragraph of the review ran as follows:

What we are being asked to believe is, basically, a far taller story than any of the earlier theories about the Ripper – the mad surgeon, the sadistic midwife, and so on. We are asked to believe, first of all, that Eddie, the Duke of Clarence, became a close friend of Walter Sickert. This is unsupported. We are asked to believe that he became sufficiently involved with a shop assistant to actually marry her – although, like everyone in the family, he was terrified of Queen Victoria, and knew that he might – almost certainly would – be king of England one day. We are asked to believe that the queen's physician, Sir William Gull, was a party to the kidnapping of the shop assistant, and that he probably performed some gruesome operation on her to make her lose her memory. And then that Gull, with the approval of the Prime Minister, went around Whitechapel killing prostitutes with appalling sadism (when, after all, a single stab would have done the trick). Moreover, that Gull was a Freemason, and committed the murders according to Masonic ritual. (The Prime Minister and Commissioner of Police were also Masons. . .) Mr Knight admits that Gull had a stroke in the year before the murders, but insists that he was still spry enough to wield the knife. . .

The question is then asked why was Annie Crook not also murdered, if the aim was to eliminate everyone who knew about the morganatic marriage? And why not Sickert too, since he was virtually to blame? Stephen Knight answers this by saying that Sickert himself was *also* the Ripper – that he had accompanied Gull on his murder expeditions and may have killed some of the victims himself. In his Afterword to the book, Joseph Sickert concedes reluctantly that this may be true, but suggests that his father may have been blackmailed into it by threats on his life. . .

Stephen Knight's book was a considerable success – so much so that he decided to give up his job as a journalist and become a full-time writer. Regrettably, soon after a paperback edition of the book came out in 1977, a story by David May appeared in the *Sunday Times* that stated that Sickert had now admitted that his whole story was a hoax. Stephen Knight, understandably, declined to accept his view, and in his best-selling book about the Freemasons, *The Brotherhood* (1984) he reiterated the whole story. By that time, sadly, he had discovered that he was still suffering from a brain tumour – of which he had believed himself cured – and he died in 1985.

In the *Sunday Times* piece, Sickert insisted that only the Jack the Ripper part of his story was a hoax, and that he was, in fact, the grandson of the Duke of Clarence, as a result of the affair between Clarence and Annie Crook. This is, of course, the only part of his story for which there is some sort of documentary evidence: viz. the rate book for 6 Cleveland Street, and Alice Margaret's birth certificate in which the name of the father and his occupation are left blank. We may also recall that Stowell spoke of Eddie in connection with Cleveland Street – not the basement flat of 'Elizabeth Cook', but the homosexual scandal at the brothel at 19 Cleveland Street. In fact, there is no evidence that Eddie was homosexual; but in his book *The Cleveland Street Scandal* (1976), H. Montgomery Hyde reveals that the Assistant Public Prosecutor mentioned 'PAV' (Prince Albert Victor – Eddie's real name) in connection with the case. Hyde points out that the man who ran the brothel – Charles Hammond – also advertised *Poses plastiques* – the Victorian equivalent of striptease (although the nude lady had to remain as still as a statue) – and that if Clarence visited the house, it may well have been under the impression that it provided 'female entertainment'. But we might also speculate that if Gull referred to some scandal involving Eddie and Cleveland Street in his diary, he might well have been referring to the duke's affair with a common shop girl named Annie Crook. . .

Hyde mentions one more piece of evidence that adds credibility to Stowell's story. A young doctor named Alfred Fripp was called in on one occasion when Prince Eddie was ill at Scarborough; among Fripp's papers after his death (he became a famous surgeon) Fripp's biographer discovered a prescription for Eddie indicating that he suffered from gonorrhoea.

Yet this still leaves us with an interesting question. We have dismissed Joseph Sickert's statement that Sir William Gull was Jack the Ripper, and it seems fairly clear that the Duke of Clarence was – according to the Court Circular – 'otherwise engaged' at the time of the murders. Yet Stowell undoubtedly saw *something* in Gull's papers that suggested that Clarence was Jack the Ripper. Michael Harrison's identification of 'S' as Jim Stephen is plausible – until we look more closely at Stephen's personality – the young Cambridge aesthete, a member of what Harrison describes as the 'epicene literati', who wrote poetry and mixed with homosexuals. Even when he was going insane, his madness does not sound like the kind that drives a man to prowl Whitechapel looking for women to disembowel. In his biography of Virginia Woolf (Jim Stephen's cousin), Quentin Bell writes: 'One day he rushed upstairs to the nursery at 22 Hyde Park Gate, drew the blade from a sword stick and plunged it into the bread. On another occasion he carried Virginia and her mother off to his room in De Vere Gardens; Virginia was to pose for him. He had decided that he was a painter – a painter of genius. He was in a state of high euphoria, and painted away like a man possessed, as indeed he was. He would drive up in a hansom cab to Hyde Park Gate – a hansom cab in which he had been driving all day in a state of insane excitement. On another occasion he appeared at breakfast and announced, as though it were an amusing incident, that the doctors had told him that he would either die or go completely mad. . .' None of this sounds in the least like the cunning and sadistic maniac of Whitechapel.

But if we dismiss Stephen, then who was 'S'? There is one more obvious candidate – Sickert. In fact, Stephen Knight's chapter on Sickert is one of the most convincing in his book. Sickert *was* undoubtedly obsessed by Jack the Ripper. Sickert's friend Marjorie Lilly told Knight: 'After the stroke Sickert would have "Ripper periods" in which he would dress up like the murderer and walk about like that for weeks on end.' And Knight points out how many of Sickert's paintings contain gruesome-looking heads of women or similar puzzling items. Sickert painted several pictures of the Camden Town murder, in which a young artist named Robert Wood was accused of cutting the throat of a prostitute. According to Joseph Sickert (whose word, admittedly, seems to be less than reliable) these paintings were really about the Ripper murders.

Another curious and enigmatic painting shows a young woman in a large room standing underneath a bust on the wall. It is the title that is so baffling: Amphytrion, or X's Affiliation Order. Knight points out that an affiliation order fixes the paternity of an illegitimate child, and that the legend of Amphytrion tells how Jupiter disguised himself as a lesser being to seduce an ordinary woman, who becomes pregnant by him. Knight speculates that the bust on the wall is a death's head, but this seems to me an obvious misinterpretation. The ordinary-looking young woman in a blouse and long skirt is obviously the woman who was seduced by Jupiter; so the bust on the wall above her must be her seducer, the father of her illegitimate child. The picture may be regarded as strong supporting evidence for Joseph Sickert's claim that the Duke of Clarence was the father of Annie Crook's baby. This in turn suggests that the story of the friendship between Clarence and Sickert is true. If Gull knew about Annie Crook and her illegitimate child, then he also knew about Sickert's role in the story. If Sickert was obsessed by the murders – and he was known to be obsessed – then it *is* conceivable that he was the 'S' Gull referred to in connection with the Duke of Clarence and Jack the Ripper.

Does this mean that Sickert was Jack the Ripper? Almost certainly not. Artists and writers may become morbidly obsessed by certain murders, but – as observed in the 'Psychological Portrait of Jack the Ripper' in the introduction to this book – no artist has ever been known to commit a premeditated murder. Sickert may have been Gull's suspect, and therefore the man who inadvertently caused suspicion to fall on the Duke of Clarence. But there is no evidence that he was capable of harming a fly. We must look for Jack the Ripper elsewhere.

And that may sound like the last word on a fascinating if unlikely theory. But in March 1987, a new magazine called *The Bloodhound* added an interesting postscript. Its editor,

Simon D. Wood, had decided to make his own investigation into the evidence on which Stephen Knight based his book. He began by writing to Mr Alan Neate, the Record Keeper of the Greater London Record Office, to ask for any information he could furnish on the life of the unfortunate Annie Elizabeth Crook. And in fact, this information was to undermine Knight's theory even more effectively than 'Hobo' Sickert's confession.

Knight's investigation had shown that the address given on the birth certificate of Annie's daughter Alice Margaret (who was born in 1885) was 6 Cleveland Street. And the rate book for the same address in 1888 listed one 'Elizabeth Cook' as occupying the basement. 'The address', says Knight, 'shows that the Elizabeth Cook of the Rate Book and Annie Elizabeth Crook were one and the same.'

Unfortunately, it shows nothing of the kind. For between 1886 and early 1888, numbers 4 to 14 Cleveland Street were pulled down, and replaced by the block of flats that still stands there today. That means that Annie Elizabeth Crook must have left 6 Cleveland Street, at the latest, in 1886. It was after the completion of the flats that Annie *Cook* moved into the basement of number 6. And the rate book shows that she lived there until 1893, long after, according to Knight, Annie Crook was dragged off by the wicked Sir William Gull and forced to undergo brain surgery to destroy her memory. . .

Moreover, the same records show that there is no truth in the story that Annie Crook was incarcerated in a mental home for the rest of her days. In 1889 she was admitted briefly to the Endell Street Workhouse, together with her daughter Alice Margaret. She was destitute, but quite obviously free. In 1894 the records show that Annie was in prison. Her daughter, aged nine, was sent to a kind of holiday camp for two weeks, so presumably Annie received fourteen days.

In 1902 Alice Margaret was admitted to St Pancras Infirmary suffering from measles, and the records show that she and her mother were living at 5 Pancras Street, where they paid two shillings a week in rent. But in 1903 Annie Crook was admitted to the St Pancras Workhouse suffering from epilepsy. Her occupation was given as 'Casual hand – Crosse and Blackwells'. And so the sad record continues. In 1906 Annie was living, together with her mother and daughter, at the Poland Street Workhouse. In 1913 Annie and her mother were admitted to the Endell Street Workhouse. In 1920 Annie Elizabeth Crook finally died in the Lunacy Ward of the Fulham Road Workhouse. But the records show that this breakdown in her mental health occurred only at the very end of her life. There is certainly no evidence that she was imprisoned in lunatic asylums from 1888 until 1920 by a 'Freemasons' conspiracy'.

Finally, the report of her death lists her religion as Church of England. So Knight's story that she was a Roman Catholic – and that this was what caused so much consternation at Windsor – is without foundation.

Simon Wood ends his article by revealing that he placed his evidence before Stephen Knight, and that Knight remained 'smilingly unrepentant'. But, in a postscript to the paperback edition, Knight admits that 'other evidence' has now come to light, which he is in the process of examining. Sadly, says Mr Wood, he never took up the challenge.

But Wood's article makes it clear that Stephen Knight must have known, even while he was writing his book, that his theory was untrue: that Annie Crook and Elizabeth Cook were two different persons, and that Annie lived out a perfectly normal – if miserable – life until her death in 1920. I am forced to the reluctant conclusion – for Stephen Knight was an old friend and I was fond of him – that he wrote the book with his tongue in his cheek, then found himself caught up in a success that prevented him from retracting or quietly disowning it.

CHAPTER SEVEN
Black Jack

'Was Jack the Ripper a Black Magician?' demanded a headline on the cover of *True Detective* magazine for January 1973. The question sounds so preposterous that it is hard to take it seriously. Yet, oddly enough, the supporting evidence is more detailed and convincing than in most theories of the Ripper's identity.

The first suggestion that the Ripper was a black magician was made by Aleister Crowley, 'the world's wickedest man', in his 'autohagiography', *The Confessions of Aleister Crowley*, first published complete in 1969. Crowley was a man who possessed an eccentric – and sometimes cruel – sense of humour, so the critical reader might be forgiven for assuming that his 'revelations' were a joke – particularly since much of the book was dictated under the influence of heroin. But in the 1970s, the distinguished 'Ripperologist' Richard Whittington-Egan was able to track down an unpublished manuscript by the journalist Bernard O'Donnell which makes it clear that Crowley was, in fact, telling the truth as far as he knew it.

Crowley's story is as follows. In 1912, he met a tough

lesbian lady named Baroness Vittoria Cremers, and agreed to allow her to become business manager of his magical order. And it was Baroness Cremers who told Crowley the story of the identity of Jack the Ripper.

In the 1880s, one of the best-known followers of Madame Blavatsky, the founder of the Theosophical Society, was a Titian-haired, beautiful woman named Mabel Collins, the author of a theosophical classic called *Light on the Path*. Disillusioned by an unsatisfying marriage, Mabel Collins entered into an intimate relationship with Vittoria Cremers, who was then in her late twenties. But Mabel, according to Crowley, 'had divided her favours with a very strange man whose career had been extraordinary. He had been an officer in a cavalry regiment, a doctor, and I know not how many other things in his time. He was now in desperate poverty and depended entirely on Mabel Collins for his daily bread. This man claimed to be an advanced Magician, boasting of many mysterious powers and even occasionally demonstrating the same.

'At this time London was agog with the exploits of Jack the Ripper. One theory of the motive of the murderer was that he was performing an Operation to obtain the Supreme Black Magical Power. The seven women had to be killed so that their seven bodies formed a 'Calvary cross of seven points' with its head to the west. The theory was that after killing the third or the fourth, I forget which, the murderer acquired the power of invisibility, and this was confirmed by the fact that in one case a policeman heard the shrieks of the dying woman and reached her before life was extinct, yet she lay in a *cul-de-sac*, with no possible exit save to the street; and the policeman saw no sign of the assassin, though he was patrolling outside, expressly on the look-out.'

The mysterious magician apparently took a great interest in the murders, and told the ladies that the murderer ate parts of his victims at the scene of the crime, then concealed traces of bloodstains on his shirt by turning up the collar of his light overcoat.

A day came when Mabel Collins wanted to rid herself of her lover; but he was holding some compromising letters she had written. The baroness offered to steal them, and slipped into his bedroom when he was out. She then took a tin uniform case from under his bed, and untied the ropes that held it shut. It proved to contain no letters: nothing but 'seven white evening ties, all stiff and black with clotted blood'.

It all sounds silly enough. To begin with, it is unlikely that the Ripper claimed seven victims. Emma Smith, who was killed in the early hours of Easter Monday (3 April), and who is often described as the Ripper's first victim, survived until the next day, when she died of peritonitis. She told police she had been attacked and robbed by four men, and there seems to be no reason to disbelieve her. So even if we accept the murder of Martha Turner, on Bank Holiday night, as the first of the Ripper murders, the total comes to six, not seven.

There was no victim killed in a cul-de-sac – Crowley is presumably thinking of the murder of Catherine Eddowes in Mitre Square. But there were three exits from the square, and the blood in the communal sink in Dorset Street reveals that the Ripper probably left by the northern one. Invisibility was unnecessary. As to the notion of the Ripper eating parts of the bodies at the scene of the crime, we know this to be nonsense. In only two cases – Annie Chapman and Catherine Eddowes – were organs taken away, and in the second the letter-writer who signed himself Jack the Ripper claimed to have fried and eaten most of the kidney.

The article in *True Detective*, 'Was Jack the Ripper a Black Magician?' was by the crime writer Leonard Gribble, and the theory was apparently passed on to him by a friend who dabbled in 'occultism'. It sounds as if the occultist has mixed up Crowley's magician theory with the 'Dr Stanley' theory put forward by Leonard Matters in 1929; he states that Jack the Ripper was a doctor who committed the murders to revenge himself for the death of his son, who had died 'a raving idiot' after contracting VD from a prostitute.

To protect himself against discovery, the doctor employed a black magic ritual which involved using his victims as 'sacrifices'. The mutilations 'followed a precise sacrificial pattern', and the number of organs removed from the victims 'increased progressively by stages'. These organs were finally used to construct a 'power pentagram'.

'I asked,' says Mr Gribble, 'if the name of this vicious dabbler in the occult and black arts had been divulged. The reply I received left me still groping. I was told: Jack the Ripper's real identity was known to Aleister Crowley, but he wouldn't divulge it . . . He claimed he could not challenge the power of the pentagram.'

Gribble's informant was obviously pulling his leg. We know that the number of organs removed from the victims did not increase progressively. But Gribble's informant was mistaken on a more important point. Crowley *did* reveal the name of his suspect. He revealed it in article on the Ripper, written apparently for his magical journal *The Equinox*, and finally published in the Crowleyan magazine *Sothis* (vol. 1, no. 4) in 1975. The article tells his curious tale about Baroness Cremers and Mabel Collins at much greater length, and gives the name of the suspect as Captain Donstan. And Crowley goes on to say that he has discussed this matter with Bernard O'Donnell, the *'crime expert of the Empire News.'* and O'Donnell proceeded to investigate the matter.

Crowley may be taking more credit than he deserves in implying that he started O'Donnell on his investigations. When Richard Whittington-Egan tracked down O'Donnell's unpublished manuscript, he learned that it was a literary and dramatic critic named Hayter Preston who had suggested that O'Donnell should turn his attention to Jack the Ripper – this was in the year 1930 – and told him: 'I can put you on to a woman who knows the whole story – at first hand too.' This woman was Baroness Vittoria Cremers, who was then in her late sixties. The baroness was living at 34 Marius Road, Balham, and O'Donnell found her 'a rather diminutive figure with short-cropped grey hair and a pair of dark, quizzical eyes'. (Crowley's account of her is less flattering – but then he claims she swindled him out of a great deal of money.)

The result of O'Donnell's investigations was a book called *Black Magic and Jack the Ripper, or This Man was Jack the Ripper*, which ran to 372 pages in manuscript. From the account given by Whittington-Egan, it undoubtedly deserves to be published.

In 1886, when living in America, Vittoria Cremers had picked up a copy of Mabel Collins' *Light on the Path*, and been much impressed. At this time, Vittoria was married to Baron Louis Cremers, of the Russian Embassy in Washington. Presumably it was a marriage of convenience, for the baroness later assured Crowley she was still a virgin. As a result of the book, she joined the American branch of the Theosophical Society.

In 1888, now a widow, she came to London, and called on Madame Blavatsky, who was living in Holland Park. Madame Blavatsky gave her the job of business manager of the theosophical magazine *Lucifer*. Its associate editor was the lovely Mabel Collins, a tall, slim woman with an oval face, now thirty-seven years of age. The baroness was ten years her senior. The two soon became close friends.

In December 1888, the baroness found Madame Blavatsky and two more theosophists studying an article in the *Pall Mall Gazette*, which suggested that the Ripper might be a black magician. It was by the Earl of Crawford, an eminent student of occult matters, and he quotes the French 'magician' Eliphaz Levi, author of *Dogma and Ritual of High Magic* (translated into English as *Transcendental Magic*), 'who gives the fullest and clearest details of the necessary steps for [magical] evocation . . .', steps which involve candles made of human fat and a preparation made from a certain portion of the body of a harlot. The earl points out that, excluding the last murder (which was committed indoors) the sites of the murders form a perfect cross. And he points out that Levi's book on magic has sold thousands of copies, and that it had been recently translated into English. . .

It should be explained that the 1870s and 80s had seen a widespread 'magical revival' in Europe, and that this was, to a large extent, a result of the impact of 'spiritualism'. Since the 1840s, when certain 'poltergeist effects' in a house in Hydesville, New York, had caused a sensation throughout America, and made celebrities of two teenage sisters named Fox, persons known as 'mediums' had found that they could cause astonishing effects by sitting in a darkened room and invoking spirits. Madame Blavatsky began her career as a medium. Now 'magicians' of the past – men like Paracelsus and Cornelius Agrippa – had also been invokers of spirits, and were firmly convinced that magic could only be accomplished through the agency of spirits. The common-sense view is that this is pure self-delusion or wishful thinking. But no one who has studied the matter with an open mind can accept this convenient assumption. Strange things *did* happen at seances, and still do. Some students of the paranormal believe that such things are a manifestation of the unconscious mind – what Jung called 'exteriorization phenomena' – but most people who have considered the evidence arrive reluctantly at the conclusion that the hypothesis of 'spirits' cannot be excluded.

Crowley, like Levi, undoubtedly believed that when he performed a 'magical ritual', he was invoking 'spirits'. So did all the other major 'occultists' of the period. And Levi says in the necromancy chapter of *Transcendental Magic*: 'The end of procedure in Black Magic was to disturb reason and produce the feverish excitement which emboldens to great crimes . . . Sacrilege, murder, theft, are indicated or hinted at as means to realization in all these works . . .' So the Earl of Crawford's theory that the Ripper may have been engaged in black magic was, at least, an intelligent supposition. But a glance at a map of the Whitechapel area* will show that there is no justification for his assertion that the sites of the murders form a perfect cross; nor is

---

* See end of this chapter.

it likely that the Ripper selected the sites for the murders with the aid of a map, then lured the victims to the exact spot.

A year after the Earl of Crawford's article appeared in the *Pall Mall Gazette*, Vittoria Cremers went back to America; she returned in March 1890, and learned that Mabel Collins had moved to Southsea. She went to visit her, and was surprised by the shabbiness of her lodgings. Mabel was living with a man – a certain Captain D'Onston – although he was out at the time. She told the baroness how this had come about. In the early part of 1889, two articles had appeared in the *Pall Mall Gazette* about Rider Haggard's immensely popular novel *She*. The writer of the first – who signed himself simply 'R.D.', claimed that he had known the 'original' of Haggard's heroine, a mysterious white woman actually called Ayesha, as in Haggard's novel. A second article, signed 'Roslyn D'Onston', described how the author had confronted a female witch doctor named Sube, and vanquished her by means of a talisman given to him by the novelist Bulwer Lytton (who was also a student of occultism and a friend of Eliphaz Levi). In this article, D'Onston made it clear that he believed in the reality of magical powers, and hinted that he himself was an adept. Mabel Collins had written to him, and received a reply saying that he was in hospital, but would contact her when he came out. In fact, he did so, and she promptly became infatuated. She assured the baroness that D'Onston was 'a great magician who has wonderful magical secrets'.

At this point, D'Onston returned home. The baroness describes him as a 'tall, fair haired man of unassuming appearance, a man at whom one would not look twice'. He had a military bearing and a sallow complexion, and gave the impression of being 'one who would remain calm in any crisis'. His eyes were pale blue, and she described them as lacking any sparkle or vestige of life, 'the eyes one might expect to find set in the face of a patient in the anaemic ward of any hospital'. His clothes were old and worn, yet spotlessly clean.

D'Onston was also, apparently, an expert on the subject of cosmetics, and the three of them decided to go into business together. They moved to Baker Street, and formed the Pompadour Cosmetique Company. D'Onston, apparently, contributed nothing to the business, being without resources.

Mabel also told the baroness the story of D'Onston's previous great love affair. He had come of a wealthy yeoman family, and it was understood that he would marry the daughter of a well-to-do local family. He joined the army and was commissioned. On a jaunt with brother officers he met a 'woman of the streets' named Ada; he visited her regularly, fell in love with her, and decided to marry her. His father promptly cut off his allowance. When D'Onston lost a great deal of money at the gambling table one evening, he was forced to appeal to his father, who agreed to settle the debt only on condition that D'Onston married the local heiress. D'Onston and Ada parted, promising that, whatever happened, they would meet in one year's time on the spot where they had first met – the middle of Westminster Bridge. But Ada committed suicide the same evening. One year later, D'Onston kept his appointment on the bridge, and as he looked down at the water, and the midnight chimes of Big Ben died away, he heard the click of heels coming towards him. He could see no one, but knew that Ada had come to keep her appointment . . .

D'Onston himself told many stories: he had been a prospector in the California gold rush, had fought under Garibaldi, and been connected with the African slave trade. He also let it drop that he had been married, and the baroness was left with the suspicion that he had murdered his wife.

D'Onston occasionally wrote articles under the odd pseudonym 'Tautriadelta'. He explained to the baroness that it was derived from the Hebrew *tau*, a letter that used to be in the form of a cross, and from the Greek *tria*, three, and the Greek delta, whose capital letter is written as a triangle. So the name signified 'Cross three triangles'. However, he declined to explain himself any further.

It was soon after this that Mabel Collins told the baroness that she suspected D'Onston of being Jack the Ripper. She declined to explain why, but said that it was because of 'something he showed me'.

Crowley's story of how the baroness went into D'Onston's room – after luring him away by telegram – is (predictably) an exaggerated version of what actually happened. She merely entered his room when he was not there and used a key to open his tin box. In it she found a few books, and some old fashioned black ties (not white, as Crowley stated) with ready-made knots. At the backs of the ties – and of the knots – there was some stain that made them stiff.

But what finally convinced the baroness that D'Onston was Jack the Ripper was a conversation she had with him when London newspapers were speculating that Jack the Ripper was back on the streets. (This was probably after a prostitute named Frances Coles had been found stabbed to death in February 1891.) D'Onston told the baroness authoritatively that there would be no more Ripper murders, then added: 'Did I ever tell you that I knew Jack the Ripper?' He had met him, he explained, when he was in hospital, at the time when Mabel first wrote to him. 'He was one of the surgeons, and when he learned I had also been a doctor, he became very chummy. Naturally, we talked about the murders . . . One night he opened up and confessed that he was Jack the Ripper.' The doctor had explained that the Ripper had killed his victims from behind, cutting their throats, and this explained why his clothing was never bloodstained. When he took away the missing organs, he 'tucked them into the space between his shirt and tie'. D'Onston added: 'And he told me that he always selected the spot where he intended to murder the woman for a very special reason. A reason which you would not understand.' D'Onston was obviously hinting at the black magic theory.

This, then, is the case against Roslyn D'Onston. It seems to depend largely on the word of Vittoria Cremers –

for although Crowley told O'Donnell that he had known D'Onston, and that D'Onston had actually given him the ties, the Crowley story seems to be basically merely a repetition of the baroness's.

Apart from the rather absurd story about the ties, there seems to be nothing to link D'Onston with Jack the Ripper. And the ties story is obviously valueless as evidence. To begin with, we know that the Ripper did not eat parts of the victims at the scene of the crime – he would not have had time, even if he had the hardihood to try and chew and swallow uncooked flesh. And the idea that he concealed Annie Chapman's uterus or Catherine Eddowes' kidney by pushing it between his shirtfront and tie is equally absurd – it would stain the shirtfront, and drip blood down his chest. D'Onston was either a mythomaniac, or had a peculiar sense of humour.

But O'Donnell was intrigued by the baroness's story, and felt that it was worth following up. He tracked down the various articles written by D'Onston, including one on African magic, published in the magazine of the Theosophical Society *Lucifer* and signed 'Tautriadelta'. This contained the observation that 'the necromancer must outrage and degrade human nature in every way possible. The very least of the crimes necessary for him (or her) to commit, to attain the powers sought, is actual murder . . .' But then, D'Onston is writing about African magic, so the comment may be less significant than it seems.

O'Donnell also tracked down an article signed Tautriadelta in W.T. Stead's spiritualist magazine *The Borderland*. It was introduced by Stead himself, who declared: 'The writer of the following extraordinary fragment of autobiography has been known to me for many years.' (Stead had been editor of the *Pall Mall Gazette*.) 'He is one of the most remarkable persons I have ever met. For more than a year I was under the impression that he was the veritable Jack the Ripper; an impression which, I believe, was actually shared by the police, who at least once had him under arrest, although, as he completely satisfied them, they liberated him without bringing him to court.' D'Onston had apparently told the baroness that he had been taken in for questioning by the police on two occasions – but then, so had thousands of others. It sounds as if he had wanted to give Stead the impression that he might be Jack the Ripper . . .

In the autobiographical article that followed, D'Onston claimed to have been interested in 'occult science' since he was fourteen, and had been initiated into the Hermetic Lodge of Alexandria by Bulwer Lytton himself. He was, he claimed, a medical student at the time. At the age of eighteen, D'Onston had studied chemistry at the University of Giessen under Dr Allen Liebig, and, together with a student named Karl Hoffman, had carried out 'successful experiments in connection with the Doppelgänger phenomenon'. The Doppelgänger is also known as the 'astral double', and in a well-known case of 1881, a student named Beard had decided to try 'projecting' himself to the house of his fiancee, Miss L.S. Verity. Miss Verity and her young sister had seen Beard in the room before he suddenly disappeared. D'Onston's experiments, according to his article, must have been successful, for he claims that 'I became obsessed by the idea that the revelation of the Doppelgänger phenomena would make me an instrument of the Gods; henceforth, on occasion, I would destroy to save; I would become as Hermes, son of God . . .'

When O'Donnell eventually tracked down D'Onston's only full-length book, *The Patristic Gospels*, published in 1904, he was surprised to find that it was a religious work, and that D'Onston claimed to have completed it 'with the undeniable guidance of the Holy Spirit'. It is a critical analysis of the four gospels. Crowley told O'Donnell that D'Onston died in 1912.

The Patristic Gospels would certainly seem to rule out D'Onston as a possible candidate for Jack the Ripper. It is possible to believe that the Ripper was a black magician, but quite impossible to imagine a man who had committed the Whitechapel murders finally writing a large book on the gospels 'with the undeniable guidance of the Holy Spirit'.

In fact, a closer look at the mysterious Captain D'Onston makes it clear that he was not Jack the Ripper, and never pretended to be. Yet he was, oddly enough, telling Baroness Cremers the truth when he said he thought he had been acquainted with Jack the Ripper. The authors have in their possession a photostat of a document from the Home Office files that proves this beyond all doubt. It is a letter written to Scotland Yard by D'Onston on 26 December 1888, and signed Roslyn D'O Stephenson – his real surname. And according to this letter – or statement – D'Onston was convinced that Jack the Ripper was a doctor called Morgan Davies, who was a house surgeon at the London Hospital, and who lived at 9 King Street, Finsbury Square. And if D'Onston is telling the truth, it seems he could very well be right.

The story behind this letter is told by Richard Whittington-Egan in *A Casebook on Jack the Ripper* (a book to which we are heavily indebted for this account of D'Onston). On 24 December 1888 – six weeks after the last Ripper murder – an ironmongery salesman named George Marsh, from Camden Town, went to Scotland Yard and told them that he suspected a man called Stephenson of being Jack the Ripper. He had met Stephenson in a pub in St Martin's Lane – the Prince Albert – and Stephenson had confided to him that he believed he knew the identity of the murderer: a certain Dr Morgan Davies. But Marsh was convinced, from Stephenson's manner, that he himself was Jack the Ripper. Stephenson had asked Marsh to go and see Dr Davies, and drew up an agreement to share any reward for the conviction of Dr Davies as Jack the Ripper. Marsh tried getting Stephenson drunk, hoping to obtain a more detailed confession, but did not succeed.

We do not know whether the police were interested in Marsh's story. But we do know that, two days later, D'Onston Stephenson called at Scotland Yard, either taking with him a five-page document, or writing it out

when he was there. In his signed statement, headed 'In Re –
The Whitechapel Murders', D'Onston recorded, 'I beg to
draw your attention to the attitude of Dr Morgan Davies of –
Street, Houndsditch, E with respect to these murders.' He
explained how he had been a patient in a private ward at the
London Hospital suffering from typhoid and was visited
almost nightly by Dr Davies, a physician who worked at the
hospital. Their topic of conversation was, of course, the
Ripper murders. D'Onston's statement went on:

Dr Davies always insisted on the fact that the murderer was a man of sexual powers almost effete, which
could only be brought into action by some strong
stimulus – such as sodomy. He was very positive on
this point, that the murderer performed on the
women from behind – in fact, *per ano*. At that time he
could have had no information, any more than myself
about the fact that the post-mortem examination
revealed that semen was found up the woman's rectum, mixed with her faeces. Many things, which
would seem trivial in writing, seemed to me to connect him with the affair – for instance – he is himself a
woman-hater although a man of powerful frame, and,
(according to the lines on his sallow face) of strong
sexual passions. He is *supposed*, however, by his intimates never to touch a woman.

One night when five medicos were present,
quietly discussing the subject, and combatting his
argument that the murderer did not do these things to
obtain specimens of uteri (wombs) but that in his case
it was the lust of murder developed from sexual lust –
a thing not unknown to medicos, he acted (in a way
which *fairly terrified* those five doctors) – the whole
scene – he took a knife, 'buggered' an imaginary
woman, cut the throat from behind: then, when she
was apparently laid prostrate, ripped and slashed her
in all directions in a perfect state of frenzy. *Previously*
to this performance, I had said: 'After a man had

275

done a thing like this, reaction would take place, and he would collapse and be taken at once by the police, or would attract the attention of the bystanders by his exhausted condition.' Dr D said 'No! he would recover himself when the fit was over and be as calm as a lamb. I will show you!' Then he began his performance. At the end of it he stopped, buttoned up his coat, put on his hat and walked down the room with the most perfect calmness. Certainly, his face was as pale as death, but that was all.

It was only a few days ago, after I was *positively* informed by the Editor of the 'Pall Mall Gazette' that the murdered woman *last* operated on had been sodomized – that I thought – 'How did *he* know?' His acting was the most vivid I ever saw. Henry Irving was a fool to it. Another point. He argued that the murderer did not want specimens of uteri, but grasped them, and slashed them off in his madness as being *the only hard* substances which met his grasp, when his hands were madly plunging into the abdomen of his victim.

I may say that Dr Davies was for some time House Physician at the London Hospital, Whitechapel; that he has lately taken this house in Castle St., Houndsditch; that he has lived in the locality of the murders for some years; and that he professes his intention of going to Australia shortly should he not quickly make a success in his new house.

Roslyn D'O Stephenson

P.S. I have mentioned this matter to a pseudo-detective named George Marsh of 24 Pratt St., Camden Town, NW with whom I have made an agreement (enclosed herewith), to share any reward which he may derive from my information.

Roslyn D'O Stephenson

P.P.S. I can be found at any time through Mr Iles of the 'Prince Albert', St Martin's Lane – in a few minutes – I live close to; but do not desire to give my address.

Roslyn D'O Stephenson

The agreement which he made with Marsh and to which he was not so reticent about adding his address was worded: '24 Dec 88 – I hereby agree to pay to Dr R D'O Stephenson (also known as "Sudden Death") one half of any or all rewards or monies received by me on a/c of the conviction of Dr Davies for wilful murder. (Signed) Roslyn D'O Stephenson MD, 29 Castle St, WC, St Martin's Lane.'

The reader will recall that the editor of the *Pall Mall Gazette* at the time was W.T. Stead who knew D'Onston and had accepted one of his articles for publication in *Borderland*, a spiritualist magazine. The article appeared under the pen name of Tautriadelta and was introduced by Stead who wrote that the author 'is one of the most remarkable persons I have ever met. For more than a year I was under the impression that he was the veritable Jack the Ripper; an impression which, I believe, was shared by the police who at least once had him under arrest . . .'

D'Onston was never arrested. As Constable Robert Spicer discovered, police inspectors paid considerable courtesy to doctors. After D'Onston's visit to the Yard, Inspector J. Roots wrote a short report on the affair.

With reference to the statement of Mr George Marsh, of 24th inst., regarding the probable association of Dr Davies and Stephenson with the murders in Whitechapel. I beg to report that Dr Stephenson came here this evening and wrote the attached statement of his suspicions of Dr Morgan Davies, Castle St., Houndsditch; and also left with me his agreement with Marsh as to the reward. I attach it.

When Marsh came here on 24th I was under the impression that Stephenson was a man I had known 20 years. I now find that impression was correct. He is a travelled man of education and ability, a doctor of medicine upon diplomas in Paris and New York; a major from the Italian Army – he fought under Garibaldi; and a newspaper writer. He says that he wrote the article about Jews in the Pall Mall Gazette, that he occasionally writes for that paper, and that he offered his services to Mr Stead to track the murderer. He showed me a letter from Mr Stead, dated Nov 30, 1888 about this and said that the result was the proprietor declined to engage upon it. He has led a Bohemian life, drinks very heavily and always carries drugs to sober him and stave off delirium tremens.

He was an applicant for the Orphanage Secretaryship at the last election.

Apart from his drinking habits, Inspector Roots clearly had a high regard for D'Onston. It appears that no further action was taken either against D'Onston or the man against whom he made accusations – Dr Morgan Davies. The *Medical Directory* for 1888 listed Dr Davies, then living at 9 King Street, Finsbury Square, EC, as, 'London Hospital late house physician and house surgeon. Res. Acc. London Hospital'.

Marsh referred to D'Onston as 'a regular soaker' who could 'drink from eight o'clock in the morning until closing time but keep a clear head'. Possibly he was drunk when he wrote the agreement regarding his suspicions of Dr Davies for he appears to be promising to pay himself in the event of being proved right. As Stephen Knight pointed out in his *Jack the Ripper: The Final Solution* (1976), D'Onston's statements were strewn with clues pointing suspicion at himself – he called himself 'Sudden Death' and referred to his suspect as 'Dr D', an abbreviation that also fitted himself, and the addresses he gave for Dr Davies and himself were in streets of the same name. Such self-advertisement pre-dated Dr Neill Cream's more effective use of the ploy although D'Onston's description of Dr Davies's behaviour might have been perfectly accurate but taken too seriously. No doubt doctors of the day spent a great deal of their time discussing theories on Jack the Ripper and debating his *modus operandi*. It was odd though that Davies was not investigated by the police.

And this, unfortunately, is all that O'Donnell was able to discover about D'Onston. Does it really amount to evidence that he may have been Jack the Ripper? Obviously not. It is quite clear that D'Onston believed that Morgan Davies was Jack the Ripper, and this is the story he told to George Marsh and to Baroness Cremers. It may have pleased a certain innate exhibitionism to be suspected of being the Ripper, and to be known as 'Sudden Death', just as it pleased him to be known as a black magician and a slave trader. But the notion that he was Jack the Ripper obviously arose – as in the case of George Marsh – from a misunderstanding.

Richard Whittington-Egan was slightly more successful in learning about Captain D'Onston, although he apparently came by the information so late that he was forced to relegate it to a footnote in his book. What he discovered was that D'Onston was born on 20 April 1841 at 35 Charles Street, Sculcoates, in the East Riding of Yorkshire, son of Richard Stephenson, a seed crusher – that is, a man working in a mill where seeds are crushed for oil. His real name was Robert Donston Stephenson. The address was 'a humble one', so Stephenson's father was not a member of the gentry, as Stephenson told Mabel Collins – which in turn means that the story about marrying a local heiress was also an invention. In short, Stephenson was a mixture of Walter Mitty and confidence man, and it is probable that most of the biographical details he gives in the *Borderland* article are pure invention – the initiation by Lord Lytton, the years at a German university, the service as a doctor in Garibaldi's army, and probably the medical degree. Dr Roslyn D'Onston was ordinary Robert Donston Stephenson, son of a mill worker. The army commission was probably genuine – since he looked like a soldier – but it seems likely that he rose from the ranks. Otherwise, it appears probable that Stephenson was just an unsuccessful fantasist.

And what of his suspicion that Dr Morgan Davies was Jack the Ripper? It is clear that Stephenson was totally convinced. But the doctor's gruesome pantomime proves nothing – many doctors enjoy producing an effect by talking casually about violence and sudden death. It is obvious that Davies did *not* tell D'Onston he was Jack the Ripper. The only corroborative evidence is the comment about sodomy. Was Mary Kelly sodomized? We do not know, for the inquest was adjourned after a few hours, and the coroner said that Dr George Bagster Phillips would not go into medical details at this stage, and that these could be given at a later date. The main account we possess of the mutilations to Mary Kelly is taken from the *Illustrated Police News*. Yet even if Dr Phillips' notes on the case still exist, and reveal that Mary Kelly was sodomized, this would still not prove Dr Morgan Davies to be Jack the Ripper. D'Onston was in hospital in early December, a month after the Mary Kelly murder; he could easily have learned about the sodomy from Bagster Phillips, or from some old acquaintance at the London Hospital.

In his autobiography *Inquest*, the Central London coroner S. Ingleby Oddie mentions his friend Arthur Diosy, a journalist, criminologist and student of the occult, who formed a dining club for criminologists. Diosy, says Oddie, was convinced that there was a black magic element in the murders, and thought that the oddly ritualistic manner in which the belongings of Annie Chapman were arranged around her body was proof of it – he thought they had been arranged in the form of a pentagram, a five-pointed star. Diosy thought that the murderer may have been searching for the elixir of life, 'one of the ingredients of which must come from a recently killed woman'. Scotland Yard, apparently, was unconvinced by his theories.

But Whittington-Egan feels that Bernard O'Donnell scored one minor triumph in his investigations – in deciphering the true significance of D'Onston's pseudonym Tautriadelta. The pentagram consists of three overlapping triangles:

280

'And if you draw straight lines between the five loci of the five Jack the Ripper murders, you will . . . construct a pentagram.'

But anyone who looks at the map of Whitechapel showing the murder sites will agree that a man who could connect the dots labelled 2, 3, 4, 5 and 6 to create a pentagram must have an oddly lopsided notion of geometry. And so one more fascinating theory must be abandoned in the face of a cool scrutiny of the evidence.

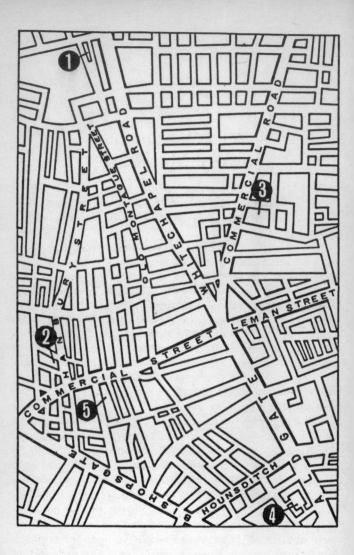

The Whitechapel District
The numbers indicate the sites of the murders.

CHAPTER EIGHT
Jack of all Trades

The uproar created by the Whitechapel murders put great pressure on the police at the time to lay their hands on the perpetrator. A succession of suspects ran the gauntlet of suspicion and most were completely exonerated for one reason or another. Some had stout defences, including in at least two cases the strongest alibi of all which was to be languishing in police custody at the time another murder was committed.

The police were kept busy enough following legitimate lines of investigation not to mention chasing after the whims and fancies with which they were bombarded by the public. Sir Charles Warren's biographer noted that Scotland Yard was said to have received 1,200 letters a day offering various suggestions. In the passionate atmosphere evoked in the East End by the horror of the murders, suspicion most frequently focused on local suspects. These were not the toffs, the princes or international criminals of later years but the jacks of all trades – the fish porters, seamen and butchers of the East End itself.

In the wake of Mary Nichols' murder on 31 August

1888, the police spent a considerable amount of their energies looking for a character called 'Leather Apron'. *The Star* in its edition of 5 September referred to this man who 'has ranged Whitechapel for a long time' and who was reported to influence the local prostitutes with 'a sway that is based on universal terror'. It was alleged that 'he has kicked, injured, bruised and terrified a hundred of them who are ready to testify to the outrages. He has made a certain threat, his favourite threat, to any number of them and each of the three* dead bodies represents the threat carried out. He carries a razor-like knife and two weeks ago drew it on a woman called "Widow Annie" . . . threatening to "rip" her up.'

The name of this individual was not known but the shared belief among the sisterhood of prostitutes was that he was a Jew. He habitually wore a leather apron – hence his nickname – and if the police were interested in him after the murder in Bucks Row, they intensified their efforts to find him following the killing of Annie Chapman when a leather apron was found in the back yard at 29 Hanbury Street. A hue and cry developed although the police had little to act on except several misleading and confusing reports. Urged on by the newspapers and acting on information received, detectives finally located the elusive 'Leather Apron'. Detective Sergeant William Thicke arrested a Polish Jew named as John Pizer at 22 Mulberry Street on 10 September and told him he was wanted for questioning in connection with the murder of Annie Chapman.

Pizer, a boot-finisher by trade who, like all such workmen, wore a leather apron, also kept several sharp, long-bladed knives at home. He was taken to Leman Street Police Station and great efforts were made to establish a link between him and the character known as 'Leather

---

* The three were Emma Smith, Martha Turner and Mary Nichols who were all counted as victims of the same murderer in this press report.

'Apron' who had been menacing the local populace. The police maintained that when local people talked of 'Leather Apron' they were referring to Pizer. He denied having that nickname and when he was put on an identity parade, several women who claimed to know 'Leather Apron' failed to pick him out.

John Pizer said that he went home on Thursday night, two days before Chapman was killed, where he stayed until the time he was arrested because he realized that false accusations were being made against him. His alibi for the murder night was confirmed by his brother and by other relatives with whom he lodged at Mulberry Street. He also had an alibi for the night Mary Nichols was murdered – by a little after 11 p.m. he was in his bed at the 'Round-house', a lodging house in Holloway Road.

Inspector Abberline himself in his report of the investigation into Nichols' murder referred to 'Leather Apron' who it was alleged had been terrorizing and blackmailing local prostitutes. He reported that, 'On his being interrogated, he was able, however, to give such a satisfactory account of his movements as to prove conclusively that the suspicions were groundless.' Pizer was released on 14 September and was called as a witness at the inquest on Chapman's death. The coroner completely exonerated the man of all the allegations made against him. According to Stephen Knight, the boot-finisher then set about suing the newspapers which had libelled him after he was arrested, and won substantial damages.

The accusations against him were not entirely laid to rest for, several years later, Sir Robert Anderson in his memoirs, *The Lighter Side of My Official Life*, identified Jack the Ripper as a 'Polish Jew', an assertion that he described as a 'definitely ascertained fact'. Donald Rumbelow in his analysis of this allegation pointed out that as Pizer was the only Polish Jew to be arrested, he must be the person against whom Anderson made his charge but lacked the courage to name. Apart from casting a slur on the character of a man freed of any suspicion, Anderson stretched the imagination by the certainty of his identification. If taken at his word he was virtually acknowledging that the police knew the identity of Jack the Ripper yet allowed him to commit three murders without apprehending him.

The hounding of John Pizer clearly showed that the determination of public and police to catch Jack the Ripper had been joined by the press. This powerful combination of forces weighed heavily on local suspects who were frequently harassed by vocal and angry mobs waiting outside police stations. Despite the criticisms levelled at the police, it says a great deal for their discipline that they maintained law and order at times when feelings ran so high. Sir Charles Warren's anxieties about a social backlash directed against the Jews in light of the infamous message on the wall can be respected even if his imagination may be faulted.

'Leather Apron' was a popular villain and, denied the head of John Pizer, the public looked for another candidate. Even before Pizer was released from custody, reports were made to the police concerning the behaviour of Joseph Isenschmid, a pork butcher who lodged at 60 Milford Road, Holloway. On 11 September two doctors practising in the area told the police that they believed the butcher might be connected with the murders in Whitechapel. Inspector John Styles, accompanied by two other officers, called at this address and learned about Isenschmid's movements during the week that he had lodged there. Apparently, he was living apart from his wife who, when interviewed, said she had not seen her husband for two months, adding that, 'he was in the habit of carrying large butcher's knives about with him'.

The matter was handed over to the CID and a watch kept for Isenschmid both at his lodgings and at the address where his wife lived. On 13 September, the pork butcher was detained at Holloway Police Station and, having been certified as a dangerous lunatic, was transferred to the Infirmary at Fairfield Road, Bow. His clothing was examined for bloodstains but none was found. His movements on the nights of the recent murders were investigated. It was ascertained that Isenschmid had failed in business about a year previously and the chief suspicion against him appeared to be his irregular hours. George Tyler who rented him a room at 60 Milford Road gave a detailed catalogue of his lodger's comings and goings to the police. It seemed that he frequently left the house at about 1 a.m. and was absent for several hours at a time.

Detective Sergeant Thicke reported to his superiors that he had made several attempts to pin down Isenschmid's movements but had failed. He also called at the Infirmary at Bow and spoke there to the Medical Superintendent, Dr Mickle. The doctor told him that Isenschmid had said the girls in the Holloway area called him 'Leather Apron'. A possible explanation of the former butcher's early morning excursions was that he went to the market to buy sheeps' heads and other meat products which he dressed prior to selling them to restaurants and coffee houses. This was the man's only means of obtaining a livelihood. The sergeant noted in his report made on 17 September, 'The Superintendent would like for police to give instructions what to do with Isenschmid.'

On 18 September, Inspector Abberline reported on the matter, referring plainly to Isenschmid as a 'lunatic'. It appeared that the pork butcher had been confined in a mental institution before and had a history of violent behaviour. 'Although at present,' he wrote, 'we are unable to procure any evidence to connect him with the murders he appears to be the most likely person that has come under our notice to have committed the crimes . . .' The following day, Detective Sergeant Thicke reported on his enquiries which included an interview with Mrs Isenschmid. She told him that her husband had become depressed after his pork butcher's shop in Holloway failed as a business enterprise and he repeatedly stayed away from home. He later spent ten weeks in Colney Hatch Lunatic Asylum and was discharged at the end of 1887 apparently returned to health. But he quickly returned to his erratic ways, spending time away from home and only visiting the house when his wife was absent in order to pick up some clothes. Mrs Isenschmid said, 'When he left he had two bone knives and his butcher's clothes with him . . . I do not think my husband would injure anyone but me. I think he would kill me if he had the chance.' She added, 'He is known as the mad butcher.'

Events overtook poor Joseph Isenschmid, for while he was detained under observation at the asylum, quietly drifting into insanity, the real Jack the Ripper struck again and enabled the police to close another of their suspect files. The mad pork butcher who for a brief period looked the brightest candidate was not heard of again.

Another local man who came under suspicion more with the benefit of hindsight than because of the strength of contemporary evidence was Joseph Barnett. When he had work he was a porter at Billingsgate but his real significance lay in being Mary Kelly's common-law husband. He was also the man named as Jack the Ripper in an article by Bruce Paley which appeared in *True Crime* magazine in April 1982. Barnett was known to have quarrelled with Kelly and during their final row at 13 Miller's Court on 30 October 1888, blows were exchanged and a window was broken.

Barnett was regarded by those who knew him as an honest, straightforward man who fought a losing battle to steer Mary Kelly away from drink and prostitution. According to neighbours, Kelly kept off the streets when her companion was in work and their arguments usually arose when she was drunk or he was jobless. In the statement he made to the police at the time of Kelly's murder, Barnett said he had been living with her at Miller's Court for eighteen months. For a period of three to four months prior to her death he had been unemployed and their relationship had been rocky. Matters came to a head at the end of October when Barnett left her 'in consequence of not earning sufficient money to give her and her resorting to prostitution', as he put it at the time.

Julia Venturney, a widow who lived at 1 Miller's Court and who knew Mary Kelly and Joe Barnett, spoke kindly of the man Kelly liked to call 'my husband'. 'I have heard him say that he did not like her going out on the streets,' she told the police. 'He frequently gave her money. He was very kind to her. He said he would not live with her while she led that course of life.' The police found Barnett helpful and he readily answered their questions, furnishing them with the information that the key to the locked door at 13 Miller's Court had been missing for some time. He explained that he and Mary gained entry to the room by pushing back the inside door bolt through a broken window. As Don Rumbelow noted, this did not entirely explain the mystery of the locked door, for someone had access to the key and used it on the day of the murder, thereby necessitating the door to be broken open by the police. Nevertheless, Barnett seemed to be an obliging fellow and provided numerous details about Mary Kelly's background.

In his statement to the police Barnett said of Kelly, 'I was friendly with her and called to see her between seven and eight p.m. Thursday (8th) and told her I was very sorry not to give her any money. I left her about 8 o'clock same evening and that was the last time I saw her alive.' He mentioned also that, 'There was a woman in the room when I called.' This was probably a reference to Maria Harvey, a fellow prostitute whom Kelly had invited to share her accommodation. Her presence was a powerful factor in the argument which led to Barnett's departure to lodgings at 24–25 New Street, Spitalfields, on 30 October. From a purely practical point of view it was plain that Kelly's room, which measured a mere twelve feet square, could not accommodate three persons. Moreover, the suspicion that Kelly and Harvey were lesbians would have put Barnett out of court.

The possibility that Kelly was a lesbian is discussed in Chapter 4, but there were other factors too which may have soured her relationship with Barnett. For one thing, she was pregnant, a fact discovered after her death but the effects of which she was probably experiencing as the autumn of 1888 slid into winter. The economic consequences of that condition would not have been welcome news at 13 Miller's Court. Added to this was pressure from the landlord to pay up the outstanding rent money and pressure of a different kind from Barnett himself. It is generally acknowledged that he tried to dissuade Kelly from the dissolute life that she was leading and there were indications that she resented his attempts at moral reform. After all, he was frequently unemployed and consequently unable to support her, yet he insisted she kept off the street which was the only way she knew of paying the rent which, by November 1888, was thirty-five shillings in arrears.

Perhaps the moral dilemma proved too much for Kelly and she turned against Barnett, telling Julia Venturney that 'she could not bear the man . . . although he was very good to her'. Mary Kelly at the age of twenty-five with not so distant memories of a different and better life saw yawning before her a path of drink and debilitation which was far from inviting. She talked to an acquaintance about committing suicide and advised a young friend, 'Whatever you do, don't go wrong and turn out as I have.' She said she was sick of the life she was leading and wanted to return to Ireland. It appeared too that there was another man in her life, Joseph Fleming, whom she had known before meeting Barnett. She told Julia Venturney that she was fond of this man although he 'often ill used her because she cohabited with Joe (Barnett)'. This suggests continued liaison after she and Barnett began living together and either man could have been the cause of her pregnancy.

To add to her trials it is suggested that Kelly's landlord was pressing her for rent money and urged her to take in a friend who would be better able than Barnett to contribute to the rent. This was the point at which Maria Harvey turned up at 13 Miller's Court and her presence may have been welcomed by Kelly for various reasons – there was the prospect of earning some rent money, Barnett's overbearing demands could be decisively rejected and the two women could be lovers if they wished. No matter what the reason, Harvey's presence precipitated the famous quarrel on 30 October and Barnett had no alternative but to leave. While he subsequently told the police that his reason for leaving was because he was unable to support Kelly, he changed this at the inquest when he told the coroner it was 'Because she had a woman of bad character there . . . that was the only reason . . . My being out of work had nothing to do with it.'

From every standpoint Barnett was a figure of rejection and failure. The theory published in *True Crime* magazine is that part of his ploy to frighten Mary Kelly off the path of prostitution was to murder and mutilate a number of her fellow practitioners. The idea came to him when he realized that he was losing control over her and after reading about the murder of Martha Turner on 7 August 1888. He therefore embarked on a series of murders, selecting as victims older, enfeebled women who would offer least resistance to attack and whose brutal murder would surely bring Kelly to her senses.

Thus began the Jack the Ripper murders and there seemed to be some evidence to suggest that Barnett's ruse was working. Mary Kelly was reported as fearing that she might fall to the Ripper's knife as she saw her colleagues in Whitechapel and Spitalfields, some of whom she probably knew, being butchered in the streets and alleyways. She had apparently been a regular at the Britannia public house in Fish Street Hill but stopped drinking there after the double murder of 30 September. Barnett said that Kelly was keen to read the newspaper reports of the murders and used to ask him 'whether the murderer was caught'.

When Kelly provoked the break with Barnett by inviting Maria Harvey to share her room, he knew his reforming zeal had been defeated and he retired a beaten and humiliated man. Bruce Paley's thesis is that Barnett, who claimed that he last saw Mary Kelly during the evening of 8 November, returned to 13 Miller's Court later that night for a final showdown. Perhaps he started out by seeking reconciliation but, whatever was discussed, violence was the outcome. It is argued that Barnett's mind snapped and he killed Kelly in a fit of maniacal fury.

The article in *True Crime* argued with considerable logic that Joe Barnett fitted many of the requirements to qualify as Jack the Ripper. He would certainly have been a familiar and reassuring figure in the East End environment and it was quite likely that many of the prostitutes in the area would have recognized him as Mary Kelly's 'husband'. He would have had an intimate working knowledge of the ways of the East End and of its geography. Interestingly too, on the occasion of the double murder on 30 September 1888, the killer's trail led northwards to Dorset Street where he washed his bloody hands in a public sink. If Barnett had been the killer, he was simply heading for home and the warmth and safety of Mary Kelly's room at Miller's Court.

The Ripper letters whose author on one occasion referred to being 'down on whores' showed a desire to frighten prostitutes which was certainly in keeping with the theory regarding Barnett's ambitions. It is suggested that the incredible response accorded by the public to the Whitechapel murders fuelled his self-esteem and he delighted in his new-found notoriety. 'If he had been something of a nonentity beforehand, Jack the Ripper had suddenly become the most feared man in the entire country,' suggested *True Crime*. He secretly revelled in the glory that the Ripper attracted, for which he found expression in the gloating and sarcastic phrases contained in the letters.

When questioned by the police to whom he reported voluntarily after the murder of Mary Kelly, Barnett was reported as being in an agitated state. Nevertheless, he successfully countered any suggestion that he was involved in the murder although there is no record of his alibi apart from a claim that he was asleep at his lodgings at the crucial time. The real explanation of the missing key to the door of 13 Miller's Court is given by Bruce Paley as an act of premeditation on Barnett's part. After the quarrel with

Kelly he simply took the key on his departure knowing that he could return to her room at any time which, according to this theory, he did late on the night of 8 November.

Barnett's nomination as the Ripper solves at least one anomaly in the series of murders. The killing of Mary Kelly was out of tune with the preceding murders inasmuch as she was much younger than all the other victims and was done to death indoors whereas they were killed in the street. This would be explained if the earlier victims were selected for their feebleness and killed in order to frighten Kelly off the streets. When the ploy failed and she, the object of devotion, was sent to the sacrifice in an act of passion, she became the odd victim out.

What does not fit easily is the suggestion that Barnett through his work as a porter at the fish market would have thereby acquired a rudimentary anatomical knowledge. But in many other respects he fits the bill. Bruce Paley traced a Joseph Barnett to Stepney where he is recorded as having died in 1926 at the age of sixty-eight and posed the question as to whether he had been a friend of Mary Kelly and her eventual killer as Jack the Ripper. The article pointed out that Barnett, like the Yorkshire Ripper a century later, had been questioned and released by the police and was an ordinary man living in the area where the crimes were committed.

It is tempting to seek to counterbalance the tendency to enfold Jack the Ripper in Masonic plots aimed at protecting royal honour with the simple explanation that he was, like Peter Sutcliffe, the Yorkshire Ripper, an ordinary man with the motive, means and opportunity to commit murder. Yet the simple explanation, while it may be instinctively believable still requires proof to raise it to the realms of real credibility. The present state of knowledge regarding Joseph Barnett does not admit of proof but, as *True Crime* concluded, 'Not all avenues of research have been exhausted.'

The desire to bring Jack the Ripper's crimes home to

their perpetrator or, perhaps, to anyone whose character was black enough to make the charge stick, did not diminish with the years. A clutch of murderers convicted of other crimes became tarred with the Ripper brush. The poisoners, Dr Neill Cream and George Chapman, and the murderous bigamist, Frederick Deeming, were megastars in the hall of villainy on whose shoulders some would have placed the Ripper's mantle.

Again the interests of public, police and press found a common goal in heaping further evils on these dogs with bad names. The public liked its villains to be monsters without compare and the press did its best to satisfy this craving. As far as the police were concerned, apart from carrying out their duty, there was always the possibility of closing the file on their greatest unsolved murder case. Cream and Chapman had their individual claims to fame in the Ripper story and both are dealt with in Chapter 3. Deeming, truly a jack of all trades, proved to be a master of murder, but was he also Jack the Ripper?

Frederick Bayley Deeming, a black-hearted villain who murdered two wives and four of his children, was dubbed by the Australian newspapers 'The Jack the Ripper of the Southern Seas'. This accusation stemmed from a report that while in custody at Perth he had confessed to two of the Ripper murders. After his execution a plaster death mask was sent to Scotland Yard where, according to Don Rumbelow, it was described to visitors as the death mask of Jack the Ripper. A contemporary piece of doggerel also pointed the finger at Deeming:

> On the twenty-third of May,
> Frederick Deeming passed away;
> On the scaffold he did say –
> 'Ta-ra-da-boom-di-ay!'
> 'Ta-ra-da-boom-di-ay!'
> This is a happy day,
> An East End holiday,
> Jack The Ripper's gone away.

Deeming was born in Birkenhead in either 1853 or 1854 and abandoned his parents at the age of fourteen when he ran away to sea. He travelled the world and opted for an elusive life by acquiring several aliases. He was variously known as Druin, George, Dawson, Lawson, Duncan, and Williams to name but a few. It was as Albert O. Williams that he became acquainted with the Australian authorities in March 1892 and the newspapers painted him as a 'desperate ruffian'. He was alleged to have married and murdered in at least three continents and to have committed a variety of frauds and extraordinary acts. Not least of these was the claim that he murdered a Zulu in the South African Cape with a jack-knife and killed thirteen lions in a single day.

While Deeming alias Williams was a black-hearted character there were limits even to his infamy. When he gave up seafaring, he worked as a plumber and gas-fitter and married a Birkenhead girl, Marie James. The couple had four children who, with their unfortunate mother, were destined to become pawns in Deeming's plans for murder. Those plans, carefully-laid, might have earned the stamp of perfection but for the arch-schemer's repetition of a successful *modus operandi*.

In July 1891, Deeming appeared in Rainhill, at the time a town of some two thousand inhabitants, east of Liverpool. He took the lease on a cottage called Dinham Villa, explaining that he was acting on behalf of a Colonel Brooks. He stayed with his family at a hotel while renovation work was carried out at the cottage. Colonel Brooks, he explained, hated uneven floors and it was necessary, therefore, to have the stone floors covered with cement; 'We go in for cementing,' he commented.

The lease was signed on 24 July and, having passed his wife off as his sister, he began to court Emily Mather, a local girl. For the next few days Deeming was kept busy at Dinham Villa and employed some labourers to assist him. Unknowingly they helped him entomb the bodies of his wife and children under the floor where he had concealed them. When the work was completed, he apparently sang and danced a hornpipe. On 22 September 1891, Deeming married Emily Mather at St Anne's Church, Rainhill, and, a few weeks later, they travelled to Australia on board the *Kaiser Wilhelm II* using the name Williams.

Fellow passengers on board the Imperial German Mail Line vessel later recalled some of the antics of Mr Albert Williams. He told tall stories of his adventures in Mexico, the United States, India and the Congo and upset several of the ship's officers. He brought charges of theft against another passenger and usurped the doctor's responsibility by giving advice about heat exhaustion and other health matters. Williams demonstrated a fascination for wearing jewellery and there were those who thought him untrustworthy and a poseur.

On arrival in Melbourne on 15 December 1891, Williams rented a house at 57 Andrew Street in the surburban district of Windsor and moved in with his recently-wedded wife. In March 1892 a woman applied to the landlord of 57 Andrew Street enquiring about the tenancy which she believed was vacant. Indeed it was, and the landlord accompanied her to the house so that she could view the accommodation. The inspection proceeded favourably until the bedroom was entered. The smell pervading this room was so powerfully disagreeable that the woman had to leave and the landlord fumbled for excuses about dead household pests.

The source of the smell seemed to be the fireplace and close examination revealed that the hearthstone had been moved. Where it had once been level with the floor of the room it now stood proud by about an inch. With the help of another man, the landlord prised up the hearthstone and, in so doing, released the full force of the unbearable stench of decomposition. The police were called and the cement under the hearthstone was broken up to reveal a hollowed out grave containing the doubled-up corpse of a woman. The skull had been fractured in three places and the woman's throat was cut.

The last tenant of 57 Andrew Street was a Mr Druin who had disappeared without giving notice. From descriptions given by witnesses who had met Druin and by the discovery in the house of a luggage ticket, the police traced the man they wanted to interview to his arrival in Melbourne on board the *Kaiser Wilhelm II* as Mr Williams. Further information was collated about Druin alias Williams and a description of the wanted man was circulated. By this time, the corpse under the fireplace had been identified as Mrs Williams by a passenger who had met her on the ocean liner.

The newspapers had a field day, describing Williams as a 'bloodthirsty savage' and a 'monster in human form'. It was suggested that he might have killed other women and buried them, and a Melbourne newspaper asked outright if he had killed his first wife. While fireplaces in a number of houses at Sydney were being excavated, the press decided to extend their enquiries to England. Meanwhile, on 11 March 1892, Williams was arrested in Southern Cross and, two days later, detectives called at Dinham Villa in Rainhill. As details of the discovery of Emily Williams's body in Melbourne emerged in the British newspapers, so the police began to take an interest in Dinham Villa's fine cement floor.

The cement was broken up and the original flagstones levered up in a back-breaking operation which eventually uncovered the bodies of a woman and four children. The woman's throat had been cut and the children had been either strangled or slashed across the throat. The discoveries at Rainhill were an overnight sensation and the road leading to Dinham Villa was thronged for weeks with curiosity seekers. Questions about the case were asked in the House of Commons, and at the inquest evidence of identification was given by one Albert Deeming who tearfully declared that the murder victims were the wife and children of his brother, Frederick Bayley Deeming. A crowd of ten thousand people watched the funeral of the Rainhill murder victims and the minister at the graveside firmly denounced Deeming as a monster.

297

While Deeming awaited trial in Melbourne, the newspapers vied with each other for stories of his infamous behaviour. These were mostly prejudicial and the man was publicly condemned long before he stood in the dock. His name, already blackened in countless press reports, was further attacked in abusive letters which the newspapers had no compunction about publishing to their readers. The newspaper circulation figures in Melbourne had never been better.

One of the accusations against Deeming was that in addition to murdering five times in Rainhill and once at Melbourne, he was also Jack the Ripper. He was said to have acknowledged this while detained in the Waterside Lockup at Perth after his arrest. His lawyer, Richard S. Haynes, sought to dismiss this damaging rumour by writing to the leading newspapers. In a letter dated 31 March 1892, he wrote, 'I have seen it published in the eastern colonies that Baron Swanston (another of Deeming's aliases) had confessed to me that he was the perpetrator of the Rainhill and Whitechapel murders . . . this statement is absolutely false and unfounded in every respect . . .'

The interests of justice and of a fair hearing for his client mentioned in Haynes's letter were not concepts which sold newspapers. Scurrilous stories continued to appear about Deeming and, in the minds of the public, Deeming's exploits in Rainhill and Melbourne were regarded as a continuation of the Ripper's activities in Whitechapel. On 8 April 1892, the Melbourne *Evening Standard* carried the headline, JACK THE RIPPER: DEEMING AT ALDGATE ON THE NIGHT OF THE WHITECHAPEL MURDERS. The report which followed originated from a London dressmaker who said that on the night Catherine Eddowes was murdered in Mitre Square, she was in the company of a man called Lawson. On the day following the murder her companion 'evinced an intimate knowledge of the mutilations of the murdered woman'. She was convinced this man was Deeming.

Deeming's early career as a seafaring man now caught up with him, contributing to the general air of malice. There was a report from Halifax, Nova Scotia, that Deeming had received a letter written to him by Catherine Eddowes and from Johannesburg and New York came stories linking his visits to the sinister presence of a Jack the Ripper. An Australian account placed him in Plymouth, Devon, in 1888 and added, 'He left that place suddenly for London and two days later the Jack the Ripper Murders commenced.' Specimens of Deeming's handwriting were compared to those attributed to the Ripper and his motive for committing the Rainhill murders was given as the need to silence his wife, Marie, who had learned his awful secret.

And so it went on in a clear demonstration of the old adage about giving a dog a bad name. A shop which sold cutlery in Melbourne was said to have been paid a visit by Deeming/Williams who wanted some surgical knives cleaned. Suspicious marks on the knives were explained away by Deeming as lemon stains! On examining the implements, the cutler remarked, 'Hullo! These knives have done some work. They seem regular Jack the Rippers.' J.S. O'Sullivan in his book on Deeming, *A Most Unique Ruffian*, commented that in the months leading up to the trial, 'no story was too absurd to be believed if it was to Deeming's discredit'. The Melbourne *Evening Standard* published 'The Old Lady's Dream' in which a woman travelling on board a ship overhead a conversation from an adjoining berth:

Woman's voice:	If you say that again I shall expose you.
Man's voice:	What do you mean?
Woman:	Oh nothing, Jack the Ripper.
Man:	Silence! Go back to sleep.
Woman:	I cannot.
Man:	You will sleep sound enough when you get on shore.

When the old lady caught sight of this mystery man, he proved to be none other than Mr Deeming, of course.

The *Evening Standard* in its edition published two days before Deeming went on trial urged against haste in the proceedings, for although he was undoubtedly guilty of the murder at Windsor, time was needed to gather conclusive proof that he was also Jack the Ripper. Such was the confidence of this accusation that there was even talk of the police officers who had arrested Deeming sharing in the reward money which had been offered for the capture of Jack the Ripper.

Deeming was tried in 1892 at Melbourne on the charge of murdering his wife Emily. He was tried under the name Albert O. Williams and his defence counsel was a young barrister, Alfred Deakin, who later served on three occasions as Australia's Prime Minister. The proceedings were distinguished by contributions from both Deakin and Deeming. Deakin first argued that the body of the woman found buried under the floor at Windsor was not Emily Mather and then sought to show that Deeming was not responsible for his acts on account of insanity. Deeming, on the final day of his trial, obtained the court's permission to address the jury. He spoke for an hour, occasionally referring to notes, and plainly declared that he had not been given a fair trial. In view of the shabby pre-trial publicity he had received, this criticism was more than justified. The initial reasonable tone of Deeming's speech gradually gave way to boastfulness and then to anger. He made accusations against his family and berated the prosecution witnesses. 'The only two countries I have not been in,' he said, 'are New Zealand and Russia, and if I had done this thing do you think I would remain in the colony? I may be a madman,' he added, 'and sometimes beside myself, but I don't think I would do that.'

The jury believed otherwise and returned a guilty verdict after thirty minutes' deliberation. Asked by the judge if he had anything further to say, Deeming embarked on a second piece of oratory and told the court, '. . . though

I may die for this I shall not be dead long before they know my innocence.' He asked the judge to spare him any lengthy speeches, 'I have been here four days, and I have been here since 10 o'clock this morning, and it is time I was released from it,' he said. Sentence of death was passed and Deeming went to the scaffold on 23 May 1892. In a letter to his brother he denied his guilt but in a note of thanks to the prison chaplain, he wrote, 'I did not intend to kill my poor Emily – I can only look upon my execution as a murder – still death will be a relief to me.' A crowd of between ten and twelve thousand people gathered outside the prison during the execution. Perhaps they thought that Jack the Ripper really had been brought to justice.

When Deeming's body was removed from the scaffold, a group of phrenologists and waxworks specialists were allowed to take measurements and make plaster casts of the head. In due course, Deeming's skull and a thigh bone were delivered into the hands of the anatomists when reconstruction work at Melbourne Prison led to the disinterment of a number of executed criminals' remains. In February 1923, Sir William Colin Mackenzie, a noted anatomist, presented a paper to a meeting of the Anthropological Society of New South Wales. His subject was Frederick Bayley Deeming whose skull he said bore a resemblance to the skull of the male gorilla. Serle's *Dictionary of Australian Biography* described Deeming as 'extremely long-armed' with 'other physical characteristics that suggested some affinity with the anthropoid apes'. Poor Deeming, even in death he could not escape opprobrium. Refusal of an application at the time of his execution to turn his brain over for medical examination inspired this little verse, headed 'A Buried Question':

> Was Deeming mad, and could his brain
> Be reckoned rotten?
> What odds if he were sane or mad?
> Unopened let his skull remain
> Whilst all the doctors rage in vain
> Till he's forgotten.

Doubtless there were many who thought Deeming should have his head examined, but beyond showing that his cranial capacity of about 1400 cc was lower than the average for the normal adult male (1500 cc), his anatomical remains produced only controversy.

Deeming was a restless character who travelled widely and was always involved in some incident or other. Even during his sea voyages he usually managed to create a disturbance or draw attention to himself in some way. On his last voyage to England, the ship's captain threatened to put him in irons because of his unacceptable behaviour towards a woman passenger. A considerable amount is known about his activities between the years 1881 and 1887 and a great deal about his movements between July 1891 and his death in May 1892. But the period between 1887 and 1891, crucial to any thesis nominating Deeming as Jack the Ripper, is more sketchy.

It is known for certain that Deeming was arraigned on bankruptcy charges in Australia at the end of 1887. He appeared before Mr Justice McFarland on 15 December and was sentenced to fourteen days' imprisonment at Darlinghurst Gaol. After completing his sentence, Deeming left Sydney with his wife and children and travelled to South Africa, arriving at Cape Town in January 1888. He perpetrated frauds at Klerksdorp and Johannesburg where he posed as a mining engineer. At some stage during the year, he returned to Cape Town from whence he despatched his wife and family to England. Deeming went on to Port Elizabeth where he was reported to be active as late as August 1889 before rejoining his family in Liverpool.

This timing would seem to rule out Deeming as Jack the Ripper and, if a South African detective by the name of Brandt was correct, the Rainhill and Winsdor murderer was active in Johannesburg in September 1888. In the month that Jack the Ripper killed three women in Whitechapel, Deeming was accused of murdering three persons in South Africa: a former British army officer and two natives. Brandt travelled to Melbourne in 1892 when

Deeming was in custody there and accused him of both fraud and murder. This would certainly have distanced Deeming from the events in London during the autumn of 1888.

No doubt the thought of being branded as Jack the Ripper would have appealed to the ego of 'Mad Fred' as Deeming was dubbed by the newspapers. In his account of the murderer's life published in 1948 under the title *The Demon Killer*, Frank Clune wrote that Deeming was asked 'in circumstances when a confession would not have harmed him', if he was Jack the Ripper. The man who had been so verbose at his trial 'remained stubbornly silent. He would neither confirm nor deny the accusation.'

Modern commentators on Jack the Ripper have given little credence to the Deeming link. Neither Dan Farson nor Stephen Knight thought it worthy of mention and Richard Whittington-Egan merely gave it a passing reference. Don Rumbelow, Tom Cullen and Arthur Douglas rated it worth a paragraph and the doggerel verse about Deeming's passing, although the versions disagree over the date of his demise. Douglas ruled out Deeming as the Ripper on the grounds that he 'was otherwise engaged at the relevant time, being in prison in England . . .' This was also the view of L.C. Douthwaite who was adamant in his book *Mass Murder*, published in 1928, that Deeming could not have been the Whitechapel murderer as he was incarcerated at the time the murders were committed.

Donald McCormick thought the Deeming link was 'a preposterous suggestion for which there is not the slightest foundation or any police evidence'. He thought one of the attributable factors was a statement alleged to have been made by Deeming to the effect that he murdered the women because they 'spread a vile infection'. Any reasonable interpretation of the facts suggests that 'Mad Fred's' ambition lay much more with bigamy, fraud and wife murder than with ridding the world of prostitutes.

In 1962 while researching his *Jack the Ripper in Fact and Fiction*, Robin Odell received a number of letters from a gentleman living in Blackpool who claimed that his father was the Whitechapel murderer. This candidate for the Ripper was born in Dundee in 1873 – which would have made him fifteen years old at the time of the murders – and he worked as an apprentice to an engineer's wood pattern maker.

Described by his son as an 'honest, kind and gentle fellow', this teenage Ripper was an apprentice in more ways than one it seems. Apparently, his master, a journeyman tradesman in his early thirties, contracted venereal disease from an East End prostitute and died at the London Hospital in 1889. Revenge against prostitutes who would be 'healthier dead' was the familiar motive. The murder weapon was described as a Swedish lock knife.

Another correspondent, in October 1970, informed Robin Odell that the copy of his book held at Beckenham Public Library in Kent had been annotated by a borrower. On the page containing the foreword by the late Dr Lindesay Neustatter was a note written in red ink which declared, 'Jack the Ripper died at Tooting Beck Hospital, Ward G III.' No further information was offered in this cryptic note signed by 'M A B'.

This is all in much the same vein as an article published in the *Daily Express* on 1 April 1985 with the headline 'Pub Skeleton could be Jack the Ripper'. The dramatic discovery was reported of a skeleton in the bricked-up cellar of the Old Bull and Bush public house in North End Road, Hampstead. Remnants of clothing attached to the bones indicated that the individual had been a 'toff' and the presence of rusting surgical knives suggested his likely profession. Preliminary tests on the remains were thought to indicate that the teeth might be matched to curious wounds found on the victims' bodies.

It was believed that the man may have been hiding in the cellar when he was overcome by the lack of ventilation and was entombed when building work was put in hand to seal off the cellar at the end of the last century. There were numerous local accounts claiming that the pub was haunted by a Victorian gentleman. It was also believed that the pub cellar was linked by a tunnel to a nearby house owned by a surgeon who worked in the Whitechapel area.

A novel candidate for the Ripper was one put forward in March 1976 in the pages of the weekly publication *Reveille*. Asking the question 'Was the most notorious murderer in British history a pasty-faced fish gutter who could never make love?' the paper carried an account of Charlie the Ripper based on the beliefs of Mrs Carmen Rogers, a medium. She described the Ripper as a nondescript sort of man with a thin face and pasty complexion but deceptively strong in the arms and hands. He was aged about thirty-four or thirty-five and worked in the fish trade. Unable to form a normal sexual relationship with a woman, he worked off his frustration by killing and mutilating prostitutes. 'Ripping them was the only way he could get inside a woman' was the graphic description of his motive. While this has the ring of psychological truth about it, the suggestion that he stopped from a sense of self-preservation does not hold up.

Carmen Rogers believed that Jack the Ripper took one of his victims, probably Annie Chapman, to the Ten Bells public house in Commercial Street, Whitechapel, before murdering her in Hanbury Street. Now renamed the Jack the Ripper, the public house operates from its original eighteenth-century building and contains an attic room in which a number of disturbing phenomena have occurred. The glass in the window which opens out onto the slated roofs of Whitechapel frequently breaks for no apparent reason and it has been known for a radio placed in the room to switch itself on.

It is suggested that the room was used by one of the barmaids who was also a part-time prostitute. Perhaps she was entertaining the Ripper when the manhunt for him came too close and he made his escape out of the window and across the rooftops. Perhaps this was one of the room's secrets – perhaps indeed.

CHAPTER NINE
Summing-Up

Perhaps you the reader will consider yourself a member of a jury trying the Jack the Ripper murders case. You have been selected for jury service, one of a select band of twelve men and women, to try England's most notorious murderer, *in absentia*, of course. Your task is to weigh the evidence and consider the burden of proof. A great deal of testimony has been heard, some of it expert but most of it from ordinary witnesses relying on their memories of great events or powers of observation and interpretation. As is customary in these proceedings, a judicial summing-up is given to assist you to distinguish between what is important and that which is peripheral in order to help you reach a verdict.

The case you have before you is a most unusual one. In every other murder trial there has been no doubt whatever about the identity of the defendant, and very little about those of the victims. But in considering the facts of the present case, which took place a century ago, we are confronted with a situation in which we are deprived of both these basic certainties. There is some doubt as to whether there were five, six or even, possibly, ten victims. Worse still, we seem to have a least a dozen defendants. It is therefore necessary to begin by pointing out to you an obvious yet extremely important fact: that at least eleven of these defendants are completely innocent of the crimes with which you have heard them charged. It is important to understand this because the various counsels for the prosecution have not only presented their cases with admirable skill, but have also, without exception, been totally convinced of the guilt of their candicate. Now the law has nothing whatever to do with this kind of conviction. Our task is a purely scientific one: to endeavour, to the best of our ability, to weigh the evidence, and to decide, upon purely logical criteria, how much of it can be taken seriously. Powerful convictions and imaginative prejudices have no place in this courtroom.

Before we consider these candidates in more detail, please consider a remark made earlier in the course of this trial: that no theory of the Ripper's identity makes sense that fails to recognize that he was a sadistic maniac. Imagine that you are holding a knife in your hand, and that you are about to make stab wounds in a tailor's dummy lying at your feet. Now make thirty-nine stabbing motions with your knife. Notice how long it takes. After about a dozen stabs it seems pointless to continue – your victim is already dead. For a man to administer more than two dozen stab wounds, he must have been in the grip of a passion akin to sexual frenzy. Members of the jury, it makes no difference whether you decide that the murder in question – that of Martha Turner was committed by the man who murdered five other women in Whitechapel. The point is that the murderer of Martha Turner must have been a sadistic maniac, not a man with some other motive, such as a desire to discourage prostitutes or to eliminate a blackmailer. And the same applies to the man who, having been interrupted when killing Elizabeth Stride, immediately went off in search of another victim, whom he then disembowelled, and to the man who spent two hours inflicting horrible injuries on the body of Marie Jeanette Kelly. The Ripper may have had some secondary motivation, such as a desire for revenge on a prostitute who had infected him – or someone he loved – with venereal disease. But the evidence shows that the primary motive must have been sexual sadism. And from our knowledge of other similar cases, we are in a position to state that such a man remains in the grip of his sadistic obsession, and usually continues to commit similar crimes either until he is caught, or until he is interrupted by death – or by confinement in some place from which he cannot escape, such as a lunatic asylum. Since Jack the Ripper was never caught, it seems to me highly likely that one of the other two alternatives must apply.

What is being suggested is that before you begin your deliberations about any individual suspect, you should first of all be quite clear in your mind about the mind of person you are looking for. You would be well advised to familiarize yourselves with other killers who were driven by perverse sexual urges, such as Peter Kürten, the Düsseldorf sadist, Earle Nelson, Albert Fish, and Peter Sutcliffe, the Yorkshire Ripper. There is only one thing we can say about Jack the Ripper with absolute certainty: that he was a man who was driven by what one psychiatrist, Melvin Reinhardt, has called 'mutilation madness'. As soon as this is clearly grasped, we can see that the basic weakness in many of the theories of the killer's identity is a certain lack of psychological realism. The proponents of these theories are approaching the problem in the spirit of a writer of detective fiction rather than of a criminologist or a policeman looking for a real murderer. So, for example, William Stewart takes as his starting point his discovery that the last victim, Mary Kelly, was pregnant, and evolves from this a theory that Jack the Ripper was a woman, most likely a midwife/abortionist, who escaped detection by burning her own bloodstained garments and dressing up in the clothes of the victim. He goes on to name a suspect – Mary Eleanor Pearcey, executed in December 1890 for the murder of her

309

lover's wife and baby. Though not a midwife, her *modus operandi* resembled the Ripper's. But Mrs Pearcey, described as 'small and insignificant looking', murdered Phoebe Hogg because she was the victim of a violent passion for Mrs Hogg's husband Frank. She begged him to come and see her in prison, but he refused. It is impossible to imagine this lovesick young woman – she was only twenty-four at the time of her execution in 1890 – killing prostitutes for the sheer joy or murder. And it is equally difficult to imagine any woman performing the mutilations that make the nickname 'Jack the Ripper' so appropriate. Stewart's assertion that 'mutilation is the supreme expression of spitefulness, and spitefulness is a vice to which female criminals are addicted' is quite simply untrue. The injuries inflicted on Mary Kelly were the outcome of 'mutilation madness', not of mere spite, and many cases could be cited to demonstrate that mutilation madness is sexual in origin – a perverted substitute for the sexual act. In the century since the Whitechapel murders, there have been a great many female killers, some of them – like Belle Gunness and Jeanne Weber – as brutal as any man. Yet it is difficult if not impossible to call to mind a single case involving 'mutilation madness'. Consequently, one is forced to the conclusion that sexual mutilation is a crime of the male sexual pervert, and that the notion of a female Jack the Ripper is a grotesque impossibility.

We can detect this same failure of psychological realism in the story of 'the satanic Dr Stanley', the man named as the killer in the first full-length book on the case, *The Mystery of Jack the Ripper* by Leonard Matters. There is no need to dwell on the inherent implausibilities of Matters' account, such as his insistence that Dr Stanley was a brilliant and highly respected London surgeon, followed immediately by the admission that he has been unable to trace him in the records of the Medical Council of Great Britain. It is enough simply to consider the motive that, according to Matters, drove Dr Stanley to commit the murders: a desire to avenge the death of his son Herbert, who died of syphilis

310

picked up from Mary Kelly. We are given to understand that Stanley killed Martha Turner, Mary Nichols, Annie Chapman, Elizabeth Stride and Catherine Eddowes after questioning them about Mary Kelly, his motive being to prevent them from warning the woman he hated. This is Matters' account of the murder of Martha Turner: 'Up the rickety stairs they went, and halted on the first floor landing. There Stanley asked the woman whom she knew among those of her kind. She named them all. Then he plied her with direct questions. The woman did not know Marie – had never heard of her. In the darkness a sinewy hand shot out . . . No cry escaped her lips. No struggle was possible, for as she sank unconscious to the ground, the knife was at her throat.' What the author omits to tell us is that the victim was then stabbed thirty-nine times. The moment we know this, his tale becomes absurd, for the surgeon described by Matters is a brilliant and rational human being, not a sadistic madman. Like Stewart, Matters has approached the crimes in the spirit of Agatha Christie rather than of Sir Bernard Spilsbury. He has simply failed to grasp the psychological reality behind the murders.

The same weakness seems to characterize a number of the other theories – for example, Dr Stowell's identification of the Ripper with the Duke of Clarence, and Michael Harrison's suggestion that he was a homosexual poet, J.K. Stephen. Stowell attempts to explain his suspect's 'mutilation madness' by saying: 'With his father's friends he stalked deer on the family estate in Scotland. This gave him many opportunities of watching the dressing of carcasses . . . The sex instinct of the psychopath is sometimes stimulated by watching dissections or mutilations.' It is very difficult to imagine a young man's sexual instinct being stimulated as he watches deer being dressed for the table. We should also recognize that in most cases, the development of sexual violence is the outcome of frustration, and that a young and good-looking member of the royal family must have had many opportunities to satisfy his sexual desires. Please bear in mind that the majority of sexual psychopaths are inhibited, introverted men in whom the normal male desire for sexual domination has been intensified to the point of cruelty. Then ask yourselves whether you can imagine such tendencies in a young and popular heir to the throne, or in a brilliant and languid man about town like J.K. Stephen. The notion that venereal disease or a blow on the head could turn a normal young man into a sadistic mutilator of women seems inherently unlikely – otherwise the incidence of sadistic sex crime would be far higher than it is.

We may also apply this argument to Oscar Wilde's friend Frank Miles, a painter who was committed to an asylum near Bristol in 1887 with syphilis, and who died of general paralysis of the insane in 1891. Miles was apparently a bisexual, with an odd predilection for exhibiting himself to young girls. But by the time he and Wilde separated in 1881, Miles was well on his way to becoming a successful and fashionable painter. This combination of qualities – artistic talent, homosexuality and sexual exhibitionism – seems totally at variance with our 'psychological profile' of Jack the Ripper, with his grim obsession with mutilation. And since there is no evidence whatever to suggest that Miles left the mental home after 1887, we may safely dismiss the case against him.

Psychologically speaking, Donald McCormick's murderer, Alexander Pedachenko, the homicidal maniac from Tver, sent to England by the Czarist government to embarrass the British police, is a far more likely candidate, for Jack the Ripper undoubtedly *was* a homicidal maniac. Unfortunately, the evidence for Pedachenko's existence is based upon the word of a notoriously dishonest journalist, William Le Queux. In *Things I Know*, published in 1923, Le Queux claims that after the Russian revolution, the Kerensky government allowed him to see a manuscript called *Great Russian Criminals*, written in French by the 'mad monk' Rasputin. It was found, according to Le Queux, in the cellar of Rasputin's house in St Petersburg. In fact,

Rasputin had no cellar – he lived in a flat on the third floor – and he did not speak a word of French. Le Queux's reliability may be gauged by a book he wrote about Rasputin called *Minister of Evil*, in which he claims that Rasputin worked as a German spy during the First World War, and even went on a secret mission to Berlin, during which he had an interview with the Kaiser. The book claims to be a translation of a manuscript by Rasputin's Italian secretary Rayevsky – a person who never existed. A glance at any reputable biography of Rasputin will reveal that he was a patriotic Russian, and that he never left Russia during the war. You will probably agree, therefore, that there would be no point in wasting further time on Le Queux's totally unsubstantiated story about Pedachenko.

So far, our suspects have fallen into two rather disappointing groups: those whose very existence is doubtful – like Dr Stanley, Pedachenko and Jill the Ripper – and those who, although they undoubtedly existed, seem to be unconnected to the murders by any genuine thread of evidence. For the sake of completeness, we should also consider Robin Odell's theory that the Ripper was a Jewish slaughterman or *shochet*, which seems to fall somewhere between the two. Odell points out that there is no evidence that the Ripper possessed the medical skill of a surgeon, but that he certainly possessed the kind of basic anatomical knowledge required by a butcher or *shochet*. Unfortunately, he has no specific candidate to suggest, and points out that the records of the London Board of Shechita were destroyed in an air raid in 1940. It seems doubtful, in any case, that these records could have offered any clue to Jack the Ripper's identity. This is the main objection to Odell's theory – that it is too general to be either proved or disproved. Unless more positive evidence can be discovered, the theory must be regarded as a useful but unverifiable suggestion.

Daniel Farson's identification of the Ripper as Montague John Druitt is the most interesting and plausible theory so far. Here, at last, there is a thread of evidence to connect the suspect with the murders. In his autobiography *Days of My Years*, published in 1914, Sir Melville Macnaghten states: 'Although ... the Whitechapel murderer, in all probability, put an end to himself soon after the Dorset Street affair in November 1888, certain facts, pointing to this conclusion, were not in the possession of the police till some years after I became a detective officer.' Macnaghten joined the force, as Assistant Commissioner, in June 1889, at the age of thirty-six. The 'Dorset Street affair' had taken place seven months earlier. Macnaghten adds little more information in this chapter except to say that 'the probability is that, after his awful glut on this occasion, his brain gave way altogether and he committed suicide ... The man, of course, was a sexual maniac . . .'

In *Mysteries of the Police and Crime*, Major Arthur Griffiths, writing ten years after the murders, has slightly more to say. He notes that by the time of the Miller's Court murder, the police 'had brought their investigations to the point of strongly suspecting several persons, all of them known to be homicidal lunatics, and against three of these they held very plausible and reasonable grounds of suspicion'. He goes on to say that one was a Polish Jew, the second a Russian doctor, 'also insane', and that 'the third person was of the same type, but the suspicion in his case was stronger, and there was every reason to believe that his own friends entertained grave doubts about him. He also was a doctor in the prime of life, was believed to be insane or on the borderland of insanity, and he disappeared immediately after the last murder ... On the last day of that year, seven weeks later, his body was found floating in the Thames, and was said to have been in the water a month.'

When Daniel Farson was researching Jack the Ripper for a television programme in 1959, he stumbled upon Macnaghten's original notes, in which the three suspects are named: the Polish Jew was called Kosminski, the Russian doctor was called Michael Ostrog, and the third suspect was called Montague John Druitt. Macnaghten also describes Druitt as a doctor, and he makes it clear that Druitt is his chief suspect. With considerable difficulty, Farson tracked down Druitt's death certificate. Macnaghten and Griffiths had been mistaken in stating that he was a doctor; Druitt was a barrister – a very unsuccessful one. And he was thirty-one at the time of his death, not forty-one, as Macnaghten had stated.

We know that Macnaghten believed Druitt to be the Ripper. What we do not know is why he thought so. And the researches of Daniel Farson and Tom Cullen into Druitt's life provide us with no clue. On the contrary, they leave us baffled that such an apparently 'normal' person could ever have been suspected of being the Ripper. Druitt had been born in August 1857 at Wimborne, in Dorset; his father was a surgeon and a Justice of the Peace. The family lived in one of the largest houses in the town. He went to Winchester public school and distinguished himself academically; he was also secretary of the debating society, and played Sir Toby Belch in *Twelfth Night*. He was a good footballer and an excellent cricketer, playing for the school's eleven at Lords in 1876. He was one of nineteen candidates to be successful for the university exams, and was awarded a scholarship to Oxford. His academic career there was less brilliant – he only managed a third in Greats – but was elected Steward for the junior common room, which indicates his popularity with his fellow students.

Farson states that it was after Winchester that Druitt's life seems to have gone into decline. He was called to the Bar in 1885, at the age of twenty-seven, but seems to have had few, if any, clients. He had to borrow money from his father to keep going.

But Farson's statement that he went into decline does not seem wholly accurate. Irving Rosenwater, a cricket enthusiast, conducted an investigation into Druitt's cricketing career, which appeared in *The Cricketer* for December 1972. He discovered that Druitt was a member of the Kingston Park and Dorset County Cricket Club, the principal club side in Dorset, and played regularly for them through the 1880s until the time of his death. He seems to have been an excellent player, taking eleven wickets in one match in 1883. He became a member of the MCC in the following year. Rosenwater also discovered that he accepted the teaching post at a Blackheath 'crammers' as early as 1884, and this no doubt explains how he was able to survive three years at the Bar without a case. Rosenwater notes that Druitt played for many sides, in dozens of matches, throughout the 1880s. It is conceivable that he made no attempt to practise as a barrister, preferring teaching and cricket. He played for the Blackheath Cricket Club, and was one of its principal bowlers, playing more matches in 1886 than anyone else. Blackheath was a fine team, and many of its members were county cricketers. So the picture that emerges of Druitt during the 1880s is of an upper-class young man who has been popular at school and university, and who prefers to continue to live the life of a kind of permanent public schoolboy. It is extremely difficult to perceive in this career any hint of the obsessive mania of Jack the Ripper.

The blow that seems to have made Druitt doubt his sanity fell in July 1888, when his mother became insane – she was to die of disease of the brain in 1890. But he continued to play cricket – on 21 July he played against Beckenham; on 3 and 4 August he played for the Gentlemen of Bournemouth. On 1 September he was playing in Canford in Dorset, three days after the murder of Mary Ann Nichols in Bucks Row, which Macnaghten regarded as the first of the Ripper murders. And on the morning of Saturday 8 September, six hours after the murder of Annie Chapman, Druitt was playing cricket on the Rectory Field at Blackheath.

When the Michaelmas term ended on 1 December 1888, Druitt was dismissed from the Blackheath school, but it is not clear why. The obvious suspicion is that he may have been guilty of a homosexual offence. But if, as he believed, he was going insane, then he may simply have become unpunctual and unreliable. That Sunday he went to see his mother, and seems to have been acutely depressed, for on his return to his chambers he wrote a note to his brother William, a Bournemouth solicitor, saying: 'Since Friday I felt I was going to be like mother and the best thing for me was to die.' On Monday 3 December he went for a walk by the river and threw himself in, his pockets weighted with stones.

What is immediately clear is that Druitt did not commit suicide because – as Griffiths and Macnaghten imply – his mind had snapped after the final murder of 9 November. He committed suicide because he was in a state of acute depression about his mother's breakdown and his own mental condition. Macnaghten also implies that 'the Ripper' committed suicide soon after the final murder; in fact, we know that it was nearly a month later. Albert Backert, a member of the Whitechapel Vigilance Committee, complained to the police in March 1889 that they were being too complacent because there had been no new Ripper murders in five months, and was told that the Vigilance Committee could be disbanded because the Ripper was known to be dead: 'He was fished out of the Thames two months ago.'

It seems perfectly clear that there is not a shred of real evidence that Montague Druitt was Jack the Ripper. All that we know is that Macnaghten, who joined the Yard after the murders, chose to believe he was. The real question that remains to be answered, then, is: had Macnaghten any reason for believing that Druitt was the Ripper, or was it merely a kind of wishful thinking? Bear in mind that the murders took place over a very brief period indeed – between August and the beginning of November 1888. We are told by Macnaghten: 'No one who was living in London that autumn will forget the terror created by these murders. Even now I can recall the foggy evenings, and hear again the raucous cry of the newspaper boys: "Another horrible murder, murder, mutilation, Whitechapel." Such was the burden of their ghastly song; and when the double murder of 30 September took place, the exasperation of the public

317

at the non-discovery of the perpetrator knew no bounds . . .' This exasperation became so great that the Commissioner of Police, Sir Charles Warren, was forced to resign on the eve of Mary Kelly's murder. And then, after this particularly horrific crime, the murders ceased. Why? What had happened? The natural assumption was that the murderer had committed suicide, or been confined in a mental home – Griffiths mentions both these possibilities, so it is clear that he does not take it for granted that Druitt was the Ripper. Yet his wording is close enough to that of Macnaghten's notes – made in 1894 – to make it relatively certain that he was quoting Macnaghten. He also repeats Macnaghten's assertion that the body of the suspect was taken from the Thames seven weeks after the murder of Mary Kelly. So we can see that although Griffiths is aware of the Druitt theory, he does not wholly accept it.

But then Macnaghten – who apparently did accept it – reveals that he knows very little about Druitt. In his memoirs he says: 'I do not think there was anything of religious mania about the real Simon Pure (i.e. Jack the Ripper) . . . I incline to the belief that the individual who held up London in terror resided with his own people; that he absented himself from home at certain times, and that he committed suicide on or about the 10th of November 1888.'

This is completely incomprehensible. It would surely be reasonable to assume that if Druitt was one of three chief suspects after the last murder, the police would have checked on his background. They would have visited the Blackheath school to find out why he was dismissed, and would have known that he lived in chambers at 9 King's Bench Walk in the Temple. They would certainly have known that he was taken out of the water on 2 January, and that he had vanished almost exactly a month before that. Yet Macnaghten makes the mistake of asserting that Druitt was a doctor, that his mind collapsed as a result of his 'awful glut' in Miller's Court, that he committed suicide on the day after the final murder, and that he lived with his family. It suddenly becomes very clear that Macnaghten actually knew very little about Montague Druitt and about his suicide. We must assume that there was no police file about Druitt, and that Macnaghten was operating largely upon hearsay. This also throws doubt on his statement: 'From private information, I have little doubt that his own family suspected this man of being the Whitechapel murderer; and it was alleged that he was sexually insane.' If, in fact, the police suspected Druitt *because* some member of his family had reported their suspicion, surely Macnaghten would say so, not 'I have little doubt . . .' And again, if there was some kind of evidence that Druitt was 'sexually insane' it seems reasonably certain that Macnaghten would say so. Phrases like 'it was alleged' and 'I have little doubt' reveal that there was no real evidence against Druitt.

To summarize: the case against Druitt rests solely on the word of Macnaghten, and as soon as we examine Macnaghten's statements critically, it becomes obvious that he knew little or nothing about Druitt. Certainly our own knowledge of Druitt makes him as unlikely a suspect as J.K. Stephen or the Duke of Clarence. Young men of this type – men who have enjoyed a successful public school and university career, men who are popular, articulate and good at sport – lack the peculiarly morbid and obsessive temperament of the sadistic maniac.

Then why did Macnaghten come to suspect him in the first place? It may be supposed that when the Ripper crimes suddenly came to an end, the police made the natural assumption that the criminal was either dead or confined in an asylum. They were already predisposed to believe that the man they were looking for was a doctor, and that he either lived in Whitechapel or within easy walking distance. When Druitt's body was taken from the Thames, they felt that this could easily be the man they were looking for. The belief that they had finally located a likely suspect led them to overlook the fact that he was not a doctor, then to forget it, and then to create the myth that Druitt had been, in fact, a medical man. What we are seeing here is the perfectly normal human tendency to believe what we want to believe.

Druitt is the last of our major suspects. Others, like Sir William Gull, Walter Sickert, George Chapman, Neill Cream and D'Onston Stephenson, seem so unlikely – for reasons already considered – that it would be a waste of time to discuss them further. Regrettably, none of the current theories about the identity of Jack the Ripper can stand up to close examination.

Most of the Ripper theories are based upon an unstated fallacy: that the Whitechapel murderer was a 'somebody'. Because we find the crimes so appalling, and because they have achieved so much notoriety, we are inclined to think of Jack the Ripper as the criminal equivalent of a great actor or a famous general. He puts us in mind of Conan Doyle's Professor Moriarty: 'He is the Napoleon of crime, Watson. He is the organizer of half that is evil and nearly all that is undetected in this great city . . . He sits motionless, like a spider in the centre of its web.' Yet a man needs very little talent, or even bravery, to skulk through dark alleyways at night and stab a few helpless women. We now know a great deal more than the Victorians knew about the psychology of the sadistic killer, and what we know suggests that Jack the Ripper was not a 'somebody' but a nobody, and that it was precisely because he was a nobody that he became a murderer. If we think of sadistic murderers of the past century – Joseph Vacher, Peter Kürten, Neville Heath, Albert Fish, Ian Brady, Dean Corll – the most obvious thing about them is that none of them could be described, by any stretch of the imagination, as 'remarkable men'. They were all, in a basic sense of the world, 'little' men, all psychologically immature, all driven by a destructive urge that had a strong component of self-pity. And we should also bear in mind that if any one of them had escaped detection, we could discuss his crimes for ever without getting any closer to his identity.

This is not to say that there is now no chance of solving the mystery of Jack the Ripper. On the contrary, the number of books about him in the past twenty years, and the profusion of new theories, indicates that there are still clues waiting to be uncovered. It is probably a question of painstaking research rather than of brilliant detective work. It is significant that Macnaghten's notes about the Ripper have been in existence since 1894; yet it was not until 1959 that a television research team decided to try and track them down.

It is also, of course, conceivable that Jack the Ripper was one of the many 'lesser' suspects who have been mentioned in the course of this investigation – for example, Dr Morgan Davies, who was reported to Scotland Yard by Donston Stephenson. Another interesting candidate is to be found in Daniel Farson's book on the Ripper. He tells how, in 1961, he received a letter from a 77-year-old man who lived in Melbourne, and who only signed his initials – G.W.B. This man told Farson: 'When I was a nipper about 1889 I was playing in the streets about 9 p.m. when my mother called: "Come in Georgie or Jack the Ripper will get you." That night a man patted me on the head and said: "Don't worry Georgie. You would be the last person Jack the Ripper would touch." ' Farson adds that this man was Georgie's own father. 'My father was a terrible drunkard and night after night he would come home and kick my mother and us kids about something cruelly. About the year 1902 I was taught boxing and after feeling proficient to hold my own I threatened my father that if he laid a hand on my mother or brothers I would thrash him. He never did after that, but we lived in the same house and never spoke to each other. Later I emigrated to Australia. I was booked to depart with three days' notice and my mother asked me to say goodbye to my father. It was then he told me his foul history and why he did these terrible murders, and advised me to change my name because he would confess before he died. Once settled in Melbourne I assumed another name. However, my father died in 1912 and I was watching the papers carefully expecting a sensational announcement.' This announcement never came. The man then goes on to explain why his father committed the murders. 'His greatest wish was for his first born to be a girl, which came to pass. She turned out to be an imbecile. This made my father take to drink more heavily . . . During the confession of those awful murders, he explained he did not know what he was doing but his ambition was to get drunk and an urge to kill every prostitute that accosted him.'

This story has far more of the ring of truth than theories about the Duke of Clarence or the satanic Dr Stanley. It *is* possible that Jack the Ripper was an ordinary labourer – G.W.B.'s father worked at delivering manure – who got very drunk periodically, then found himself in the grip of a sadistic urge. The only implausibility in the story is the notion that the father simply gave up committing murder; a knowledge of criminal history brings to mind only one case of a sadistic killer – the Boston Strangler – who simply outgrew the urge to kill. But by 1890, G.W.B.'s father would be forty years old, an age at which the sexual urge begins to diminish in many men, particularly heavy drinkers. It now remains for some researcher, or team of researchers, to track down G.W.B.'s identity – which should not be too difficult, since we know his initials and roughly when he moved to Australia – and to find out whether there are any medical records concerning his father. The result could well be the kind of positive proof of the Ripper's identity that our investigation has so far failed to provide.

Members of the jury, on the basis of the evidence you have heard and having carefully considered all the arguments put forward in the case, you must be directed to find all the defendants not guilty – no other verdict is possible. Let us console ourselves with the thought that we *shall* have another defendant standing in the dock one day, and that this time the evidence will persuade you to bring in a different verdict.

Appendix One
The Ripper's Disciples

When Jack the Ripper committed his murders, sexual murder was rare, and sadistic sex murder was virtually unknown. To speak of 'murder for sex' would have struck a Victorian as slightly absurd, unless it meant murder committed in a blind passion for some particular woman, like the Rev. James Hackman's shooting of Margaret Reay, mistress of the Earl of Sandwich. Sex was surely plentiful enough for any man to obtain without murder. Even the children indulged. Donald Rumbelow recounts a story of a man who was going down a slum court when he saw a boy and a girl of ten or eleven trying to have sexual connection. He pulled the lad off, and the boy protested: 'Why do you take hold of me? There are a dozen of them at it down there.'

The Jack the Ripper murders were the first sex crimes in our modern sense of the word (although I would be perfectly willing to concede that anyone with an intimate knowledge of continental or oriental crime might find a better candidate). Yet when we compare them with later sex crimes, one obvious and immediate difference emerges. Nearly all later sex murders involved sexual intercourse, or an attempt at it. But as far as we know, the Ripper's sole motivation was to disembowel his victims (although, of course, we do not know enough about the post-mortem on Mary Kelly to know whether intercourse had taken place). This is why his contemporaries were inclined to see them as crimes of revenge, of a man who had a 'down on whores'. And although it is perfectly conceivable that he had a 'down on whores' – perhaps because he had contracted venereal disease from one of them – the mutilations make it clear that he was driven by an obsessive sexual fever.

This means the 'ordinary' sex crimes do not offer us a

great deal of insight into the psychology of Jack the Ripper. In 1895, a 24-year-old Sunday school superintendent, Theodore Durrant, lured two girls into a Baptist church in San Francisco and raped and murdered them both. In 1902, a man who called himself John Bennett advertised for a babysitter in San Francisco, and raped and mutilated the fifteen-year-old girl, Norah Fuller, who applied. In America, sex crimes of this type became increasingly frequent after the turn of the century, while in Europe they continued to be rare. And this is undoubtedly because America was more of a 'melting pot' than Europe, where old traditional values continued to exert their influence. It is significant that San Francisco was more of a 'melting pot' than most American cities. It indicates clearly – what should probably be obvious in any case – that sex crimes are related to social stress, to a lack of a sense of 'roots'. In Europe in the 1890s, two of the worst sex criminals – Joseph Vacher, the French 'Ripper', and the German Ludwig Tessnow – were both travelling journeymen, with no permanent home. Vacher, a man who had spent some time in a lunatic asylum, raped and disembowelled fourteen people – males as well as females – between 1894 and 1897. (Vacher was bisexual.) He was 'caught in the act' when attempting to strangle a peasant woman, and later executed. Tessnow murdered young children – four altogether – then literally hacked them to pieces; he was convicted when stains on his clothes – which he claimed to be wood stain – were proved to be human blood, by the new method developed by Paul Uhlenhuth.

Germany was to produce some of the worst sex murderers of the first half of the twentieth century: Fritz Haarmann, Georg Grossmann, Adolf Seefeld, Karl Denke, Peter Kürten, Rudolf Pleil, Heinrich Pommerenke, Werner Boost. Peter Kürten, the Düsseldorf sadist, stands out from this list of names because he was a sadist in the precise, technical sense of the word: the thought of pain and mutilation caused him excitement to the point of orgasm. The others were simply sex killers, in the sense of being

324

motivated by sexual desire (although Grossman ate his victims, and Haarmann sold them for meat). Kürten, who murdered eight people in an orgy of killing in 1929, was morbidly fascinated by the sight – or even the thought – of blood. His sadism had developed during long periods of solitary confinement in prison, when his sexual fantasies became steadily more violent – a consequence of 'the law of diminishing returns'. The result was that when he came out of prison, he found sex unsatisfactory unless it was accompanied by violence or pain. He made a habit of playfully throttling his girlfriends during intercourse, and many of them seem to have found this completely natural. He also crept up behind people in the street – men as well as women – and experienced an orgasm as he stabbed them or struck them with a hammer. As soon as he had experienced orgasm, he lost interest in the victim, which is why many who were attacked escaped with their lives. Just before his execution by beheading, he told the police doctor that his greatest wish was to hear the sound of his own blood dripping into the basket.

In Kürten we can see that the normal 'aggressive' element in male sexuality has been pushed to a point where it has totally *replaced* the ordinary desire for penetration. He admitted to the doctor, Karl Berg, that he kept looking at the white throat of the stenographer who was taking down his confessions, and wishing he could throttle it. Most 'sex maniacs' would only have thought about undressing her. So what we are dealing with here is not sex crime in the usual sense of the word, but a crime which almost deserves a new classification; bearing in mind Melvin Reinhardt's 'mutilation madness', we might almost call it 'destruction madness'.

The point may be underlined by reference to a curious case of the early 1900s, the 'Great Wyrley mystery'. In 1903 there was a series of mutilations of animals in the area of Great Wyrley in Staffordshire; someone was creeping up on the animals in the night and cutting open their bellies with a razor or very sharp knife. Horses, sheep, cows and a pit pony were butchered in this way. Suspicion fell on a 27-year-old solicitor, George Edalji, son of a Parsee clergyman, against whom there was a great deal of racial discrimination. There was also a series of gloating Jack the Ripper type letters to the police. Edalji was convicted on circumstantial evidence – mud on his shoes and alleged horsehairs on his coat – and sentenced to seven years in prison. Released for good conduct after three years, he appealed to Conan Doyle for help. Doyle went to Great Wyrley, and conducted a careful investigation after the manner of his own Sherlock Holmes. This not only convinced him that the frail, short-sighted Edalji must be innocent, but that the culprit was an ex-schoolfellow of Edalji's called Royden Sharp. The British establishment stood firm and refused to reconsider the case, but Doyle's articles excited so much public indignation that the result was the creation of the Court of Criminal Appeal.

Whoever mutilated the cattle also perpetrated on the Rev. Edalji a series of malicious hoaxes – ordering expensive goods in his name and placing advertisements in newspapers signed by the clergyman – but it is also apparent that he was a sadist in the same sense as Kürten and Jack the Ripper. The cattle mutilations were not an attempt at a hoax; they were performed for pleasure (although anonymous letters then blamed Edalji). Although Doyle built up a watertight case against Royden Sharp – including the evidence of a handwriting expert that the 'Ripper' letters were in Sharp's handwriting – there was no prosecution.

So it is to Sharp that we should look for instructive parallels about Jack the Ripper. Sharp had been expelled from school in Walsall at the age of thirteen for forgery and destructive tendencies. He loved using a knife. On the way to school by train he would turn over cushions and slice open the underside so that the horsehair emerged; he would also cut the leather straps on the windows. When he left school he was apprenticed to a butcher. A schoolmate he detested was deluged with anonymous letters. In 1895 he went to sea, and Doyle discovered that whenever Sharp was at sea, the malicious hoaxes and anonymous letters ceased. The animal mutilations all occurred when Sharp was at home between voyages. Sharp had worked on a cattle ship, from which he obtained a large and sharp instrument known as a horse lancet (Conan Doyle succeeded in getting possession of it). Doyle established that the shallow incisions in the animals' bellies must have been made with a similar instrument. And he himself began to receive anonymous letters as soon as he began to defend Edalji publicly – letters in the same handwriting as all the other anonymous letters.

So if, as seems highly probable, the Jack the Ripper postcards to Mr Lusk and the Central News Agency were written by the Whitechapel murderer, then we should probably be looking for a man with some characteristics in common with Royden Sharp: a juvenile delinquent type with a strong streak of malice and a fascination with knives and cutting instruments. If, in fact, Sharp had been in his twenties in 1888 – instead of a schoolboy – he would be the ideal suspect for the Ripper murders, since nothing is more likely than that such a person would graduate from killing animals to killing 'fallen women', as Peter Kürten graduated from torturing animals to killing human beings. It is also interesting to note that Sharp was unable to resist boasting about his attacks. In 1903, a friend of the Sharp family, Mrs Emily Smallking, went to call at their cottage. She spoke of the cattle mutilations to Sharp, who took a large horse lancet from a cupboard and said: 'Look, this is what they kill cattle with.' Mrs Smallking reported this to Doyle, who included it in his dossier on the case. Sharp spoke with a kind of gleeful malice, evidently enjoying shocking Mrs Smallking – the same kind of gleeful malice we find in the Ripper letters. All this should at least make it clear that the kind of person who committed the Whitechapel murders was not a brilliant but unbalanced surgeon, or a misogynistic poet, or a cricket-playing barrister – or even a retired army officer who practised ritual magic – but a malicious overgrown schoolboy who had probably been in trouble for as long as he could remember.

Other cases of sex crime can offer us fragmentary clues about the psychology of Jack the Ripper. Earle Nelson, born in Philadelphia in 1897, went on a rampage of murder and rape between February 1926 and November 1927, killing twenty-two women. Nelson's mother died when he was a baby and he was brought up by an aunt; at the age of ten he was knocked down by a tram car and was unconscious for six days; for the rest of his life he suffered from headaches. Soon after his twenty-first birthday, he tried to rape a child in a basement, and was sent to prison; he escaped several times, and in the following year married a young schoolteacher who knew him as Roger Wilson. He proved to be a difficult husband, screaming at his wife a great deal, beating her, and accusing her of infidelity on the slightest pretext. When she had a nervous breakdown, he visited her in hospital and forced her to have intercourse; interrupted by a doctor, he accused him of having an affair with his wife, then left.

Nelson disappears from sight for the next six years. But in February 1926 he called at a San Francisco boarding house to enquire about a room. The sixty-year-old landlady showed him to an empty room, and was strangled and raped. Ten days later, another sixty-year-old landlady was strangled and raped in San Jose. In June, two more women were murdered in the same manner. In October, three women were murdered in three days. In November there were victims in San Francisco, Seattle and Oregon City; two days before Christmas a 49-year-old woman was strangled and raped in Council Bluffs, Iowa; two days after Christmas, he strangled a 23-year-old woman, then a 28-year-old woman and her eight-month-old baby girl; both were violated. During the next five months there were five more victims – in Detroit, two in the same lodging house. Then the 'Gorilla murderer' – as the press now called him – crossed into Canada. In Winnipeg he took a room in the house of a Mrs Hill, and quickly lured a fourteen-year-old girl called Lola Cowan to his room. Lola was found four days later – after Nelson had left – under his bed, her body badly mutilated. Nelson had slept with her under his bed for three days. He called on another landlady, Mrs Emily Patterson, killed her with a hammer and raped her; her husband found her body later when he went on his knees beside the bed to pray. Mrs Patterson was Nelson's last victim; he was recognized from his description in the post office at Wakopa, and arrested. He was hanged in Winnipeg in January 1928.

Two interesting points emerge. One was that Nelson was an extremely jealous and violent husband, who finally caused his wife to have a nervous breakdown. The other is that most of the murders and rapes were committed in a hurry, like Jack the Ripper's murders, although on occasions when he felt he was not likely to be interrupted he violated the body more than once. But on the one occasion when he no longer felt in a hurry – with the body of Lola Cowan concealed in his room – he mutilated the body to such an extent that it was unrecognizable – as Jack the Ripper mutilated Mary Kelly. We can infer that when Nelson's urge was allowed to satisfy itself at leisure, it ran to 'mutilation madness', exactly like that of the Ripper.

We can also observe that the majority of Nelson's victims were elderly women, many in their sixties, suggesting a revenge motive against a 'mother' figure. Since his mother died when he was very young, it may be safe to infer that the mother figure was the aunt who brought him up, the highly religious Mrs Lily Fabian. (Nelson liked to pose as a religious man, which explains why so many landladies trusted him.) But Mrs Fabian was also young enough to have an attractive young daughter, Rachel, at whom Nelson peeped through keyholes. After one of his prison escapes he was found outside her bedroom window, watching her undress. The mother-revenge motive can be found in many cases of sexual murder, and it may be significant that in one of his murders Jack the Ripper removed the uterus. In fact, all the mutilations suggest that the Ripper's basic obsession was with the womb, and therefore that he was a man who had reason to hate his mother. Yet if this is so, then the destruction of the womb suggests a basic suicidal urge.

In his classic study *The Sexual Criminal*, Paul de River, a Los Angeles criminologist, analyses a case of a Ripper-type killer, whom he calls K. K, who killed two prostitutes, leaving them mutilated and disembowelled; the first victim was left in much the same state as Mary Kelly – in fact he went further and disarticulated both her arms and legs. He had been placed in an orphanage at the age of six, and hardly knew his mother, although he was fifteen when she died. He had contracted both syphilis and gonorrhoea, and was a heavy smoker and drinker. He was also bisexual, but there was no sadistic element in his relations with men, with whom he performed mutual fellatio. (He admitted, 'I have more satisfaction from females.') He had been married, and had threatened his wife with a knife and cut her on the buttock with a safety razor blade. He claimed that he had first experienced the urge to destroy women four years before, and had contracted venereal disease since, so the two were not directly connected. De River makes it clear that K is not insane, or even apparently abnormal. 'He likes people . . . He has no enemies. He is not anti-social; has no illusions, delusions or hallucinations. He is co-operative and polite and fairly well orientated as to time, places, dates and persons. His insight and judgement are good . . . His wealth of knowledge is good for one of his education.' But it seems obvious that K himself was unable to understand his desire to mutilate women. 'I don't know what made me do it . . . I was completely insane.' He went on to describe how he had bought a knife when he was drunk, then picked up the prostitute and went up to her room. Then, after an act of oral sex, he throttled her unconscious, and stabbed her. Then he went into a frenzy and mutilated the body. From his own account of the murder, it is strangely difficult to understand why he did it, except that when he was drunk, his sexual excitement drove him to perverse lengths, and

330

sexual desire somehow became mixed up with a deep resentment of his mother.

It is scarcely necessary to say that if K – whose real name was Wilson – had remained uncaught, and had committed two or three more murders, he would have remained a horrible legend in Los Angeles, as Jack the Ripper was in London. Yet he was an extremely ordinary little man, aged thirty-four, an ex-soldier and a labourer who, apart from his 'mutilation madness', was in every way normal. De River says of him that he was 'a pitiless, ruthless sadist who in his mind entertained but one thought, namely murder and the dissection of his victims. They were the victims of a playful, sadistic dissectionist, the objects of the caprices of a butcher. He was not a rapist. He was highly perverted with a lust for murder . . . He denied sexual intercourse with either victim, and his was not the action of a man seeking the gratification of his general sexual impulse. He sought above all the satisfaction of an urge to kill and to destroy the object that was once symbolic of love . . .' Here, one suspects, we have an accurate psychological portrait of Jack the Ripper. K was finally executed.

If, in fact, Jack the Ripper shared with 'K' a 'lust for murder' that was unconnected with a desire for normal sexual intercourse, then it could be misleading to classify him with most sex killers. Albert DeSalvo, the Boston Strangler, left many of his thirteen victims in 'obscene' positions, with bite marks on their bodies and objects – like a wine bottle – inserted into their vaginas, and some were stabbed repeatedly. Yet the basic motivation was always sex. And although many of the victims were elderly women, DeSalvo was extremely fond of his mother. His motivation was a raging sexual hunger. The same seems to be true of Albert Fish, the American child murderer, a 'polymorphous pervert' who cooked and ate his last victim. One of the few American murder cases that seems to offer a true parallel to the crimes of Jack the Ripper is the Cleveland torso killer, also known as 'the mad butcher of Kingsbury Run'. Between 1935 and 1938, the 'mad butcher' killed a dozen men and women, sometimes two at a time, and left their bodies in chopped-up piles. He usually removed the heads, and in half a dozen cases these were never found. Most of the victims were derelicts and prostitutes, and the killer – like 'K' – was clearly bisexual. Cleveland's public safety director Elliot Ness finally came to suspect a well-to-do young man who owned his own house and motor car – reasoning that the 'butcher' must have had a place where he could work undisturbed for many hours dismembering his victims, and some means of transporting their bodies to the places where they were found. The man was aware that he was under suspicion and, according to Ness's chronicler Oscar Fraley, took a kind of sneering pleasure in being able to outwit the police. Just as Ness thought he had enough evidence to arrest him, the suspect had himself confined in a mental asylum. The murders stopped, but Ness received a series of postcards jeering about his failure to catch the mad butcher; these ceased when the suspect died.

Here we have touched again on one of the most important elements in the Ripper's psychology, and a key to the morbid fascination they continue to inspire. Melvin Reinhardt, writing about the seventeen-year-old sadist who killed and dismembered an eight-year-old boy, remarked, 'His ego is of the sort that demands cruelty,' and added the significant comment, 'It seemed as if he were saying, "Now I am even." ' The Jack the Ripper crimes also seem to suggest the feeling of a man who is shaking his fist at society; even the words 'Dear Boss' seem to convey a sneer at authority.

There is one theory of the Ripper's motivation that seems to be as likely as any. One of the mysteries of the case is how he succeeded in killing his victims so silently – sometimes, as in the case of Mary Nichols and Annie Chapman, within a few yards of people who were lying asleep with open windows. We have so far made the assumption that the Ripper was a sadistic maniac who was only interested in murder and mutilation. Yet we know that even a habitual sadist like Peter Kürten often had normal

332

sexual intercourse with women he picked up. We also know that he often squeezed the throats of these women in the act of intercourse, and that many of them seemed to feel that this was perfectly natural, and were even willing to go out with Kürten again. Could this not also explain how the Ripper killed his victims so silently? We may presume that, when his victims accompanied him into some dark corner, they assumed that his only interest was in sexual intercourse. They would probably raise their own clothing, and lie down on the ground. The woman would have felt no alarm if, as the man was lying on top of her, he raised his hands to her throat. Francis Camps is on record as believing that the Ripper strangled his victims before killing them. Or he may, like Kürten, only have squeezed their throats until they lost consciousness.

We may also recall the letter received by Daniel Farson from a man who signed himself 'G.W.B.', who declared that his father, an ordinary labourer, had confessed to being Jack the Ripper and told his son that he experienced the urge to kill prostitutes when he was drunk. This again rings true. There are many cases on record of men who – like De River's 'K' – experience the sadistic urge after drinking heavily. The Ripper may have been a man of this type – an ordinary labourer who made a habit of picking up prostitutes whenever he had money in his pocket, and who was carried away by 'mutilation madness' when he was drunk.

All this only underlines the point already made: that the chief mistake of 'Ripperologists' may be in assuming that Jack the Ripper was some kind of criminal genius, a cunning madman who was able to convince those who knew him that he *was* a perfectly normal individual, who only became abnormal when he was very drunk. Possibly this explains why the murders stopped. A sadistic killer like Earle Nelson or Peter Sutcliffe feels the compulsion to go on killing until he is caught. But a man who knows that he becomes virtually insane when he drinks too much has another choice – to give up getting drunk. Reformed sex murderers are rare, but the world is full of reformed alcoholics.

A final comment on the peculiar fascination that the Ripper has continued to exercise for the past century. In *A New Theory of Human Evolution*, Sir Arthur Keith suggests that man's tribal ancestors had two basic codes of conduct, which he calls the code of amity and the code of enmity. They felt amity towards members of their own tribe, and enmity towards strangers. Up to the time of the Ripper, the code of amity had prevailed in Victorian society, in spite of its inequalities – symbolized by the music hall comedian with the battered hat pretending to be a 'toff'. There were, of course, certain people who did not share the code of amity – people like Karl Marx, who longed to see the gutters running with blood and the bourgeoisie hanging from lampposts. But the Victorian poor were deeply shocked by such proposals, and felt that it was the revolutionaries who deserved to hang from lampposts.

With Jack the Ripper, it was as if the code of enmity had arrived with a vengeance. All societies have been plagued with crime, ever since the earliest cities in Mesopotamia, but the criminal always took care not to flaunt his activities; he operated in secret, as befits a parasite. This maniacal killer represented a new attitude; he seemed to be screaming his defiance at the forces of law and order. And everyone, from Members of Parliament to costermongers and prostitutes, felt that his attitude embodied a new kind of threat to society. Karl Marx had talked about alienation, but Jack the Ripper symbolized it. He seems to represent the beginning of our modern age, with its terrorists who plant bombs in crowded railway stations, its 'motiveless' serial killers who leave a trail of bodies behind them, its sadistic rapists searching for the 'ideal sex slave'. The crimes form a watershed between an age of innocence and an age of violence. It is because we instinctively recognize this that the Ripper murders continue to arouse a feeling of uneasy fascination.

Appendix Two
Sir Melville Macnaghten's Notes

The case referred to in the sensational story told in 'The Sun' in its issue of 13th inst, & following dates, is that of Thomas Cutbush who was arraigned at the London County Sessions in April 1891, on a charge of maliciously wounding Florence Grace Johnson, and attempting to wound Isabelle Frazer Anderson in Kennington. He was found to be insane and sentenced to be detained during Her Majesty's pleasure.

This Cutbush, who lived with his mother and aunt at 14 Albert St. Kennington, escaped from the Lambeth Infirmary, (after he had been detained there only a few hours, as a lunatic) at noon on 5th March 1891. He was rearrested on 9th idem. A few weeks before this, several cases of stabbing, or jabbing from behind had occurred in the vicinity, and a man named Colicutt was arrested, but subsequently discharged owing to faulty identification. The cuts in the girls dresses made by Colicutt were quite different to the cut made by Cutbush (when he wounded Miss Johnson) who was no doubt influenced by a wild desire of morbid imitation. Cutbush's antecedents were enquired into by Ch. Inspr. (now Supt.) [unreadable], by Inspr. Race, and by P.S. McCarthy C.I.D. (The last named officer had been specially employed in Whitechapel at the time of the murders there) and it was ascertained that he was born, and had lived in Kennington all his life. His father died when he was quite young, and he was always a 'spoilt' child. He had been employed as a clerk and traveller in the Tea trade at the Minories, & subsequently canvassed for a Directory in the East End, during which time he bore a good character. He apparently contracted syphilis about 1888, and, – since that time, – led an idle and useless life. His brain seems to have become affected, and he believed that people were trying to poison him. He wrote to Lord Grimthorpe, and others, and also to the Treasury, complaining of Dr Brooks, of Westminster Bridge Rd, whom he threatened to shoot for having supplied him with bad medicines. He is said to have studied medical books by day, and to have rambled about at night, returning frequently with his clothes covered with blood, but little reliance could be placed on the statements made by his mother or his aunt, who both appear to have been of a very excitable disposition. It was found impossible to ascertain his movements on the nights of the Whitechapel murders. The knife found on him was bought in Houndsditch about a week before he was detained in the Infirmary. Cutbush was a nephew of the late Supt. Executive.

Now the Whitechapel Murderer had 5 victims and 5 victims only, – his murders were

(i) 31st Aug '88. Mary Ann Nichols – at Buck's Row – who was found with her throat cut – & with (slight) stomach mutilation.

(ii) 8th Sept '88 Annie Chapman – Hanbury Street: throat cut – stomach & private parts badly mutilated & some of the entrails placed round the neck.

(iii) 30th Sept '88. Elizabeth Stride – Berner's Street: throat cut, but nothing in shape of mutilation attempted, & *on same date* Catherine Eddowes – Mitre Square, throat cut, & very bad mutilation, both of face & stomach.

(iv) 9th November. Mary Jane Kelly – Miller's Court, throat cut, and the whole of the body mutilated in the most ghastly manner.

The last murder is the only one that took place in a *room*, and the murderer must have been at least 2 hours engaged. A photo was taken of the woman, as she was found lying on the bed, without seeing which it is impossible to imagine the awful mutilation.

With regard to the *double* murder which took place on *30th* Sept. there is no doubt but that the man was disturbed by some Jews who drove up to a Club (close to which the body of Elizabeth Stride was found) and that he then, 'mordum satiatus', went in search of a further victim whom he found at Mitre Square.

It will be noticed that the fury of the mutilations *increased* in each case, and, seemingly, the appetite only became sharpened by indulgence. It seems, then, highly improbable that the murderer would have suddenly stopped in November '88, and been content to recommence operations by merely prodding a girl behind some 2 years and 4 months afterwards. A much more rational theory is that the murderer's brain gave way altogether after his awful glut in Miller's Court, and that he immediately committed suicide, or, as a possible alternative, was found to be so hopelessly mad by his relations, that he was by them confined in some asylum.

No one ever saw the Whitechapel Murderer, many homicidal maniacs were suspected, but no shadow of proof could be thrown on any one. I may mention the cases of 3 men, any one of whom would have been more likely than Cutbush to have committed this series of murders:–

(1) A Mr M.J. Druitt, said to be a doctor and of good family, who disappeared at the time of the Miller's Court murder, and whose body (which was said to have been upwards of a month in the water) was found in the Thames on 31st Dec. – or about 7 weeks after that murder. He was sexually insane and from private info I have little doubt but that his own family believed him to have been the murderer.

(2) Kosminski a Polish Jew and resident in Whitechapel. This man became insane owing to many years indulgence in solitary vices. He had a great hatred of women, especially of the prostitute class, and had strong homicidal tendencies: he was removed to a lunatic asylum about March 1889. There were many crimes connected with this man which made him a strong 'suspect'.

(3) Michael Ostrog, a Russian doctor, and a convict, who was frequently detained in a lunatic asylum as a homicidal maniac. This man's antecedents were of the worst possible type, and his whereabouts at the time of the murders could never be ascertained.

And now with regard to a few of the inaccuracies and misleading statements made by the 'Sun'. In its issue of 14th Feb., it is stated that the writer has in his possession a facsimile of the knife with which the murders were committed. This knife (which for some unexplained reason has, for the last 3 years, been kept by Insp. Race, instead of being sent to Prisoners' Property Store) was traced and it was found to have been purchased in Houndsditch in Feb. '91 or 2 years and 3 months *after* the Whitechapel murders ceased!

The statement, too, that Cutbush 'spent a portion of the day in making rough drawings of the bodies of women, and of their mutilations' is based solely on the fact that 2 *scribble* drawings of women in indecent postures were found torn up in Cutbush's room. The head and body of one of these had been cut from some fashion plate, and legs were added to show a woman's naked thighs and pink stockings.

In the issue of 15th Inst. it is said that a *light* overcoat was among the things found in Cutbush's house, and that a man in a *light* overcoat was seen talking to a woman in Backchurch Lane whose body with arms attached was found in Pinchin St. This is hopelessly incorrect! On 10th Sept. '89 the naked body, with arms, of a woman was found in some sacking under a railway arch in Pinchin St: the head and legs were never found nor was the woman ever identified. She had been killed at least 24 hours before the remains (which had seemingly been brought from a distance) were discovered. The stomach was split up by a cut, and the head and legs had been severed in a manner identical with that of the woman whose remains were discovered in the Thames, in Battersea Park, and on the Chelsea Embankment on 4th June of the same year; and these murders had no connection whatever with the Whitechapel horrors. The Rainham mystery in 1887, and the Whitehall mystery (when portions of a woman's body were found under what is now Scotland Yard) in 1888 were of a similar type to the Thames and Pinchin St. crimes.

It is perfectly untrue to say that Cutbush stabbed 6 girls

behind – this is confounding his case with that of Colicutt.

The theory that the Whitechapel murderer was left-handed, or, at any rate, 'ambidextrous', had its origin in the remark made by a doctor who examined the corpse of one of the earliest victims; *other doctors did not agree with him.*

With regard to the *4* additional murders ascribed by the writer in the Sun to the Whitechapel fiend:–

(1) The body of Martha Tabram, a prostitute was found on a common stair case in George Yard buildings on 7th August 1888; the body had been repeatedly *pierced*, probably with a *bayonet*. This woman had, with a fellow prostitute, been in company of 2 soldiers in the early part of the evening. These men were arrested, but the second prostitute failed, or refused, to identify, and the soldiers were accordingly discharged.

(2) Alice McKenzie was found with her throat cut (or rather *stabbed*) in Castle Alley on 17th July 1889; no evidence was forthcoming and no arrests were made in connection with this case. The *stab* in the throat was of the same nature as in the case of the murder.

(3) Frances Coles in Swallow Gardens, on 13th February 1891 – for which Thomas Sadler, a fireman, was arrested, and, after several remands, discharged. It was ascertained at the time that Sadler had sailed for the Baltic on 19th July '89 and was in Whitechapel on the night of 17th idem. He was a man of ungovernable temper and entirely addicted to drink and the company of the lowest prostitutes.

(4) The case of the unidentified woman whose trunk was found in Pinchin St on 10th Sept. 1889 – which has already been dealt with.

M. L. Macnaghten
23rd Feb. 1894

Bibliography
A Hundred Years of Ripperature
by Alexander Kelly

What has made the Ripper case so attractive to generations of crime writers? And why do so many readers, film buffs and television-watchers find these crimes irresistible? There are some obvious reasons for our continuing fascination with these murders – sex crimes always seem to attract special attention (ask any journalist), the murderer appeared and disappeared at will in almost supernatural manner, and the drama was acted out in an alien and mysterious underworld of poverty and refugees, prostitution and squalor, a world normally hidden behind a curtain of Victorian middle-class respectability.

In the end, what makes the Ripper different, though, is that he was never caught. Crime coverage in the Victorian period and in our own day usually follows a pattern. First we have the discovery of 'orrible murder, then a sensational hunt, and arrest, and finally we are told more than we could wish to know during (or after) the trial. In the Ripper case there was a (not very fully reported) hunt and there were arrests, but of course there was no trial – at least at the time. Instead, each of the main books on the case sets out an elaborate statement for the prosecution of their chosen villain, but with no convincing defence offered. If a defence counsel had been able to get to work on the Matters theory, for instance, one challenge of 'Call your South American witness or sit down!' would have been enough to see the case out of court. Only once, when the Duke of Clarence was put in the dock and then swiftly exonerated (with the aid of the Court Diary published in *The Times*) has anything like a forensic debate taken place when a new theory emerged. What usually happens is that the case for the defence is put much later, in the next book on the subject.

For this reason a number of more or less daft ideas have been given time to take hold. For the same reason, most books on the case start off well with a thorough demolition job on the latest theory or crop of theories before descending into an Alice in Wonderland presentation of the prosecution case against somebody else. The result has been an irresistible potpourri of charges, countercharges and dispute, so much so that some of the recent books have not bothered to add to the list of candidates.

Only a sensible solution could ruin the Ripper case. Fortunately the combined effects of passing years, an absence of key facts and endlessly fertile inventing make a solution increasingly unlikely. How about Queen Victoria as the next candidate with Sir William Gull as her accomplice?

Speculation about the identity of the Ripper began almost as soon as it became clear that these were not isolated murders. The daily and Sunday newspapers were soon competing furiously to be first with details of the next murder and to give the most gory evidence from each inquest. In the absence of any real news from the police about their murder hunt, the press started one of their own and packed their columns with fresh suspects (the *Daily News* excelled at this, pointing the finger at everyone from Texans to policemen) or new ways of catching him (this was the forte of the *Pall Mall Gazette*, which offered bloodhounds, women detectives and prize fighters dressed as women, amongst many suggestions). If one *Gazette* idea had been adopted, Jack's work would have been made much easier. This was for 'Everyone to report to the police before going to bed', presumably so that they could be killed on the way home.

The first signs of the Ripper industry were now showing in Britain and the USA with the pamphlets by Brewer and Fox. A number of broadsheets were also issued to celebrate the latest atrocity. Not to be outdone, all sorts of contemporary magazines and journals, from the *British Medical Journal* to *Fun, Moonshine* and *Punch* pitched in with comments or specialist advice. For a survey of all these publications, see the Facts and the Theories' which follows.

Dr Arthur MacDonald, an early American criminologist, can probably be claimed as the first writer to try to find a serious explanation for the murders, although he got no further than giving 'pathological sexual passion' as the cause in his *Criminology* (1893). His French contemporary, Professor Jean Lacassagne, went one better when reprinting MacDonald's account in his own book on Joseph Vacher (known as 'the disemboweller') by including police photographs of the corpses of two Ripper victims.

When William Le Queux came to write his collection of tall stories and reminiscences, *Things I Know about Kings, Celebrities and Crooks* (1923), he drew upon his early experience covering the murders for the *Globe* in putting together an unlikely case against a Dr Pedachenko. From here on the theories begin to flow thick and fast. Of the key publications, the first classic book on the case was *The Mystery of Jack the Ripper* (1929) by Leonard Matters. This is a classic only in the sense that it was the first book devoted entirely to the Ripper; the theory put forward is best regarded as pure fiction, with the idea of Dr Stanley avenging his son's death probably being inspired by a retelling of the 'discovery of the guilty doctor by clairvoyant Robert Lees' story which had been current since at latest 1895, when a version had apparently appeared in the *People*.

William Stewart's *Jack the Ripper: A New Theory* (1939) is a feeble book which argues improbably that Jack was a woman. Much better written but shored up with a recycled version of the Pedachenko notion is *The Identity of Jack the Ripper* (1959 and 1970) by Donald McCormick.

Apart from Stewart, who described himself as an artist, the early writers from Le Queux onwards were all journalists and their books have the flavour of the news cuttings file and of saloon bar chats with dubious witnesses rather than of rigorous research. Robin Odell's *Jack the Ripper in Fact and Fiction* (1965) changed all that. His suggestion of the Ripper as a *shochet*, or Jewish ritual slaughterman, was not strongly supported but there was no doubt about the painstaking effort that went into establishing the facts of the case and reviewing the theories. Publication of this book by Harrap also led to the fruitful association with that publisher's expert on crime, Joe Gaute, the results of which can be seen listed below and in the present book.

Following Odell's breakthrough came the first serious candidate for the Ripper mantle. Television broadcaster and writer Dan Farson had been 'pursuing' Montague Druitt for some time when an American crime writer, Tom Cullen, became interested in the same person. Cullen's book *Autumn of Terror* (1965) at last offered a plausible suspect even if neither Cullen nor Farson in his *Jack the Ripper* (1972) were able to prove that Druitt had ever been to Whitechapel. Both Cullen's and Farson's books are still worth seeking out although they have been overtaken by several new theories.

Dr Thomas Stowell never actually identified his suspect in print but he told enough people to ensure that the 'S' referred to in his *Criminologist* article (published in 1970) was soon identified as the Duke of Clarence. Soon afterwards the historian Michael Harrison challenged this attribution in *Clarence* (1972) and turned the spotlight on J.K. Stephen instead. As a dilettante poet and misogynist, Stephen had some promising attributes for a Ripper, but seekers after this book should be warned that it is a worthy biography of a minor and not very interesting duke.

The golden age of Ripper theories was now well advanced and two more offerings came almost at once, this time on television. In the BBC series *Jack the Ripper* (1973), fictional detectives Barlow and Watt proposed either a conspiracy by high-ranking Freemasons or a bizarre scheme involving the royal doctor and a coachman beating off the Catholic threat to the throne. Sanity was restored for the moment by Donald Rumbelow's *The Complete Jack the Ripper* (1975). This book, by a City of London policeman, was easily the best guide to the crimes and the theories published before the present book. One word of warning is necessary, though: you should try to get hold of the hardback version; the paperback edition (published in 1976) lacks both Colin Wilson's lively introduction and an index – a small crime in itself!

Although the flow of Ripper books continued for three more years, on the whole they were disappointing fare. Stephen Knight's *Jack the Ripper: The Final Solution* returned to the royal doctor and coachman, adding painter Walter Sickert and a surreal but amusing plot that transforms conspiracy theory into a new art form. The books by Whittington-Egan (1976) and Douglas (1979) add no new theories and little by way of fact and Spiering's book is not recommended. Ripper fans can look forward to a treat in the next year or two as the centenary publications appear but, unless Jack decides to put in a reappearance, there must be a limit to the possible variations on a good yarn. The next hundred years will tell . . .

Turning for a moment to the Ripper stories that do not pretend to be true, *The Lodger* (1911) by Mrs Belloc Lowndes deserves special mention as one of the most popular and successful variations on the theme, alongside Colin Wilson's *Ritual in the Dark* (1960).

An honourable mention is also earned by Robert Bloch who persistently returned to the subject. Two of his finest offerings are the short story 'Yours Truly, Jack the Ripper' (1945) and his most recent sally *The Night of the Ripper* (1984) which is a clever blend of fact and fiction. *The Ruling Class* (1968), a powerful play by Peter Barnes which later became one of Peter O'Toole's best films, is the other outstanding work, ahead of a field that includes an episode of the TV programme *Star Trek*, various American TV police dramas, and stories offering almost all of the main Sherlock Holmes characters as the Ripper, including Dr Watson and the maestro himself!

The Facts and the Theories

Aberconway, Lady Christabel Letter in *New Statesman* (London) on 7 November 1959. Lady Aberconway, Macnaghten's daughter, claimed to possess 'my father's notes on Jack the Ripper' naming three suspects.

Adam, Hargrave Lee (editor) *Trial of George Chapman* 223 p. Hodge (London) 1930. In 'Notable British Trials' series. Dismisses the unsupported testimony of Macnaghten, Anderson and Sir Henry Smith who claimed to know the Ripper's identity. Tabulates 'the case for supposing' that Chapman was the Ripper.

Adam, Hargrave Lee 'George Chapman' in *The Black Maria or The Criminals Omnibus* edited by Harry Hodge, Gollancz (London) 1935. Reiterates his earlier material.

Alexander, Marc *Royal Murder* 221 p. Muller (London) 1978. Includes a chapter by Colin Wilson on the Ripper outlining the events and the Clarence, Stephen and Gull/Netley theories.

Ambler, Eric *The Ability to Kill and Other Pieces* 191 p. Bodley Head (London) 1963. Includes nine pages outlining the crimes and the suggestion that 'Having achieved an apotheosis of horror, he had at last exorcized the evil that had haunted him.'

Anderson, Robert *Criminals and Crime: Some Facts and Suggestions* 182 p. Nisbet (London) 1907. The then head of the Criminal Investigation Department makes a passing reference to the Ripper being 'safely caged in an asylum'.

Anderson, Robert *The Lighter Side of My Official Life* 295 p. Hodder (London) 1910. The Ripper was a 'low class Polish Jew', but no evidence is offered.

Anderson, Robert 'The Lighter Side of My Official Life: XI. At Scotland Yard' in *Blackwood's Magazine* (Edinburgh) March 1910. Pages 357–8 give a similar account to that in his book of the same title but a footnote adds that a witness identified the Ripper who was 'Caged in an asylum . . . but when he learned that the suspect was a fellow-Jew he declined to swear to him'.

Anderson, Robert In his preface to *The Police Encyclopaedia* vol. 1 by Hargrave Lee Adam, 237 p. Routledge (London) 1911. Anderson claimed that 'there was no doubt as to the identity of the criminal'.

Archer, Fred *Ghost Detectives: Crime and the Psychic World* 176 p. W.H. Allen (London) 1970. Retells the story of clairvoyant Lees. See *Daily Express*.

Atholl, Justin 'Who was Jack the Ripper?' in *Reynolds News* (London) of 15 September 1946. He was an epileptic medical student.

Barker, Richard H. (editor) *The Fatal Caress and Other Accounts of English Murders from 1551 to 1891* 210 p. Duell, Sloan and Pearce (New York) 1947. Pages 164–209 carry *The Times* reports of 1888.

Barnard, Allan (editor) *The Harlot Killer: The Story of Jack the Ripper in Fact and Fiction* 248 p. Dodd Mead (New York) 1953. Anthology of more or less relevant pieces.

Barnett, Henrietta Octavia Weston *Canon Barnett: His Life, Works and Friends by His Wife* 2 vols. Murray (London) 1918. Second volume has a chapter on Whitechapel conditions when he went there as vicar, including reactions to the Ripper outrages.

Baverstock, Keith *Footsteps Through London's Past; A 'Discovering' Guide* 56 p. Shire Pubs. (London) 1972. The Ripper walks are on pages 4-10.

Beattie, John *The Yorkshire Ripper Story* 160 p. Quartet (London) 1981. This account of the recent spate of murders concludes with two pages on the East End crimes.

Beaumont, F.A. 'The Fiend of East London: Jack the Ripper' pp. 243–53 of *The Fifty Most Amazing Crimes of the Last 100 Years* 768 p. Odhams (London) 1936. Describes six murders, then tails off into the Matters theory.

Bell, Donald ' "Jack the Ripper" – The Final Solution?' in *The Criminologist* vol. 9 no. 33 (Summer 1974) pp. 40–61. Conjectures that Dr Thomas Neill Cream bought himself out of an American prison and performed the Ripper murders.

Bell, Quentin *Virginia Woolf: A Biography: Volume One. Virginia Stephen 1882–1912* 230 p. Hogarth Press (London) 1972. Details of the madness of cousin James Kenneth Stephen (pp. 35–6).

Bermant, Chaim *Point of Arrival: A Study of London's East End* 292 p. Eyre Methuen (London) 1975. Chapter 9 discusses the suggestion that the killer was a Jew.

Binney, Cecil *Crime and Abnormality* 176 p. Oxford U.P. (Oxford) 1949. Relays an account of the Ripper as a religious maniac who conducted open-air services on Margate beach.

Bloch, Ivan *Sexual Life in England Past and Present* 664 p. Aldor (London) 1938. 'Said to have been identified as an insane student.'

Blundell, Nigel *The World's Greatest Mysteries* 224 p. Octopus (London) 1980. A good six-page summary of the main theories.

Boar, Roger and Blundell, Nigel *The World's Most Infamous Murders* 192 p. Octopus (London) 1983. Pages 92–7 offer the Druitt theory and some *Illustrated Police News* pictures.

Bocock, John Paul Article in the *New York World* (1888) ascribed the murders to Nicolas Vassili, a Russian member of the 'Shorn' sect (according to R.K. Fox).

Borchard, Edwin Montefiore *Convicting the Innocent: Errors of Criminal Justice* . . . with the collaboration of E. Russell Lutz 421 p. Yale U. Institute of Human Relations (Connecticut) 1932. Chapter on 'Frenchy: Ameer Ben Ali' which links the Algerian with the Ripper.

Brewer, John Francis *The Curse upon Mitre Square AD 1530–1888* 72p. Simpkin, Marshall (London) 1888. The return of Brother Martin after three and a half centuries to wreak more vengeance upon womankind.

British Journal of Photography (London) 19 October 1888 pp. 659–60. Critical of police for failure to use photography at scenes of crime and suggests divisional photographers. Comments on facsimile posters relating to the case. Its 16 November 1888 issue p. 723 records use of photographs at Kelly murder, reiterates suggestion for divisional photographers.

Brookes, John Alfred Rowland *Murder in Fact and Fiction* 284 p. Hurst and Blackett (London) 1925. Mentions Macnaghten's suspects and concludes that the murders were 'probably the work of a doctor or medical student' (pp. 116–17).

Browne, Douglas G. *The Rise of Scotland Yard: A History of the Metropolitan Police* 392 p. Harrap (London) 1956. Lists the pertinent facts.

Buckle, George Earle (editor) *The Letters of Queen Victoria: Third Series. A Selection from Her Majesty's Correspondence and Journal between the Years 1886 and 1901. Volume One 1886–1890* 688 p. Murray (London) 1930. Page 447 has the text of a cypher telegram to Lord Salisbury instructing 'these courts must be lit, and our detectives improved'. Page 449 carries a draft letter listing 'some of the questions that occur to the Queen'.

Butler, Arthur 'Was Jack the Ripper a Woman?' in the *Sun* (London) 29 August to 1 September 1972. A former Chief Superintendent introduces a variation on Stewart's theory involving a female abortionist and male accomplice.

Butler, Ivan *Murderers' London* 238 p. Hale (London) 1973. The opening chapter tours 'The Ripper streets'. Factually sound.

Camps, Francis E. 'More About Jack the Ripper' in *London Hospital Gazette* April 1966, reprinted in *The Criminologist* (London) February 1968 and in *Camps on Crime* 181 p. David and Charles (Newton Abbott) 1973. Includes a plan and pencil sketches of a victim.

Camps, Francis E. and Barber, Richard *The Investigation of Murder* 143 p. Michael Joseph (London) 1966. The Professor of Forensic Medicine at London University devotes his opening chapter to the Ripper, considered from the viewpoint of detection methods used. Concludes that the murderer may not have been caught even using modern methods.

Cargill, David and Holland, Julian *Scenes of Murder: A London Guide* 230 p. Heinemann (London) 1964. Records the locations of the murders.

Chambers' Guide to London the Secret City 160 p. Ocean Books (London) 1974. The author has four pages on the Ripper, concludes that he was a female abortionist and claims the theory as his own!

Chester, Lewis, Leitch, David and Simpson, Colin *The Cleveland Street Affair* 236 p. Weidenfeld and Nicolson (London) 1976. Found no evidence for the Duke of Clarence as the Ripper.

Chicago Sunday Times-Herald 28 April 1895. Knight quotes an article entitled 'Capture of Jack the Ripper' in which Dr Howard discloses that the Ripper was another doctor who was declared insane and incarcerated. Includes the earliest known version of the Lees theory.

Clark-Kennedy, Archibald Edmund *The London: A Study of the Voluntary Hospital System, Volume 2. The Second Hundred Years 1840–1948* 310 p. Pitman (London) 1963. Covers the usual ground.

Cobb, Geoffrey Belton *Critical Years at the Yard: The Career of Frederick Williamson of the Detective Department and the CID* 251 p. Faber (London) 1956. Recounts top-level police reaction to the murders. Critical of Anderson; Williamson took no part.

County of Middlesex Independent 2 and 5 January 1889, reported the death of suspect Druitt.

Crowley, Aleister *The Confessions of Aleister Crowley: An Autobiography* Abridged edition by John Symonds and Kenneth Grant 1058 p. Cape (London) 1969; Hill and Wang (New York) 1970. Originally six volumes of which two were published as *The Spirit of Solitude* in 1929. Page 755 records the view that the Ripper committed seven murders to obtain supreme black magic power by forming a Calvary cross of seven points. After the third killing he achieved invisibility!

Cullen, Tom A. *Autumn of Terror: Jack the Ripper, His Crimes and Times* 254 p. Bodley Head (London) 1965, Illustrated. American edition published as *When London Walked in Terror* Houghton (Boston) 1965. The 1966 British paperback edition was reprinted as *The Crimes and Times of Jack the Ripper* in 1973. A painstaking book which considers various theories and identifies 'for the first time' the three prime suspects. Has Montague Druitt, a barrister, as the killer.

Daily Dispatch (Manchester) 10 April 1905 p. 5 'Jack the Ripper: A Startling Confession in New York'. Charles Y. Hermann takes a bow but 'police believe that the man is suffering from hallucinations'.

Daily Express (London) 'How I Caught Jack the Ripper!' 7 March 1931 p. 7; 'Clairvoyant Who Tracked Jack the Ripper' 9 March 1931, p. 3; 'Jack the Ripper's End' 10 March 1931 p. 3. Three articles tell how Robert James Lees tracks down the killer, a prosperous West End doctor who was certified insane by a 'commission de lunatico inquirendo' after his seventeenth murder.

Daily News (London) The issues for 1888 carry a continuous commentary on the murders and inquests. Theories propounded feature the Ripper in women's clothes, as a Texan or fanatical vivisectionist, as a policeman, and using the sewers as an escape route.

Daily Telegraph (London) Contemporary issues. That for 4 October 1888 carried a facsimile of a 'Ripper' letter and postcard. Also advocated police right to stop and search people for knives.

Davis, Derek ' "Jack the Ripper" – The Handwriting Analysis' in *The Criminologist* vol. 9 no. 33 Summer 1974 pp. 62–9. Examines two Ripper letters and asserts that both were written by poisoner Dr Cream.

Deacon, Richard *The Cambridge Apostles: A History of Cambridge University's Elite Intellectual Secret Society* 214 p. Robert Royce (London) 1985. Inconclusive discussion of whether J.K. Stephen was the Ripper.

Deacon, Richard *A History of the British Secret Service* 440 p.

Muller (London) 1969. Pages 29–30 recount the Le Queux story. Deacon is a pseudonym of Donald McCormick.

Deacon, Richard *A History of the Russian Secret Service* 568 p. Muller (London) 1972. Donald McCormick has another go at his theory.

Dearden, Harold 'Who Was Jack the Ripper?' in *Great Unsolved Crimes* by A.J. Alan and others, 351 p. Hutchinson (London) 1935. Attributes the murders to 'some doctor or medical student'.

Dew, Walter *I Caught Crippen* 242 p. Blackie (London) 1938. Devotes a third of the book to the Ripper; describes events with plenty of local colour because he was stationed with the CID in Whitechapel. No theory.

Dictionary of National Biography Smith, Elder (London) 1898. Entries for J.F. Stephen and his son.

Douglas, Arthur *Will the Real Jack the Ripper* 72 p. Countryside Pubs. (Chorley, Lancs.) 1979. Illustrated. His account of the murders concentrates on the discrepancies in other commentaries. Decides that the Ripper was 'a mere nobody after all'.

Douthwaite, Louis Charles *Mass Murder* 288 p. Long (London) 1928. Disposes of the Deeming Ripper assertion by claiming that 'At the time of the . . . murders Deeming was in prison'.

East, John M. *'Neath the Mask: The Story of the East Family* 356 p. Allen and Unwin (London) 1967. Refers to an encounter between a stall attendant and a suspect.

Eisler, Robert *Man into Wolf: An Anthropological Interpretation of Sadism, Masochism and Lycanthropy* . . . 286 p. Routledge (London) 1951. Makes a passing reference in support of the possibility that the Ripper was a woman.

Empire News (Manchester) 28 October 1923 pp. 1–2 'New Story of Jack the Ripper'. An '*Empire News* student of criminology' asserted that 'Every head of police knows that Jack the Ripper died in Morris Plains lunatic asylum in 1902.' The Ripper was Mr Fogelma, a Norwegian sailor.

Evening News (London) 5 March 1954 p. 6 Obituary of Chief Inspector James Stockley notes that he was disguised as a 'loafer, costermonger, milkman, chimney sweep and itinerant musician' as part of Ripper operation.

Farson, Daniel *The Hamlyn Book of Horror* 157 p. Hamlyn (London) 1977. Eight pages of illustrated text on the Ripper.

Farson, Daniel *Jack the Ripper* 144 p. Joseph (London) 1972. Arrives at the same conclusion as Cullen, but by a somewhat different route. More evidence is offered against M.J. Druitt. The first recent book to include photographs of the corpses of Eddowes and Kelly (two of these appeared in Lacassagne). The paperback edition, Sphere (London) 1973, carries additional information.

Farson, Daniel 'The Truth, the Whole Truth' in the London *Evening News* for 18–22 September 1972. Five articles on the murders based on his book. Nothing new until part four in which Montague Druitt is identified.

Feigenbaam, Benjamin Article in *Arbeter Fraint* (London) 21 December 1888 denies a *Church Times* claim that Jack was a Russian anarchist.

Fishman, William J. *East End Jewish Radicals 1875–1914* 336 p. Duckworth (London) 1975. Passing references to the Ripper and to the suggestion that he was a Russian anarchist.

Fishman, William J. *The Streets of East London* 139 p. Duckworth (London) 1979. Four illustrated pages.

Forbes, Archibald 'The Motive of the Murders' Letter to the *Daily News* published on 3 October 1888 p. 6 labels the killer as a monomaniac seeking 'revenge against the class a member of which has wrought him his blighting hurt'. Perhaps an 'excitable medical student'.

Ford, Ford Madox *Return to Yesterday* 438 p. Gollancz (London) 1931. Claims that his nurse, Mrs Atterbury, discovered the body of one of the victims and saw a man vanish into the fog. (What fog?)

Fox, Richard Kyle *The History of the Whitechapel Murders: A*

Full and Authentic Narrative of the above Murders with Sketches 48 p. Fox (New York) 1888. The editor of the *National Police Gazette* rehashes news reports of nine murders padded out by a paraphrase of de Quincey's version of the Ratcliffe Highway murders. Attributes crimes to Nicolas Vassili.

Franklin, Charles *The World's Worst Murderers: Exciting and Authentic Accounts of the Great Classics of Murder* 320 p. Odhams (London) 1965. Pages 13–23 sketch in the events and the theories then current. Suggests that the Ripper may have 'retired' after the Kelly killing.

Friedland, Martin L. *The Trials of Israel Lipski* 219 p. Macmillan (London) 1984. Suggests that the anti-Semitic press response to the murders may have been orchestrated to curtail Jewish immigration.

Gaute, Joseph H.H. and Odell, Robin *Murder 'Whatdunit': An Illustrated Account of the Methods of Murder* 247 p. Harrap (London) 1982. Jack is the only murderer to receive an entry under his own name.

Gaute, Joseph H.H. and Odell, Robin *Murder Whereabouts* 286 p. Harrap (London) 1986. Only passing references to Whitechapel's favourite son/daughter.

Gaute, Joseph H.H. and Odell, Robin *The Murderer's Who's Who: Outstanding International Cases from the Literature of Murder in the Last 150 Years* 269 p. Harrap (London) 1979. Includes two pages on the crimes and favourite suspects and a passing reference to the subject by Colin Wilson in his introduction.

George, Earl Lloyd *Lloyd George* 248 p. Muller (London) 1960. Similar account to that by Owen (below).

Ghastly Murder in the East End 1888. Broadsheet reproduced in Cullen.

Goodman, Jonathon *Bloody Versicles: The Rhymes of Crime* 224 p. David and Charles (Newton Abbot, UK) 1971. Three pages on the Ripper ditties.

Green, Jonathon *The Directory of Infamy: The Best of the Worst* 288 p. Mills and Boon (London) 1980. A small entry on the master.

Gribble, Leonard Reginald 'The Man They Thought Was Jack the Ripper' in *True Detective* (London) March 1977 pp. 4–12, 49. George Chapman examined and dismissed.

Gribble, Leonard Reginald 'Was Jack the Ripper a Black Magician?' in *True Detective* (London) January 1973 pp. 16–25. An illustrated and inaccurate account explores this idea.

Griffiths, Arthur George Frederick *Mysteries of Police and Crime* vol. 1 464 p. Cassell (London) 1898. Records three suspects – a Polish Jew, a Russian doctor and a doctor who was later found drowned.

Haines, Max *Crime Flashback: Book 2* 230 p. Toronto Sun (Canada) 1981. Eight pages on the Ripper. Supports Druitt.

Halsted, Dennis Gratwick *Doctor in the Nineties* 206 p. Johnson (London) 1959. Halsted was at the London Hospital at the time and described the atmosphere and general suspicion which fell on medical men. Outlines six murders and suggests that Jack was a syphilitic sailor of the North Sea fishing fleet.

Hansard's Parliamentary Debates (Commons). The record of what is said in the Lower House of Parliament. An index is available for the period.

Harris, Melvin 'The Murders and the Medium' in *The Unexplained: Mysteries of Mind, Space and Time* 65 (1981) 1290–3. Illustrated article in this part-work looks at and dismisses the Lees legend.

Harrison, Fraser *The Dark Angel: Aspects of Victorian Sexuality* 288 p. Sheldon Press (London) 1977. Jack rates only two pages but is credited with eight murders.

Harrison, Michael *Clarence: The Life of the Duke of Clarence and Avondale, KG 1864–1892* 253 p. W.H. Allen (London) 1972. Reattributes Stowell's Clarence theory to J.K. Stephen.

Hayne, W.J. *Jack the Ripper: or The Crimes of London* 1889. Stolen from the Library of Congress and untraced elsewhere.

Herd, Richard 'The Secret of Ex-Convict SY5 45' in the London *Evening News* 8 September 1955. Old lag's tale of his wife as Jill the Ripper.

Hibbert, Christopher *The Roots of Evil: A Social History of Crime and Punishment* 524 p. Weidenfeld and Nicolson (London) 1963. Passing account of events.

Hill, William Boyle *A New Earth and a New Heaven* 312 p. Watts (London) 1936. Pages 119–27 of this spiritualist book recount the Lees story as reported by the *Daily Express*.

Honeycombe, Gordon *The Murders of the Black Museum 1870–1970* 296 p. Hutchinson (London) 1982. Pages 5–14 outline the events and regurgitate some of the usual illustrations. He favours Druitt.

Howard, Philip *We Thundered Out: 200 Years of The Times 1785–1985* 176 p. Times Books (London) 1985. Two pages of reports (and pictures) from the *Illustrated Police News* and from *The Times* of 10 November 1888.

Hubler, Richard Gibson 'A Stunning Explanation of the Jack the Ripper Riddle' in *Coronet* (New York) November 1956 pp. 100–6.

Hyde, H. Montgomery *Carson: The Life of Sir Edward Carson, Lord Carson of Duncairn* 515 p. Heinemann (London) 1953. Pages 182–3 link George Chapman with the Ripper.

Hynd, Alan Article in *True Magazine* (New York) 1956 has Griffith S. Salway discovering a Spanish Ripper's identity via a trunk with a false bottom.

Hynd, Alan 'Murder Unlimited' in *Good Housekeeping* (New York) February 1945 pp. 29, 197–200. Describes contacts between Mathew Parker (a fruiterer) and the Ripper in otherwise orthodox account.

Illustrated Police News Law Courts and Weekly Record (London) The issue for 18 August 1888 carried a report and illustration of *Tragedy in Whitechapel. A woman stabbed in thirty-nine places*; then from 8 September to 8 December inclusive this sensation sheet kept the murders 'on the boil' with a weekly report, always on page 2, and a total of 184 cover pictures of uniformly crude appearance. Sporadic coverage to 1892.

The issues for 8 and 22 September, 6 and 20 October, and 17 November 1888 were reproduced in *Great Newspapers Reprinted* 25 February 1974 published by Peter Way Ltd (London).

Inglis, Norman 'Was Jack the Ripper Caught?' in *Tit-bits* (London) 12 May 1962. A sighting.

'Jack the Ripper: The Story of the Whitechapel Murders' in *Famous Crimes Past and Present* (London) 1903 vol. 2 no. 15 pp. 25–30, no. 16 pp. 49–58, no. 17 pp. 73–81. no. 18 pp. 97–102. Published by Harold Furniss. Jack is 'a lunatic suffering from erotomania . . . he was a doctor, not Neill Cream, was mad, and is now probably dead'.

Jack the Ripper at Work Again. Another terrible murder and mutilation in Whitechapel 4 p. (No publisher given) 9 November 1888. Broadsheet with pictures of the 'supposed murderer' and 'the victim', two columns of news and four of doggerel.

Jackson, Robert *Francis Camps: Famous Case Histories of the Celebrated Pathologist* 208p. Hart Davis (London) 1975. Chapter 9 'Camps on the Ripper' outlines the events of the time and claims that Camps 'came down in favour of the Farson theory'.

Jannino, E.A. *Jack the Ripper*. Paper presented to a discussion session at the Third International Meeting on Forensic Pathology, London 1963. Postulated 'moon madness' theory for Boston and Whitechapel murders.

Jones, Elwyn and Lloyd, John *The Ripper File* 204 p. Futura Barker (London) 1975. The book of the television series. Ignore the Barlow and Watt linking passages and this represents one of the best collections of factual readings on the case, complete with the Freemason conspiracy and Sickert theories.

Keating, P.J. 'Fact and Fiction in the East End' in *The Victorian City: Images and Realities: Vol. 2* edited by H.J. Dyos and Michael Wolff, Routledge (London) 1973. Suggests (pp. 594–5) that the murders reinforced an image of the East End as violent and outcast rather than monotonous and outcast.

Kelly, Alexander Garfield *Jack the Ripper: A Bibliography and Review of the Literature* 55 p. Association of Assistant Librarians, S.E.D. (London) 1973; second edition 83 p. 1984. Includes an introduction to the murders and the theories by Colin Wilson.

Kingston, Charles *The Bench and the Dock* 290 p. Stanley Paul (London) 1925. Pages 203–4 describe James Monro's supposed involvement in the Ripper search. Reports the suspects as a West End doctor and a medical student at St Bartholomew's Hospital.

Knight, Stephen *Jack the Ripper: The Final Solution* 284 p. Harrap (London) 1976. Illustrated. Painter Walter Sickert, Sir William Gull and John Netley go to endless trouble to eliminate four prostitutes who were party to Royal blackmail. A paperback edition by Treasure (London) in 1984.

Knight, Stephen 'Jack the Ripper: The Final Solution' in the *Evening News* (London) June 21st (pp. 15–17), 22nd (pp. 12–13), 23rd (pp. 10–11), 24th (12–13), 25th (16–17) 1976. Adapted from the book by Arthur Pottersman and Simon Brodbeck.

Knight, Stephen *The Brotherhood: The Secret World of the Freemasons* 336 p. Granada (London) 1984. Four-page reiteration of bits of his earlier book.

Knight, Stephen 'Why Sickert Denied Ripper Tale' in the *Sunday Times* (London) July 2nd 1978. His reply to David May (q.v.).

Lacassagne, Jean Alexandre Eugene *Vacher L'Eventreur et les crimes sadiques* 314 p. Storck (Lyons); Masson (Paris) 1899. Pages 254–265 carry MacDonald's account for comparison with the crimes of Joseph Vacher. Notable for photographs of the Kelly and Eddowes corpses.

Lamb, David C. 'On active service for humanity: he found his soul on Devil's Island' in *Tit-bits* (London) 23 September 1939 pp. 6–7. The memoirs of the Salvation Army Commissioner recall a sign-writer visitor who had predicted the death of Carroty Nell. Lamb adds 'Remembering my visitor's exceptional dexterity, his story of seeing visions of blood, his strange demeanour and his remarkable forecast, I have now little doubt in my mind that he was Jack the Ripper'.

Lancet (London) This medical journal challenged the view that the Ripper was a lunatic (15 September 1888) and carried a letter from Dr Henry Sutherland on 22 September which diagnosed that 'he or they are of perfectly sound mind'(!). It commented on coroner's court evidence (29 September) and urged sanitary reform in Whitechapel (6 October).

Le Queux, William *Things I Know about Kings, Celebrities, and Crooks* 320 p. Nash and Grayson (London) 1923. Covered the events for *The Globe*. Quotes from 'Rasputin's own manuscript' which revealed the Ripper as Dr Alexander Pedachenko.

Leeson, Benjamin *Lost London: The Memoirs of an East End Detective* 187 p. S. Paul (London) 1934. Tells how he was called to the scene of the Coles murder, the rest is hearsay. Claims thirteen victims and hints at 'a certain doctor, known to me'.

Linklater, Magnus 'Did Jack the Ripper Have Royal Blood?' in the *Sunday Times* (London) 1 November 1970. Elaborates on the Stowell theory naming Edward, Duke of Clarence as the suspect.

Lithner, Klas *Vem var Jack Uppskäraren?* (Who Was Jack the Ripper?) in *Jury* (Stockholm) no. 2 1973 pp. 12–16. Surveys the case and theories.

Logan, Guy B.H. *Masters of Crime: Studies of Multiple Murders* 288 p. Paul (London) 1928. Chapter on the Ripper concludes that he was a victim of syphilis from America who had 'declared war on the special class from which he chose his victims'.

Lowndes, Susan (editor) *Diaries and Letters of Marie Belloc Lowndes 1911–1947* 291 p. Chatto and Windus (London) 1971. Pages 96–8 describe origins of *The Lodger* and record Hemingway's enthusiasm for the book.

Lustgarten, Edgar *The Illustrated Story of Crime* 223 p. Weidenfeld and Nicolson (London) 1976. Pages 208–13 give a brief resumé of the case, with pictures.

McCormick, (George) Donald (King) *The Identity of Jack the Ripper* 192 p. Jarrolds (London) 1959; second edition 256 p. Long (London) 1970. Illustrated. Detailed account of the murders and leading suspects. Postulates Dr Alexander Pedachenko as a Czarist secret agent who committed the murders to discredit London anarchists. Colin Wilson commented that he 'accepts the evidence of Le Queux . . . a pathological liar', but this claim is refuted in the second edition.

MacDonald, Arthur *Le criminel type dans quelques formes graves de la criminalité* Storck (Lyons) 1893. Includes an account of eleven Ripper murders between 1887 and 1889.

MacDonald, Arthur *Criminology* 416 p. Funk and Wagnalls (New York) 1893. The pioneering American criminologist found that 'the atrocities . . . are without doubt caused by a pathological sexual passion'.

McGowan, Bill 'Who Was Jack the Ripper?' in the London *Evening News* 1 September 1964 p. 7. Various conjectures including the Ripper as a woman, policeman, mad surgeon. American sailor.

MacLeod, C.M. 'A Ripper Handwriting Analysis' in *The Criminologist* (London) August 1968 pp. 120–7. A Canadian graphologist analysed two letters reproduced in the Camps article and concluded that they were written by different people, the first of whom may have been the Ripper.

Macnaghten, Melville L. *Days of My Years* 300 p. Arnold (London) 1915. Treacly memoirs by a chief of CID suggest that the 'Boss' letter came from a journalist and that the Ripper committed suicide.

Marjoribanks, Edward *The Life of Lord Carson. Volume One* 455 p. Gollancz (London) 1932. The life of the great advocate who prosecuted George Chapman the poisoner. Conjectures that Chapman was the Ripper (pp. 304–5).

Marjoribanks, Edward *The Life of Sir Edward Marshall Hall* 483 p. Gollancz (London) 1929. Contains anecdotes about Neill Cream who confessed to being the Ripper. Hall dismissed the idea (pp. 48–50).

Marne, Patricia *Crime and Sex in Handwriting* 150 p. Constable (London) 1981. 'Analysis' of two possible Ripper letters.

Marx, Roland *'L'énigme Jack l'Eventreur'* in *L'Histoire* 62 (Dec. 1983) pp. 10–21. Detailed review of the facts, theories and fictional variations.

Masters, R.E.L. and Lea, Eduard *Sex Crimes in History: Evolving concepts of sadism, lust-murder, and necrophilia from ancient to modern times* 323 p. Julian P. (New York) 1963. Pages 81–8 attribute nine (and possibly twenty) murders which 'were not committed without a certain redeeming grace, a saving wit, a mitigating sophistication and savoir faire'(!).

Matters, Leonard W. *The Mystery of Jack the Ripper* 254 p. Hutchinson (London) 1929. Illustrated. Variously reprinted since. The first classic work on the subject has a conjectural theory based on a confession relayed at secondhand. The murderer is a doctor revenging his son. The 1948 reissue published by W.H. Allen has a new introductory chapter.

Matters, Leonard W. 'Will We Ever Solve the Mystery of Jack the Ripper?' in the *Sunday Express* (London) 4 May 1930. Discusses the Chapman Ripper proposition and refutes it because 'it is directly opposed to my own theory'.

May, Betty *Tiger-woman: My Story* 232 p. Duckworth (London) 1929. Written by Bernard O'Donnell, originally as a series of articles for the *World's Pictorial News*. Includes an incident in which Aleister Crowley claimed to have the ties of the Ripper, who was a surgeon-magician.

May, David. 'Jack the Ripper "Solution" Was a Hoax, Man Confesses' in the *Sunday Times* (London) 18 June 1978. Joseph Sickert disowns the Stephen Knight story.

Moore-Anderson, Arthur P. *Sir Robert Anderson and Lady Agnes Anderson* 173 p. Marshall, Morgan and Scott (London) 1947. Records the notions that Jack was a Malay seaman on shore leave, that a vital clay pipe was destroyed and that 'the only person who ever had a good view of the murderer identified the suspect without hesitation . . . but refused to give evidence'.

Morland, Nigel 'Jack the Ripper: A Final Word' in *The Criminologist* (London) Autumn 1971 pp. 48–9. A handwriting analysis by Prof. C.L. Wilson showed 'no justification whatsoever for identifying Jack the Ripper with the Duke of Clarence'.

Moylan, John *Scotland Yard and the Metropolitan Police* 398 p. Putnam (London) 1929. The former Receiver to the Metropolitan Police said that 'It is almost certain that he escaped by committing suicide.'

Muusmann, Carl *Hvem var Jack the Ripper?* 102 p. Hermann-Petersen (Copenhagen) 1908. He was Alois Szemeredy, a Hungarian who perfected his art in Argentina and eventually in Austria. He committed suicide.

Nash, Jay Robert *Compendium of World Crime* 452 p. Harrap (London) 1983. Originally published as *Almanac of World Crime* 433 p. Anchor/Doubleday (New York) 1981. Skimpy treatment of the case (three pages plus five passing references). Favours Cream.

Neil, Arthur Fowler *Forty Years of Man-hunting* 288 p. Jarrolds (London) 1932. Police Superintendent presents the 'strong theory' that poisoner George Chapman was the Ripper.

Neil, Charles (editor) *The World's Greatest Mysteries* 50 p. Neil (Australia) (c. 1936) pp. 5–19 'How Jack the Ripper Was Caught' retells the clairvoyant Lees story.

Neustatter, Walter Lindesay in the foreword to *Jack the Ripper in Fact and Fiction* by Robin Odell. Neustatter dismissed various medical theories before suggesting that the Ripper may have been schizophrenic.

New York Daily Graphic October 4th 1888 p. 744 'London's Ghastly Mystery.' Records Dr J.G. Kiernan's view that the Ripper was a cannibal.

New York World Telegraph and Sun 15 February 1960. The killer as Alonzo Maduro from South America.

Newton, H. Chance *Crime and the Drama or Dark Deeds Dramatized* 284 p. S. Paul (London) 1927. Refers to brief performances of 'horrible dramatic depictions of certain of the unspeakable murders committed by Jack the Ripper'.

Nicholson, Michael *The Yorkshire Ripper* 197 p. Star W.H. Allen (London) 1979. Has a four-page account of the Whitechapel murders.

Oddie, S. Ingleby *Inquest* 255 p. (London) 1941, pp. 57–62. Describes seven crimes and Oddie's visit to the sites with Conan Doyle. Notes Arthur Diosy's theory that the murders were part of a black magic ritual and the objects found at the scenes of crime formed magical 'pentacles'.

Odell, Robin (Ian) *Jack the Ripper in Fact and Fiction* 275 p. Harrap (London) 1965. Illustrated. The first thorough book on the subject. Examines the major suggestions, quoting at length from some protagonists. Advances the argument that Jack was a *shochet* or Jewish slaughterman. A revised paperback edition was published by Mayflower in 1966.

O'Donnell, Elliott *Confessions of a Ghost Hunter* 323 p. Thornton Butterworth (London) 1928. Tales of Whitechapel hauntings by Elizabeth Stride and Mary Kelly.

O'Donnell, Elliott *Great Thames Mysteries* 288 p. Selwyn and Blount (London) 1929. A chapter on the Ripper speculating about links between the murders and cases of dismemberment in 1887–8.

O'Donnell, Elliott *Haunted Britain* 192 p. Rider (London) 1948. Page 36 has accounts of ghostly events in Whitechapel, recorded in 1895.

O'Neil, P. 'Parting Shots: Clarence the Ripper?' in *Life* (New York) 13 November 1970 pp. 85–8. Speculation on the Duke of Clarence theory.

Owen, Frank *Tempestuous Journey: Lloyd George, His Life and Times* 784 p. Hutchinson (London) 1954. Tells of Lloyd

George's shock at seeing East End conditions on a jaunt to catch the killer.

Paley, Bruce 'A New Theory on the Jack the Ripper Murders' in *True Crime Monthly* April 1982 pp. 3–13. Now it is the turn of Joseph Barnett, who is at least known to have met (and lived with) Mary Kelly.

Pall Mall Gazette: An evening newspaper and review (London) Plethora of material includes details of murders and inquests and a host of suggestions e.g. bloodhounds, beagles, women detectives, and pugilists in drag; pictures the Ripper as a Malay, Russian, Frenchman or policeman. An index is available.

Pearsall, Ronald *The Worm in the Bud; The World of Victorian Sexuality* 560 p. Weidenfeld and Nicolson (London) 1969. Pages 306–13 provide an account of the murders with a wealth of background material, some of it rather remote.

Pearson, Edmund Lester *More Studies in Murder* 232 p. Random House (New York) 1936. A chapter on the murders is reprinted in Barnard. Adds nothing except a delightful comment on the theory of Matters. 'The deathbed confession bears about the same relation to the facts of criminology as the exploits of Peter Rabbit . . . to zoology'.

The People (London) 19 May 1895 'A Startling Story'. Relays the Lees theory from the *Chicago Sunday Times Herald*, according to Whittington-Egan.

People's Journal 26 September 1919. Rumbelow (q.v.) quotes an item about the retirement of a detective named Steve White who had seen and almost arrested the Ripper.

Pimlott, John Alfred Ralph *Toynbee Hall: Fifty Years of Social Progress 1884–1934* 315 p. Dent (London) 1935. Pages 81–2 describe the efforts of a vigilance association to apprehend the Ripper.

Platnick, Kenneth B. *Great Mysteries of History* 224 p. David and Charles (Newton Abbot) 1972. The main themes appear on pages 58–73.

Police Gazette (London) The issue for 26 October 1888 has a series of descriptions of the wanted man.

Pulling, Christopher *Mr Punch and the Police* Butterworths (London) 1964, pp. 120–30 describe reactions to the murders in *Punch* and elsewhere. Reproduces anti-establishment cartoons from *Fun* one of which demands the resignation of the Home Secretary. Remarks on friction between the City and Metropolitan Police.

Reilly, B.E. 'Jack the Ripper: The Mystery Solved?' in *City* (City of London Police magazine) February 1972. 'Doctor Merchant' is condemned because of his home (Brixton) and date of death (1888) although no evidence is offered that he had ever been to Whitechapel!

Revill, Joan 'Read all abaht it. The 'orrible 'oroscope of Jack the Riper' in *Prediction* (London) June 1973 pp. 6–9. Yes, it could have been M.J. Druitt or the Crown Prince of Austria!

Reynolds News and Sunday Citizen (London) 8 February 1959 p. 9 'Blacksmith gives Yard vital clue: Jack the Ripper was my cousin'. The Ripper as Frank Edwards, cousin of a retired Worthing blacksmith.

Richardson, Joseph Hall *From the City to Fleet Street: Some Journalistic Experiences* 302 p. S. Paul (London) 1927. Describes the case, quotes a letter from Anderson and a description of the Ripper in the *Police Gazette* (London).

Robertson, Terence 'Madman Who Murdered Nine Women' in *Reynolds News and Sunday Citizen* 29 October 1950 p. 3. Journalistic rehash of the nine murders committed by a Polish sailor.

Robinson, Tom *The Whitechapel Horrors: Being an authentic account of the Jack the Ripper murders* 32 p. Daisy Bank Pub. (Manchester) (no date). Attributes seven murders to the killer.

Rosenwater, Irving 'Jack the Ripper – Sort of a Cricket Person?' in *The Cricketer* January 1973 pp. 6–7, 22. Information about M.J. Druitt's cricketing career. The title refers to that of E.W. Swanton's autobiography.

Rumbelow, Donald 'The City of London Police Museum and Exhibition' in *Police Journal* (Chichester) July 1970 pp. 343–4. Reports that Metropolitan Police were forbidden to disturb Kelly corpse before the arrival of bloodhounds. Meanwhile City Police entered the premises and took photographs. Four photographs of the body of Eddowes are in the museum.

Rumbelow, Donald *The Complete Jack the Ripper* 286 p. W.H. Allen (London) 1975. Illustrated. The best book yet. Offers no new theory but Colin Wilson's introduction adds artist Frank Miles to the roll of dishonour. The paperback edition (Star: 1976) lacks both introduction and index. A new edition is expected soon.

Sabben-Clare, James 'Jack the Ripper' in the *Trusty Servant* no. 34 December 1972 pp. 3–5. The Old Wykehamist magazine celebrates one of its distinguished old boys – M.J. Druitt.

Saxon, Peter 'The Man Who Dreamed of Murder' in *Sexton Blake Library* 3 November 1958. Medium Lees rides again.

Scott, Harold (editor) *The Concise Encyclopaedia of Crime and Criminals* Deutsch (London) 1961. Ripper article appears to have been written by McCormick.

Shaw, George Bernard 'Blood Money for Whitechapel' a leading article putting the socialist viewpoint in the *Star* of 24 September 1888. Shaw also wrote an unpublished letter to the *Star* as from J.C., abhorring capital punishment and repudiating attempts to catch the murderer. See his *Collected Letters 1874–1897* (p. 197) Reinhardt (London) 1965.

Shew, Edward Spencer *A Companion to Murder* 303 p. Cassell (London) 1960; Knopf (New York) 1962. Repeats the evidence of Adam that Chapman may have been the Ripper.

Sims, George Robert *The Mysteries of Modern London* 192 p. Pearson (London) 1906. Passing references to the Ripper 'a man of birth and education'.

Sitwell, Osbert (editor) *A Free House: or The Artist as Craftsman, being the writings of Walter Richard Sickert* 362 p. Macmillan (London) 1947. Preface has the same story as recorded in *Noble Essences*.

Sitwell, Osbert *Noble Essences of Courteous Revelations: Being a book of characters and the fifth and last volume of left hand, right hand* Macmillan (London) 1950. Pages 189–91 record painter Walter Sickert's claim to have lived in lodgings formerly occupied by the killer, a veterinary student who died in Bournemouth.

Smith, Henry *From Constable to Commissioner: The story of sixty years, most of them misspent* 137 p. Chatto and Windus (London) 1910. Smith was Chief Superintendent of Police in the City of London 1885–90 and includes details of the Ripper's City murder and of a rendezvous with a suspect.

Snyder, Louis Leo and Morris, Richard Brandon (editors) *Treasury of Great Reporting: Literature under pressure from the sixteenth century to our time* 784 p. Simon and Schuster (New York) 1949. Includes *Times* article by John Williams 'I sent you half a kidne . . .'

Southern Guardian (Wimbourne, UK) Issue for 5 January 1889 carried inquest report on suspect Druitt.

Sparrow, Gerald *Crimes of Passion* 154 p. Barker (London) 1973. Pages 90–8 carry a thoroughly slipshod rehash of the Clarence theory with at least fifteen mistakes in four pages.

Spectator (London) 27 July 1889 pp. 107–8 'False Clues' quotes a *New York Herald* article about a sailor suspect and concludes 'It is hoped that others . . . will act on a less simple and easy assumption than that of hunting for a man who will fit their theories'.

  In its 7 March 1891 issue pp. 335–6 'The Whitechapel Murder' suggests that Frances Coles was a Ripper victim and that he would have remained equally undetected in Paris, Vienna or New York.

Spicer, Robert Clifford 'I Caught Jack the Ripper' in *Daily Express* (London) 16 March 1931. He arrested a doctor who was released by Spicer's police superiors.

Spiering, Frank *Prince Jack: The True Story of Jack the Ripper* 192 p. Doubleday (New York) 1978. A careless elaboration of Stowell's theory. Jack was the Duke of Clarence but J.K. Stephen wrote the letters. No sources are quoted for many significant statements.

Springfield, Lincoln *Some Piquant People* 287 p. Fisher Unwin (London) 1924. Claimed that the finger was levelled at 'Leather Apron' by Harry Dam, a journalist on the *Star* and that when Pizer was released from custody they headed off any libel suit by paying him £10 'being little more than a pound a murder'.

Stephen, Leslie *The Life of Sir James Fitzjames Stephen, A Judge of the High Court of Justice, by his brother* . . . 504 p. Smith, Elder (London) 1895. Includes a chapter on James Stephen.

Stewart, William *Jack the Ripper: A New Theory* 223 p. Quality Press (London): Saunders (Toronto) 1939. Argued that the Ripper was a woman. The second major book on the theme.

Stowell, Thomas E.A. 'Jack the Ripper – A Solution?' in *The Criminologist* (London) November 1970. Announced that the murders were committed by 'S' 'the heir to power and wealth'. Subsequent reports suggested that S was the Duke of Clarence but Stowell denied this. Also discusses the clairvoyant Lees story and recounts details about Sir William Gull the royal physician.

Stowell, Thomas E.A. In a letter to *The Times* published on 5 November 1970, denied that Clarence was his suspect but repeated that 'he was a scion of a noble family'. Stowell died on the previous day and his son destroyed the Ripper papers (according to *The Times* of 14 November).

Sunday Chronicle (Manchester) of February 6th 1949 'She was a decoy to catch Jack the Ripper'. Concerns Mrs Amelia Brown, a police whistle, and a rope dropped over the wall of the London Hospital.

Symonds, John *The Great Beast: The Life and Magick of Aleister Crowley* 413 p. Macdonald (London) 1971. A previously unpublished note on p. 16 says 'The Victorian worthy in the case of Jack the Ripper was no less a person than Helena Petrovna Blavatsky'. Not unnaturally Symonds describes the notion as preposterous.

Symons, Julian Gustave *Crime and Detection: An Illustrated History from 1840* 288 p. Studio Vista (London) 1966. Two pages with illustrations. American edition entitled *A Pictorial History of Crime* Crown (New York) 1966.

Symons, Julian Gustave 'The Criminal Classes'. A chapter in *Rule Britannia: The Victorian World* 255 p. Times Newspapers (London) 1974 edited by George Perry and Nicholas Mason. Two pages on the Ripper including several pictures. Claims six murders.

Thomson, Basil *The Story of Scotland Yard* 324 p. Grayson (London) 1935. Page 178 mentions the case and reports that CID officers suspected an insane Russian doctor who committed suicide in 1888.

Thorwald, Jurgen *The Marks of Cain* 239 p. Thames and Hudson (London) 1965. Pages 65–6 record the principal facts and the McCormick theory.

Time (New York) 'Who Was Jack the Ripper?' 9 November 1970 p. 29. Speculation on the Clarence supposition.

The Times (London) The index for 1888–9 has a series of relevant entries.

The Times of 4 November 1970 p. 12 'Court Circular Clears Clarence'. 'A loyalist on the staff at Buckingham Palace' cites court circulars which suggest that (Albert Victor) Edward was otherwise engaged at the times of the murders.

The Times of 16 August 1973. 'New Ripper' previews an episode of the BBC television series in which Joseph Sickert accuses Sir William Gull of political murders.

Two More Horrible Murders in the East End 1888. Broadsheet reproduced in Cullen.

Two Worlds (London) 21 February 1959 'Medium Solved Britain's Vilest Murders'. The Lees story.

Umpire (Manchester) 31 July 1910 p. 2 'Who Was Jack the Ripper?' Dr Forbes Winslow appeared before Bow Street magistrate Mr Marsham on behalf of William Grant, an Irish medical student turned cattle-boat fireman, who had served a prison sentence for wounding a Whitechapel woman. The article implied that London solicitor George Kebbell had appeared for Grant at his preliminary hearing and had later announced not only that Grant was the Ripper but that he died in prison! Winslow reported receipt of a 'confession' from the Melbourne former fiancée of the Ripper who had also denounced her beloved to the Australian police with the result that 'Jack' emigrated to South Africa. Interviewed after the hearing Winslow gave his suspect as 'an epileptic maniac' who 'wore Canadian snowshoes' for quietness.

Vincent, William 'Jack the Ripper' in the *Police Review* (London) 16 December 1977 to 14 April 1978. A detailed review of the main facts and theories. Concludes that they amount to very little.

Volta, Ornella *The Vampire* translated from the Italian by Raymond Rudorff 160 p. Tandem (London) 1965. Claims nine murders for the Ripper between 1887–9, most of her other facts are equally shaky. He 'showed a surrealist sense of composition' in arranging intestines!

Walbrook, H.M. *Murders and Murder Trials 1812–1912* 366 p. Constable (London) 1932. Surveys the known facts.

Warden, Rob and Groves, Martha (editors) *Murder Most Foul and Other Great Crime Stories from the World Press* Ohio U.P. (Chicago) 1980. A chapter reprints *The Times* reports on the death of Annie Chapman.

Warren, Charles 'Sir Charles Warren Defends the Force' in *Pall Mall Gazette* and the *Daily News* on 4 October 1888. The Commissioner of Police replies to the Whitechapel District Board of Works.

Weiskopf, J.S. 'Jack the Ripper' in *History Makers* (London) 16 January 1870 pp. 432–5. Summary of the case, no theories but two contemporary posters.

Wensley, Frederick Porter *Forty Years of Scotland Yard: The Record of a Lifetime's Service in the Criminal Investigation Department* 312 p. Garden City Pub. Co. (New York) 1930; published in England as *Detective Days* Cassell (London) 1931. Describes the near capture of the murderer of Frances Coles and speculates that this may have been the Ripper.

White, Jerry *Rothschild Building: Life in an East End Tenement Block: 1887–1920* 301 p. History Workshop Series Routledge (London) 1980. Claimed that 'Large-scale redevelopment was Jack the Ripper's most important legacy'.

The Whitechapel Murders or The Mysteries of the East End Nos. 1–5 (incomplete) 40 p. Purkess (London) 1888. A strange collection of fact and fantasy preserved in the John Johnson collection of the Bodleian Library.

Whittington-Egan, Richard *A Casebook on Jack the Ripper* 174 p. Wildly (London) 1976. Reprints the *Contemporary Review* articles and extends the coverage through to 1975. An interesting review of the literature.

Whittington-Egan, Richard 'The Identity of Jack the Ripper' in *Contemporary Review* (London) November 1972 pp. 239–43; December 1972 pp. 317–21; January 1973 pp. 13–18, 24. Surveys the main theories.

'Who Was Jack the Ripper?' in *Crimes and Punishment* (London) no. 17 July 1975 pp. 455–70. Discusses the facts and major theories. Well illustrated. Authoritative, as befits a magazine which employed Joe Gaute, Robin Odell, Donald Rumbelow and Colin Wilson.

Williams, Guy R. *The Hidden World of Scotland Yard* 270 p. Hutchinson (London) 1972. Pages 28–33 have a brief note on Commissioner Warren's fate and several pictures from contemporary journals.

Williams, Montagu *Round London: Down East and Up West* 387 p. Macmillan (London) 1892. Describes his visits to a penny peepshow in the Whitechapel Road showing wax models of the Ripper victims.

Williams, Watkin Wynn *The Life of General Sir Charles Warren: By His Grandson* 450 p. Blackwell (Oxford) 1941. Pages 221–2 have an unreliable account of murders. Denies that all the victims were prostitutes; describes the Ripper as reticent; claims that Scotland Yard received 1,200 letters daily. Warren's bloodhound tests seen as 'very successful' but claims that no murders took place when the bloodhounds were in London. Favours the doctor theory of Griffiths.

Williamson, Linda 'R.J. Lees: Did He Find Jack the Ripper?' in *Two Worlds* (London) July 1986. The most-repeated Ripper yarn repeated again.

Wilson, Colin *A Casebook of Murder* 288 p. Frewin (London) 1969: Cowles (New York) 1970. Good arguments against existing propositions. Ascribes a suicidal tendency to the killer indicated by destruction of the womb. Disposes of Odell and Stewart arguments by suggesting that 'The essence of the sadistic crime is the fantasy beforehand, and fantasy flourishes in a vacuum'. The most imaginative approach so far.

Wilson, Colin *A Criminal History of Mankind* 702 p. Granada (London) 1984. Several references to the Ripper; claims that the Victorians were only dimly aware that these were sex crimes.

Wilson, Colin 'The Duke and the Ripper' in *Books and Bookmen* (London) December 1972 pp. 92–3. A commentary on the Stephen and Druitt theories based on Harrison and Farson.

Wilson, Colin 'My Search for Jack the Ripper' series in *Evening Standard* (London) 8–12 August 1960. Gives the Matters, Adam and McCormick theories. Reprinted in *Unsolved* 240 p. Xanadu Publishers (London) 1987.

Wilson, Colin *The Occult* 601 p. Hodder (London) 1971. Footnote to p. 446 accuses Volta (q.v.) of wild inaccuracies.

Wilson, Colin *Order of Assassins: The Psychology of Murder* 242 p. Hart Davis (London) 1972. Reprints *Leicester Chronicle* article and comments on the Reilly theory.

Wilson, Colin *Rasputin and the Fall of the Romanovs* 240 p. Barker (London) Farrar Straus (New York) 1964. Le Queux (q.v.) claimed to have read a manuscript dictated in French by Rasputin and recovered from his cellar, giving the facts behind the Ripper murders. According to Wilson, Rasputin had neither cellar nor French. See pp. 204–6.

Wilson, Colin 'Was the Ripper the Highest in the Land?' in *Leicester Chronicle* of 28 January 1971 pp. 14–15. Elaborates on Stowell's theories and confirms that the Duke of Clarence was suspect. Prefers Cullen's view.

Wilson, Colin and Pitman, Patricia *Encyclopedia of Murder* 576 p. Barker (London) 1961. Summary of the main suggestions then on offer about the Ripper's identity.

Winslow, Lyttleton Stewart Forbes *Recollections of Forty Years: Being an account at first hand of some famous criminal lunacy cases* . . . Ousley (London) 1910. Chapter on the Ripper. Author offered many suggestions to the police including replacement of Whitechapel police by attendants experienced with lunatics. Records the story that Jack was a gorilla. Winslow received several Ripper letters and decided that he was a well-to-do man living near St Paul's and suffering from religious mania. Claimed to have stopped the murders by publishing his clues.

Woodhall, Edwin Thomas *Crime and the Supernatural* 282 p. Long (London) 1935. Chapter 4 has yet another version of the Lees theory.

Woodhall, Edwin Thomas *Jack the Ripper: or When London Walked in Terror* 96 p. Mellifont Press (London) 1937. Pulp paperback which presents Jill the Ripper as Olga Tchkersoff revenging the death of her prostitute sister, adds another rehash of the Lees story, then lifts Matters' theory. Reaches new heights in a tour de force account of the escape and suicide of a suspect based on a misunderstanding of five lines of Macnaghten.

Wulffen, Erich *Der Sexualverbrecher: En Handbuch für Juristen, Verwaltungsbeamte und Ärzte* (Berlin) 1922. Eleven murders committed between 1887–9 as a surrogate for the sexual act.

Yallop, David A. *Deliver Us From Evil* 375 p. Macdonald Futura (London) 1981. This book on the Yorkshire Ripper includes five pages outlining Jack's career.

Fiction and Drama: A Selection

An attempt has been made in my published bibliography (listed earlier) to record as many of the fictional variations on the Ripper theme as possible. A small selection of the more interesting and accessible items is given below.

Alexander, David *Terror on Broadway* 243 p. Random (New York) 1954; Boardman (London) 1956. Jack (call me Waldo) on Times Square.

Alexander, Karl *Time After Time* 320 p. Granada (London) 1980. The book of the film in which Dr Leslie John Stephenson (alias Jack) is sent into eternity by H.G. Wells. An imaginative idea (involving time travel) but in the end it doesn't really work. The film (same title) was released in 1979 with Malcolm McDowell as H.G. Wells chasing David Warner as Jack. Directed and written by Nicholas Meyer.

Baring-Gould, William S. *Sherlock Holmes: A Biography of the World's First Consulting Detective* 284 p. Hart-Davis (London) 1962. Chapter XV tells how Holmes (in drag) is almost killed by the Ripper but is rescued by Watson in the nick of time. Revealed as Inspector Athelney Jones.

Barnes, Peter *The Ruling Class: A Baroque Comedy* 115 p. Heinemann (London) 1969. This spendid play has Jack Gurney spreading his time between the streets of Whitechapel and the House of Lords. First performed in 1968, it appeared in film version in 1972, with Peter O'Toole as Jack.

Barry, John Brooks *The Michaelmas Girls* 262 p. Deutsch (London) 1975. The Ripper teams up with a procuress.

Bloch, Robert *The Night of the Ripper* 240 p. Doubleday (New York) 1984; Robert Hale (London) 1986. Jack and Jill the Ripper emerge from an intricately woven tale involving all the main protagonists.

Block, Robert 'A Toy for Juliette' in Ellison, Harlan (editor) *Dangerous Visions*. Jack as an involuntary time-traveller provides a solution to the *Marie Celeste* mystery in passing.

Bloch, Robert 'Yours truly, Jack the Ripper' in his *The Opener of the Way* Arkham House (Sauk City, USA) 1945. An ageless Ripper stalks his 88th victim in contemporary Chicago. Originally published in *Weird Tales* (1943).

Borowitz, Albert *The Jack the Ripper Walking Tour Murder* 256 p. St Martin (New York) 1986.

Boucher, Anthony 'Jack El Distripador' in *Ellery Queen's Mystery Magazine* (New York) 1945, reprinted in Allan Barnard's *The Harlot Killer*.

Burroughs, William S. *Nova Express* 251 p. Grove (New York) 1962. Jack's murder notes are 'cut' into the text (p. 45).

Cendrars, Blaise *Moravagine* 1926, translation published by Peter Owen (London) 1968. A chapter entitled 'Jack the Ripper' has Moravagine extending his musical scope as the Ripper in Berlin.

Chaplin, Patrice *By Flower and Dean Street and the Love Apple* Duckworth (London) 1976. Jack returns as an advertising jingle writer.

Chetwynd-Hayes, R. 'The Gatecrasher' in his *The Unbidden* 224 p. Tandem (London) 1971. An uninvited guest at a seance.

Desmond, Hugh *Death Let Loose* 189 p. Wright and Brown (London) 1956. The Ripper story retold with the Chief of Police in a leading role.

Dibdin, Michael *The Last Sherlock Holmes Story* Cape (London) 1978. Holmes finishes the Ripper and Moriarty at a stroke.

Ellison, Harlan 'The Prowler in the City at the Edge of the World' in Ellison, Harlan (editor) *Dangerous Visions*. *Volume One* 359 p. Doubleday (New York) 1967: David Bruce and Watson (London) 1970. Sequel to Bloch's 'A Toy for Juliette'.

Farmer, Philip José *A Feast Unknown* 286 p. Essex House

(New York) 1969; Quartet (London) 1975. The son of Jack!

Gardner, John *The Return of Moriarty* Weidenfeld and Nicolson (London) 1974. Druitt as the Ripper, disposed of through the good offices of Professor Moriarty!

Gordon, Richard *The Private Life of Jack the Ripper: A Novel* 279 p. Heinemann (London) 1980. Dr Bertie Randolph anaesthetizing his victims before performing 'surgery'. Pretty feeble.

Greer, Terence *Ripper* 1973. A musical staged at the Half Moon Theatre in East London featuring a series of Rippers.

Hagen, Orlean *Who Done It? A guide to detective, mystery and suspense fiction* 834 p. Bowker (New York) 1969. The most fruitful source of fictional Ripperana.

Hatherley, Frank *The Jack the Ripper Show and How They Wrote It* (1973). A British musical (with music by Jeremy Barlow) in which the killer changes with each performance.

Heine, Maurice *'Regards sur l'enfer anthropoclassique'* in *Minotaure* (Paris) No. 8, 1936 pp. 41–45. The Ripper, disguised as a vicar, in conversation with the Marquis de Sade and others.

Keating, H.R.F. *The Sheriff of Bombay: An Inspector Ghote Novel* Collins (London) 1984. A modern Indian Jack the Whipper '. . . very much the same as the British fellow'.

Law, John *In Darkest London* (London) 1889. Deathbed confession of the Ripper as a slaughterhouse worker.

Lovesey, Peter *Swing, Swing Together* 190 p. Macmillan (London) 1976. A former Ripper suspect is suspected of two further murders – or was he the intended victim? Good period flavour.

Lowndes, Marie Belloc *The Lodger* Scribner (New York) 1911; Methuen (London) 1913 and many editions since. A best-selling novel which first appeared as a short story in *McClure's Magazine* January 1911 pp. 262–77 and was reprinted by Barnard in that form. The classic of Ripper fiction, it inspired several films: Alfred Hitchcock's *The Lodger: A Story of the London Fog* (1926) starring Ivor

Novello; The Lodger (1932) directed by Maurice Elvey (released in the USA as *The Phantom Fiend*); *The Lodger* (1944) directed by John Brahm, with Laird Cregar as the killer; and *The Man in the Attic* (1953) directed by Hugo Fregonse, with Jack Palance as Jack. A two-act opera, *The Lodger* by Phyllis Tate, was first performed in 1960 and televized in 1964.

Oliver, N.T. *The Whitechapel Mystery: Jack the Ripper, A Psychological Problem* 225 p. Continental Pub. Co. (Chicago) 1891. Number 8 of the bi-weekly *Patrol Detective Series* according to the title page. John Dewey a New York policeman tracks down Dr Westinghouse (the Ripper) in London and becomes his accomplice!

Parry, Michel (editor) *Jack the Knife: Tales of Jack the Ripper* 160 p. Mayflower (London) 1975. Anthology of Ripper fiction. Worth seeking out.

Pember, Ron and de Marne, Denis *Jack the Ripper: A Musical Play* 53 p. French (London) 1976. Play with music by Pember first presented at the Ambassador's Theatre, London on 17 September 1974. Montague Druitt as the villain (and magician).

Queen, Ellery *Sherlock Holmes versus Jack the Ripper* 271 p. Gollancz (London) 1967. Published in USA as *A Study in Terror* Lancer (New York) 1966. Inspired by a film of that title. The duke did it!

Reade, Leslie *The Stranger*. A three-act play staged at the Playhouse, New York, for sixteen performances from 12 February 1945.

Reid, Hugh 'Dulcie' in the *Fourth Pan Book of Horror Stories* 271 p. Pan (London) 1963. The murderer collects heads for his mantelpiece.

Russell, Ray *Unholy Trinity* 141 p. Bantam (New York) 1967; Sphere (London) 1971. 'Sagittarius', the third novella of the trilogy, proceeds via Stevenson's Mr Hyde/Jack the Ripper, through a reincarnation or disciple of Bluebeard . . .

Shew, Edward Spencer *Hand of the Ripper* 160 p. Sphere (London) 1971. The book of the film – *Hands of the Ripper*

(1971) directed by Peter Sasdy. This is a splendid film and it would be a shame to reveal the killer.

Stevens, Shane *By Reason of Insanity* Weidenfeld and Nicolson (London) 1979. Thomas Bishop pursues a Ripper-style career in modern America. Or does he?

Tapper, Oscar *Jack the Knife* Elam (London) 18 p. 2nd edition 1970. Verse drama first published in *East London Arts Magazine* autumn 1964 and performed April 1965.

Thomas, Donald *The Ripper's Apprentice* 245 p. Macmillan (London) 1986. A fictionalized life of Thomas Neill Cream and very good of its kind. Cream makes a full confession.

Trow, M.J. *The Adventures of Inspector Lestrade* 224 p. Macmillan (London) 1985. The Ripper as Melville Macnaghten's daughter – but of course!

Vachell, Horace Annesley *The Lodger*. Play produced at Maxine Elliott Theatre, New York from 8 January 1917 for fifty-six performances. Adapted from the Lowndes novel and starring Lionel Atwill as the innocent lodger.

Veheyne, C. *Horror* 160 p. Brown, Watson (London) 1962. The Ripper is a frustrated clergyman encouraged by his Mum.

Walsh, Ray *The Mycroft Memoranda* 186 p. Deutsch (London) 1984. Holmes seeks his man. A Watson did it!

Wedekind, Frank *Der Erdgeist* 1895 and *Die Büchse der Pandora* 1904. Two plays by the German dramatist translated as *Earth Spirit* 1914 and *Pandora's Box* 1918, both published in New York. New translation by Stephen Spender, Vision (London) 1952. The heroine is murdered by the Ripper. Adapted by film director G.W. Pabst as *Pandora's Box (Lulu)* (1922) starring Louise Brooks and with Gustav Diessl as the Ripper. The screenplay was published by Lorrimer (London) in 1971. Alban Berg's unfinished opera *Lulu* had its premier in 1937 and was released on record in 1952.

Wilson, Colin *Ritual in the Dark* 416 p. Gollancz (London); Houghton (Boston, USA) 1960. Ripper in a contemporary setting.

Films, Television and Radio

I have tried to round-up most of the films, as well as the TV and radio programmes on the theme in my bibliography. A few of those not already mentioned are:

Dr Jekyll and Sister Hyde 1972. Hammer film written by Brian Clemens and directed by Roy Ward Baker. Martine Beswick does her thing.

Jack the Ripper 1958. Mid-century film (distributed by Regal films) featuring Lee Paterson and directed by Robert S. Baker. The screenplay by Jimmy Sangster was based on a story by Peter Hammond and Colin Craig.

Jack the Ripper 1973. BBC Television dramatization in six parts (13 July to 17 August 1973) has Detective Chief Superintendents Barlow and Watt in pursuit of the Ripper after having given him eighty-five years' start. Introduces the Freemason theory and attempts to link the Cleveland Street Scandal with the painter Sickert and the murders.

Murder by Decree 1980. English film by John Hopkins, directed by Bob Clark and based on the Sickert story. Christopher Plummer is Sherlock Holmes, James Mason is Watson. Highlight Theatrical Productions.

Smiler With a Knife. A documentary programme about the murders broadcast by BBC Radio on 12 April 1967. Written by Tony Van den Bergh.

Study in Terror 1965. Based on a story by Donald and Derek Ford and starring John Neville as Holmes. Directed by James Hill. Georgia Brown's singing makes it all worthwhile.

Who Was Jack the Ripper? BBC Radio programme in the *Other Victorians* series broadcast on 1 June 1972. Written by Michell Raper; the text was later (1974) published by the Tabaret Press.

Index

Abberline, Inspector Frederick, 41, 45, 78, 87, 88, 90, 145, 146, 147, 179 , 285, 287
Aberconway, Lady Christabel, 206, 212, 220
Acland, Caroline, 247, 249
Acland, Theodore Dyke, 247
Adam, Hargrave Lee, 146, 147
Adams, Fanny, 17
Adler, Dr Hermann, 175
Albert Victor, Prince *see* Clarence
Allsop, Kenneth, 246, 249
Anderson, Sir Robert, 73, 95, 101–4, 107, 115, 120, 171–3, 240, 285
Andrew, PC Walter, 93
Arnold, Superintendent J., 58, 78, 89–90

Backert, Albert, 212, 220, 317
Baderski, Lucy, 146
Bailey, L. W., 236–8
Baker, Frederick, 18
Baring-Gould, William S., 239
Barnett, Joseph, 77, 80, 85, 87, 91, 187, 288–93
Barnett, Revd Samuel, 213
Barry, John Brooks, 187–91
Baxter, Wynne E., 38, 46, 50, 51, 53, 59, 61, 86
Bell, Donald, 140–2
Bell, Professor Quentin, 232, 258
Belloselski, Prince Serge, 150, 152
Bell Smith, G. Wentworth, 113
Bermant, Chaim, 175
Billington, James, 135
Blackwell, Dr Frederick, 54, 59, 163, 185
Blavatsky, Madame Helena, 264, 267–8
The Bloodhound, 259
Bond, Dr Thomas, 95, 161, 163–4
Bonner, Paul, 253, 254
Bowyer, Thomas, 77

Bradford, Sir Edward, 99
Brady, Ian, 22, 320
Broadbent, Dr William Henry, 139
Brown, Dr F. Gordon, 55–6, 62–6, 71, 94, 124, 160, 163, 164, 165, 171, 174
Brown, James, 61
Burn, Gordon, 23
Burridge, Mary, 15
Butler, Arthur, 191–6, 202

Callaghan, E, 113
The Cambridge Review, 252
Camps, Professor Francis, 159, 174, 217,
Chapman, Annie, 15, 30, 41, 44, 47–9, 68, 73, 75, 104, 121, 124, 171–3, 182, 193, 195, 216, 226, 236, 238, 254, 265, 272, 280, 284, 311, 336
Chapman, Annie (wife of Chapman, George), 146
Chapman, George, 118–19, 144, 178, 294, 320
Chandler, Inspector Joseph, 41–2
Chicago Tribune, 136
Clarence, Duke of, 95, 226, 232, 245–51, 253, 255, 257, 259, 311, 319, 322
Cleland, John, 20
Clover, Matilda, 138
Clune, Frank, 303
Coles, Frances, 96–9, 118–19, 124, 230, 232, 339
Collins, Mabel, 264–7, 269–71, 279
Cooper, Liza, 47
Coram, Thomas, 60
Corll, Dean, 320
Cotton, Mary Ann, 180
County of Middlesex Independent, 208
Cox, Mary Ann, 83, 87
Crawford, Earl of, 267–8
Crawford, (City of London solicitor), 64–6

Cream, Dr Thomas Neill, 134–44, 147, 278, 294
Cremers, Baroness Vittoria, 264, 266–7, 269, 271–4
The Cricketer, 225, 315
The Criminologist, 226, 245, 249–50, 252, 342
Crook, Alice Margaret, 253–61
Crook, Annie Elizabeth, 253–61
Cross, George, 36
Crow, Albert, 34
Crowley, Aleister, 263–8, 271–3
Cullen, Tom, 155, 187, 212–17, 220–3, 303, 315, 343
Cutbush, Thomas, 205, 222, 335–8

Daily Chronicle, 139
Daily Express, 157, 304
Daily Mail, 215
Daily Mirror, 149
Daily Telegraph, 88, 159, 162, 215
Davies, Dr Morgan, 274–80, 321
Davis, Derek, 143
Davis, John, 41, 46
Deakin, Alfred, 300
Deeming, Frederick Bayley, 294–303
Delhaye, William, 153
De River, Paul, 330–1,
De Salvo, Albert, 331
Dew, Walter, 83, 120–21
Diemschutz, Louis, 53–4
Dilnot, George, 240
Diosy, Arthur, 280
Donner, Gerald Melville, 223–4
Donovan, Timothy, 48
Donston, *see* Stephenson
Donworth, Ellen, 138–9
Douglas, Arthur, 196, 210, 226, 233, 303, 344
Doyle, Sir Arthur Conan, 187, 326–7
Druitt, Anne, 224
Druitt, Edward, 224, 236
Druitt, Lionel, 210–11, 217, 224
Druitt, Montague John, 92, 101, 155, 205–19, 228, 236, 313–19, 337
Druitt, Dr Robert, 215
Druitt, William, 209, 219, 317
Durrant, Theodore, 324

Dutton, Dr Thomas, 145–7, 152–5, 179, 214

Edalji, George, 326–7
Eddowes, Catherine, 23, 56, 64–70, 104–5, 110, 124, 144, 159–60, 162, 164, 171, 175, 182, 185, 189, 194–5, 230, 254, 265, 272, 298, 311, 336
Evans, John, 48
Evening News, 224
Evening Standard, 246, 298

Farmer, Amelia, 47
Farmer, Annie, 92, 230–1
Farson, Dan, 132, 139, 187, 202, 206, 210–2, 217–25, 249, 313–15, 343
Fell, W. G., 210–11
Fish, Albert, 22, 309, 320, 331
Fripp, Dr Alfred, 257
Furniss, Harold, 39, 62

Gaute, J. H. H., 343
Gladstone, William Ewart, 213
Gold, Eliza, 64
Gould, Maurice, 211
Grant, William, 115
Gribble, Leonard, 266
Griffiths, Major Arthur, 99–101, 122, 156, 219, 314, 317
The Guardian, 136, 159
Gull, Sir William, 178, 228–9, 233, 247–8, 251–2, 257, 260, 320, 341
Gunness, Belle, 310
Gustaafsdotter, Elizabeth, *see* Stride

Haarmann, Fritz, 324
Halse, Daniel, 57
Hansen, Robert, 27, 29
Harris, Frank, 20
Harrison, Michael, 226–33, 250–3, 343
Harvey, Lou, 143
Harvey, Maria, 85, 86, 187, 289–91
Haynes, Richard S., 298
Heath, Neville, 22, 320
Helson, Inspector, 38, 39–40
Herd, Richard, 196, 198

Hogg, Phoebe, 310
Howard, Sir Charles, 99
Hutchinson, George, 89–90,
141–3, 154, 189
Hyde, H. Montgomery, 257

Illustrated Police News, 79, 280
Isenschmid, Joseph, 286–88

Jewish Chronicle, 175

Keith, Sir Arthur, 334
Keleene, Dr Timothy, 34
Kelly, Alexander, 143, 340
Kelly, John, 64, 65
Kelly, Mary Jane, 26, 30, 77,
82–91, 111, 127–30, 141, 142,
154, 158, 161–3, 179, 183, 187,
189–91, 194, 196, 198, 239, 249,
254, 280, 288, 289–93, 309, 311,
318, 330, 336
Kent, Constance, 180
Kidney, Michael, 59
Kiss, Bela, 29
Klosowski, Severin Antoniovitch,
145–7, 153, 154, 156, *see also*
Chapman, George
Knight, Stephen, 161, 233, 255,
256, 258–61, 278, 344
Konovalov, Vassily, 150, 151, 157
(alias for Pedachenko)
Kosminski, 155, 156, 314, 337
Kroll, Joachim, 30
Kürten, Peter, 22, 23, 309, 320,
324, 325

The Lancet, 44, 162
Langham, S. F., 64, 67
Lave, Joseph, 153–4
Lawende, Joseph, 67, 106
Lee, A. L., 132–3
Lees, Robert James, 247–8
Leeson, Detective Sergeant
Benjamin, 96–7, 119, 124, 154
Le Queux, William, 148–55,
312–13, 342
Levi, Eliphas, 267–8,
Levisohn, Wolff, 146, 153
Levitski, 149
Lewis, Sarah, 85, 87, 184
Lewis, Matthew Gregory, 19
Linklater, Magnus, 245

The Listener, 238
Llewellyn, Dr Ralph, 36–7, 123,
163
Loftus, Philip, 223–4
London Hospital Gazette, 159
Long, PC Alfred, 56, 66
Long, Elizabeth, 48
Lowndes, Marie Belloc, 117, 344
Luiskovo, Andrey, 151 (alias for
Pedachenko)
Lusk, George, 30, 70, 143, 327
Lynder, Frank, 249–50
Lytton, Bulwer, 269, 273, 279

M'Carthy, John, 77–8
McCormac, John, 93
McCormick, Donald, 133,
144–57, 179, 186, 198, 214–5,
223, 249, 303, 312, 342
MacDonald, Arthur, 342
Macdonald, Dr Roderick, 86–7,
161
McKenzie, Alice, 93–5, 99, 111,
163, 230, 339
Mackenzie, Sir William Colin,
301
McLaren, Lady Rose, 206
Macnaghten, Sir Melville,
99–100, 116–19, 122, 155–6,
185, 205–6, 210, 213, 217,
220–3, 239, 314–19, 335–9
MacWilliam, Inspector James,
58, 64, 67
Mallett, ?, 230, 231
Manson, Charles, 22
Marjoribanks, Edward, 135
Marne, Patricia, 143
Marsh, Alice, 139, 144
Marsh, George, 274
Marsh, Maud, 146–7
Marshall, William, 60
Marshall Hall, Sir Edward, 135,
140
Mather, Emily, 295, 300
Matters, Leonard, 21, 26, 125,
130–4, 142, 265, 310, 340, 342
Matthews, Henry, 72
Maxwell, Caroline, 87, 179–80,
184
May, David, 256
Maybrick, Florence, 108, 228
Medical Directory, 278

Medical News, 159
Medical Register, 158, 210, 217
Menesclou, Louis, 17, 18
Merchant, Dr, 158–9
Miles, Frank, 234–6, 312
Monro, James, 72–3, 81–2, 95, 99,
  240–3
Morland, Nigel, 249–50
Moylan, Sir John, 220, 240
Murray's Magazine, 81

Neate, Alan, 260
Neil, Arthur Fowler, 118
Neil, PC John, 35–6
Neilson, Donald, 23
Nelson, Earle, 22, 309, 328–9, 333
Netley, John, 255
Neustatter, Dr Lindesay, 304
New York Herald, 113
Nichols, Mary Ann, 38–40, 42,
  124, 193, 216, 225, 254, 283–5,
  316, 356
Nichols, William, 38
Nideroest, Johann, 149–50

Ochrana Gazette, 151
Odell, Robin, 165, 220, 242,
  303–4, 313, 343
Oddie, S. Ingelby, 280
O'Donnell, Bernard, 263, 266,
  272, 273, 280
O'Donnell, Elliott, 181
Openshaw, Dr Thomas, 71, 143
Ostrog, Michael, 155–6, 314, 337
O'Sullivan, J. S., 299

Paley, Bruce, 288, 291–2
Pall Mall Gazette, 267, 269, 272,
  277, 341
Paul, John, 36, 38
Pearcy, Mary, 108–9, 184–5, 309
Pearson, Edmund, 132
Pearson, Hesketh, 234
Pedachenko, Dr Alexander,
  148–57, 312–13, 342
Pelham, Camden, 18
Phillips, Dr George Bagster, 42–3,
  49, 54, 60–2, 78–9, 82, 87, 94–6,
  124, 134, 160–4, 171
Piggott, William Henry, 45
Pizer, John, 45, 172, 284–6
Police Gazette, 61, 67

Prater, Elizabeth, 85, 87
Preston, Hayter, 266
Punch, 23, 53, 82, 241, 341

Rasputin, Grigori, 148, 153, 313
Reilly, B. E., 58–9
Reinhardt, James Melvin, 26, 28,
  332
Richardson, Emilia, 46
Richardson, John, 47
Richardson, J. Hall, 151
Rogers, Carmen, 305
Roots, Inspector J., 277
Rosenwater, Irving, 225, 226, 315
Rumbelow, Donald, 132, 140,
  142, 149, 152, 155, 164, 173,
  182, 187, 194–5, 209, 212, 220,
  224, 229, 231, 233–4, 253, 285,
  289, 294, 303, 343

Saddler, James, 98–9
Salisbury, Lord, 254
Saunders, Dr William Sedgwick,
  62, 163
Seefeld, Adolf, 324
Sequiera, Dr George William, 55,
  62, 160, 163
Sharp, Royden, 326–7
Shaw, George Bernard, 20
Shepherd, C. W., 152
Shrivell, Emma, 139, 144
Sickert, Joseph, 233, 253–9
Sickert, Walter, 216, 217, 233,
  253, 256, 259, 320
Simenon, Georges, 28
Sitwell, Sir Osbert, 216
Smith, Emma Elizabeth, 33, 35,
  120, 192, 230–1, 265, 284
Smith, Sir Henry, 55–6, 64, 71,
  101, 104–7, 116, 118
Smith, Madeleine, 180
Smith, Robert, 23
Smith, PC William, 61
Southern Guardian, 209
The Spectator, 99, 203
Spicer, Robert, 157–8, 277
Spiering, Frank, 252, 344
Spink, Isabella, 146
Spratling, Inspector, 39
Stanley, Dr, 21, 26, 125–34, 144,
  265, 310, 322
The Star, 284

Stead, W. T., 272, 277
Stephen, Sir James Fitzjames,
    227–8
Stephen, James Kenneth, 226–33,
    250–2 258, 311, 319
Stephen, Sir Leslie, 227
Stephenson, Dr Roslyn D'Onston,
    162, 269–80, 320
Stewart, William, 21, 181–3, 194,
    203, 309, 342
Stott, Daniel, 136, 137
Stowell, Dr. T. E. A., 226, 229,
    233, 245–52, 257, 311, 343
Straume, Peter, 150
Stride, Elizabeth, 23, 26, 59–61,
    110, 144, 194, 202, 230–1, 311,
    336
Swanson, Chief Inspector
    Donald, 113, 160
The Sun, 191, 335
Sunday Express, 215
Sunday Times, 245, 256, 257
Sutcliffe, Peter, 23–9, 110, 309, 333

Tabram, Martha, *see* Turner
Tchkersoff, Olga, 198–203
Tessnow, Ludwig, 324
Thicke, Detective Sergeant John,
    45, 284, 287
Thomson, Sir Basil, 119, 122,
    124, 148, 150, 156, 220
Thompson, PC Ernest, 96, 99
The Times, 69, 71, 73, 90, 242, 246,
    250, 340
Toughill, Thomas, 234–5
True Crime, 288, 291, 293
True Detective, 263, 265
Turner, Martha, 34–5, 112, 185,
    193, 195, 230–31, 265, 284, 291,
    308, 311

Vacher, Joseph, 320, 324
Valentine, George, 208
Vassilyev, A. T., 152
Venturney, Julia, 289–90
Victoria, Queen, 74, 178, 232,
    236, 245, 247, 255, 341
Vincent, Sir Howard, 240
Violenia, Emanual, 173

Warren, Sir Charles, 51, 58, 72–4,
    78, 81, 92, 105, 176, 194, 240,
    242–3, 283, 286, 318
Watkins, PC, 55, 165
Weber, Jeanne, 310
Webster, Kate, 180
Wedekind, Frank, 15
Wells, H. G., 20
Wensley, Frederick Porter, 118
Whitman, Charles, 22
Whittington-Egan, Richard, 162,
    217, 232–3, 235, 263, 274, 279,
    344
Wilde, Oscar, 234, 235, 312
Wilder, Christopher, 29
Williams, Dr J. F., 153, 155
Williams, Watkin Wynn, 220
Wilson, Colin, 22, 132, 234, 246,
    344
Wilson, Harry, 98
Winberg, 149
Winslow, Dr L. Forbes, 75, 101,
    108–17
Wood, Simon, D., 260–1
Woodhall, Edwin, 131, 198, 200,
    202
Woolf, Virginia, 227, 258

Zverieff, Nicholas, 149, 150

BEYOND THE OCCULT
by Colin Wilson

Colin Wilson has been exploring the field of the paranormal ever since he began the research for his first highly successful book on the subject, *The Occult* (1970). Approaching these phenomena with the training and attitudes of a scientist rather than a committed occultist, he eventually became convinced that the evidence for what we call the paranormal is at least as powerful as the evidence for the existence of atomic particles.

Now, after twenty years of further research, he sets out to show in *Beyond The Occult* that the 'world picture' of the modern occultist is as consistent and comprehensive as that of the scientist. He begins with the human mind, and with vivid examples of its unseen powers: ESP, precognition, clairvoyance, psychokinesis, psychometry, dowsing, out-of-the-body experiences, mystical experiences of all kinds. From there he moves on to the profoundly mysterious phenomena – poltergeists, spirit possession, reincarnation – that have convinced him of the reality of disembodied spirits.

Hundreds of fascinating glimpses into the universe of the paranormal are linked with the latest scientific thinking about the uncertain nature of ultimate 'physical' reality to support Colin Wilson's powerful case: that our so-called 'normal' experience may in fact be sub-normal, and that evolution may have brought us near to the edge of a quantum leap into a hugely expanded human consciousness.

A BANTAM PRESS HARDBACK

0 593 01174 0